Consent

Consent: Legacies, Representations, and Frameworks for the Future examines the conceptualisation of 'consent' across various historical periods, cultures, and disciplines to offer an expansive, pluralistic vision for future articulations of consent as it circulates throughout contemporary life in sexual encounters, medical contexts, and media representations.

This volume is distinctive in its diverse conceptual scope and commitment to cross-disciplinary dialogue, accommodating perspectives on consent that are contextually sensitive and culturally diverse. The chapters examine a range of topics, from socio-cultural engagements with consent in Latin American music, feminist movements in Pakistan, and BDSM in Poland, to theoretical and pedagogical ones exploring alternative possibilities for framing and understanding consent through intersectional approaches and institutional curricula.

Consent: Legacies, Representations, and Frameworks for the Future is of value to researchers, practitioners, undergraduate and postgraduate students, and general readers interested in histories, representations, and future possibilities of consent in its many manifestations.

Sophie Franklin is a postdoctoral researcher in English literature at the Ludwig-Maximilian University of Munich, Germany. She specialises in nineteenth-century literature, cultural legacies, and representations of violence from the late eighteenth century to the present.

Hannah Piercy is a postdoctoral researcher and assistant in Medieval English Studies at the University of Bern, Switzerland. She works on medieval insular romance, consent and coercion, and sensory studies.

Arya Thampuran is Assistant Professor at Durham University's Institute for Medical Humanities, UK, and the Principal Investigator on the Black Health and the Humanities Network. Her research engages with how creative practitioners across the African diaspora express mental health and healing through non-biomedical modes.

Rebecca White teaches in the Department of English Studies at Durham University, UK, where she completed an AHRC-funded doctorate on screen adaptations of nineteenth-century fiction.

Consent

Legacies, Representations, and Frameworks for the Future

Edited by
Sophie Franklin, Hannah Piercy, Arya Thampuran, and Rebecca White

Routledge
Taylor & Francis Group
LONDON AND NEW YORK

First published 2024
by Routledge
4 Park Square, Milton Park, Abingdon, Oxon OX14 4RN

and by Routledge
605 Third Avenue, New York, NY 10158

Routledge is an imprint of the Taylor & Francis Group, an informa business

British Library Cataloguing-in-Publication Data
A catalogue record for this book is available from the British Library

Library of Congress Cataloging-in-Publication Data
Names: Franklin, Sophie, editor. | Piercy, Hannah, editor. | Thampuran, Arya, editor. | White, Rebecca Arwen, 1982- editor.
Title: Consent : legacies, representations, and frameworks for the future / edited by Sophie Franklin, Hannah Piercy, Arya Thampuran, and Rebecca White.
Description: Abingdon, Oxon [UK] ; New York, NY : Routledge, 2024. | Series: Interdisciplinary research in gender | Includes bibliographical references and index.
Identifiers: LCCN 2023028538 (print) | LCCN 2023028539 (ebook) | ISBN 9781032429625 (hardback) | ISBN 9781032429632 (paperback) | ISBN 9781003365082 (ebook)
Subjects: LCSH: Consent (Law) | Consent (Law)--Social aspects. | Duress (Law) | Gender identity--Law and legislation. | Gender identity--Social aspects.
Classification: LCC K579.I6 C66 2024 (print) | LCC K579.I6 (ebook) | DDC 346.01/62--dc23/eng/20230926
LC record available at https://lccn.loc.gov/2023028538
LC ebook record available at https://lccn.loc.gov/2023028539

ISBN: 978-1-032-42962-5 (hbk)
ISBN: 978-1-032-42963-2 (pbk)
ISBN: 978-1-003-36508-2 (ebk)

DOI: 10.4324/9781003365082

Typeset in Times New Roman
by Taylor & Francis Books

The Open Access versions of the Introduction and Afterword were funded by the University of Bern.
The Open Access version of chapter 11 was funded by Durham University.

Contents

Contributors

Rebecca Barnes is Senior Research Adviser in Qualitative and Social Research Methods at the NIHR Research Design Service East Midlands, based at the University of Leicester. She has researched domestic violence and abuse for 20 years, focusing particularly on LGBTQ+ people's intimate relationships.

Megan Batterbee is a PhD candidate at the University of Kent's School of English. Her PhD thesis, entitled 'Hidden in Plain Sight: The Problem of Consent in the Novel, 1748–99', examines consent and rape discourse within the feminist novels of the late eighteenth century.

Rosanna Bellini is a Postdoctoral Scholar at Cornell Tech in New York City, US. In her research, she focuses on the misuse of digital technologies in intimate partner contexts, with a specialisation in working first-hand with adversarial users ('abusers') and financial harms. To mitigate the ongoing risks of sexual abuse and harm, she is determined to identify the tenets of meaningful, consentful technology design, deployment, and evaluation.

Kate Butterby is a Research Associate at Durham University and Glasgow Caledonian University. Her research focuses on domestic abuse, with a particular focus on abuse within LGBTQ+ people's relationships. She is currently working on a European project focused on developing digital and other approaches to eliminating domestic abuse, and research exploring sexual violence in higher education.

Sudeshna Chatterjee is currently the Director of Equity and Social Justice at the Town of Reading in Massachusetts. She has a PhD from the University of Massachusetts Boston and is a scholar-practitioner in the field of human rights, social justice, and inclusive governance.

Hazel Dixon is a researcher at Newcastle University, UK. Their current research focuses on how we can use embodiment, playful design, and co-creation for the design and delivery of Relationships and Sex Education. They are particularly interested in understandings of the body within technology and how we can create technologies and services that build in principles of radical disability justice.

Catherine Donovan is Professor and Head of Department in Sociology at Durham University. She has been researching the intimate and family lives of LGBTQ+ people for over twenty years, focusing mainly on domestic and sexual violence and abuse and hate. She is also working on sexual violence victimisation of students in higher education.

Sophie Franklin is a postdoctoral researcher in English literature at the Ludwig-Maximilian University of Munich. She specialises in nineteenth-century literature, cultural legacies, and representations of violence from the late eighteenth century to the present. Her first monograph, *Violence and the Brontës: Language, Reception, Afterlives*, is forthcoming with Edinburgh University Press.

Shelby Judge is an Early Career Academic at the University of Derby, researching feminist responses to the manosphere. Her doctoral research was 'Contemporary Feminist Adaptations of Greek Myth', and her work in this field is ongoing. Shelby's overarching research interests are in feminist and queer theory and contemporary women's fiction.

Natashia Lindsey is an Assistant Professor of Theatre and faculty associate in Africana and Black Studies at Central Washington University in the US. An interdisciplinary scholar, her work focuses on the many intersections of race and performance including racial performativity and the unmasking and dismantling of white supremacy.

Christina Mansueti is in the final year of her doctoral studies at the University of Sunderland. Her research focuses on contemporary comedy and the female voice. Her doctoral thesis explores how contemporary feminisms are negotiated in two UK-based female comedies: Michaela Coel's *Chewing Gum* and Phoebe Waller-Bridge's *Fleabag*.

Kyle L. Murray is a Lecturer of Law at City Law School, University of London. He has research and teaching expertise across various areas of law and philosophy, including consent, deception, and mistake in sexual offences. He has given media comment and been published in leading national and international peer-reviewed journals. He holds LLB (hons), Master of Jurisprudence, and PhD degrees from Durham Law School.

Hannah Piercy is a postdoctoral researcher and assistant in Medieval English Studies at the University of Bern. Her first book, *Resistance to Love in Medieval English Romance: Negotiating Consent, Gender, and Desire*, was published by D. S. Brewer in 2023. She works on medieval insular romance, consent and coercion, and sensory studies.

Eunice Rojas is the Herman N. Hipp Professor of Modern Languages and Literatures and Chair of the Interdisciplinary Minor in Latin American and Latinx Studies at Furman University. She studies contemporary Latin

American literature and music dealing with discourses of political, social, or cultural resistance to oppression.

Emily A. Rollie is an Associate Professor of Theatre at Central Washington University, US. A professional theatre director and intimacy choreographer as well as scholar, Emily's artistic and scholarly work focuses on consent-based practices and intimacy choreography as well as queer and intersectional feminist approaches to directorial artistic practices.

Iqra Shagufta Cheema is an Assistant Professor of Humanities and coordinator of the Social Change programme at Graceland University, Iowa, US. Her research focuses on media cultures, transnational feminism, postcolonial literature, and film studies. She is the editor of *The Other #MeToos* (Oxford University Press, 2023) and primary author of *ReFocus: The Films of Annemarie Jacir* (Edinburgh University Press, 2023).

Jay Szpilka is a post-doctoral fellow at the SWPS University in Warsaw. They completed their doctorate on BDSM practices in contemporary Poland at the University of Warsaw's Institute of Polish Culture. Their current work focuses on the intersection between transness and sexual desire, especially in the context of fringe kinky practices.

Arya Thampuran is Assistant Professor at Durham University's Institute for Medical Humanities and the Principal Investigator on the Black Health and the Humanities Network. Her research engages with how creative practitioners across the African diaspora express mental health and healing through non-biomedical modes.

Caroline West is an outreach coordinator with Active* Consent. She holds an MA and PhD in sexuality studies from Dublin City University. Caroline hosts the sexual wellness podcast Glow West and is a relationship columnist with the Irish Independent newspaper.

Rebecca White teaches in the Department of English Studies at Durham University, UK. She is an Associate Editor for *The Year's Work in English Studies* (Oxford University Press) and is currently working on a monograph exploring Jane Austen's afterlives, including her reception during the COVID-19 pandemic.

Acknowledgements

This book began life as a series of conversations between the editors during our time as doctoral students and early career researchers at Durham University. Discussing our shared research interests across time periods and specialisations led us to organise a conference, 'Consent: Histories, Representations, and Frameworks for the Future' at Josephine Butler College, Durham University, in 2019. We are grateful to everyone who attended this conference and participated as speakers or delegates; we were inspired by the papers presented and the productive conversations sparked across disciplines. We would also like to thank the organisations who provided funding to support the conference, Durham Centre for Academic Development and the Institute of Advanced Study at Durham University. Our initial vision was that this volume would collect and develop research presented at the conference, but it grew beyond our original plans and we are delighted to have welcomed many new contributors to extend the focus of this volume in exciting ways. We were grateful for the response to the Call for Papers we issued and would like to thank all those who applied – we only wish we could have included more of the excellent submissions we received here. We owe huge thanks to every single contributor, whose work has inspired us to think afresh about the topic of consent. We would especially like to thank those who have been involved in this project from the start for their patience and dedication.

Thank you to the editorial staff at Routledge, especially Charlotte Taylor and Jodie Collins, for their input and help with this volume. Sincere thanks to the anonymous peer reviewer, whose generous feedback helped us to improve the collection and nuance our discussions in important ways. Finally, we are grateful for the friendships and solidarity that have sustained this volume through the COVID-19 pandemic and the upheavals of early career academia; we hope that the enjoyment we have found in editing this collection together is evident to those who read it.

1 Introduction

Sophie Franklin, Hannah Piercy, Arya Thampuran, and Rebecca White

A man is led into a dark room, to meet a woman he thinks is his lover. He is given a cup of wine, which causes him to become so intoxicated that he cannot wait to get into bed. He believes throughout the encounter that the woman whom he has sex with is someone else. In the morning, he opens the window to let the sunlight in, and the deception is over. When he recounts this episode afterwards, he insists 'that I did was against my will' ['that I ded was ayenste my wylle'].[1]

This man is Launcelot, the supreme knight of King Arthur's Round Table, and the episode as recounted appears in Sir Thomas Malory's version of the Arthurian legend, *Le Morte Darthur*, completed in England in 1469–70 and published in a print version by William Caxton in 1485.[2] It predates what Katherine Angel refers to as our contemporary 'consent culture' by 550 years, and yet its concerns are those of this moment.[3] It engages with issues of deceptive sex or rape by fraud, intoxication and what degrees or methods invalidate consent, and whether it is possible for a man to be raped by a woman.[4] In contemporary Britain, this would be legally classified as sexual assault: UK law holds that only people with a penis can be the perpetrators of rape, although people of any gender can be rape victims.[5] In medieval English law, the crime of *raptus* (which could mean rape or abduction) was punishable in two distinct ways. A trespass could be brought by a woman's father or husband, framing it as a crime of property (whereby the woman's family could also seek recompense for cases of consensual adulterous sex, or consensual elopement), or women themselves could bring an appeal of *raptus*. In contrast, male victim-survivors of rape or sexual assault had no way of defining their experiences in legal terms.[6] Yet Launcelot's own words are clear: 'that I ded was ayenste my wylle'. He does not name the episode as rape, but he does clearly assert that he has been coerced into doing something against his will.

We open this book with this episode for several reasons.[7] Firstly, because it illustrates the long historical legacy and perennial relevance of discussions about consent and coercion. Secondly, because it demonstrates the value of *representations* of consent and coercion – in literature, art, music, film, and TV – for thinking critically on this topic. Launcelot's own words for his experience go against contemporaneous and modern legal practices,

DOI: 10.4324/9781003365082-1

illustrating the limitations of legal frameworks for ethical sexual practices and the relation of experience. Where the law is silent, inadequate, or unclear, literary or artistic portrayals open up new questions, offer radically different perspectives, or explore greater levels of nuance. Our third reason for including this episode is because it engages with several key frameworks used by the contributors to this volume: deceptive sex, intoxication, gendered power dynamics, and authorial agency. The presence of this episode in Malory's *Morte* raises important questions about authorial testimony, literature, and ethics, because Malory was himself accused of two counts of *raptus* against Joan Smith in 1450. These accusations are uncertain and unclear: because of the capacious nature of medieval *raptus* law, the charges (brought by Joan's husband, Hugh Smith) may be aiming to punish consensual adultery, or they may have been fabricated or exaggerated by Malory's political enemies.[8] And yet such interpretations also offer an easy way to avoid confronting the ethical issue of how we read authors' real-life experiences of and potential involvement in rape or coercion alongside their – sometimes highly sensitive – literary accounts. A fourth reason is that the episode urges us to attend to the voices of survivors, while interrogating whose survivor testimonies are granted visibility and credibility within particular cultural configurations, including the Western context of this example. While this volume features relatively few pieces that are explicitly written by survivors, this is in part because we feel strongly that disclosure itself is a matter of consent; it should remain optional within academic work, as the demand for survivor testimonies can place a disproportionate burden of representation on certain figures. Finally, we include this episode at the start of this introduction because it foregrounds the often-unacknowledged experiences of men whose consent is violated. We recognise that the perspectives of men as victim-survivors remain underrepresented in this volume; however, several of the chapters, including those by Jay Szpilka, Rebecca White, and Christina Mansueti, engage with men's experiences of consent across a range of sexual orientations and dynamics. Acknowledging the full range of experiences of consent, coercion, and assault, across the spectrum of gender, sexuality, and relationships, is vital to enable more holistic understandings of how we can create a safer and more equitable world for all.[9]

This book aims to take stock of 'consent' at a time in which its cultural prevalence as a framework for sexual ethics in particular is being questioned and challenged. Consent, as many scholars have recently argued, has been taken as an all-encompassing term, obscuring the nuances of the conflicting and ambiguous issues that fall within its remit.[10] In its use in everyday experience, it has come to be equated with negotiation, desire, and pleasure, to stand in for the whole domain of ethical sexual practice, a conceptual conflation that is problematic and misleading.[11] So what, then, *is* consent? What does it mean and what is it useful for at this junction in contemporary thought? And what bearing should it have on future principles, practices, and policies?

For the purposes of this introduction, we define consent as voluntary agreement, which sets boundaries of what is and is not acceptable to the participants in a particular interaction, whether this interaction constitutes a sexual encounter, engagement in a medical practice, or an agreement between an author and audience.[12] However, this is simply a working definition, and the collection puts in dialogue the definitions offered by individual contributors to co-produce a more nuanced framework for understanding consent. Because our book takes a cross-disciplinary approach to consent across a wide range of specialisms, spatialities, and temporalities, definitions of consent necessarily vary in accordance with individual authors' particular areas of focus. Consent does not remain static throughout history and across the globe – though we argue that the concept of voluntary agreement underlies most formulations of consent, even as whose agreement matters changes, from the focus on patriarchal consent that understands women's bodies as property to the grounding of consent in individual subjectivity. Consent is an important legal standard and remains key to opening up conversations about ethical conduct in many areas of life, from sexual to artistic to biopolitical.

Current Contexts of Consent Studies

Consent moves across boundaries of the popular and the theoretical, and is often considered both self-evident and fraught with complexity.[13] Approaches to the term have tended to diverge into two broad fields: those that perceive consent to be a productive framework as a critical, political, and practical tool, and those that view consent as restrictive and even outdated, especially in the context of sex and intimacy. In drawing attention to some of the key critical debates around consent in contemporary thought, we wish to tease out the ways in which this volume speaks to and expands upon such discussions.

While recognising its limitations, this edited collection reveals the capacious possibilities of consent. We acknowledge the frequent denouncements and querying of consent, especially through its history as a liberal contract and property relation that can perpetuate, as Tina Sikka outlines, 'heteronormative and ethnocentric structures by fixing normative Western heterosexuality as the default' and 'its racializing elision of liberal consent's imbrication in a history in which consent was not afforded to enslaved women and distorted with respect to enslaved men'.[14] Recent critical work on consent has argued, as Angel does in *Tomorrow Sex Will Be Good Again*, that it 'has a limited purview, and it is being asked to bear too great a burden, to address problems it is not equipped to resolve'.[15] Meanwhile, Mithu Sanyal sets out how consent is 'not a cure-all, and it is more complex than it may initially seem', to which our own collection attests.[16] For Linda Martín Alcoff, 'consent is an imperfect instrument, descriptively as well as juridically' when it comes to '*understanding* sexual violations'.[17] Yet, as Alcoff also asserts, the etymology of consent means 'a "feeling with" or a "feeling together"', which gives 'a different connotation than the association of consent with contracts, and brings it closer to the concept of "mutuality" that legal theorist Martha Chamallas (1988) argues would be a better approach to norming sex than contractual consent'.[18] Following

Alcoff, we perceive restrictions in the history of consent and its associations with contractualism and property, while simultaneously seeking to contextualise, nuance, and potentially redefine its meaning and significance.

The #MeToo movement led to a resurgence of wider conversations around consent and its parameters. Yet it also reflected, as Angela Onwuachi-Willig writes, 'the longstanding marginalization and exclusion that women of color experience within the larger feminist movement in U.S. society' and beyond, which Rebecca White's chapter in this volume addresses.[19] The failure of Western feminist movements like #MeToo to be truly intersectional in outlook is further evident in consent's own frequent obscuring of marginalised identities and communities through the promotion of the myth that 'we are all free autonomous agents capable of exercising choice, and that choice is a purely rational act', a myth deeply connected to liberal philosophers of the Western Enlightenment.[20] As Sikka delineates, however, there are numerous movements in the non-Anglophone world that 'aim to deconstruct and rearticulate sexual norms and laws around gender-based violence' through a more complex engagement with consent.[21] Eunice Rojas's and Iqra Shagufta Cheema's chapters in this volume examine feminist activist movements beyond a narrow white, 'Western' perspective often associated with #MeToo, through Latin American feminist campaigns against gender-based violence and the significance of the slogan *Mera Jism, Meri Marzi* (my body, my choice) in contemporary feminist politics in Pakistan; additionally, Arya Thampuran's chapter seeks to 'elasticise the conceptual boundaries of consent' through the decolonisation of traumatic testimony in Inuit and Nigerian contexts.

Consent is routinely aligned with heteronormativity, individualism, and white subjectivity, leading to feminist calls against the widespread and exclusive use of consent as an intersectional and international theory and practice.[22] While some critics have therefore argued for a move away from consent, Robin Bauer and Melanie Beres make a case for the queering of consent and the expansion of consent studies through a more sustained consideration of queer stories.[23] In the process, 'rather than starting off [with] the premise of an autonomous subject with free will', consent can emerge as 'an affective process that is situated in complex social power dynamics', and as a 'complex and open-ended process that needs to be situated in one's personal history as well as social contexts'.[24] This position resonates with Alexandre Baril's opposition to the legal notion of consenting to the public distribution of images, which defines consent as a 'singular and irrevocable event', specifically in the context of marginalised groups such as trans people: 'What happens when consent is no longer constructed as either given or not, is understood as a process instead of an event, and is conceptualized as a social relation instead of defined by a neoliberal, individualist notion of subject and agency?'[25] In *Unsafe Words: Queering Consent in the #MeToo Era* (2023), Shantel Gabrieal Buggs and Trevor Hoppe write of how contributors 'poke and prod in search of more capacious, queer, and kink-friendly notions of consent'.[26] Several of the authors in this volume also seek to queer the boundaries of consent: Jay Szpilka's chapter explores consensual non-consent within BDSM communities in Poland; Catherine Donovan, Kate Butterby, and Rebecca Barnes's essay spotlights rarely researched assumptions around sexual consent within abusive LGBTQ+ relationships; Kyle Murray's chapter examines the limitations of the British court's heteronormative conceptualisation of sexual activity and suggests an alternative model of consent that will enable a move away from the legal emphasis on so-called 'gender fraud'.

While many of the chapters in this volume examine sexual dynamics and intimate interpersonal relationships, consent has a wider remit, as exemplified in recent scholarship. Kalidas D. Chavan and Rajendra S. Bangal's *Informed Consent in Medical Practice* (2019), for example, offers a comprehensive view of the issue of informed consent in medical practice from a medicolegal perspective.[27] Meanwhile, *The Ethics of Consent* (2009), edited by philosophers Franklin Miller and Alan Wertheimer, provides a 'systematic analysis of the concept of consent and the moral and legal work that it performs', such as in healthcare, clinical research, and work contracts.[28] Andreas Müller and Peter Schaber's more recent *Routledge Handbook of the Ethics of Consent* (2018) examines some of the discussions around consent 'often reignited or reshaped by the progress of medicine, new technologies, or social developments'; like Miller and Wertheimer's volume, however, it predominantly spotlights perspectives from philosophers, legal scholars, and political theorists, rather than highlighting more cross-disciplinary approaches.[29] What distinguishes our collection is its diverse conceptual scope and commitment to cross-disciplinary dialogue, accommodating perspectives on consent that are contextually sensitive and culturally diverse.

Contexts of this Collection

To capture this spirit of open dialogue on consent, and actively interrogate its significance through time and space, we have titled this collection *Consent: Legacies, Representations, and Frameworks for the Future.* This reflects the historical roots, enduring relevance, and possible potential of consent – and the significance of sustaining conversations on this contested term. Indeed, our collection itself is a legacy of a conference co-organised by this editorial group in 2019 at Durham University (UK), where the editors met as doctoral and early career researchers. The conference, 'Consent: Histories, Representations, and Frameworks for the Future', originated as a series of conversations facilitated by shared office spaces and intra-departmental events, demonstrating the value of these spaces at a time when they are increasingly rare due to workloads and pressure on room bookings within universities that have benefited from the removal of the student cap. The conference was conceptualised in response to contemporary #MeToo and #TimesUp campaigns, as well as the work of the 1752 Group, an organisation addressing sexual misconduct in academic spaces.[30] We held the event at one of Durham's historic colleges, Josephine Butler, named after the nineteenth-century activist and social reformer who advocated for consent in healthcare, campaigning against the UK's Contagious Diseases Acts and against sexual slavery as a violation of consent. Butler was also a vocal critic of child prostitution and sex trafficking, championing women's right to consent in a society that sought to stymy it.[31]

Our overarching aim, with both the conference and this present collection, was to facilitate a collaborative space for dialogue on consent as it circulates in both pedagogy and practice – from the textual encounter to media and technology, and institutional policy-making. This collection was initially conceived of as a space to sustain the critical cross-disciplinary and cross-sectoral conversations generated from the conference, from literary analyses of medieval rape testimonies to legislative and technological considerations of consent, cutting across borders from England to South Asia. As it stands, however, this body of work has grown beyond this initial aim, reflecting the changing cultural and political climates over the intervening years; indeed, only a third of this collection comes from research originally presented at the conference. This evolution is captured in our taxonomic tweak, from 'Histories' in the conference title to 'Legacies' in this collection, as one of the representative components of our transtemporal and transgeographical approach to consent. Its historically entrenched significance notwithstanding, we have sought here to house a host of perspectives on consent that cut across contextual boundaries. While these issues remain embedded in sociocultural histories, their evolving expressions are inflected by contemporary realities, not just since Butler's work, but – as we editors became acutely aware – since our 2019 conference itself: from the COVID-19 pandemic, which radically transformed interpersonal dynamics and our relationships with work and technology, to heightened confrontations with the intersectional entanglements of embodied experience in healthcare. Our collection has thus expanded to reflect these shifting positionalities and landscapes, integrating perspectives far beyond the scope and space of the conference, whilst remaining firmly committed to an intersectional and interdisciplinary approach.

We have reflected on the term 'Representations' as this body of work has developed; the protracted process of producing this collection, since the conference and through the pandemic, has proven to be a critically self-reflexive space for us as editors and academics.[32] In their heightened urgency, we have included here perspectives on racial and sexual issues pertaining to embodied expressions of consent; consent and governmentality in post-Roe America; and pedagogical practices engaging with consent, to name a few. Acknowledging that these issues will resonate with and affect different readers in specific ways, we invited contributors to add content notes prefacing their chapter where they felt it appropriate to do so. Given the nature of the volume, some content warnings will already be evident, and some authors therefore chose to omit content notes. We felt it important to leave this decision to individual contributors, facilitating a specific and plural approach that is registered also in the formal and methodological diversity this collection accommodates: these creative and critical engagements with consent reflect its significance – thematically, theoretically, and experientially – across a range of cultural productions and platforms, from literature and film to music, performance art, and theatre.

But we remain mindful of the selective scope of our collection, in both its content and the process of co-production itself. While this collection takes care to foreground non-heteronormative formations and formulations of consent, and incorporates a robust range of queer approaches, crip and neurodiverse perspectives in particular remain notably absent; these are oft-marginalised, under- and/or mis-represented voices in academic spaces, and the difficulty in accessing and accommodating material from within disability studies may attest to broader structural issues of institutional access and representation.

We are mindful that our authorship is predominantly situated within UK, European, and North American academic contexts, and while the contributions offer important perspectives, it is worth acknowledging the representational privilege wielded in the academic milieu from which this collection is produced and within which it circulates. This space is itself not immune to the forms of cultural gatekeeping, barriers to access, and issues over rights of representation that exist within the broader socio-political landscape.

The lack of survivor narratives and survivor-led work in our own collection is a gap we have critically reflected on. Indeed, these voices have become more visible and audible in the wider literary landscape, with experiencer-centred testimonies such as Jonathan Dollimore's *Desire: A Memoir* (2017), Samra Habib's *We Have Always Been Here: A Queer Muslim Memoir* (2019), Carmen Maria Machado's *In the Dream House* (2019), and Vanessa Springora's *Consent: A Memoir* (2020) coming to the cultural fore. These works critically interrogate how consent is navigated when the body in question occupies multiple culturally defined and institutionally imposed forms of marginality: when the body occupies spaces where homosexual relationality, religion, and nationhood become sources of vulnerability. Shedding light on the oft-suppressed discourse on sexual violence and rape in the Indian socio-legal context, Sohaila Abdulali's *What We Talk about When We Talk about Rape* (2018) offers incisive theoretical critique on localised and globalised expressions of rape and sexual consent through the lens of Abdulali's personal experience as a survivor-activist. In a similar methodological vein, albeit with an unexpected re-orientation of representation, Tara Kaushal provocatively enfolds the perspectives of men involved – in various forms and contexts – with sexual crime in India in *Why Men Rape: An Indian Undercover Investigation* (2020). Moreover, Tanaka Mhishi's *Sons and Others: On Loving Male Survivors* (2022) addresses the barriers to understanding the experiences of male victim-survivors, including queer men's experiences of rape.[33] These accounts speak to the value of hybrid modalities of expression, and the urgency of broadening the remit of representation – creatively and contextually – to facilitate nuanced conversations on consent.

However, we are also cautious of the ethical quandaries involved in enfolding such work into what is largely an academic collection; we are wary of representation for its own sake, and the traps of forfeiting meaningful, ethically oriented engagement in the calls for inclusivity and inclusion that have come to dominate much of the discourse surrounding decolonial practice in academic spaces. We are also mindful of the challenging demands of personal disclosure that expert-by-experience accounts might raise, particularly when switching between theoretical and testimonial modes. Perhaps this speaks more deeply to certain vexities in the value-laden epistemic hierarchies erected between the academic and the anecdotal – boundaries which we seek to actively deconstruct here by demonstrating how institutional and popular cultures coalesce to construct and condition consent. How, then, might we accommodate and treat survivor accounts within 'conventional' academic forms of output? Can we meaningfully engage with these accounts through the methodological toolkit and modes of reception we are acculturated to in academic practice? What ethical and epistemic considerations might we need to address in multi-disciplinary work; how might we develop a sensitive space for meaningful cross-institutional and cross-sectoral collaboration?

These are questions that exceed the scope of this body of work. In gesturing towards 'Frameworks for the Future', this collection does not purport to answer or resolve these critical questions. We offer here a space for these complexities to be challenged and contested through the collection. These chapters are disciplinarily distinct but not discrete; they bridge boundaries by speaking to some of these core questions, attesting to the potential of such cross-contextual conversation in formulating effective, ethical modes of engaging with consent. And perhaps it is worth leaving these provocations as a critical frame for both authors and readers while engaging with this collection as well.

Overview of the Volume

This volume is divided into four parts, each of which incorporates diverse disciplinary perspectives. Shelby Judge opens Part I, 'Culture and Resistance', examining divergent adaptations of *The Iliad* in contemporary Anglophone women's writing. Judge explores shifting portrayals of Briseis, considering her as male possession, dispossessed of the right to consent. Her contribution provides a framework for the volume, pointing to transhistorical and transcultural debates about consent that resonate through subsequent chapters, albeit beginning with a narrative of particular importance to Western culture; the volume as a whole, however, seeks to move beyond this framework. Initiating this more expansive interrogation of consent, Eunice Rojas takes up Judge's discussion of sexual violence, moving from Ancient Greece to twenty-first-century Latin America in Chapter Three. In place of Homer's 'Song of Ilium', Rojas examines songs composed in 2016 as part of the #NiUnaMenos movement; attuned to the power of art as activism, she investigates music and performance as both protest against femicide and as a reassertion of women's agency. Iqra Shagufta Cheema similarly examines the provocative power of sound in the following chapter, interrogating the significance of the slogan *Mera Jism, Meri Marzi* ('my body, my choice') within Pakistan's contemporary feminist politics. As both spoken and written chant, Shagufta

Cheema traces the ways in which *Mera Jism, Meri Marzi* has reverberated beyond the Aurat March of 2018, becoming a focal point for debates about women's right to sexual consent, safety, and autonomy. However, although the slogan potently unites speech and sentiment, Shagufta Cheema exposes the tensions between older and younger generations of Pakistan's feminists that *Mera Jism, Meri Marzi* invoked, unwittingly reasserting patriarchal sexual anxieties and religio-political confusion. Just as Shagufta Cheema confronts conservative narratives of sexual agency, Jay Szpilka expands the interpretative parameters of consent through the concept of 'consensual non-consent' in Chapter Five, exploring BDSM practices in Poland. Informed by ethnographic research and queer and feminist theories, Szpilka examines the tension underpinning kink, its participants both chained to the need to maintain consent while yearning to break free of its bondage. All four chapters in Part I demonstrate that while 'culture' embeds concepts of consent, it also provides the means for evolution, scrutinising and shaping definitions and practices of consent across time and space. The chapters themselves protest against rigid and restrictive understandings of consent; revision becomes a form of resistance.

(Re)vision indeed underpins Part II, 'Consent on Stage and Screen', which explores the myriad ways consent is visualised in film, television, theatre, and online videos. Rebecca White's study of African American slave narratives in Chapter Six casts Szpilka's commentary on consent in 'bondage' in a different light, focusing on black women who – recalling Briseis – forcibly became (white) male property, subjected to sexual violence, scientific violation, and denied the right to (refuse) consent.[34] White traces the ongoing legacy of this abuse as it confronts twenty-first-century black US women, interrogating enslavement's complex and conflicted afterlives on screen and online. Christina Mansueti then returns to the question of non-consensual sex discussed in Part I, exploring Michaela Coel's television series *I May Destroy You* (BBC, 2020). In doing so, Mansueti engages with the dynamics of racial and sexual representation in relation to consent, trauma, and past and present British attitudes towards sexual assault. Taking up the often-blurred line between acting, role play, and reality raised by Szpilka in Chapter Five and by White in Chapter Six, Natashia Lindsey and Emily A. Rollie then illuminate the theatrical stage as a space in which consent can become problematic. Noting the potential for theatre artists to be driven into performing acts of physical intimacy through compulsion rather than consent, Lindsey and Rollie draw attention to the work of theatrical intimacy educators and choreographers; while applauding the tools they offer to help artists voice consent, they argue that such consent education should be expanded into a complete curriculum that moves beyond the stage and into the classroom. In scrutinising the visual, White, Mansueti, and Lindsey and Rollie make sometimes invisible issues regarding consent visible, demonstrating the ways in which visual culture can confirm, create, and contest discourses about consent.

Part III, 'Lived Experience and (Authorial) Expressions', then extends the discussion of coercion and violence traced in earlier chapters in the volume.

Megan Batterbee returns to the issue of rape that forms a connective thread between chapters, exploring the works of Mary Wollstonecraft and Mary Hays, whose Enlightenment feminism helped shape later, particularly Eurocentric, feminist discourses referenced throughout the volume. Recalling White's retrieval of nineteenth-century African American testimony, Batterbee recovers the voices of eighteenth-century England, examining Hays's and Wollstonecraft's rape survival narratives as vehicles for the re-establishment of violated female identity. Arya Thampuran, in Chapter Ten, takes up Batterbee's discussion of non-consent and recasts it, analysing epistemic and corporeal violence within the politics of (neo)colonial biopower and interrogating both literary and lived accounts of skin-based practices and perceptions of selfhood. Her work uncovers resistance to limiting and pathologising therapeutic discourses, resituating Akwaeke Emezi's *Freshwater* (2018) and autobiographical accounts of Inuit skin grafting beyond prescribed narratives of wellness. In Chapter Eleven, Catherine Donovan, Kate Butterby, and Rebecca Barnes locate Hays's and Wollstonecraft's concern with legitimising agency within the twenty-first century, interrogating the relationship power dynamics of LGB and/or T+ people; like Thampuran, they challenge 'normative' narratives, breaking down patriarchal public stories about love and intimacy that hinge upon binaries. The transhistorical, transcultural, and transnational questions regarding violence and violation posed by the chapters in this section resonate through the volume as a whole.

In many ways, such questions are answered by the practices, pedagogies, and developments explored by the contributions to the volume's final section, the 'Futures of Consent', which seeks to shape positive and proactive new attitudes towards, and activism about, consent. The transhistorical issues which connect chapters throughout the book speak to constant, yet ever-evolving, debates about consent. In Chapter Twelve, Rosanna Bellini and Hazel Dixon draw attention to the ways in which shifting technologies have shaped such debates. They return to the issues of sexual violence, violation, and consent pursued throughout this volume, placing them within a twenty-first-century digital age and scrutinising the relatively overlooked intersection between technology and sexuality. Noting the growing influence of digital systems (such as smartphone apps) in shaping sexual communication, Bellini and Dixon expose the dubious messages around consent that technological artefacts reinforce. They instead suggest improved practices for future technological design, spotlighting embodiment, flexibility, and reality. Kyle Murray, in Chapter Thirteen, similarly exposes troubling contemporary messages around consent, exploring the concept of 'deceptive sex' within the law in Wales and England; tracing twenty-first-century reforms to nineteenth-century legislation which centralises sexual autonomy in understanding consent, he uncovers a contemporary return to restrictive parameters in defining such autonomy and conceptualises a new approach through 'defined consent'. Caroline West then turns from courtroom to classroom and other educational contexts in Chapter Fourteen. Like Rollie and Lindsey, West considers the future of consent education, exploring Irish innovations in delivering college workshops addressing sexual violence and violation, including the use of textiles and dress as vehicles for conversation and change through social media. A recognition of the need to continually interrogate consent through conversation and change reverberates throughout the volume, culminating in Sudeshna Chatterjee's concluding chapter. She pursues feminist-decolonial approaches to frame consent through a critical-governmentality lens, scrutinising its redeployment in conservative narratives in twenty-first-century America. As foregrounded by Chapter Six's discussion of nineteenth-century African American enslavement, constitutional understandings of consent hold a complex and troubled history in the US. Chatterjee takes up this history, testing interpretations of consent at the core of the nation's social contract, complicating binary definitions that hinge around 'individual' and 'public', 'common good' and 'corruption'. Instead, Chatterjee draws upon the rescindment of Roe v. Wade (2022) to demonstrate the ways in which consent and the social contract are exclusionary practices, and to explore paths forward for racial and gendered equity. While the four chapters in this section scrutinise current debates surrounding consent, their transhistoricism also points to the persistence of violence and violation across time, an issue we unpack in the Afterword. Yet, in exposing embedded iniquities and troubling regressions, a pathway towards positive future practice is opened up, in which individual agency and choice are foundational to understandings of consent. It is such movement towards positive future practice that this volume as a whole seeks to celebrate and confirm.

Notes

1 Sir Thomas Malory, *Le Morte Darthur*, ed. by P. J. C. Field, Arthurian Studies, 80, 2 vols (Cambridge: Brewer, 2013), I, 631. Translation by Hannah Piercy.

2 On this episode, see Hannah Piercy, *Resistance to Love in Medieval English Romance: Negotiating Consent, Gender, and Desire*, Studies in Medieval Romance, 25 (Cambridge: Brewer, 2023); Kristina Hildebrand, '"I love nat to be constreyned to love": Launcelot and Coerced Sex', *Arthurian Literature*, 37 (2022), 175–92; David Grubbs, 'The Knight Coerced: Two Cases of Raped Men in Chivalric Romance', in *Teaching Rape in the Medieval Literature Classroom: Approaches to Difficult Texts*, ed. by Alison Gulley (Leeds: Arc Humanities Press, 2018), pp. 164–82; Catherine Batt, 'Malory and Rape', *Arthuriana*, 7.3 (1997), 78–99.

3 Katherine Angel, *Tomorrow Sex Will Be Good Again: Women and Desire in the Age of Consent* (London: Verso, 2021), p. 7.

4 For a definition of deceptive sex or rape by fraud, see Michael Mullen, 'Rape by Fraud: Eluding Washington Rape Statutes', *Seattle University Law Review*, 41.3 (2018), 1035–52 (p. 1035); or Kyle Murray's chapter in this volume.

5 'Sexual Offences Act 2003', legislation.gov.uk <https://www.legislation.gov.uk/ukpga/2003/42/section/1> [accessed 22 May 2023].

6 Corinne Saunders, *Rape and Ravishment in the Literature of Medieval England* (Cambridge: Brewer, 2001), pp. 20, 60–61.

7 Throughout this book, we have asked contributors not to use 'we' in a universalised sense. 'We' here and throughout this introduction denotes our collective editorial

team. Because issues of consent are specific to unique contexts, which are shaped by intersectional factors including but not limited to gender, sexuality, race, class and socioeconomic status, cultural backgrounds, colonialism, and capitalism, it is especially important to acknowledge our own positionality. We met whilst pursuing our doctorates at Durham University, a UK-based Higher Education Institution that has historically been a privileged, research-focused institution, presenting barriers to access for individuals from marginalised communities. We acknowledge that our positionality as editors is shaped by and reflects this sociocultural context: three of us are white scholars from the UK, and one of us is Southeast Asian by heritage with higher education pursued in the UK. We are all cisgender women and early career scholars working in varying degrees of academic precarity in the UK and Europe.

8 See Saunders, pp. 235–36; P. J. C. Field, *The Life and Times of Sir Thomas Malory*, Arthurian Studies, 29 (Cambridge: Brewer, 1993), p. 106; Christine Carpenter, 'Sir Thomas Malory and Fifteenth-Century Local Politics', *Bulletin of the Institute of Historical Research*, 53.127 (1980), 31–43 (pp. 37–38 n. 54). For a contrasting view, see Batt, p. 82.

9 While sexual violence is overwhelmingly a crime perpetrated by men upon women, Tanaka Mhishi argues powerfully against the idea that 'male survivors' stories are exceptions or irrelevances', pointing out that 'we share a world and our experiences are closely interwoven'. See *Sons and Others: On Loving Male Survivors* (n.p.: 404 Ink, 2022), p. 3.

10 See particularly Amia Srinivasan, *The Right to Sex* (London: Bloomsbury, 2021), pp. xiii, 36; Angel; Joseph J. Fischel, *Screw Consent: A Better Politics of Sexual Justice* (Oakland: University of California Press, 2019).

11 See further Fischel, p. 4. On negotiation, see Rebecca Kukla, 'That's What She Said: The Language of Sexual Negotiation', *Ethics*, 129.1 (2018), 70–97.

12 We draw here on the *OED* definition of consent as 'voluntary agreement' or 'acquiescence': 1. a, 'consent, n.', *OED* online. See also the discussion in Quill R. Kukla, 'A Nonideal Theory of Sexual Consent', *Ethics*, 131.2 (2021), 270–92.

13 For an overview of such approaches to consent, see Melanie Beres, '"Spontaneous" Sexual Consent: An Analysis of Sexual Consent Literature', *Feminism & Psychology*, 17.1 (2007), 93–108.

14 Tina Sikka, *Sex, Consent and Justice: A New Feminist Framework* (Edinburgh: Edinburgh University Press, 2021), pp. 31–32.

15 Angel, p. 27.

16 Mithu Sanyal, *Rape: From Lucretia to #MeToo* (London: Verso, 2019), p. 159.

17 Linda Martín Alcoff, *Rape and Resistance: Understanding the Complexities of Sexual Violation* (Cambridge: Polity, 2018), p. 174 (emphasis in original).

18 Ibid., p. 129.

19 Angela Onwuachi-Willig, 'What About #UsToo?: The Invisibility of Race in the #MeToo movement', *Yale Law Journal Forum*, 105 (2018), 105–20 (p. 107).

20 Sikka, p. 31.

21 Ibid., p. 26. See also the edited collection, *The Other #MeToos*, ed. by Iqra Shagufta Cheema (Oxford: Oxford University Press, 2023).

22 See, for example, Carol Pateman, 'Women and Consent', *Political Theory*, 8.2 (1980), 149–68; Catharine A. MacKinnon, *Toward a Feminist Theory of the State* (Cambridge, MA: Harvard University Press, 1989); Daniel Loick, '"… as if it were a thing." A Feminist Critique of Consent', *Constellations*, 27.3 (2019), 412–22; Srinivasan.

23 See Robin Bauer, 'Queering consent: Negotiating critical consent in les-bi-trans-queer BDSM contexts', *Sexualities*, 24.5–6 (2021), 767–83; Melanie Beres, 'From ignorance to knowledge: Sexual Consent and Queer Stories', *Feminism & Psychology*, 32.2 (2022), 137–55.

24 Bauer, pp. 779–80.

25 Alexandre Baril, 'Confessing Society, Confessing Cis-tem: Rethinking Consent through intimate images of trans* people in the media', *Frontiers: A Journal of Women Studies*, 39.2 (2018), 1–25 (pp. 1, 19).
26 Shantel Gabrieal Buggs and Trevor Hoppe, 'Introduction', in *Unsafe Words: Queering Consent in the #MeToo Era*, Q+ Public (New Brunswick, NJ: Rutgers University Press, 2023), pp. 1–18 (p. 10).
27 See Kalidas D. Chavan and Rajendra S. Bangal, *Informed Consent in Medical Practice: Principles and Convention* (New Delhi: Jaypee Brothers Medical Publishers, 2019).
28 Franklin Miller and Alan Wertheimer, 'Preface: The Ethics of Consent: Theory and Practice', in *The Ethics of Consent: Theory and Practice*, ed. by Franklin Miller and Alan Wertheimer (Oxford: Oxford University Press, 2009), pp. ix–xiii (p. x).
29 Andreas Müller and Peter Schaber, 'The Ethics of Consent: An Introduction', in *The Routledge Handbook of the Ethics of Consent*, ed. by Andreas Müller and Peter Schaber (Abingdon: Routledge, 2018), pp. 1–6 (p. 2).
30 For information on the work of the 1752 Group, see <https://1752group.com/>. For further reading on the intersectional approach to staff and student issues pertaining to sexual conduct in higher education, see Tiffany Page, Anna Bull, and Emma Chapman, 'Making Power Visible: "Slow Activism" to Address Staff Sexual Misconduct in Higher Education', *Violence Against Women*, 25 (2019), 1309–30; Susan Oman and Anna Bull, 'Joining up well-being and sexual misconduct data and policy in HE: "To stand in the gap" as a feminist approach', *Sociological Review*, 70 (2022), 21–38.
31 For further reading on Butler's advocacy in healthcare, see Margaret Hamilton, 'Opposition to the Contagious Diseases Acts, 1864–1886', *Albion*, 10 (1978), 14–27; for a robust engagement with Butler's campaigning against the sex and slave trades, and an analysis of what is contentiously termed the 'White Slave' beyond Europe, see Susan Mumm, 'Josephine Butler and the International Traffic in Women', in *Sex, Gender, and Religion: Josephine Butler Revisited*, ed. by Jenny Daggers and Diana Neal (New York: Peter Lang, 2006), pp. 55–71.
32 While the length of this process has been largely due to personal and external circumstances, including efforts to expand the scope of this volume and invite new contributors, we acknowledge the significance of slow scholarship, which has emerged in recent years in resistance to increasing demands placed on scholars working within neoliberal university structures to generate research and teaching at an increasingly accelerated, and often unsustainable, pace. In a collaborative article, Alison Mountz et al. argue that 'slow scholarship enables a feminist ethics of care that allows us to claim some time as our own, build shared time into everyday life, and help buffer each other from unrealistic and counterproductive norms that have become standard expectations'. Indeed, as Gita R. Mehrotra notes, 'slow scholarship calls on us to slow down in order to build deep, trusting relationships and to create space for dialog', a practice and ethos that we, as co-editors, have certainly benefitted from. See Alison Mountz et al., 'For Slow Scholarship: A Feminist Politics of Resistance through Collective Action in the Neoliberal University', *ACME: An International E-Journal for Critical Geographies*, 14.4 (2015), 1235–59 (pp. 1253–54); Gita R. Mehrotra, 'How We Do the Work Is the Work: Building an Intersectional Queer Praxis for Critical Feminist Scholarship', *Affilia: Feminist Inquiry in Social Work* (2022), 1–15 (p. 6) <https://doi.org/10.1177/08861099221137561>.
33 Mhishi.
34 In this volume, B/black is stylised according to authors' preference, as we are mindful of the sociopolitical valence of both versions of the term. A capital 'B' has often been used as a diasporic identity marker in popular media, one that also designates group solidarity in certain allied activist circles; a lowercase 'b' is

sometimes critiqued as being problematically suggestive of colour or a 'naturalised' biological category. However, the assumption of shared identity with the term 'Black' is also a source of contention, as it might elide intra-group differences engendered by sex, class, and other variable identity metrics. In the spirit of accommodating plural, intersectional viewpoints, and adopting a decolonial perspective on the way terminology circulates in popular culture and academic disciplines, we have left this decision to individual authors. This is also our practice for terms like people of colour, BIPOC, and global majority, the usage of which we have left to individual authors.

Bibliography

Abdulali, Sohaila, *What We Talk about When We Talk about Rape* (New York: New Press, 2018)

Alcoff, Linda Martín, *Rape and Resistance: Understanding the Complexities of Sexual Violation* (Cambridge: Polity, 2018)

Angel, Katherine, *Tomorrow Sex Will Be Good Again: Women and Desire in the Age of Consent* (London: Verso, 2021)

Baril, Alexandre, 'Confessing Society, Confessing Cis-tem: Rethinking Consent through Intimate Images of Trans* People in the Media', *Frontiers: A Journal of Women Studies*, 39.2 (2018), 1–25

Batt, Catherine, 'Malory and Rape', *Arthuriana*, 7.3 (1997), 78–99

Bauer, Robin, 'Queering Consent: Negotiating Critical Consent in Les-bi-trans-queer BDSM Contexts', *Sexualities*, 24.5–6 (2021), 767–83

Beres, Melanie, 'From Ignorance to Knowledge: Sexual Consent and Queer Stories', *Feminism & Psychology*, 32.2 (2022), 137–55

Beres, Melanie, '"Spontaneous" Sexual Consent: An Analysis of Sexual Consent Literature', *Feminism & Psychology*, 17.1 (2007), 93–108

Buggs, Shantel Gabrieal, and Trevor Hoppe, 'Introduction', in *Unsafe Words: Queering Consent in the #MeToo Era*, Q+ Public (New Brunswick, NJ: Rutgers University Press, 2023), pp. 1–18

Carpenter, Christine, 'Sir Thomas Malory and Fifteenth-Century Local Politics', *Bulletin of the Institute of Historical Research*, 53.127 (1980), 31–43

Chavan, Kalidas D., and Rajendra S. Bangal, *Informed Consent in Medical Practice: Principles and Convention* (New Delhi: Jaypee Brothers Medical Publishers, 2019)

Dollimore, Jonathan, *Desire: A Memoir* (London: Bloomsbury Academic, 2017)

Field, P. J. C., *The Life and Times of Sir Thomas Malory*, Arthurian Studies, 29 (Cambridge: Brewer, 1993)

Fischel, Joseph J., *Screw Consent: A Better Politics of Sexual Justice* (Oakland: University of California Press, 2019)

Grubbs, David, 'The Knight Coerced: Two Cases of Raped Men in Chivalric Romance', in *Teaching Rape in the Medieval Literature Classroom: Approaches to Difficult Texts*, ed. by Alison Gulley (Leeds: Arc Humanities Press, 2018), pp. 164–82

Habib, Samra, *We Have Always Been Here: A Queer Muslim Memoir* (London: riverrun, 2019)

Hamilton, Margaret, 'Opposition to the Contagious Diseases Acts, 1864–1886', *Albion*, 10 (1978), 14–27

Hildebrand, Kristina, '"I love nat to be constreyned to love": Launcelot and Coerced Sex', *Arthurian Literature*, 37 (2022), 175–92

Kaushal, Tara, *Why Men Rape: An Indian Undercover Investigation* (Delhi: Harper Collins Publishers India, 2020)

Kukla, Quill R., 'A Nonideal Theory of Sexual Consent', *Ethics*, 131.2 (2021), 270–92

Kukla, Rebecca, 'That's What She Said: The Language of Sexual Negotiation', *Ethics*, 129.1 (2018), 70–97 [cited according to author's preference]

Loick, Daniel, '"… as if it were a thing." A Feminist Critique of Consent', *Constellations*, 27.3 (2019), 412–22

Machado, Carmen Maria, *In the Dream House* (Minneapolis: Graywolf Press, 2019)

MacKinnon, Catharine A., *Toward a Feminist Theory of the State* (Cambridge, MA: Harvard University Press, 1989)

Malory, Sir Thomas, *Le Morte Darthur*, ed. by P. J. C. Field, Arthurian Studies, 80, 2 vols (Cambridge: Brewer, 2013), I

Mehrotra, Gita R., 'How We Do the Work Is the Work: Building an Intersectional Queer Praxis for Critical Feminist Scholarship', *Affilia: Feminist Inquiry in Social Work* (2022), 1–15 <https://doi.org/10.1177/08861099221137561>

Mhishi, Tanaka, *Sons and Others: On Loving Male Survivors* (n.p.: 404 Ink, 2022)

Miller, Franklin, and Alan Wertheimer, 'Preface: The Ethics of Consent: Theory and Practice', in *The Ethics of Consent: Theory and Practice*, ed. by Franklin Miller and Alan Wertheimer (Oxford: Oxford University Press, 2009), pp. ix–xiii

Mountz, Alison, Anne Bonds, Becky Mansfield, Jenna Loyd, Jennifer Hyndman, Margaret Walton-Roberts, Ranu Basu, Risa Whitson, Roberta Hawkins, Trina Hamilton, and Winifred Curran, 'For Slow Scholarship: A Feminist Politics of Resistance through Collective Action in the Neoliberal University', *ACME: An International E-Journal for Critical Geographies*, 14.4 (2015), 1235–59

Müller, Andreas, and Peter Schaber, 'The Ethics of Consent: An Introduction', in *The Routledge Handbook of the Ethics of Consent*, ed. by Andreas Müller and Peter Schaber (Abingdon: Routledge, 2018), pp. 1–6

Mullen, Michael, 'Rape by Fraud: Eluding Washington Rape Statutes', *Seattle University Law Review*, 41.3 (2018), 1035–52

Mumm, Susan, 'Josephine Butler and the International Traffic in Women', in *Sex, Gender, and Religion: Josephine Butler Revisited*, ed. by Jenny Daggers and Diana Neal (New York: Peter Lang, 2006), pp. 55–71

Oman, Susan, and Anna Bull, 'Joining Up Well-Being and Sexual Misconduct Data and Policy in HE: "To stand in the gap" as a Feminist Approach', *Sociological Review*, 70 (2022), 21–38

Onwuachi-Willig, Angela, 'What About #UsToo?: The Invisibility of Race in the #MeToo Movement', *Yale Law Journal Forum*, 105 (2018), 105–20

Page, Tiffany, Anna Bull, and Emma Chapman, 'Making Power Visible: "Slow Activism" to Address Staff Sexual Misconduct in Higher Education', *Violence Against Women*, 25 (2019), 1309–30

Pateman, Carol, 'Women and Consent', *Political Theory*, 8.2 (1980), 149–68

Piercy, Hannah, *Resistance to Love in Medieval English Romance: Negotiating Consent, Gender, and Desire*, Studies in Medieval Romance, 25 (Cambridge: Brewer, 2023)

Sanyal, Mithu, *Rape: From Lucretia to #MeToo* (London: Verso, 2019)

Saunders, Corinne, *Rape and Ravishment in the Literature of Medieval England* (Cambridge: Brewer, 2001)

'Sexual Offences Act 2003', legislation.gov.uk <http://www.legislation.gov.uk/ukpga/2003/42/section/3> [accessed 22 May 2023]

Shagufta Cheema, Iqra, ed., *The Other #MeToos* (Oxford: Oxford University Press, 2023)
Sikka, Tina, *Sex, Consent and Justice: A New Feminist Framework* (Edinburgh: Edinburgh University Press, 2021)
Springora, Vanessa, *Consent: A Memoir* (London: Harper Collins, 2021)
Srinivasan, Amia, *The Right to Sex* (London: Bloomsbury, 2021)

Part I
Culture and Resistance

2 Could Briseis Consent? A Critical Comparison of Contemporary Women Writers' Adaptations of Briseis's Narrative

Shelby Judge

Content Notes: This chapter contains references to rape, sexual violence, degradation, war and conflict, including brief references to Ukraine and the Rohingya.

Raped women have been artists' muses for centuries. How are we, as twenty-first-century readers, expected to contend with the litany of sexual violence in Greek myth, and how can we address centuries of fetishised depictions of sexual violence? Through an investigation of Briseis and Achilles's relationship in contemporary feminist adaptations of Greek myth, namely in Emily Hauser's *For the Most Beautiful* (2016), Pat Barker's *The Silence of the Girls* (2018) and *The Women of Troy* (2021), and Madeline Miller's *The Song of Achilles* (2011), this chapter will consider whether Briseis could be capable of consent. Could Briseis ever consent to a relationship with Achilles since he literally owned her, and what questions are generated by a consenting or raped Briseis, in light of discourses surrounding #MeToo? In asking whether Briseis can consent, an insight is gained into what the expectations are for portraying consent in post-#MeToo literature. In addition, by using Briseis's adaptations as a case study, a discussion is opened on how twenty-first-century readers deal with the omnipresent theme of rape in Greek myth.

'Go into any art museum', directs Helen Morales, and you will see Daphne metamorphosing into a tree, *The Rape of Europa, The Rape of the Sabine Women, The Rape of Proserpina*, 'Lucretia, Leda, Polyxena, Cassandra, Deianeira…'.[1] Furthermore, myths provide a repertoire of rape narratives, including Phaedra who lied about being raped, Cassandra who was punished for revoking consent, and Medusa who was punished for being raped. For Morales, 'predatory men still silence women; the removal of Philomela's tongue is the original nondisclosure agreement' and 'the myth of Helen is perhaps the most dangerous of all the rape myths' because it has been told and retold in so many different ways that it is impossible to discern whether she consents.[2] She continues that these rape myths – that is, myths depicting rape, rather than untruths about rape itself – are 'firmly entrenched in our culture' and they certainly contribute to the normalising of sexual violence and rape culture in the West.[3] As much as these myths concerning sexual violence provide the framework for rape culture, they also contain the seeds

DOI: 10.4324/9781003365082-3

for #MeToo, which Morales finds in the sisterhood of Philomela and Procne, and the determination of Ceres/Demeter in her search for Proserpina/Persephone.[4] Because such myths focus on the trauma, strength, and survival of victims, they can still resonate even in this post-#MeToo world. It is these threads that are often pulled by contemporary feminist adapters, who can draw upon nuanced portrayals of women in myth or, alternatively, can weave in new narrative threads where the women have not previously been given voices. The Trojan Saga has become a particular source of interest for writers seeking a mythological framework through which to discuss #MeToo, power, and consent, due to its variety of female characters, opportunities to write about women's experiences in wartime, and its ability to use the martial conflict as an analogue for gender-based power imbalances and violence. For the purposes of this study, *consent* will be understood within a framework of feminist philosophy and sexual ethics, in which affirmative consent requires enthusiastic and informed approval before and throughout any interaction. This framework is not without its limitations. Ellie Anderson lists seven key problems with consent, including that consent functions primarily to shield individuals from sexual assault; consent reinforces the idea that men ask for sex and women respond; consent fails to register the temporally unfolding nature of sexual encounters, nor their ambiguity; and it can stifle nuanced understandings of consent and pleasure.[5] Anderson proposes focusing on the felt dimensions of sexual subjectivity, rather than the current legalistic approach, to prioritise the ways that feelings exist in relation to sex, taking into account social scripts and power relations.

Before addressing the central question of this chapter – could Briseis consent? – one must first contextualise the present literary landscape. The current vogue for feminist adaptation of myth in contemporary women's writing can hardly be overstated. Some of the most prominent contemporary writers – Margaret Atwood, Ali Smith, Jeanette Winterson, Pat Barker – have contributed to this trend, while some authors' entire oeuvre is in this genre, such as Natalie Haynes, Jennifer Saint, and Madeline Miller. Literature within this genre has won the Women's Prize for Fiction (*The Song of Achilles*, 2012), and garnered much online attention from reviewers and fandoms. Greek myths offer an interconnected network of characters and stories: when texts such as Saint's *Ariadne* (2021) and Miller's *Circe* (2018) include many of the same characters, plot points, and stylistic choices, the novels can be considered paraquels.[6] Adrienne Westenfeld recently compared this to the Marvel Cinematic Universe. Just as Spiderman's origin can be told in multiple superhero movies, the mythic narratives of Penelope, Clytemnestra, or Antigone are ripe for retelling by different authors. There is a consumerist hope — held by publishers, producers, and fans alike — for 'a Marvel-style Mythology Cinematic Universe', which will begin with HBO Max's forthcoming eight-part miniseries based on Miller's *Circe*.[7] This proliferation of women's myth writing and the huge popularity of the novels has not only inspired other authors, but has also signalled to the publishing industry an extremely profitable niche in the market.

It is also necessary to ask: who is Briseis? 'Rage—Goddess, sing the rage of Peleus' son Achilles': the *Iliad* opens with Achilles's rage at losing Briseis – his 'war prize', his sex slave – to Agamemnon, who claims her in compensation for losing his own prize, Chryseis.[8] Though the loss of Briseis opens the *Iliad*, she has since fallen into relative obscurity, particularly in comparison to Helen, ostensibly the motivator of the Trojan War itself, and Penelope, the heroine of the domestic plot of the *Odyssey*. In the *Iliad*, Briseis's background is only mentioned once, and it is focused on the experiences of 'The brilliant runner Achilles' who 'lay among his ships, / raging over Briseis, the girl with lustrous hair, / The prize he seized from Lyrnessus— / After he had fought to exhaustion'.[9] This scene is dedicated to Achilles's present heartbreak at losing Briseis to Agamemnon and his previous victory. Briseis's only other presence in the epic is when Agamemnon returns her and when we see her mourn for Patroclus.[10] As Harold Isbell indicates, in the *Iliad*, Briseis is 'scarcely developed and she is little more than a pivot around which the fabled wrath of Achilles is developed'.[11] The fact that Briseis is relatively forgotten in modern culture makes her a prime candidate for feminist reimaginings. Susan Sellers theorises that feminist rewriting can be organised into two categories: 'as an act of demolition, exposing and detonating the stories that have hampered women, and a task of construction – of bringing into being enabling alternatives'.[12] Briseis's myth falls into the latter category, as her comparative obscurity means that her myth is ripe for 'revitalising', and adapting her is 'a task of construction' more than of exposition or revisitation.

In *For the Most Beautiful*, Hauser presents the most dissimilar iteration of Briseis and Achilles's relationship compared to other novelistic retellings, as it is a romantic, consensual relationship. Achilles raids Briseis's land and kills her three brothers, as well as her father and her husband. Yet, when Briseis sees Achilles kill her entire family, she focuses on 'His eyes glitter[ing] in the dark, the skin of his arms and chest tight over smooth muscles, […] His strangeness [that] was painfully gorgeous, [and] his slim height'.[13] The focus on Achilles's sexually alluring physical features demonstrates Briseis's initial attraction to him, covered as he is in the blood of his victims, namely her family and the people of Lyrnessus. The portrayal of Achilles and Briseis's relationship as mutually passionate has its roots in ancient literature. In *Heroides* III, Ovid has Briseis recount their mutual passion, 'You will remember when my arms touch your neck; / the sight of my breasts will stir your heart'.[14] However, Isbell notes that, for Ovid's Briseis, 'the attraction identified as love is dangerously close to the fear of abandonment' and that their relationship is not 'that of two lovers made equal by the intensity of their affection'.[15] For Ovid, Briseis's feelings are necessarily informed by her uncertain future as Achilles's prize in Agamemnon's camp and her subjugation under a man who killed her family and who is at once her 'lover and lord'.[16] Hauser's choice to portray their relationship as a romance is perhaps a response to what Sarah Pomeroy calls the 'grim picture' of the 'endless catalogue of rape in Greek myth'[17] – a consenting Briseis does not become one of the 'endless catalogue' of victims of sexual violence in Greek myth.

Pomeroy offers 'the erotic fantasies of modern women' as another perspective from which to view myths about rape.[18] She suggests that 'women frequently enjoy the fantasy of being overpowered, carried away, and forced to submit to an ardent lover' so perhaps 'Greek women dreamed of being Leda enfolded by the soft, warm caress of Zeus'.[19] Within this interpretation, Briseis consenting to the conquering Achilles becomes a sexual fantasy, though one that admittedly is 'a symptom of masochism, [and] the result of women's repression by society'.[20] This theory from Pomeroy is jarring, since her monograph *Goddesses, Whores, Wives, and Slaves* (1975) is considered a feminist polemic in the field of Classics. It is worth noting that the misapprehension that violence was welcome in sexual initiation was still ingrained in law until the 1970s, which may account for Pomeroy's stance.[21] It is therefore evident that Hauser's choice to portray Briseis and Achilles's relationship as a romance recalls troubling and outdated perspectives on sexual violence, namely that it can be explained away by women's sexual fantasies. This discussion gestures towards a significant contention in classical scholarship, that which an introduction to feminist classicist scholarship calls the 'fertile and seminal topic' of the theme of rape: 'What are we today to make of the many classical myths of ardent pursuit as well as those of amorous conquest? Are they religious stories, are they love stories, or are they in the end all fundamentally horrifying tales of victimisation?'[22] Put simply: how do we contend with the prevalence of rape in Greek myth and literature? In the case of *For the Most Beautiful*, changing the central relationship into one shaped by mutual lust and affection redresses the omnipresence of rape in Greek myth.

However, Hauser perpetuates troubling traditions in romance literature when it comes to consent. Rachel Brownstein points out that the 'heroine [in the romantic tradition] may say or even think she is of no importance; people may try to use her as a pawn, a mere means to their ends'.[23] Romance heroines often lack agency beyond choosing who to marry and, despite often being the protagonists, their (sexual and social) desires are secondary to what society and the male characters demand. The paucity of informed consent in romance literature has faced renewed scrutiny in recent years: the '#MeToo movement has sparked a reckoning about power, sex, and consent that has already reached deep into the entertainment industry, inspiring conversations about how to build a better popular culture'.[24] Although romantic and erotic fiction was initially 'marked by consent that was questionable at best and totally absent at worst', the genre has progressed to the point where 'Navigating consent [is] an essential element of the romance novelist's craft'.[25] Because of the prominence of consent in contemporary discourse, there is a certain expectation for this to be reflected in recent women's writing. As Mithu Sanyal explains in *Rape: From Lucretia to #MeToo* (2019), '#MeToo isn't just about sexual crimes but about a much wider discussion of sexual ethics'.[26] Can Briseis consent in a way that encompasses the sexual ethics of a post-#MeToo era? In *For the Most Beautiful*, Briseis consents 'Because nothing else made sense, except the closeness of his body against [hers] [...] and that [they] were together'.[27] The typically romantic language is intended to suggest a modern romance, and it is arguable that this portrays a sex-positive feminist message in which Briseis is making her own choice. However, when Achilles takes Briseis as his war prize and sex slave in the novel, he says: '"I shall not force you, [...] No one should make love because they have to. [...] But remember this, Briseis, [...] You *will* come to my bed. I shall not wait forever."'[28] Achilles tells Briseis that he will not rape her, but that she '*will*' have sex with him, and that his patience has limits. This is the man who killed her entire family, razed her city, and has enslaved her. While the language of romance is an attempt to recast Achilles and Briseis's relationship in terms of modern romance literature, the coercive consent suggests that this is an outdated model of romantic literature, marked by dubious consent practices. Although *For the Most Beautiful* was published in 2016, a year before #MeToo became a global phenomenon, the novel's readership increased as the feminist adaptation of myth genre boomed in 2018, meaning that many readers expected a novel that aligned with post-#MeToo ethics. It is also worth noting that the novel was published after Margaret Atwood's *The Penelopiad* (2005) and Ursula Le Guin's *Lavinia* (2007), both overtly feminist retellings of Greek myth, which Hauser studied in her doctoral thesis.[29] Briseis's consent 'doesn't break with gender scripts of women as passive recipients of men's violent desires',[30] and therefore fails to redress the litany of sexual violence in classical and romance literature.

In terms of power dynamics, Achilles is literally Briseis's owner, and therefore she cannot consent, since she does not have the power to withhold consent. The US National Sexual Violence Resource Centre (NSVRC) clarifies that consent can be complicated when one partner holds more power than the other. Relevant to Briseis and Achilles, the NSVRC specifies that 'Someone may have more social privilege than their partner – [...] White privilege, male privilege, and other unearned advantages are part of the power some of us bring to relationships'.[31] Achilles is a man in a patriarchal society, as well as the leader of the Myrmidon army and the best hero among the Greeks, while Briseis is a slave. In relation to modern conceptions of consensual relationships, Briseis and Achilles's relationship in *For the Most Beautiful* is ultimately problematic. As Aimee Hinds Scott argues, a reception is not automatically feminist because it has a female narrator; if motifs of sexual violence and systemic oppression are ignored or glossed over in the retelling, misogynistic tropes that can lead to actual violence are perpetuated, rather than remedied.[32] Hauser's novel cannot therefore be categorised as a *feminist* adaptation of Greek myth simply because Briseis is a narrator.[33] Having Briseis consent to Achilles indicates that the novel chooses romance over remedying the recurrent themes of coercion to violent rape that have persisted throughout the centuries.

In the novel's 'Author's Note', Hauser states that Briseis and Chryseis's experiences as women in wartime can be generalised to 'female prisoners of war' throughout history which 'makes us reflect on the experience of war for everyone'.[34] Similarly, Pat Barker's intention in *The Silence of the Girls* was to use the ancient story to bring awareness to 'issues such as the Rohingya women and the Democratic Republic of Congo, which is […] the rape capital of the world. I was very much aware of rape as an instrument of war'.[35] Briseis's experience as a rape victim and enslaved person during the Trojan War can therefore narrate women's experiences in wartime throughout history. *The Silence of the Girls* opens with 'Great Achilles. Brilliant Achilles, shining Achilles, godlike Achilles […] how the epitaphs pile up. We never called him any of those things; we called him "the Butcher"'.[36] This opening specifically engages with the classical tradition by quoting Achilles's epithets from the *Iliad*, therefore asserting that Barker's novel is not interested in preserving Achilles's legend – it is focused on women's experiences in wartime. Barker also recounts that 'the #MeToo movement was happening when I was in the very final stages of editing the book, and I had this extraordinary thing where I had written a book about the Bronze Age and suddenly it sounds more and more topical, every day'.[37] As Morford et al. note, 'Feminist authors too are creating new versions of traditional tales designed to illuminate their point of view about political, social, and sexual conflict between men and women in our world today'.[38] In the case of Barker's interpretation of Briseis, Briseis's experiences relate to women who are sexually abused during wartime and the sexual exploitation of women in contemporary society more generally. The following analysis of Briseis's experiences in the novel as unflinchingly brutal is not only Barker's interpretation of Briseis's myth, but also a confrontation of the long history of women's violent sexual oppression within patriarchy.

The candid portrayal of 'rape as an instrument of war' in *The Silence of the Girls* is illustrated when Achilles chooses Briseis as his 'prize of honour'.[39] Briseis remarks 'What can I say? He wasn't cruel […] He fucked as quickly as he killed, and for me it was the same thing. Something in me died that night'.[40] The idiom 'What can I say?' communicates the unspeakable trauma of rape; unlike Hauser and Miller, who attempt to rewrite Briseis's rape and preserve Achilles's honour, Barker is showing the reality of captured women in wartime, that they will be dehumanised, raped, and brutalised. This bleak reality is initially supplemented by the matter-of-fact tone, but the equating of rape and death and the short clauses show the emotional and physical horror of rape. Briseis continually refers to herself as a slave – a sex slave, a bed slave, an enslaved symbol of Achilles's honour – as well as comparing herself to the kings' assets and dogs, because she is aware of how she is valued and commodified. Briseis reflects that 'A slave isn't a person who's being treated as a thing. A slave *is* a thing, as much in her own estimation as in anybody else's'.[41] This demonstrates the motif of dehumanisation in the novel, and the use of the feminine pronoun asserts Barker's intention to focus on the lived experiences of enslaved women in war encampments. She also compares her relative luck at being Achilles's prize to the fortunes of 'the common women around the campfires', who are repeatedly brutalised and then have to fight the stray dogs for scraps and sleeping spaces.[42] Relatedly, Barker's adaptation does not forswear the grotesque realities of life in war encampments, as we see in gruesome detail the filth of the living conditions: 'I noticed a rat running between piles of rotting food. [... Blood erupted from its mouth; [...] maggots [were] busy underneath its skin'.[43] The visceral imagery not only foreshadows the plague; it also reveals the disgusting realities of war encampments, literally in terms of the filth and ideologically in terms of the abuse of women.

In the *Iliad*, Agamemnon takes Briseis from Achilles, and when he later returns her, he swears he has not raped her. In both Hauser's and Miller's adaptations, that remains true. Again, Barker departs from this: her Agamemnon 'prefers the back door'.[44] This euphemism undermines his ultimate power, since the enslaved women mock him when they are alone. In an interview, Barker remarked that the conversations between women are significant because they reflect the way that 'women have always gotten together to speak about men in a kind of ribald, passive-aggressive way, because they have no actual power'.[45] Agamemnon's proclivity for anal sex causes the women to view him as a sadistic sexual deviant, because it causes more physical pain for his victims (indeed, the women's network offers support to Agamemnon's victims, emotionally as well as pragmatically with a healing salve made of goose fat and herbs). Agamemnon's brutality is furthered by his favourite prize being 'the youngest of us, Chryseis, [who] was fifteen years old; the [sweet] daughter of a priest'.[46] The youth and sweetness of Chryseis is emphasised to render Agamemnon the most sadistic rapist in the Greek army. When Briseis remembers being seized by Agamemnon, she narrates that 'Achilles cried when I was taken away. *He* cried; *I* didn't. [...] *But I cried that night*'.[47] This simultaneously demeans Achilles's legend as a hyper-masculine hero, shows that she does not love Achilles, and expresses her trauma. Perhaps the most demeaning action in the novel is carried out by Agamemnon, as Briseis describes: 'inserting a finger between my teeth to prise my jaws apart, he worked up a big gob of phlegm – leisurely, taking his time about it – and spat it into my open mouth'.[48] This is an act of ownership, domination, and dehumanisation, capturing his privilege and her lack of agency. Agamemnon's irredeemability as a character is a common trope amongst such adaptations. While Achilles is cast as a 'Butcher' or, more often, a tragic hero, Agamemnon is a politician, warmonger, and sexual deviant. This depiction is quite a departure from Agamemnon's characterisation in the *Iliad*, where he is chosen by the gods to lead the Greeks. Instead, Agamemnon's irredeemability owes more to his portrayal in Aeschylus's *Agamemnon*, where he has earned *dikē* (punishment) for sacrificing Iphigenia; the sack of Troy with its attendant atrocities; and the inherited crimes of his father.[49] Clytemnestra calls him 'that polluted criminal';[50] and it is this iteration and condemnation of Agamemnon that survives in contemporary retellings, perhaps due to anti-war sentiments and the familiarity of a corrupt, profiteering politician to modern readers. Although Barker's portrayal of Briseis's experience is the most upsetting to read in terms of women's experiences of brutalisation, rape, and dehumanisation, it is also the account that affords Briseis the most opportunity to tell her own story, without focusing on Achilles's legend.

In *The Silence of the Girls*, Briseis survives in a number of ways. First, she outlives Achilles. She also survives in terms of her pregnancy and her story. Before Achilles dies, he impregnates her, and she views this as a reclamation of her body, concluding that 'this flesh, this intricate mesh of bone and nerve and muscle, belonged *to me.* In spite of Achilles, in spite of my aching hips and thighs'.[51] Raping local women is a typical aspect of warfare in the same way that pillaging property is; men's possessions – gold and women – are claimed like their land.[52] However, Briseis reclaims her body and therefore, despite the physical atrocities that she has experienced, she cannot be conquered in the same way that Troy has been. Brooke Ophardt argues that the commodification of reproduction strips women of their bodily autonomy during their pregnancies and, throughout history, women have been valued for predominantly reproductive purposes.[53] Yet this concept is subverted in Briseis's narrative because she had no bodily autonomy to begin with, due to her being a war bride, so her pregnancy actually re-establishes her bodily autonomy.

Additionally, Briseis considers her literary afterlife a form of survival, which is evident when she contemplates the vital role women play in oral history:

> *We're going to survive* — our *songs,* our *stories. They'll never be able to forget us. Decades after the last man who fought at Troy is dead, their sons will remember the songs their Trojan mothers sang to them.* [54]

While the Greeks can 'claim' these women, marry them and impregnate them, they are still 'Trojan', which is to say, they still have their identities separate to the ones that the invading armies ascribe onto them. Furthermore, despite the Greeks' victory, Trojan heritage will continue with the Trojan women, and in the Greeks' future lineage because of the children that they have with the captured Trojan women. However, Barker's Briseis does not romanticise the masculine domination of literature, as she bitterly reflects that the surviving narrative will be 'His story. *His*, not mine', here referring to the fact that the surviving stories of the Trojan War will be remembered by men and about men.[55] The phrasing 'His story' orally becomes 'history' which, when followed by the emphasised '*His*', suggests a reference to 'Herstory'. Herstory was first coined over fifty years ago by feminist activist Robin Morgan in her creative writing anthology *Sisterhood is Powerful* (1970) and refers to women's often-overlooked positions in history. Herstory is particularly significant here, because Briseis's role in this ancient story and in later receptions was minimised and relatively forgotten. When considering the erasure of women in history, Briseis also criticises the sanitisation of the epics in order to preserve the heroic reputations of the men: 'They won't want to know we were living in a rape camp'.[56] Briseis's ending in *The Silence of the Girls* overcomes the historic suppression of women's voices and thus counters the patriarchal notion that '"*Silence becomes a woman*"' while also giving Briseis a narrative in which she reclaims her bodily autonomy.[57]

In the sequel to *The Silence of the Girls, The Women of Troy*, Briseis's freedom and autonomy manifest in contrast to the fates of Helen and Amina. The novel is set after the fall of Troy, but before the ships have departed for Greece. Briseis is technically free from slavery and she has freedom of movement – she is even free from sexual assault, since she is married to Achilles's charioteer, but he has not consummated the marriage, due to his continued loyalty to Achilles. This contrasts to Helen's fate in the novel as a victim of domestic violence – she is visibly bruised, due to Menelaus punishing her for what he perceives to be her role in instigating the war. Briseis sees through the guise of the Trojan War: 'Poor Helen. All that beauty, all that grace – and she was really just a mouldy old bone for feral dogs to fight over'.[58] Consequently, Helen becomes as much a victim of the war as Briseis. The issue of Helen's blame in the Trojan War is a contentious one: either Helen is an evil seductress entirely to blame for the thousands of deaths in a decade-long war, or she completely lacks agency because she was stolen and then used as an excuse for a war about trade.[59] In Barker's *The Women of Troy*, she is a victim of domestic violence resulting from the perception that she is to blame. There is also the invented subplot of Barker's character Amina, who buries Priam in defiance of Neoptolemus's ruling that he shall remain unburied. This is, of course, an importation of the plot of Sophocles's *Antigone*. Like Antigone's call to honour the laws of the gods over those of Creon, Amina challenges Neoptolemus's ruling with the words 'you can't just overrule the laws of god. Nobody can – I don't care how powerful you are'.[60] Barker's Briseis becomes Ismene in this subplot. In Sophocles's drama, Ismene calls to be martyred alongside her sister, declaring 'I share the guilt, / the consequences too', but she is ultimately excluded from the consequences.[61] This is also the case for Briseis: Neoptolemus kills Amina (a more direct version of Creon's condemnation of Antigone), while Briseis is spared due to her pregnancy with Achilles's child. Why has Barker chosen to import this myth into her retelling, and what does it tell us about the enduring legacy of Antigone's myth? As Daniel Mendelsohn argues, it is 'a clever means of infusing all the abjection and the moralising with some genuine drama'.[62] In deploying Antigone in this uncanny context (familiar in its Greek mythological setting; unfamiliar in the Trojan, rather than Theban, Cycle), Barker is borrowing and redeploying the instantly recognisable symbol of a powerless girl standing up to a corrupt, patriarchal power. Hence, in *Women of Troy*, the motifs of sexual violence and moral degradation in wartime from the novel's predecessor are expanded upon, as the most beautiful woman in the world is abused and Antigone traverses sagas to once again oppose unjust patriarchs.

Barker's novels foreground women's abuse, and they therefore sharply contrast to Hauser's romanticisation of Achilles and Briseis's relationship. Finally, Miller's *The Song of Achilles* also eclipses the abuse and lack of consent at the heart of Briseis's story by completely desexualising and sanitising the relationship between Achilles and Briseis in order to accentuate the romance between Achilles and Patroclus. Achilles and Patroclus rescue Briseis from the soldiers who seek to brutalise her. This starkly contrasts to the other women in the Greek camps who are dressed in rags and have to serve the people who murdered their families, then 'At night they served in other ways, and I [Patroclus] cringed at the cries that reached even our corner of the camp'.[63] This completely sanitises Briseis's story to keep Achilles's legend untarnished, in order to make him an acceptable queer romantic lead, thereby placing more value on his character than on her suffering. Briseis's captivity is told through the lens of Achilles and Patroclus's heroism in saving her, and the women's experiences of being brutalised focuses on Patroclus's discomfort in hearing it. In *Down Girl: The Logic of Misogyny* (2018), Kate Manne coins the term 'himpathy' to refer to 'the flow of sympathy away from female victims towards their male victimizers'.[64] Manne points to the 'golden boy' narrative that surrounded Brock Turner as evidence of 'the excessive sympathy sometimes shown toward male perpetrators of sexual violence'.[65] This is a useful framework when considering Miller's treatment of Briseis, because Achilles is specifically exonerated from the crime of rape that he had committed in previous versions of the story, to present a more sympathetic romantic lead. Briseis's victimhood is completely unwritten to achieve the romantic relationship between Achilles and Patroclus. Of course, adaptations can be selective, choosing which elements of the stories to include to fit their aims; they do not have to incorporate all the original stories. Both Julie Sanders and Linda Hutcheon emphasise this in their critical texts on adaptation. Sanders states that 'the rewrite [...] invariably transcends mere imitation, serving instead in the capacity of incremental literature', demonstrating this idea of adapting authors selectively rewriting in order to meet the aims of 'not replication as such, but rather complication, expansion rather than contraction'.[66] Hutcheon concurs that selection is a key part of adaptations, since 'the appeal of adaptations [...] lies in their mixture of repetition and difference, of familiarity and novelty'.[67] Though adapting authors benefit from the familiar mythic templates, their divergences from the originals are an essential part of the adaptation.

Finally, Natalie Haynes's *A Thousand Ships* shares the blame for Briseis's maltreatment between Achilles and Patroclus. While Achilles 'slaughtered Lyrnessus as easily as drawing breath', he claims Briseis as a gift for Patroclus, who rapes her: 'She did not weep when Patroclus took her to his bed, even though the memory of her husband was still so raw'.[68] 'Gentle' Patroclus – a reputation that he often keeps in modern retellings – becomes complicit in Achilles's violence and a beneficiary of it.[69] The entirety of the *Iliad* is told from the points of view of Briseis and Chryseis in this chapter of Haynes's polyphonic novel, highlighting the glaring limitations of any version of a story that only tells the men's side. Instead, the novel is 'not offering [...] the story of one woman during the Trojan War'; rather, it offers 'the story of all the women in the war'.[70] Briseis cannot consent in any way that aligns with our current understandings about sex and power. In concluding that Briseis can never consent, that enslaved women cannot consent, this research contributes to wider understandings of wartime sexual violence throughout history, from the mythological Bronze Age to the present day conflict in Ukraine.[71] Moreover, it contributes significantly to emerging research into the role of #MeToo in contemporary feminist fiction. The #MeToo movement constituted a reckoning about power and consent, and we can find in the Trojan Cycle familiar archetypes: Agamemnon is the man with ultimate power and control, Achilles is the golden boy who engenders sympathy despite his acts of violence, Patroclus is complicit in the patriarchal hegemony, and the women are silenced victims and outspoken survivors. When women reclaim Greek myths from their violent and patriarchal roots, it is a reclamation of victims' experiences, and a challenge to the dominant narratives upheld *by* powerful men, *for* powerful men.

Notes

1 Helen Morales, *Antigone Rising: The Subversive Power of Ancient Myths* (London: Wildfire, 2020), p. 66.
2 Ibid., pp. 72, 67.
3 Ibid., p. 67.
4 Ibid., pp. 72–74.
5 Ellie Anderson, 'Women in Philosophy: The Limits of Consent in Sexual Ethics', *Blog of the American Philosophical Association*, 24 April 2019 <https://blog.apaonline.org/2019/04/24/women-in-philosophy-the-limits-of-consent-in-sexual-ethics/> [accessed 2 May 2023].
6 Shelby Judge, 'Review of Saint, Jennifer, *Ariadne*', *New Classicists*, 7 (2022), 82–87.
7 Adrienne Westenfeld, 'It's Time to Get Into Mythology', *Esquire*, 16 September 2021 <https://www.esquire.com/entertainment/books/a37578874/greek-mythology-boom-best-books/> [accessed 2 May 2023].
8 Homer, *Iliad*, trans. by Robert Fagles (London: Penguin, 1998), I: 1.
9 Ibid., II: 784–87.
10 Ibid., XIX: 210, XIX: 333–58.
11 Harold Isbell, 'Introduction: Briseis to Achilles', in *Heroides*, trans. by Harold Isbell (London: Penguin, 1990; repr. 2004), pp. 19–20 (p. 19).
12 Susan Sellers, 'Myth and Fairy Tale in Contemporary Women's Fiction', in *Feminist Literary Theory: A Reader*, ed. by Mary Eagleton (Oxford: Wiley-Blackwell, 2011), pp. 187–90 (p. 189).
13 Emily Hauser, *For the Most Beautiful* (London: Penguin, 2016), p. 133.
14 Ovid, *Heroides*, trans. by Harold Isbell (London: Penguin, 1990, repr. 2004), III.
15 Isbell, pp. 19–20.
16 *Heroides*, III.
17 Sarah Pomeroy, *Goddesses, Whores, Wives, and Slaves: Women in Classical Antiquity* (London: Penguin, 1975, repr. 2015), p. 12.
18 Ibid.
19 Ibid.
20 Ibid.
21 See Mithu Sanyal, *Rape: From Lucretia to #MeToo* (London: Verso, 2019), p. 11.
22 Mark Morford, Robert Lenardon, and Michael Sham, *Classical Mythology*, 9th edn (Oxford: Oxford University Press, 2011), pp. 19–20.
23 Rachel Brownstein, *Becoming a Heroine* (New York: Penguin, 1984), p. 35.
24 Kelly Faircloth, 'The Romance Novelist's Guide to Hot Consent', *Jezebel*, 14 February 2018 <https://jezebel.com/the-romance-novelists-guide-to-hot-consent-1822991922> [accessed 2 May 2023].
25 Ibid.

26 Sanyal, p. 181.
27 Hauser, *Beautiful*, p. 253.
28 Ibid., pp. 187–88.
29 See Emily Hauser, 'Since Sappho: Women in Classical Literature and Contemporary Women's Writing in English' (unpublished doctoral thesis, Yale University, 2017).
30 Sanyal, p. 105.
31 'I Ask How Power Impacts Consent', *National Sexual Violence Resource Centre* (Pennsylvania: NSVRC, 2019), p. 1.
32 Aimee Hinds Scott, 'Rape or Romance? Bad Feminism in Mythical Retellings', *Eidolon*, 3 September 2019 <https://eidolon.pub/rape-or-romance-1b3d584585b8> [accessed 2 May 2023].
33 In the 'Author's Note', Hauser does comment on the silencing of Briseis and Chryseis despite their necessity to the plot of the *Iliad* and considers how faithful her own text is to Homer's. Hauser notes that 'all the main events and facts come from the *Iliad*' but she has created the backstories, characteristics, and endings for Briseis and Chryseis due to their lack thereof in the *Iliad* (p. 457). Hauser herself has a doctorate in Classics from Yale University, and is a Lecturer in Classics and Ancient History at the University of Exeter. Her academic background accounts for the geographical and social accuracy of Briseis's backstory, and her research into women's literature and classical reception inspired *For the Most Beautiful*, with a view to completing the unfinished stories of Briseis and Chryseis. Although Hauser's interpretation of Achilles and Briseis's relationship is problematic, her work is valuable due to its historical accuracy over feminist concerns.
34 Ibid., p. 456.
35 Pat Barker, quoted in 'Pat Barker with Katy Brand', *The Penguin Podcast*, 5 December 2018 <https://podcasts.apple.com/gb/podcast/pat-barker-with-katy-brand/id89411073?i=1000425178252> [accessed 2 May 2023].
36 Pat Barker, *The Silence of the Girls* (London: Penguin, 2018), p. 3.
37 Barker, 'Pat Barker with Katy Brand'.
38 Morford et al., p. 17.
39 Barker, *Girls*, p. 28.
40 Ibid.
41 Ibid., p. 38.
42 Ibid., p. 48.
43 Ibid., pp. 66–67.
44 Ibid., p. 48.
45 Barker, 'Pat Barker with Katy Brand'.
46 Barker, *Girls*, p. 48.
47 Ibid., p. 110.
48 Ibid., p. 119.
49 Sarah Ruden, 'Introduction' in 'Oresteia: Agamemnon', in Aeschylus, *The Greek Plays*, ed. by Mary Lefkowitz and James Romm (New York: Modern Library, 2016), pp. 45–50 (p. 49).
50 Aeschylus, 'Oresteia: Agamemnon', trans. by Sarah Ruden, in *The Greek Plays*, l. 1419.
51 Barker, *Girls*, p. 279.
52 See Kelly Dawn Askin, *War Crimes Against Women: Prosecution in International War Crimes Tribunals* (Leiden: Martinus Nijhoff Publishers, 1997), pp. 19–21.
53 Brooke Ophardt, 'Body Autonomy During Pregnancy: Where Did It Go?', *Dissenting Voices*, 5 (2016), 79–94 (p. 79).
54 Barker, *Girls*, p. 296 (emphasis in original).
55 Ibid., p. 324.
56 Ibid.
57 Ibid., p. 294.

58 Pat Barker, *The Women of Troy* (London: Penguin, 2021), p. 48.
59 See Bettany Hughes, *Helen of Troy: Goddess, Princess, Whore* (London: Pimlico, 2005); Laurie Maguire, *Helen of Troy: From Homer to Hollywood* (Oxford: Wiley-Blackwell, 2009).
60 Barker, *Women*, p. 159.
61 Sophocles, *Antigone*, in *The Three Theban Plays: Antigone, Oedipus the King, Oedipus at Colonus*, trans. by Robert Fagles (London: Penguin, 1984), ll. 603–04.
62 Daniel Mendelsohn, 'The Many Wars of Pat Barker', *New Yorker*, 18 October 2021 <https://www.newyorker.com/magazine/2021/10/25/the-many-wars-of-pat-barker> [accessed 2 May 2023].
63 Madeline Miller, *The Song of Achilles* (London: Bloomsbury, 2011), p. 218.
64 Kate Manne, *Down Girl: The Logic of Misogyny* (Oxford: Oxford University Press, 2018), p. 23.
65 Ibid., p. 197.
66 Julie Sanders, *Adaptation and Appropriation* (London: Routledge, 2006), p. 12.
67 Linda Hutcheon, *A Theory of Adaptation* (London: Routledge, 2006), p. 114.
68 Natalie Haynes, *A Thousand Ships* (London: Macmillan, 2019), pp. 84, 100.
69 *Iliad*, XVII: 234.
70 Haynes, p. 40.
71 Bethan McKernan, 'Rape as a Weapon: huge scale of sexual violence inflicted in Ukraine emerges', *The Guardian*, 4 April 2022 <https://www.theguardian.com/world/2022/apr/03/all-wars-are-like-this-used-as-a-weapon-of-war-in-ukraine> [accessed 2 May 2023].

Bibliography

Aeschylus, 'Oresteia: Agamemnon', trans. by Sarah Ruden, in *The Greek Plays*, ed. by Mary Lefkowitz and James Romm (New York: Modern Library, 2016)

Anderson, Ellie, 'Women in Philosophy: The Limits of Consent in Sexual Ethics', Blog of the American Philosophical Association, 24 April 2019 <https://blog.apaonline.org/2019/04/24/women-in-philosophy-the-limits-of-consent-in-sexual-ethics/> [accessed 2 May 2023]

Askin, Kelly Dawn, *War Crimes Against Women: Prosecution in International War Crimes Tribunals* (Leiden: Martinus Nijhoff Publishers, 1997)

Barker, Pat, quoted in 'Pat Barker with Katy Brand', *The Penguin Podcast*, 5 December 2018 <https://podcasts.apple.com/gb/podcast/pat-barker-with-katy-brand/id89411073?i=1000425178252> [accessed 2 May 2023]

Barker, Pat, *The Silence of the Girls* (London: Penguin, 2018)

Barker, Pat, *The Women of Troy* (London: Penguin, 2021)

Brownstein, Rachel, *Becoming a Heroine* (New York: Penguin, 1984)

Faircloth, Kelly, 'The Romance Novelist's Guide to Hot Consent', *Jezebel*, 14 February 2018 <https://jezebel.com/the-romance-novelists-guide-to-hot-consent-1822991922> [accessed 2 May 2023]

Hauser, Emily, *For the Most Beautiful* (London: Penguin, 2016)

Hauser, Emily, 'Since Sappho: Women in Classical Literature and Contemporary Women's Writing in English' (unpublished doctoral thesis, Yale University, 2017)

Haynes, Natalie, *A Thousand Ships* (London: Macmillan, 2019)

Hinds Scott, Aimee, 'Rape or Romance? Bad Feminism in Mythical Retellings', *Eidolon*, 3 September 2019 <https://eidolon.pub/rape-or-romance-1b3d584585b8> [accessed 2 May 2023]

Homer, *Iliad*, trans. by Robert Fagles (London: Penguin, 1998)

Hughes, Bettany, *Helen of Troy: Goddess, Princess, Whore* (London: Pimlico, 2005)

Hutcheon, Linda, *A Theory of Adaptation* (London: Routledge, 2006)

'I Ask How Power Impacts Consent', National Sexual Violence Resource Centre (Pennsylvania: NSVRC, 2019)

Isbell, Harold, 'Introduction', in *Heroides*, trans. and ed. by Harold Isbell (London: Penguin, 1990; repr. 2004), pp. 19–20

Judge, Shelby, 'Review of Saint, Jennifer, Ariadne', *New Classicists*, 7 (2022), 82–87

Maguire, Laurie, *Helen of Troy: From Homer to Hollywood* (Oxford: Wiley-Blackwell, 2009)

Manne, Kate, *Down Girl: The Logic of Misogyny* (Oxford: Oxford University Press, 2018)

McKernan, Bethan, 'Rape as a Weapon: huge scale of sexual violence inflicted in Ukraine emerges', *Guardian*, 4 April 2022 <https://www.theguardian.com/world/2022/apr/03/all-wars-are-like-this-used-as-a-weapon-of-war-in-ukraine> [accessed 2 May 2023]

Mendelsohn, Daniel, 'The Many Wars of Pat Barker', *New Yorker*, 18 October 2021 <https://www.newyorker.com/magazine/2021/10/25/the-many-wars-of-pat-barker> [accessed 2 May 2023]

Miller, Madeline, *The Song of Achilles* (London: Bloomsbury, 2011)

Morales, Helen, *Antigone Rising: The Subversive Power of the Ancient Myths* (London: Wildfire, 2020)

Morford, Mark, Robert Lenardon, and Michael Sham, *Classical Mythology*, 9th edn (Oxford: Oxford University Press, 2011)

Ophardt, Brooke, 'Body Autonomy During Pregnancy: Where Did It Go?', *Dissenting Voices*, 5 (2016), 79–94

Ovid, *Heroides*, trans. by Harold Isbell, 2nd edn (London: Penguin, 2004)

Pomeroy, Sarah, *Goddesses, Whores, Wives, and Slaves: Women in Classical Antiquity*, 2nd edn (London: Penguin Random House, 2015)

Ruden, Sarah, 'Introduction' in 'Oresteia: Agamemnon', in *The Greek Plays*, ed. by Mary Lefkowitz and James Romm (New York: Modern Library, 2016), pp. 45–50

Sanders, Julie, *Adaptation and Appropriation* (London: Routledge, 2006)

Sanyal, Mithu, *Rape: From Lucretia to #MeToo* (London: Verso, 2019)

Sellers, Susan, 'Myth and Fairy Tale in Contemporary Women's Fiction', in *Feminist Literary Theory: A Reader*, ed. by Mary Eagleton (Oxford: Wiley-Blackwell, 2011), pp. 187–90

Sophocles, *The Three Theban Plays: Antigone, Oedipus the King (Oedipus Tyrannos), Oedipus at Colonus*, trans. by Robert Fagles (London: Penguin, 1984)

Westenfeld, Adrienne, 'It's Time to Get Into Mythology', *Esquire*, 16 September 2021 <https://www.esquire.com/entertainment/books/a37578874/greek-mythology-boom-best-books/> [accessed 2 May 2023]

3 Stopping the Rapist in our Path

Resisting Rape Culture in Latin American Music and Performance Art

Eunice Rojas

In June of 2015, over two years before the #MeToo hashtag went viral in the United States, an Argentine feminist movement began a campaign against gender-based violence using the social media hashtag #NiUnaMenos (#NotOne[Woman]Less), calling for an end to endemic femicide in Latin America.[1] By 2016, the movement and its associated social media hashtag had spread to most of the Spanish-speaking world, sparking numerous protests throughout Latin America. In the same year, a related Spanish-language hashtag of #NoTeCalles (#Don'tBeSilent) emerged in Mexico to encourage victims of sexual assault to share their stories. In 2018, in the wake of the #MeToo movement in which English-language social media exploded with personal stories of sexual harassment, abuse, and rape, a Spanish language version emerged under the hashtag #Cuéntalo (#TellIt).

To accompany these campaigns denouncing sexual harassment and gender-based violence, musical artists from various countries in the region penned songs reflecting the messages promoted through the hashtags. Hip-hop artists throughout Latin America provided the soundtrack to the movements with provocatively titled tracks such as 'Filosofía feminista' (Feminist philosophy), 'Mi cuerpa es mía' (My [female] body is mine), and 'Paren de matarnos' (Stop killing us). Even several years before the #NiUnaMenos movement began, artists such as Chilean singer Ana Tijoux were employing hip hop to counter the hegemonic culture of sexual assault. These songs all helped pave the way for the interactive performance of 'Un violador en tu camino' (A rapist in your path) by the Chilean feminist collective Las Tesis in November 2019. Introduced in Chile amid the ongoing social upheaval in that country, the piece immediately went viral and was adapted for performances throughout the Americas as well as in the wider world. Following the work of sociologists Ron Eyerman and Andrew Jamison on music and social movements, this chapter examines how songs produced before and after the *Un violador en tu camino* phenomenon constitute a cognitive praxis in which the artists participate in collective action to educate the public on the importance of affirmative consent as a precursor to sexual activity. Their goal is to alter the hegemonic patriarchal culture of gender-based sexual violence by encouraging a sex-critical approach to consent.

DOI: 10.4324/9781003365082-4

Social Movements, Cognitive Praxis, and Sex-Critical Approaches to Consent

In *Social Movements: A Cognitive Approach* (1991), Eyerman and Jamison propose a way of viewing social movements as epistemological communities engaged in the production of knowledge. They conceive of social movements as 'movements of collective creation that provide societies with ideas, identities, and even ideals'.[2] In this way, social movements perform what Eyerman and Jamison call 'cognitive praxis', as they constitute 'the social action from where new knowledge originates' by developing and disseminating new perspectives of human understanding. In conceptualising social movements as cognitive praxis, Eyerman and Jamison view these movements 'not merely as a challenge to established power, but also and more so as a socially constructive force'.[3] They describe their approach as focusing on 'the process of articulating a movement identity (cognitive praxis), on the actors taking part in this process (movement intellectuals), and on the contexts of articulation (political cultures and institutions)'.[4] In *Music and Social Movements* (1998), Eyerman and Jamison turn their focus to the role that music plays in the cognitive praxis of social movements by examining 'the mobilization of music, and the making and remaking of musical traditions, within social movements'.[5] These scholars state that they conceive of the relationship between music and social movements as 'collective learning processes'.[6] They add that 'in social movements, musical and other kinds of cultural traditions are made and remade, and after the movements fade away as political forces, the music remains as a memory and as a potential way to inspire new waves of mobilization'.[7] In this way, musical texts can continue to educate audiences and effect cognitive praxis long after their original release or performance.

More recently, sociologist William Roy builds on the work of Eyerman and Jamison with regards to the role of culture in shaping social movements. According to Roy, 'many people doing art, doing music, doing drama, doing literature, not just consuming it, is an extraordinarily powerful mode for both solidifying commitment to social movements and for helping them achieve their goals'.[8] Similarly, journalist Helen Cordes and political sociologist Eric Selbin in their work on music in collective political action note that 'the shared experience of singing and the imagined experience of song make people feel a part of something more than themselves, empower them to dream, and inspire them to act. They sing their community/ies into being'.[9] In feminist movements that protest the prevalence of sexual and gender-based violence in Latin America, music acts as a vehicle to help change ideas about bodily autonomy and consent and form a community that vocally challenges the patriarchal roots of rape culture; endorses an affirmative and sex-critical conception of sexual consent; and commits to the unsilencing of sexual assault.

On her blog titled 'Sex Critical', sexuality studies scholar Lisa Downing explains that her use of the term 'sex critical' is intended to transcend the binary of positive/negative or healthy/harmful conceptions of sex.[10] Instead,

Downing proposes that all sexual activity and sexual representations be subject to critical interrogation. In *Sexual Consent* (2020), Milena Popova explains that sex-critical approaches to consent engage less in legal frameworks for sexual consent and more on the ways in which popular culture influences 'the conditions under which sexual violence thrives and the conditions for tackling it'.[11] Within this sex-critical approach to consent, the cognitive praxis encouraged by anti-patriarchal Latin American hip-hop helps both male and female listeners to think critically about the need for affirmative consent as an unwaiveable prerequisite for any sort of sexual activity.

Antipatriarchal Hip-Hop

In the early 2010s, several Latin American feminist hip-hop artists began to produce songs with lyrics that explicitly challenge the patriarchal hegemony of Latin American societies. Although these songs tackle an array of feminist concerns, sexual harassment and sexual assault are common topics that emerge in many of them. In 2011, for example, the Nicaraguan activist and musician Gaby Baca released the song 'Todas juntas, todas libres' (All [women] together, all [women] free) in which the poetic voice calls for collective action among women and addresses a potential unnamed male aggressor. She tells him 'ya no quiero más de tu violencia ni tu insistencia' (I don't want any more of your violence or your insistence). In 'Con la misma moneda' (Taste of their own medicine), another song from the same year, Baca's poetic voice asserts the right to dress up without being accosted and asks her male interlocutor how he would feel if he were sexually harassed on every street corner. While both songs assert women's bodily autonomy and address a potential male sexual aggressor, 'Todas juntas, todas libres' specifically educates female listeners about the need for collective action to combat sexual harassment and violence by reminding women that they should not have to submit to unwanted sexual attention and that they possess strength in numbers.

In 2014, hip-hop artist Ana Tijoux, the French-born daughter of Chilean exiles, released 'Antipatriarca' (Antipatriarch), which has become one of the most famous Latin American feminist hip-hop songs of the twenty-first century. Amid a broad vindication of strong and independent womanhood, the poetic voice proclaims her body as her own and tells her male interlocutor that he will no longer mistreat, denigrate, or oppress her, and she adds, 'tú no me vas obligar, tú no me vas a silenciar' (you're not going to force me, you're not going to silence me). Tijoux's 'Antipatriarca', like Gaby Baca's songs, engages in cognitive praxis by helping to change attitudes towards sexual aggression, consent, and expected reactions to sexual violence and harassment. Both artists use their music to denounce inappropriate sexual behaviour and to encourage a collective identity of women who defend bodily autonomy and support the idea of affirmative consent. Furthermore, the songs offer victim-survivors a script with which to confront their potential abusers. In an opinion piece, Tijoux explains the educational nature of her music in sex-critical terms. 'The masculine body is power, domination, colonization. It is that which denigrates and subjugates', she writes, and adds that she understands that her role as a woman is to question and debate this normalisation of sexual violence.[12] Tijoux claims that 'education is not carried out only in classrooms, but that all platforms of public space can be educational'.[13] Furthermore, employing both Eyerman and Jamison's rhetoric of cognitive praxis and Downing's notion of sex-critical consent, she asserts that 'singers have the imperative task of bringing about a shift through our songs and lyrics. We have to bring the issue to the fore, awaken critical thought'.[14]

#NiUnaMenos

The #NiUnaMenos hashtag went viral in Argentina in 2015 after the killing of fourteen-year-old Chiara Páez by her sixteen-year-old boyfriend, as protesters – first in Argentina and quickly thereafter throughout Latin America – mobilised to denounce violence against women and the frequent impunity of aggressors of such violence. In her examination of feminist movements in Latin America, political sociologist Marisa Revilla Blanco notes that 'Hashtags, slogans [...] performances and videos are part of the repertory of innovative tools of the women's movements'.[15] Revilla Blanco explains that the expansion of virtual social networks and increase in accessibility of apps that allow for presence, participation, and interaction on the internet have allowed for 'the emergence of young female Latin American rappers and hip-hoppers with feminist lyrics [...] who are allowing for a diversification of messages and reaching ever younger audiences'.[16] Furthermore, historian Olaf Kaltmeier and cultural studies scholar Wilfried Raussert assert that 'the Guatemalan hip-hop artist Rebeca Lane founded the feminist collective "Somos Guerreras" and empowers – through her music and through workshops – girls and young women to fight for the rights of their bodies'.[17] The type of work performed by this collective, which seeks to directly educate women on issues of sexual consent, is therefore amplified and widely disseminated through the music of other similar artists who can reach large audiences through social media.

In Rebeca Lane's 'Ni una menos' (Not one [woman] less), a song she released in 2017 in the wake of the feminist movement that used the #NiUnaMenos hashtag, the poetic voice offers statistics regarding the number of Guatemalan women raped each hour and encourages the listener to extrapolate out the number of rape victims in the rest of the world. The song employs these statistics to assert a position of collective resistance against femicide and rape culture, as the poetic voice claims to sing in the name of both her sisters and her great-grandmothers. As a trained sociologist, an activist, and a popular artist, Lane exemplifies the figure that Eyerman and Jamison describe as a 'movement intellectual'. Drawing on the concept of the intellectual described by Italian theorist Antoni Gramsci, Eyerman and Jamison acknowledge that 'all activists in social movements are, in some sense, "movement intellectuals", because through their activism they contribute to the formation of the movement's identity'.[18] For Gramsci, 'traditional' intellectuals, who help uphold the dominant order, are differentiated from 'organic' ones. The 'organic' intellectual, Gramsci writes, is 'capable of helping to overturn the existing social order and usher in new ways of thinking'.[19] This type of intellectual is not a traditional scholar but someone who participates actively in a movement 'as constructor, organizer, "permanent persuader" and not just a simple orator'.[20] With her training in sociology and her activist use of popular music, Lane uses songs as a medium to communicate counter-hegemonic ideas informed by academic theory.

The poetic voice of 'Ni una menos' explicitly distinguishes herself from traditional intellectuals who prop up the patriarchy. Contrary to the 'machos [...] que creen que con su intelectualidad nos van a venir a educar sentados en su privilegio' (machos [...] who believe that they will educate us with their intellectualism and their seat of privilege), the poetic voice asserts that she has no privilege to protect her body. Her body, she notes, makes her the perfect target on the streets. The poetic voice also offers several examples of victims of sexual violence that include a nine-year-old raped and impregnated by her brother and a woman beaten to death by a man who purported to love her. These stories help challenge the traditional view of sexual violence as crimes of passion. Performance studies scholar Marcela Fuentes explains that 'cultural products such as telenovelas and tango lyrics usually narrate the killing of women by their partners as crimes of passion, contributing to shaping perceptions about relationship violence as the effect of the victim's charms or love's true nature'.[21] By depicting sexual aggression in brutal and unromantic terms, songs such as 'Ni una menos' help to perform the cognitive praxis of changing societal understanding of sexual violence and sexual assault in Latin America and alter conceptions of consent in the process.

A Rapist in Your Path

By 2019, #NiUnaMenos shared social media space with numerous other Spanish-language hashtags that were designed to encourage victims of sexual violence and harassment to share their stories. In 2016, a group of victims of sexual assault in Mexico launched a social media campaign with the hashtag #NoTeCalles (Don'tStaySilent) to persuade other victims to report their own assaults.[22] A similar campaign began in Spain in 2018 after the initial acquittal of five men who called themselves *La manada* (The wolf pack) and were accused of raping a teenage girl and filming their assault. Despite the brutal nature of the attack and the accompanying film evidence, the five men were convicted of the lesser charge of sexual abuse rather than the more serious one of rape. The public outcry over the results of the trial prompted a Spanish journalist to urge her followers to speak out on social media about their own stories of sexual abuse with #Cuéntalo (Talk about it).[23] The *cuéntalo* hashtag, which in its first two weeks produced over 160,000 original tweets and well over two million total uses,[24] quickly spread across the Atlantic, particularly to Argentina, Mexico, Colombia, and Chile, where a group of serial kidnappers and rapists of young women became known as *la manada chilena* (the Chilean wolf pack) due to their similarity with the Spanish case.

In November 2019, a trans-inclusive Chilean feminist collective named Las Tesis staged a street performance that they called *Un violador en tu camino* (A rapist in your path) in front of a police station in Valparaiso, Chile, to denounce rape culture. Inspired and informed by the work of Argentine social anthropologist Rita Segato, Las Tesis conceived of their performance as 'an attempt to translate her theories into a format that would be accessible to those who would not ordinarily encounter them'.[25] In this way, music and performance are used deliberately as vehicles of education, further encouraging the formation of a cognitive praxis of sex-critical notions of consent. The performance consists of chanted lyrics that condemn femicide and rape, and call out the police, the justice system, and the state for inadequately handling cases of sexual assault. A simple series of movements accompany and reinforce the chants, and the blindfolded artists point straight ahead as they accuse a hypothetical individual, 'el violador eres tú' (the rapist is you). As *violador*, the Spanish term for rapist, is more ambiguous than the English term, it lends itself in this context to being either a provocative accusation of rape on individuals who have allowed sexual assaults to go unpunished or a more general indictment of the authorities as violators of rights, such as the right to seek justice.

According to the members of Las Tesis, the collective had originally planned a performance of their work in October 2019 but postponed it due to the unprecedented social upheaval that began in Chile that month.[26] Localised demonstrations that had erupted over a small increase in metro fares quickly ballooned into widespread and prolonged protests over a wide array of social issues caused by Chile's neoliberal economy, including unequal access to quality healthcare, education, and pensions. Soon thereafter, the heavy-handed police treatment of the protesters became a reason for protest in and of itself. Approximately one month into the upheaval, Las Tesis adapted the material they had already been working on for some time to also include a condemnation of the Carabineros de Chile (the Chilean body of law enforcement) due to the numerous allegations of police officers committing acts of sexual abuse on individuals detained during the protests.[27]

After the initial presentation in Valparaiso, Las Tesis and other groups of individuals performed the work flash-mob style in other Chilean cities, generally in front of courthouses, police departments, or other government buildings, and the performance was soon appropriated, adapted, and reinterpreted by women's groups worldwide. The inclusive nature and simplicity of the piece's choreography and lyrics allowed and even encouraged any interested individuals to show up and take an active part in the performance or to organise their own staging, and in the first months after the initial performance of *Un violador en tu camino* it was re-enacted in over 200 locations.[28] According to cultural activist Andrea Alejandra Gordillo Marquina, the phenomenon of *Un violador en tu camino* is 'perhaps one of the most prominent examples of the power of the public pedagogy of the arts'.[29]

In the chorus of the chanted lyrics, the first-person singular poetic voice emphatically denies typical efforts to blame the victim of sexual assaults. The line, 'la culpa no era mía, ni dónde estaba, ni cómo vestía' (it was not my fault, or where I was, or how I was dressed), which is repeated four times in succession, negates any possibility of implied consent on the part of the rape survivor. Moreover, the line 'el estado opresor es un macho violador' (the oppressive state is a macho rapist) is not only a reference to the high levels of impunity for sexual aggressors, but it is also a deliberate evocation of Segato's theories regarding the relationship between rape and structures of power. Writing on the intersection of rape and femicide with political economic power, sociologist Claudia Lozano explains that for Segato, 'the rapist does not operate independently but is linked to society and a hierarchy defined by the theft and pillage of the power of women and the relative competence of peers'.[30] Segato herself proposes that violent rapists respond to a subconscious mandate in which society demands that the sexual aggressor use the body of the victim to demonstrate, or even obtain, his own virility.[31] Although the nuances of Segato's theories are highly simplified in the performance piece, the idea that sexual violence is part of broader societal and structural issues and should not be a source of shame and silence for the victim rings through in each reinterpretation of the piece. Through music, the participants galvanise audience members to engage in a cognitive praxis that changes ideas surrounding issues of sexual consent.

The Path Forward

On 14 November 2019, less than a month into the social upheaval and less than a week before the first performance of *Un violador en tu camino*, Mon Laferte, a well-known Chilean singer-songwriter who would later release 'Plata ta tá', one of the most popular songs about the 2019 social uprising, attended the Latin Grammy Awards in Las Vegas to accept the award for Best Alternative Music Album. In front of the red-carpet paparazzi, Laferte opened her jacket to expose her bare chest, and revealed a message she had written in large block letters on her torso that read, 'En Chile violan torturan y matan' (In Chile they rape, torture, and kill). Like the performance piece by Las Tesis, Laferte was alluding to allegations that Chilean police had committed human rights violations on protesters taking part in the social uprising. Just two months after the protests began, the Chilean Public Prosecutor's Office had opened over 2,500 criminal investigations of sexual violence arising from alleged police misconduct or brutality.[32] Laferte's red-carpet performance was intended, in part, to call attention to acts of sexual violence perpetrated by Chilean police during the response to the protests.

By using a commonly sexualised part of her body to publicly express a message of resistance against systemic sexual violence, Laferte made a claim to her own bodily autonomy while also condemning the violation of others'. That same night, Laferte doubled down on the message by posting to social media a topless photo of herself taken by photographers at the event with the caption 'Mi cuerpo libre para una patria libre' (My free body for a free homeland).[33] Gender studies scholar Karina Eileraas proposes that when demonstrators employ their own bodies in protest, 'they pose a metaphysical question: What is my body—my life—worth to you?'[34] Furthermore, Eileraas explains that 'nude protest has a special capacity to reconfigure the body politic by framing vulnerability as a basis for exchange and staging intimate zones of disruption and disidentification'.[35] Laferte's use of her own body similarly re-envisions the female body from a role of silent victimhood to that of advocacy, empowerment, education, and resistance against a Chilean state that enables rape culture and whose police force is accused of engaging in other violations of human rights.

In 2021, two years after her provocative appearance at the Latin Grammy Awards, Laferte released the album *1940 Carmen*, an autobiographical and introspective work that also includes songs written in English.[36] In 'A Crying Diamond', the poetic voice describes an impoverished 13-year-old girl with musical aspirations who is sexually abused by a 40-year-old man who promises to make her famous. 'She never told anyone because she was afraid', the poetic voice explains. Laferte herself clarifies that the song describes an experience of sexual molestation that she suffered during her childhood.[37] In a line reminiscent of Segato's theories of rape as the aggressor's way of reclaiming his own virility, the song describes the sexual abuser as having taken the girl's youth from her, 'and that makes him feel good'. Although Laferte attributes her newfound candidness regarding her past sexual abuse to the hormones she was taking to boost her fertility,[38] it is also likely that she was influenced by the #Cuentalo, #NoTeCalles, and #MeToo social media campaigns and their associated songs that encouraged victims of sexual harassment, abuse, and violence to share their stories. In this way, her own music can be seen as a product of the cognitive praxis of feminist social movements denouncing sexual abuse and encouraging a sex-critical approach to consent.

Also in the wake of the 2019 social upheaval in Chile, the British television production company Freemantle teamed up with the Chilean company *Productora Fábula* to produce the television series *La jauría* (The Pack). Released in July 2020 in Latin America and Spain and later that year in the United States, *La jauría* offers a fictional account of the disappearance of a female high school student who was the leader of a feminist movement protesting the school's complicity with a teacher accused of sexual misconduct. The theme song for the series is written and performed by Ana Tijoux, who also acts in several episodes. Entitled 'No estamos solas' (We are not alone), the song alludes to women who have been raped, beaten, and disappeared as well as to a Church and State that operate as an *aparato cómplice* (accomplice apparatus). The poetic voice asserts her bodily autonomy with the line *mi cuerpo es mío* (my body is mine) and proclaims a collective identity of women who resist sexual aggression and advocate for each other. 'Tocan a una, tocan a todas' (They touch one of us, they touch all of us), the poetic voice declares at the end of the song before adding a final line that echoes the title of the song, 'no estamos solas' (we are not alone). The collective call of the song serves to encourage women to understand their sexual assaults as violations of consent that should be resisted and brought to justice, thereby effectuating cognitive praxis on the issue of sexual consent.

While Tijoux's song advocates for women collectively defending themselves and each other from sexual assault, the all-male Uruguayan rock band *No Te Va Gustar* (You're not gonna like it) teamed up with female Argentine rapper Nicki Nicole in 2021 to release a song that goes on the offensive. The lyrics of 'Venganza' (Revenge) and its official music video feature a first-person poetic voice who confronts her rapist and promises vengeance. She explicitly denies the possibility that the attack was something to which she passively consented and celebrates the opportunity to face her attacker in order to exact her revenge. The video opens with a shot of a bare-chested corpulent man draped in a black judicial robe. With the appearance of a medieval monarch, he sits on a stone block, wears a simplistic metal crown and a medallion around his neck, and he holds what appears to be a sceptre but is actually a darkly painted replica of a human arm and hand with two missing fingers. The monarchical figure looks on sceptically at first, raising his eyebrows as the members of *No Te Va Gustar* prepare their instruments and launch into the introduction of the song. The musicians are all dressed in white clothes painted with red and black to give the appearance of blood smears and even abstract bleeding faces. The entire backdrop for the video is covered with similar designs. They direct their music angrily at the man in the black robe, and by the end of the song they encircle him as he covers his ears with his hands and drops his head, cowering in apparent fear. In the second half of the song, Nicki Nicole enters the frame and raps at the man, telling him, 'te metiste en mi razón, me hiciste creer que mi forma de vestir era una provocación' (you got into my head, you made me think that the way that I dress was a provocation). The video ends with the musicians playing their final note over the clothes and crown of the man who seems to have melted away completely. One by one, they walk off, leaving Nicki Nicole gazing down at the crown with contempt before walking away as well.

The final scenes of the video appear to be a symbolic inversion of a *bukkeke,* a sex act in which a group of men ejaculate over a woman. Notably, in 2018, Guatemalan performance artist Regina José Galindo denounced the controversial Spanish gang rape case of *La manada* by representing the assault ritualistically as a *bukkeke*. Galindo's performance piece depicts the artist dressed in black and kneeling as a group of seven men in hoodies and jeans surround her, unzip their pants, and ejaculate on her. The music video for 'Venganza' presents an inverted version of that same ritual. In this case, the victim at the centre of the circle is assumed to be the original attacker himself, and the new aggressors are musicians. The moment of climax occurs during the final reverberating note of the song as all the instruments are pointed directly at the centre of the circle and the electric guitarist sustains a long vibrato, shaking the neck of his instrument at the man in the crown. He symbolically ejaculates music rather than semen onto the figure at the centre of the circle. This musical inversion of a scene of sexual assault, like Galindo's performance piece, constitutes an effort to change the paradigm of victims of sexual assault silenced by patriarchal ideas that they are responsible for and have therefore consented to their own rapes. While the idea of sexual violence being punished by another act of aggression raises important ethical concerns, rather than a literal act of revenge, the song proposes a symbolic reaction to sexual assault through the medium of musical education on the tenets of affirmative consent, as the female voice explicitly rejects the notion that the way she was dressed served as a provocation for assault.

In March 2021, just two weeks after *No Te Va Gustar* and Nicki Nicole released the 'Venganza' video, Karen Méndez, a reggaeton and pop singer born in Argentina and raised in Spain, uploaded to YouTube a song entitled 'Si algún día me toca a mí' (If it happens to me one day / If [he] touches me one day). With almost as many views as the 'Venganza' video, 'Si algún día me toca a mí' features a female poetic voice who expresses that if she is sexually attacked and killed, she wants the listener to know that she did not offer any consent to the act. In the chorus of the song, she also tells listeners never to say that her photos made someone touch her skin. Another part of the song alludes to the societal attitudes that contribute to sexual violence. The poetic voice states that she has no weapons 'pa[ra] matar una educación que me mata si voy sola' (to kill an education that kills me if I go out alone). In a pinned comment on her own video, Méndez positions her song as part of an attempt to encourage a cognitive praxis that changes traditional notions of sexual consent. 'Esta es mi forma de lucha' (This is my way of fighting), Méndez writes, and adds, 'esto soy yo, nosotras, todas. Solo tomen conciencia, y cambiemos el juego' (This is me, us, all women. Just educate yourselves, and let's change the game).[39] Méndez's urge that women 'change the game' represents an effort to transform women's understanding, thinking, and actions regarding sexual assault and consent.

In April 2022, five years after Guatemalan rapper Rebeca Lane turned the #NiUnaMenos hashtag into a hit single in 2017, she returned to the issue of consent with the release of the single 'No es no' (No is no) from her 2022 album *Florecer* (Blooming). On an Instagram post promoting the album, Lane explains the didactic purpose of one of her songs. 'No es no', she writes, 'es un tema de *Florecer* que escribí ante lo que parece ser desconocimiento total por parte de algunos a algo tan básico como el consentimiento' (is a song from *Florecer* that I wrote in light of what seems to be the complete ignorance of some people regarding something as basic as consent).[40] During the majority of the song, Lane addresses a man who tries to kiss the singer against her will, and she educates him regarding affirmative consent. In the final 30 seconds of the song, however, the poetic voice stops singing and addresses female listeners in an extended spoken voice section. After alluding to patriarchal structures that have instilled in women a fear of resisting sexual aggression, she empowers her female listeners by instructing them on when to offer consent. 'Si te están insistiendo o manipulando para que aceptes' (If they are insisting or manipulating you into accepting), she tells them, 'es un no' (it's a no).

Conclusion

From Gaby Baca's 'Todas juntas, todas libres' to Rebeca Lane's 'No es no', the music studied in this chapter traces a decade of songs that seek not just to challenge the patriarchal tenets of rape culture but to empower and educate women and men about consent and appropriate sexual behaviour. In this way, the songs, as well as the performance piece by Las Tesis, are part of a growing epistemological community dedicated to creating and disseminating new knowledge regarding affirmative and sex-critical consent among the Spanish-speaking public. Comments from the artists themselves indicate a deliberate effort to re-educate the public through their music. Ana Tijoux's statement that singers should bring about a shift and awaken critical thought through their lyrics is similar to Karen Méndez's call for women to educate themselves and change the game. Similarly, the effort by Las Tesis to make Segato's feminist theories accessible to the general public through the medium of performance is comparable to Rebeca Lane's attempt to tackle widespread ignorance regarding consent. All of the artists in this chapter, in participating in what Gordillo Marquina describes as the 'public pedagogy of the arts', engage in Eyerman and Jamison's concept of cognitive praxis by creating and circulating songs that seek to change attitudes in the Latin American public about unacceptable sexual behaviour and how to respond to it.

Notes

1 All translations in this chapter from Spanish to English are my own (unless otherwise stated).
2 Ron Eyerman and Andrew Jamison, *Social Movements: A Cognitive Approach* (Cambridge: Polity Press, 1991), p. 4.
3 Ibid.
4 Ibid.
5 Ron Eyerman and Andrew Jamison, *Music and Social Movements* (Cambridge: Cambridge University Press, 1998), p. 5.
6 Ibid., p. 7.
7 Ibid., pp. 1–2.
8 William Roy, 'How Social Movements Do Culture', *International Journal of Politics, Culture, and Society*, 23 (2010), 85–98 (p. 86).
9 Helen Cordes and Eric Selbin, 'Singing Resistance, Rebellion, and Revolution into Being', in *Sonic Politics: Music and Social Movements in the Americas*, ed. by Olaf Kaltmeier and Wilfried Raussert (Abingdon: Routledge, 2019), pp. 19–43 (p. 25).

10 Lisa Downing, 'What is "Sex Critical" and why should we care about it', *Sex Critical*, 12 July 2012 <http://sexcritical.co.uk/2012/07/27/what-is-sex-critical-and-why-should-we-care-about-it/> [accessed 1 May 2023].

11 Milena Popova, *Sexual Consent* (Cambridge: MIT Press, 2020), p. 21.

12 Ana Tijoux, '*Cultura de la basura*: Ana Tijoux on Misogyny and Pop Music', *Fourth Wall*, 2 October 2014 <https://walkerart.org/magazine/ana-tijoux-sexism-music-op-ed> [accessed 1 May 2023].

13 Ibid.

14 Ibid.

15 Marisa Revilla Blanco, 'Del ¡Ni una más! al #NiUnaMenos: movimientos de mujeres y feminismos en América Latina', *Política y sociedad*, 56 (2019), 47–67 (p. 48).

16 Ibid., p. 60.

17 Olaf Kaltmeier and Wilfried Raussert, 'Introduction', in *Sonic Politics: Music Social Movements in the Americas* (Abingdon: Routledge, 2019), pp. 1–18 (p. 3).

18 Eyerman and Jamison, *Social Movements*, p. 94.

19 Antonio Gramsci, 'Intellectuals and Education', in *The Antonio Gramsci Reader*, ed. by David Forgacs (New York: New York University Press, 2000), pp. 300–22 (p. 321).

20 Ibid.

21 Marcela Fuentes, '#NiUnaMenos (#NotOneWomanLess): Hashtag Performativity, Memory, and Direct Action', in *Women Mobilizing Memory*, ed. by Ayse Gül Altinay et al. (New York: Columbia University Press, 2019), pp. 172–91 (p. 177).

22 'Women in Mexico Launch Don't Stay Silent Campaign #NoTeCalles', *Vallarta Daily News*, 22 April 2016 <https://www.vallartadaily.com/notecalles/> [accessed 22 May 2023].

23 Tom Phillips, '#Cuéntalo: Latin American women rally around sexual violence hashtag', *Guardian*, 3 May 2018 <https://www.theguardian.com/world/2018/may/03/cuentalo-latin-american-women-rally-around-sexual-violence-hashtag> [accessed 1 May 2023].

24 Cristina Fallarás et al., 'El Proyecto #Cuéntalo', <http://www.proyectocuentalo.org/#proyecto> [accessed 1 May 2023].

25 Deborah Martin and Deborah Shaw, 'Chilean and Transnational Performances of Disobedience: LasTesis and the Phenomenon of *Un violador en tu camino*', *Bulletin of Latin American Research*, 40 (2021), 712–29 (p. 713).

26 Canal Abierto, *LASTESIS, artistas chilenas que protagonizaron el 19F*, online video recording, YouTube, 20 February 2020 <https://www.youtube.com/watch?v=u7IgDMOapvo> [accessed 2 May 2023].

27 Ibid.

28 Martin and Shaw, p. 712.

29 Andrea Alejandra Gordillo Marquina, 'The Art of Protest in Latin America: A Media Review of Ana Tijoux's *Cacerolazo* and Other Protest Art in Latin America's 2019 Uprisings', *Comparative Education Review*, 64 (2020), 325–28 (p. 327).

30 Claudia Lozano, 'The Free Market and Gender Relations: Political Economic Power, Impunity, and the Murders of Women', *Seattle Journal for Social Justice*, 5 (2007), 661–96 (p. 673).

31 Rita Segato, *Las estructuras elementales de la violencia* (Buenos Aires: Universidad Nacional de Quilmes, 2003), pp. 38–39.

32 Pascale Bonnefoy, 'Mounting Evidence of Abuse by Chile's Police Leads to Calls for Reform', *New York Times*, 19 December 2019 <https://www.nytimes.com/2019/12/13/world/americas/chile-police-protests.html> [accessed 1 May 2023].

33 Mon Laferte (@monlaferte), 'Mi cuerpo libre para una patria libre', Instagram post, 14 November 2019 < https://www.instagram.com/p/B433Ox4lQ_x/?hl=es> [accessed 18 May 2023].

34 Karina Eileraas, 'Sex(t)ing Revolution, Femen-izing the Public Square: Aliaa Magda Elmahdy, Nude Protest, and Transnational Feminist Body Politics', *Signs: Journal of Women in Culture and Society*, 40 (2014), 40–52 (p. 42).

35 Ibid.

36 Julyssa Lopez, 'How Mon Laferte Unlocked a New Honesty in Her Songwriting', *Rolling Stone*, 29 October 2021 <https://www.rollingstone.com/music/music-latin/mon-laferte-1940-carmen-1250057/> [accessed 1 May 2023].

37 Andrés de Real, 'Mon Laferte: En este disco hablo de un tema que nunca habia querido tocar un abuso que sufri en mi infancia', *La Tercera*, 6 November 2021 <https://www.latercera.com/culto/2021/11/06/mon-laferte-en-este-disco-hablo-de-un-tema-que-nunca-habia-querido-tocar-un-abuso-que-sufri-en-mi-infancia/> [accessed 1 May 2023].

38 Lopez, 'How Mon Laferte Unlocked a New Honesty'.

39 Karen Méndez (KarenMéndezKM), *Si algún día me toca a mi*, comment on online video recording, YouTube, 18 March 2021 <https://www.youtube.com/watch?v=1R5SlJGlLX8> [accessed 1 May 2023].

40 Rebeca Lane (@rebecalane6), '"No es no" es un tema de *Florecer*…', Instagram post, 11 April 2022 <https://www.instagram.com/p/CcOaBuroRlw/> [accessed 1 May 2023].

Bibliography

Bonnefoy, Pascale, 'Mounting Evidence of Abuse by Chile's Police Leads to Calls for Reform', *New York Times*, 19 December 2019 <https://www.nytimes.com/2019/12/13/world/americas/chile-police-protests.html> [accessed 1 May 2023]

Canal Abierto, *LASTESIS, artistas chilenas que protagonizaron el 19F*, online video recording, YouTube, 20 February 2020 <https://www.youtube.com/watch?v=u7IgDMOapvo> [accessed 2 May 2023]

Cordes, Helen, and Eric Selbin, 'Singing Resistance, Rebellion, and Revolution into Being', in *Sonic Politics: Music and Social Movements in the Americas*, ed. by Olaf Kaltmeier and Wilfried Raussert (Abingdon: Routledge, 2019), pp. 19–43

Downing, Lisa, 'What is "Sex Critical" and Why Should We Care About It', *Sex Critical*, 12 July 2012 <http://sexcritical.co.uk/2012/07/27/what-is-sex-critical-and-why-should-we-care-about-it/> [accessed 1 May 2023]

Eileraas, Karina, 'Sex(t)ing Revolution, Femen-izing the Public Square: Aliaa Magda Elmahdy, Nude Protest, and Transnational Feminist Body Politics', *Signs: Journal of Women in Culture and Society*, 40 (2014), 40–52

Eyerman, Ron, and Andrew Jamison, *Music and Social Movements* (Cambridge: Cambridge University Press, 1998)

Eyerman, Ron, and Andrew Jamison, *Social Movements: A Cognitive Approach* (Cambridge: Polity Press, 1991)

Fallarás, Cristina, Aniol Maria, Vicenç Ruiz, Karma Peiró, and BSC Viz Team, 'El Proyecto #Cuéntalo' <http://www.proyectocuentalo.org/#proyecto> [accessed 1 May 2023]

Fuentes, Marcela, '#NiUnaMenos (#NotOneWomanLess): Hashtag Performativity, Memory, and Direct Action', in *Women Mobilizing Memory*, ed. by Ayse Gül Altinay, María José Contreras, Marianne Hirsch, Jean Howard, Banu Karaca, and Alisa Solomon (New York: Columbia University Press, 2019), pp. 172–91

Gordillo Marquina, Andrea Alejandra, 'The Art of Protest in Latin America: A Media Review of Ana Tijoux's *Cacerolazo* and Other Protest Art in Latin America's 2019 Uprisings', *Comparative Education Review*, 64 (2020), 325–28

Gramsci, Antonio, 'Intellectuals and Education', in *The Antonio Gramsci Reader*, ed. by David Forgacs (New York: New York University Press, 2000), pp. 300–22

Laferte, Mon (@monlaferte), 'Mi cuerpo libre para una patria libre', Instagram post, 14 November 2019 <https://www.instagram.com/p/B433Ox4lQ_x/?hl=es> [accessed 18 May 2023]

Lane, Rebeca (@rebecalane6), '"No es no" es un tema de Florecer…', Instagram post, 11 April 2022 <https://www.instagram.com/p/CcOaBuroRlw/> [accessed 1 May 2023]

Lopez, Julyssa, 'How Mon Laferte Unlocked a New Honesty in Her Songwriting', *Rolling Stone*, 29 October 2021 <https://www.rollingstone.com/music/music-latin/mon-laferte-1940-carmen-1250057/> [accessed 1 May 2023]

Kaltmeier, Olaf, and Wilfried Raussert, 'Introduction', in *Sonic Politics: Music Social Movements in the Americas* (Abingdon: Routledge, 2019), pp. 1–18

Lozano, Claudia, 'The Free Market and Gender Relations: Political Economic Power, Impunity, and the Murders of Women', *Seattle Journal for Social Justice*, 5 (2007), 661–96

Martin, Deborah, and Deborah Shaw, 'Chilean and Transnational Performances of Disobedience: LasTesis and the Phenomenon of *Un violador en tu camino*', *Bulletin of Latin American Research*, 40 (2021), 712–29

Méndez, Karen (KarenMéndezKM), *Si algún día me toca a mi*, comment on online video recording, YouTube, 18 March 2021 <https://www.youtube.com/watch?v=1R5SlJGlLX8> [accessed 1 May 2023]

Phillips, Tom, '#Cuéntalo: Latin American women rally around sexual violence hashtag', *Guardian*, 3 May 2018 <https://www.theguardian.com/world/2018/may/03/cuentalo-latin-american-women-rally-around-sexual-violence-hashtag> [accessed 1 May 2023]

Popova, Milena, *Sexual Consent* (Cambridge: MIT Press, 2020)

de Real, Andrés, 'Mon Laferte: En este disco hablo de un tema que nunca habia querido tocar un abuso que sufri en mi infancia', *La Tercera*, 6 November 2021 <https://www.latercera.com/culto/2021/11/06/mon-laferte-en-este-disco-hablo-de-un-tema-que-nunca-habia-querido-tocar-un-abuso-que-sufri-en-mi-infancia/> [accessed 1 May 2023]

Revilla Blanco, Marisa, 'Del ¡Ni una más! al #NiUnaMenos: movimientos de mujeres y feminismos en América Latina', *Política y sociedad*, 56 (2019), 47–67

Roy, William, 'How Social Movements Do Culture', *International Journal of Politics, Culture, and Society*, 23 (2010), 85–98

Segato, Rita, *Las estructuras elementales de la violencia* (Buenos Aires: Universidad Nacional de Quilmes, 2003)

Tijoux, Ana, 'Cultura de la basura: Ana Tijoux on Misogyny and Pop Music', *Fourth Wall*, 2 October 2014 <https://walkerart.org/magazine/ana-tijoux-sexism-music-op-ed> [accessed 1 May 2023]

'Women in Mexico Launch Don't Stay Silent Campaign #NoTeCalles', *Vallarta Daily News*, 22 April 2016 <https://www.vallartadaily.com/notecalles/> [accessed 22 May 2023]

4 *Mera Jism, Meri Marzi*

Crisis of Consent and Digital Mediations in Pakistan

Iqra Shagufta Cheema

Mera Jism, Meri Marzi was simultaneously the most critical and the most controversial slogan at the Aurat March, Pakistan, in 2018.[1] Literally translated as 'my body, my choice', this slogan is an assertion of women's bodily autonomy and a demand for their sexual consent. It became, rather unsurprisingly, the paradoxical focal point that encapsulated the sexual safety crisis, invocations of #MeToo feminist goals, and cultural anxieties around sexual politics in Pakistan. *Mera Jism, Meri Marzi* provoked the religious and cultural conservatives but – interestingly – also provoked the older generation of feminists, some of whom found the linguistic expressions and political agendas of the younger generation of feminists rather unpalatable. Despite the ephemeral nature of most provocative events and statements in the age of social media, *Mera Jism, Meri Marzi* has sustained its semantic role as a signpost for contemporary feminist politics in Pakistan.

To explore how and why this slogan became the epicentre of the struggle for women's rights to sexual consent, physical safety, and sexual autonomy, this chapter traces the gendered intersections of culture and religion in a heteropatriarchal location to highlight how this slogan served as a multipronged intervention in the contemporary crises of sexual violence against women in Pakistan. Pakistan has witnessed a surge in cases of sexual violence or, at least, an increase in their reportage (since most cases of sexual violence remained underreported prior to wider usage of social media and the #MeToo movement) – this crisis has particularly worsened since COVID-19. Feminists have called this crisis a national femicide.[2] However, most religious and traditional conservatives have resorted to blaming victims and the West for this crisis. Approaching *Mera Jism, Meri Marzi* as the semantic site of feminist struggles for sexual safety and autonomy, this chapter analyses these unintentional provocations of masculine sentiments, religiopolitical confusion, and patriarchal sexual anxieties to suggest that *Mera Jism, Meri Marzi* – more than being one of the feminist slogans at the Aurat March – is a collective protest and demand for attention to national femicide for an eventual remediation of violence against women.

For this purpose, I first provide the context in which the slogan entered the feminist political and public sphere in Pakistan and the popular reaction to it.

DOI: 10.4324/9781003365082-5

Then I discuss the slogan's impact on feminist politics as well as on feminists, along with highlighting women's reclamation of the gendered vocabularies often deployed against them. Finally, I highlight the importance of a transnational understanding of consent and the simultaneous criticality of localising this understanding to increase the efficacy of these conversations and contestations about consent in the socioreligious context of Pakistan.

National Femicide and Aurat March in Pakistan

2020 and the following years witnessed a significant increase in cases of violence against women, so much so that it was termed a national femicide. Much of the reported violence was committed inside the family, by victims' long term romantic or marital partners. Some of the cases made it to social media, resulting in hashtag campaigns, like #JusticeforQuratulain,[3] #JusticeforSaima,[4] #JusticeforNoor,[5] and #JusticeforSara.[6] These are only a few of the cases that gained public attention because of their gruesome violence that ended in murder – but it is telling that these women were murdered by husbands or long-term partners inside homes in a country where domestic and gendered abuse remains grossly underreported. While I revise this chapter, there have been two reports of rape today: a guard raped an 18-year-old bus hostess in a moving bus,[7] and two strangers raped a woman in a park in Pakistan's capital and also told her to 'not be in the park at night'[8] – leaving us with the question of whether the rapists believed that they must punish a woman who is in a public space at night or that they perversely believed that she should not be in public if she did not want to be raped. While these cases have increased lately, the problem of men violating women's bodies is not new. It comes as no surprise that Pakistan was ranked 167 out of 170 on the Women, Peace, and Security Index,[9] with about 11 daily reported cases of rape.[10] These incidents, with all their callousness and brutality, make visible the crisis of consent in Pakistan. As the violence and disregard for sexual consent increases, so does the critical need to understand, promote, and develop a culture of consent.

Given Pakistani women's marginalised position, the responsibility of violence prevention often falls on the shoulders of the state, which itself remains tethered to the demands of the majoritarian religious and cultural conservatives. The Pakistani Constitution of 1973 grants equal status to people of all genders: 'All citizens are equal before the law and are entitled to equal protection of the law […] Nothing in this Article shall prevent the State from making any special provision for the protection of women and children.'[11] However, the 1979 Hudood Ordinances introduced during Pakistan's then military ruler, General Zia-ul-Haq's theocratic regime (1977–88), bypass the constitutionally granted gender equality. These ordinances added another layer of Islamic laws to the Pakistan Penal Code (PPC) (which is based on the Indian Penal Code, originally prepared by Lord Macaulay in 1860). As a result of this promulgation, rape, non-marital consensual sex, sodomy, enticement, attempted rape, and false allegations of adultery became criminal offences under Islamic Criminal Laws.[12] Prior to the Hudood Ordinances, these offences were governed by the secular Pakistan Penal Code, in which adultery and fornication were not criminal offences.[13] Many of these laws legislated victim blaming and victim punishment and even admission and reportage of rape resulted in 'social death' and legal punishment.[14] These conditions directed the feminist attention from postcolonial nationalistic loyalties to critique of and confrontation with the state.

This layering of the Pakistani Penal Code with colonial and then Islamic laws, also called 'Pakistan dual legal regimes', adds interpretive legislature ambiguity to enable men to commit gender-based violations with '(dual) impunity'.[15] Feminists and women's rights activists, particularly the Women's Action Forum (1981), advocated for women's rights and demanded amendments to the Hudood Ordinances. The feminist fights, under these conditions, necessitated engagement with a theocratic state and populace. Simultaneously, it determined a cautious and relatively conservative framing of women's rights and roles in a nation-state, with conversations about women's sexuality and their right to their own bodies becoming secondary or subtler. Eventually in 2006, after 30 years of feminist struggle, the Hudood Ordinances were amended by the Protection of Women Act.[16]

Decades-long investment, deliberation, and contestation of Pakistani legislative, state, and religious bodies into regulating and controlling women's bodies manifests itself in the mass imagination and public discourse as paranoia and panic about women, their sexuality, and their place in Pakistan – this is precisely what we witness in women's protest slogans and the public reception of these slogans. With this long history of public and legislated violence against women's bodies and its prevention, unsurprisingly, the crisis of consent emerged as the centre of protesters' slogans for the inaugural Aurat March. Officially, the Aurat March had a four-part manifesto that demanded an end to violence against women and called for economic, reproductive, and environmental justice. The march was 'joyous and jolting, visible and visceral' – 'a moment of collective release, resistance, and resurgence'.[17] Informally, the march's participants held placards and raised slogans saying *Mera Jism, Meri Marzi* to demand and assert their right to bodily autonomy and consent.

Mera Jism, Meri Marzi

This slogan has its roots in the feminist slogan 'my body, my choice', which feminists have used transnationally to assert their reproductive rights and sexual consent. The slogan has become a central link between historically, temporally, and geographically variegated feminisms across the globe, especially after its post-#MeToo resurgence. Due to its roots in the #MeToo movements and these shared ideological links – and despite its movement from the Global North to the Global South – the Aurat March and these attendant slogans are both transnational and national. In 2018, chants of *Mera Jism, Meri Marzi* (my body, my choice), *apni dick pics apnay pass rakho* (keep your dick pics to yourself), and *consent ki tasbeeh roz parhein* (remember the rosary of consent everyday) heralded the first time that Pakistan publicly came face-to-face with the question of women's sexuality and the national and cultural treatment of women as sexual objects, in a setting where it was women speaking about it. This 'sight of thousands of women's bodies in the public arena of the street', chanting *Mera Jism, Meri Marzi* and *pidarshahi ka janazah* (patriarchy's funeral), 'signify a historical as well as a hysterical moment in the making: historical as it is unprecedented in Pakistan's street movements' history; hysterical because the epithet captures the resistance and hysterical reactions of the detractors'.[18]

Many women experienced and described the event as revolutionary.[19] However, women's audacity to speak openly about their sexuality and its violations was declared disrespectful, subversive, and reprehensible by most – even by some from the older generation of feminists. When a human rights activist and journalist, Marvi Sirmed, tried to explain the slogan to a popular TV writer, Khalil-ur-Rehman Qamar, it quickly turned into an ugly fight where Qamar hurled sexist slurs at Sirmed, with Sirmed responding with *Mera Jism, Meri Marzi*. Many other famous public intellectuals, media celebrities, and religious scholars also attacked and reprimanded feminists for their slogans.

The nationally aired argument between Sirmed and Qamar bifurcated Pakistanis into two groups: firstly, those who imagine an ideal Pakistani Muslim woman based on their socioreligious interpretation of Pakistan as a theocratic nation-state; and secondly, those who imagine women and men as equal humans and citizens in a nation state that is increasingly captivated by regressive religious and political ideas and ideologues. The war between these two groups annually intensifies as International Women's Day and its attendant Aurat March approach. According to the public imagination of the first group, an ideal Pakistani woman remains:

> [...] [someone] who becomes available to state leaders and Islamic fundamentalists for ideological purposes. For example, when state and religious leaders restrict women to the confines of the private sphere through their politico-religious rhetoric, as well as in law, they fashion a "Pakistani Woman" almost exclusively as wife and mother. That wife and mother become useful in projects of nation-building and Muslim group identity construction.[20]

This definition holds true to a large extent. In contrast, I imagine a Pakistani woman according to the second group here, whom I call the 'post-#MeToo Pakistani woman': a woman who self-defines her roles and responsibilities and claims her right to self-determine her role in the nation-state first and foremost as an equal citizen, irrespective of her relationship with male citizens of the state. She is equally capable of constructing and critiquing the state. She is not responsible for her nation's honour internationally, but who represents her nation internationally.

This definition remains underwritten by women's relationship with a heterosexual theocratic nation-state. But this relationship with the state remains critical due to the need for state imperative and support for women's presence and protection both in the public and private spheres, especially since women's right to consent, sexual safety, and bodily autonomy remains tied to the ideological leanings of the ruling parties, as described above. Eventually, any conversation about women's rights in Pakistan, especially the conversations that occur in the context of secular or progressive politics, become enmeshed with Pakistani anxieties about female sexuality – *Mera Jism, Meri Marzi* was treated no differently.

Assailants of the slogan alleged that liberal and secular feminists wanted to turn Pakistan into a free-sex zone, perpetuate a Western-sponsored agenda of uprooting the Pakistani family system, abort pregnancies, and tear the country's moral fabric by enabling women to have consensual sex with people of their choosing. Most Pakistanis evaluate women's character solely based on their virginity and believe women's modesty to be the foundation of familial and social integrity. Women are valued for their familial roles as mothers, sisters, and daughters – and rarely as agential subjects. Hence, women's reclamation of their sexual agency and consent is akin to the familial and social ruination. Ironically, Islam grants many of these rights to women – including abortion rights, the right to choose a marriage partner, and the right to sexual consent in a marriage. These feminists were also accused of being anti-Islam, anti-Pakistan, pro-West, American agents, degenerate, and sex-maniacs. Many feminists faced threats of physical and sexual abuse in response to their attempts at eradicating physical and sexual abuse.

If we unpack the assumptions and ideas that underwrite these accusations, it becomes clear that these remain rooted in anachronistic beliefs that women's place is in the domestic space (as was determined by Zia's regime) or that women are allowed in designated public spaces only as participants in the construction of a nation-state and its ideal image (as was determined during Pervez Musharraf's regime).[21] *Mera Jism, Meri Marzi* challenges both. It signifies women's determination to exercise their own will over their own bodies both linguistically and sociopolitically via *mera* and *meri* which translate as 'my' in the Urdu language. It also invokes *jism* and *marzi*, which translate as 'body' and 'will' respectively. These assumptions about women's roles and vocabularies precisely constitute and secure the foundations of masculinities and heteropatriarchal familial and cultural structures.

Masculinities – shaped, strengthened, and secured both by national and religious dictates – are further reified via the exercise of masculine will over women's bodies, which manifests itself in various forms, including limiting women to domestic spaces, controlling their mobility, hindering their financial freedom, dictating their sexual lives, and using their bodies as a site of male honour and ego. It also results in violating women's bodies if they deviate from the prescribed moral norms, a trend that shows itself in the form of honour killings, revenge rape, or disciplinary rape. Successfully challenging these masculine privileges requires revisions to the social, religious, and national order, so it comes as no surprise that these slogans for the right to sexual consent and autonomy received such retaliation. How can a people that mansplain to women the meaning of sexual violence and consent, or that guides them as to which language to use when asking for sexual safety, imagine, let alone enact, gender and sexual equity?

Crisis of Consent and Digital Mediations

While communication, respect, and acknowledgement are the shared lexicon in many definitions of consent, feminists have been long contesting the question of how one seeks an equal right to consent in a heteropatriarchy that inherently contains and safeguards unequal gendered and sexual relations between its members. As Quill R. Kukla puts it: 'if we insist that real consent requires full autonomy, then virtually no sex will turn out to be consensual'.[22] Others have also argued against the possibility of women's consent due to the unequal power relations and sociocultural forces at work.[23] This is a conundrum that Pakistani women continue to face when asking for their right to sexual consent and bodily autonomy, as observed during the 2018 Aurat March. Below, I summarise some definitions of sexual consent to elaborate on the ways in which digital media platforms inform and mediate conversations regarding consent in a #MeToo environment.

Scholars have reduced consent to either a physical act,[24] an intellectual act,[25] or a combination of the two. Some read consent as 'an act of moral transformation',[26] since it differentiates bad sex from good sex,[27] morally problematic sex from morally unproblematic sex,[28] or a criminal act of bodily violation from making love.[29] Consent, in most of these definitions, remains gendered as it automatically assumes that men act sex while women react to men's actions.[30] Ideally then, consent means that women are able to make decisions about engaging in sexual activities without any implicit or explicit fear of negative consequences for their decision. Or to term it positively, they engage in sexual activity with the clear knowledge that their decision will not bear on their personal, familial, social, or professional lives in any way. However, this consent requires a complete rehaul of the economic and social structures within which women currently exist as less privileged members.

These facts and facets of consent assume further complexities when examined in a heteropatriarchal theocracy where only marital sex is legal, extramarital or same-sex sex is a punishable offence, religious and political conceptions of sex and permissible sexual acts vary widely, and the punishments for sexual crimes are often discretionary under the national and religious laws and lawmakers. Simultaneously, though people do not have access to healthy modes of sexual education in Pakistan, men often learn exploitative sexual behaviours from porn; Pakistan tops the list of porn-searching countries[31] despite the government's ban on porn websites since 2011.[32] Sexual information learnt from porn, combined with gendered religious beliefs, reinforces men's misogynistic and harmful beliefs about gender relations and their entitlement to women's bodies.

However, recent digital feminist movements have raised a new feminist consciousness wherein women have gained deeper understanding of their experiences.[33] This consciousness is informed and strengthened both by the progressive legislations for gender equity in Pakistan as well as from the international feminist uprisings succeeding the #MeToo movement and International Women's Marches. Thus, the new feminist consciousness is rooted in both women's ability to digitally enact their feminist politics internationally as well as in the relatively open cultural space and legal securities afforded to women nationally. But this consciousness was (in)formed by the sexual violence against women's bodies, bodies that were visible to Pakistani masses in digital spaces like the body of Qandeel Baloch. Qandeel Baloch gained notoriety through her social media videos where she challenged Pakistani masculinities and men's predatory sexual behaviours, among other things. Her life quickly became rife with many scandals, including her promise of a public strip tease and her meeting with a senior cleric, Mufti Abdul Qavi. In 2016, her brother murdered her for honour while she was asleep in her parents' house. Baloch's body, then, became the site of the sexual anxieties, projections, and fears of the entire nation. Both her life and death brought into the open the debates about sex, sexual expression, sexual agency, and sexual consent in domestic and public spaces and made visible its links to class, capital, and economic politics.[34] Hence, her murder became the fertile ground where conversations about female sexuality and public ownership of that sexuality were initiated and continued. Baloch's murder and *Mera Jism, Meri Marzi* garnered similar responses from the Pakistani public: these acts instantaneously become signifiers of women's right to sexual consent and their ownership of their bodies. Since women's bodies are made into symbols of both the national and religious heterosexual narratives, women's assertion of their right to consent both in the domestic and public sphere as sexual objects threatens the ways men assert their masculinities.

It is critical to note here that previous conversations about consent only occurred in legislative or reformist contexts. Previous generations of feminists, in their engagement with political and religious bodies, exercised cautious engagement with sexual consent framed as violence against women and not as women's right to pleasure with the partner of their choice. The younger generation of feminists is more concerned with the issues of sexual safety and consent because of women's increasing presence in public spaces. And women's presence is facilitated less by the sociolegal state structures but rather mandated by the increasing financial pressures in a country that consistently faces international financial terrorism from organisations like IMF. Besides these pressures, women realise the criticality of financial independence for freedom of mobility. This is also a reason that some senior feminists have been critical of 'cyberfeminists' who are 'unable to locate their own identities with relevance to Pakistan's politics – not wanting to engage in a critique on neo-liberal economics'.[35]

While Afiya Shehrbano Zia critiques younger feminists' disengagement and avoidance of conversation with political and legislative bodies in the country as well as their incertitude between pietist or liberal feminisms, other feminists have also critiqued what they consider immodest and indecent language which was deployed in the Aurat March. However, they admit that sexuality and issues of the transgender, gay, or other sexually marginalised communities were not central to the Woman's Action Forum or older feminists' politics.[36] They have also recognised their failure in training the new feminists to continue effective and impactful feminist politics in Pakistan. And these questions of class, faith, and language have served as scapegoats for those critical of *Mera Jism, Meri Marzi*.

After his on-screen argument with Sirmed (mentioned previously), Qamar highlighted the ways feminists ignored the class question and instead focused on questions of sexual consent and sexual autonomy. He questioned feminists' character and their agendas by noting that a group of women from the elite class, who labelled themselves feminists, only wanted sexual freedom. He suggested that feminists should instead focus on the 'real' issues facing women, namely poverty and a widening class gap. While popular feminist movements gained some traction in different time periods, more indigenous and regional feminist movements that specifically addressed income and class disparities – like the anti-military land rights peasant movement in Okara or the Lady Health Workers movement asking for job security and better income – did not receive popular attention or retain space in the public memory for long. Qamar, in his critiques, disjoints sexual violence and women's class-based vulnerability to sexual violence. Women involved in menial labour and belonging to the lower middle class are actually the ones who are the most vulnerable to sexual violence and non-consensual sex. Most of the reported cases of violence against women in the last few years have been within upper-middle-class or elite-class communities: for example, in Noor Muqaddam's case, involving the daughter of a former Pakistani diplomat, and Sara Inam's case, daughter-in-law of one of the top journalists in the country. Besides that, other famous cases of sexual violence or harassment, like the harassment case filed against the famous singer Ali Zafar by his equally famous counterpart Meesha Ali, or the domestic abuse case filed against the well-known actor Feroze Khan by his wife Alizey Fatima, have also been mostly reported from the same social strata.

This counters Qamar's critique of feminists and the Pakistani #MeToo movement as being completely elite as it shows that violence against women is an issue in every socioeconomic class, albeit to varying degrees. However, feminists have been long deliberating over the ways to bridge the class gaps. While some of Qamar's critique of class-based feminist politics holds true, conversations about consent and sexual safety in domestic and public spaces and their attendant sociocultural changes would ultimately benefit every woman. Therefore, they are a mass concern. This also makes it clear that the precautions about honour and respectability are mostly the concerns of an aspirational middle class that views women's audacity to assert the right to consent in a disruptive and appropriative lexicon as a Western import and inspiration, not in line with Pakistan's national and religious cultures.

This brings us to the questions of language and the Western influence on Pakistani women's demands for sexual safety and consensual sex. The allegation of being a Western import and not being indigenous enough has always accompanied Pakistani feminist movements, which have not been rigorously documented. So, *Mera Jism, Meri Marzi*, as a slogan raised during the Aurat March 2018, which was inspired by the international #MeToo movement and Women's Marches, automatically became more suspect for the public due to its transnational links. Many of the organisers of the Aurat March are foreign-educated academics who, due to their academic training in the West, replicate or repeat the vocabularies employed in feminist conversations in the Global North. Therefore, many feminists have also cautiously opted for local vernacular and vocabularies for their conversations as is evidenced by the Aurat March slogans.

Additionally, Aurat March participants employ an appropriative lexicon, by rebranding designated masculine vocabularies of everyday use, in their demands for sexual safety. For example, some of the slogans and placards in the Aurat March read: *Akeli, Awara, Azad* (alone, vagrant, and free), *main awara, main badchalan* (sure, I am immoral and characterless), *aaj maa behen aik ho gay hai* (today, mother and sister are together), *lo beth gai theek se* (behold, I am sitting with legs closed). These slogans are a play on gendered abuses and slurs that are employed frequently and mostly by men, but that are also a familiar part of the social vernacular for everyone. Women who do not have a male caretaker such as a husband, father, or brother are perceived to be sexually promiscuous and are often referred to as *awara* and *badchalan*. Those who are highly educated, career oriented, and who do not rely on men's financial and social support are insultingly referred to as *azad*.

Azad means being able to make decisions for oneself without anyone's interference or influence – while being *azad* or being able to make national decisions without foreign interference is an aspiration for Pakistan, women's ability to decide for themselves threatens the heteropatriarchal familial and cultural structures that rely on women's reproductive and economic labours. To show their modesty and passivity, women are often advised to sit with their legs closed as sitting with legs wide symbolises sexual immorality. And every cuss word that men employ to insult other men is rooted in sex and threats of sexual violence, which includes uninvited sexual attacks and non-consensual sex with the opposite's mother, sister, or daughter. *Aaj maa behen aik ker doon ga* (today, I'll make your mother and sister into one), which threatens to attack both the opponent's sister and mother at the same time, is among one of the most frequently used insults in Pakistani Punjabi culture. But feminists in the Aurat March revised it into *Aaj maa behen aik ho gay hai* (today, mother and sister are together). Via a playful recontextualisation of the statement, they rebranded it as a statement of feminist solidarity between sisters and mothers all around the nation.

Thus, women used the same vocabularies that are invoked and employed against them, not to attack men but to ask for safety from the abuse that this gendered masculinist lexicon threatens against them. Reactions to these demands then highlight masculine fragility as well as the effectivity of these strategies in disrupting the politics of consent when pursued and deployed consistently. However, these slogans in the Aurat March of 2018 received vehement opposition and strong reactions that also affected the succeeding Aurat Marches. In 2020, the march organisers received a bomb threat in Karachi. In Islamabad, a mural on sisterhood painted before the march was defaced. Marchers were pelted with stones by right-wing political party activists, despite security arrangements, resulting in injuries to some of the organisers. In Lahore and Islamabad, the court of law was used to petition the banning of the march on the grounds of indecency and immorality, but the cases were overruled by the high courts in each respective city. Even cases of religious blasphemy, a crime punishable by death in extreme cases, were filed against the marchers. Due to these threatening tactics, along with a lack of support from the state and critique from older feminists, the Aurat Marches and the vocabularies employed therein became more subtle and accommodating to the mass demands. In 2022, the Aurat March focused on demands for broader protection, peace, equity, and security without any reference to women's sexuality or pleasure.[37]

Afiya Zia reads this 'concession' as 'the success of the narrative of right-wing women'.[38] The leader of the pious Al-Huda movement, Dr. Farhat Hashmi, has appealed to Pakistani Muslim women to subdue their 'sexual agency for the prime purpose of serving Muslim men'.[39] She has also insisted that marital rape is a 'misnomer with respect to Muslim marriages' and instructed Muslim women to 'willingly consent and submit to, not resist, the sexual demands of their husbands'.[40] There have not been any reported cases of marital rape in Pakistan so far, so it is hard to imagine how these digital and on-the-ground conversations about women's right to consent would affect these cases.

Futures of Consent

Despite the opposition to the Aurat March and attacks on marchers and march organisers, the Aurat March and #MeToo have been instrumental in furthering and normalising conversations about consent and the critical need for consent in Pakistan. Though initially these demands were read as too disruptive and transgressive, they cracked open a socioreligious pressure point about women's right to sexual safety and consent. While feminists strategically resorted to a subdued and sanctified lexicon for sexual safety in on-the-ground spaces, post-#MeToo Pakistani women remain persistent in their demands in digital spaces. Many feminists pursue these conversations about sexual safety and consent in digital spaces under their original names or via anonymous accounts. These digitally mediated conversations about consent are 'arguably as effective as in-person gatherings and protests as a feminist political strategy'.[41] Digital spaces have proved critical in continuing these conversations about consent in a heteropatriarchal theocracy where these issues remain muddy and contested and are suspended between the religious and liberal state policies and public behaviours as well as between the Islamists and secular feminists.

Notes

1 Aurat March is an annual demonstration for women's rights, held on International Women's Day. The first Aurat March was held on 8 March 2018 in solidarity with Women's Marches internationally.

2 See, for example, Anmol Irfan, 'Pakistan's Femicide Crisis', *Think Global Health*, 25 August 2022 <https://www.thinkglobalhealth.org/article/pakistans-femicide-crisis> [accessed 12 May 2023].

3 'Quratulain Baloch murder case 2021: Husband sentenced to death', *The Current*, 12 January 2023 <https://thecurrent.pk/quratulain-baloch-murder-case-2021-husband-sentenced-to-death/#:~:text=The%20brutal%20murder%20took%20place,sparked%20nationwide%20outrage%20and%20condemnation> [accessed 12 May 2023].

4 'No place for violence against women in our society, lives, religion or culture', *Express Tribune*, 23 July 2021 <https://tribune.com.pk/story/2311826/no-place-for-violence-against-women-in-our-society-lives-religion-or-culture> [accessed 12 May 2023].

5 'Grisly murder of Noor Mukadam sparks outrage over femicides in Pakistan', *Express Tribune*, 30 July 2021 <https://tribune.com.pk/story/2313024/grisly-murder-of-noor-mukadam-sparks-outrage-over-femicides-in-pakistan> [accessed 12 May 2023].

6 Azman bin Mohd Noor, 'Prosecution of Rape in Islamic Law: A Review of Pakistan Hudood Ordinance 1979', *IIUM Law Journal*, 16.2 (2008), 283–98.

7 Shahid Mehmood, 'Bus hostess allegedly raped by guard', *Express Tribune*, 5 February 2023 <https://tribune.com.pk/story/2399426/bus-hostess-allegedly-raped-by-guard> [accessed 12 May 2023].

8 Ahmed Subhan and Ayaz Akbar Yousafzai, '"Armed men" rape girl in Islamabad's F-9 park', *The News*, 4 February 2023 <https://www.thenews.com.pk/latest/1037501-armed-men-rape-girl-in-islamabads-f-9-park> [accessed 12 May 2023].

9 'Pakistan's Performance on the Women, Peace, and Security Index', *Georgetown Institute for Women, Peace and Security*, 2021 <https://giwps.georgetown.edu/country/pakistan/> [accessed 12 May 2023].

10 '11 rape incidents reported across Pakistan every day: official data', *Geo News*, 13 November 2020 <https://www.geo.tv/latest/318448-official-statistics-unveil> [accessed 12 May 2023].

11 Pakistani Government, 'Article 25 of 1973 Constitution of Pakistan' (Islamabad: Islamic Republic of Pakistan, 1973) <https://pakistanconstitutionlaw.com/article-25-equality-of-citizens/> [accessed 12 May 2023].

12 Reportedly, due to these laws, no rape was reported throughout Zia's rule, or rates of reported rape significantly dropped. See 'Public hanging during Zia's regime', *Soch*, 23 September 2020 <https://www.sochfactcheck.com/public-hanging-during-zias-regime-did-not-eliminate-rape/> [accessed 12 May 2023].

13 Martin Lau, 'Twenty-Five Years of Hudood Ordinances – A Review', *Washington and Lee Law Review*, 64.4 (2007), 1291–1314 (p. 1292).

14 See Khawar Mumtaz and Farida Shaheed, *Women of Pakistan: Two Steps Forward, One Step Back* (London: Zed Books Ltd., 1987), p. 42. Safia Bibi's case serves as an example. She was unable to identify her rapists due to her blindness and was subjected to six months in jail and suffered 15 lashes.

15 Afiya Shehrbano Zia, '"My Body, Allah's Choice": Islamic Laws and Sexual Autonomies in Pakistan', *Australian Journal of Asian Law*, 23.2 (2022), 95–110 (p. 97).
16 'Protection of Women: Criminal Laws Amendment' (Pakistan: Islamic Republic of Pakistan, 2006) <https://www.ilo.org/dyn/natlex/docs/ELECTRONIC/81773/88938/F92328325/PAK81773.pdf> [accessed 12 May 2023].
17 Shama Dossa, 'The Aurat March: Women's Movements and New Feminisms in Pakistan', in *Routledge Handbook of Gender in South Asia*, ed. by Leela Fernandes (London: Routledge, 2021), pp. 319–34 (p. 329).
18 Shirin Zubair, '*Mera Jism Meri Marzi*: Framing the Contestations of Women's Rights in Pakistan', in *Global Contestations of Gender Rights*, ed. by A. Scheele, J. Roth, and H. Winkel (Bielefeld: Bielefeld University Press, 2022), pp. 307–26 (p. 317).
19 See Iqra Shagufta Cheema, ed., *The Other #MeToos* (New York: Oxford University Press, forthcoming 2023).
20 Nancy Cook, 'The Discursive Constitution of Pakistani Women: The Articulation of Gender, Nation, and Islam', *Atlantis: A Women's Studies Journal*, 25.2 (2001), 31–41 (p. 31).
21 See Shahnaz Khan, 'Muslim Women: Negotiations in the Third Space', *Signs: Journal of Women in Culture & Society*, 23 (1998), 463–94; Rubina Saigol, *Feminism and the Women's Movement in Pakistan: Actors, Debates and Strategies* (Islamabad: Friedrich-Ebert-Stiftung Pakistan, 2016); Cook.
22 Quill R. Kukla, 'A Nonideal Theory of Sexual Consent', *Ethics,* 131.2 (2021), 270–92 (p. 270).
23 See Catharine MacKinnon, *Toward a Feminist Theory of the State* (Cambridge, MA: Harvard University Press, 1989); Robin West, 'The Harms of Consensual Sex', in *The Philosophy of Sex: Contemporary Readings*, ed. by Alan Soble, Jacob M. Held, and Raja Halwani (Lanham, MD: Rowman and Littlefield, 2002), pp. 317–22.
24 Todd A. Ostler, 'Verbal and Nonverbal Dating Behaviors and Sexual Consent: Implications for Miscommunication between Men and Women' (unpublished doctoral thesis, University of Nevada, 2003).
25 Heidi Hurd, 'The Moral Magic of Consent', *Legal Theory,* 2 (1996), 121–46.
26 Melanie A. Beres, '"Spontaneous" Sexual Consent: An Analysis of Sexual Consent Literature', *Feminism & Psychology,* 17.1 (2007), 93–108.
27 Alan Wertheimer, *Consent to Sexual Relations* (Cambridge: Cambridge University Press, 2003).
28 See Hurd.
29 David Archard, *Sexual Consent* (Boulder, CO: Westview Press, 1998).
30 Patricia J. Morokoff, 'A Cultural Context for Sexual Assertiveness in Women', in *Sexuality, Society and Feminism*, ed. by C. B. Travis and J. W. White (Washington, DC: American Psychological Association, 2000), pp. 299–319.
31 Carrie Weisman, 'Why porn is exploding in the Middle East', *Salon*, 15 January 2015 <https://www.salon.com/2015/01/15/why_porn_is_exploding_in_the_middle_east_partner/> [accessed 12 May 2023].
32 'Pakistan blocks 8,00,000 websites to curb pornography', *Indian Express*, 18 July 2019 <https://www.newindianexpress.com/world/2019/jul/18/pakistan-blocks-800000-websites-to-curb-pornography-2005936.html> [accessed 12 May 2023].
33 See Shagufta Cheema (forthcoming).
34 Sanam Maher, *The Sensational Life and Death of Qandeel Baloch* (New Delhi: Aleph Book Company, 2018).
35 Afiya Shehrbano Zia, 'New Directions in the Pakistani Women's Movement', in *Gender, Governance and Islam*, ed. by Deniz Kandiyoti (Edinburgh: Edinburgh University Press, 2019), pp. 165–85 (p. 169).
36 See Saigol.

37 'Aurat March Launches Manifesto of Justice', *Dawn*, 19 February 2022 <https://www.dawn.com/news/1675882> [accessed 12 May 2023].
38 Zia, 'Islamic Laws and Sexual Autonomies in Pakistan', p. 106.
39 Ibid.
40 Ibid.
41 See Shagufta Cheema (forthcoming).

Bibliography

'11 rape incidents reported across Pakistan every day: official data', *Geo News*, 13 November 2020 <https://www.geo.tv/latest/318448-official-statistics-unveil> [accessed 12 May 2023]

Archard, David, *Sexual Consent* (Boulder, CO: Westview Press, 1998)

'Aurat March Launches Manifesto of Justice', *Dawn*, 19 February 2022 <https://www.dawn.com/news/1675882> [accessed 12 May 2023]

Beres, Melanie A., '"Spontaneous" Sexual Consent: An Analysis of Sexual Consent Literature', *Feminism & Psychology*, 17 (2007), 93–108

Cook, Nancy, 'The Discursive Constitution of Pakistani Women: The Articulation of Gender, Nation, and Islam', *Atlantis: A Women's Studies Journal*, 25.2 (2001), 31–41

Dossa, Shama, 'The Aurat March: Women's Movements and New Feminisms in Pakistan', in *Routledge Handbook of Gender in South Asia*, ed. by Leela Fernandes (London: Routledge, 2021), pp. 319–34

'Grisly murder of Noor Mukadam sparks outrage over femicides in Pakistan', *Express Tribune*, 30 July 2021 <https://tribune.com.pk/story/2313024/grisly-murder-of-noor-mukadam-sparks-outrage-over-femicides-in-pakistan> [accessed 12 May 2023]

Hurd, Heidi, 'The Moral Magic of Consent', *Legal Theory*, 2 (1996), 121–46

Irfan, Anmol, 'Pakistan's Femicide Crisis', *Think Global Health*, 25 August 2022 <https://www.thinkglobalhealth.org/article/pakistans-femicide-crisis> [accessed 12 May 2023]

Khan, Shahnaz, 'Muslim Women: Negotiations in the Third Space', *Signs: Journal of Women in Culture & Society*, 23.2 (1998), 463–94

Kukla, Quill R., 'A Nonideal Theory of Sexual Consent', *Ethics*, 131.2 (2021), 270–92

Lau, Martin, 'Twenty-Five Years of Hudood Ordinances – A Review', *Washington and Lee Law Review*, 64.4 (2007), 1291–1314

MacKinnon, Catharine, *Toward a Feminist Theory of the State* (Cambridge, MA: Harvard University Press, 1989)

Maher, Sanam, *The Sensational Life and Death of Qandeel Baloch* (New Delhi: Aleph Book Company, 2018)

Mehmood, Shahid, 'Bus hostess allegedly raped by guard', *Express Tribune*, 5 February 2023 <https://tribune.com.pk/story/2399426/bus-hostess-allegedly-raped-by-guard> [accessed 12 May 2023]

Morokoff, Patricia J., 'A Cultural Context for Sexual Assertiveness in Women', in *Sexuality, Society and Feminism*, ed. by C. B. Travis and J. W. White (Washington, DC: American Psychological Association, 2000), pp. 299–319

Mumtaz, Khawar, and Farida Shaheed, *Women of Pakistan: Two Steps Forward, One Step Back* (London: Zed Books Ltd., 1987)

'No place for violence against women in our society, lives, religion or culture', *Express Tribune*, 23 July 2021 <https://tribune.com.pk/story/2311826/no-place-for-violence-against-women-in-our-society-lives-religion-or-culture> [accessed 12 May 2023]

Noor, Azman bin Mohd, 'Prosecution of Rape in Islamic Law: A Review of Pakistan Hudood Ordinance 1979', *IIUM Law Journal*, 16.2 (2008), 283–98

Ostler, Todd A., 'Verbal and Nonverbal Dating Behaviors and Sexual Consent: Implications for Miscommunication between Men and Women' (unpublished doctoral thesis, University of Nevada, 2003)

'Pakistan blocks 8,00,000 websites to curb pornography', *Indian Express*, 18 July 2019 <https://www.newindianexpress.com/world/2019/jul/18/pakistan-blocks-800000-websites-to-curb-pornography-2005936.html> [accessed 12 May 2023]

Pakistani Government, 'Article 25 of 1973 Constitution of Pakistan' (Islamabad: Islamic Republic of Pakistan, 1973) <https://pakistanconstitutionlaw.com/article-25-equality-of-citizens/> [accessed 12 May 2023]

'Pakistan's Performance on the Women, Peace, and Security Index', Georgetown Institute for Women, Peace and Security, 2021 <https://giwps.georgetown.edu/country/pakistan/> [accessed 12 May 2023]

'Protection of Women: Criminal Laws Amendment' (Islamabad: Islamic Republic of Pakistan, 2006) <https://www.ilo.org/dyn/natlex/docs/ELECTRONIC/81773/88938/F92328325/PAK81773.pdf> [accessed 12 May 2023]

'Public hanging during Zia's regime', *Soch*, 23 September 2020 <https://www.sochfactcheck.com/public-hanging-during-zias-regime-did-not-eliminate-rape/> [accessed 12 May 2023]

'Quratulain Baloch murder case 2021: Husband sentenced to death', *The Current*, 12 January 2023 <https://thecurrent.pk/quratulain-baloch-murder-case-2021-husband-sentenced-to-death/#:~:text=The%20brutal%20murder%20took%20place,sparked%20nationwide%20outrage%20and%20condemnation> [accessed 12 May 2023]

Saigol, Rubina, *Feminism and the Women's Movement in Pakistan: Actors, Debates and Strategies* (Islamabad: Friedrich-Ebert-Stiftung Pakistan, 2016)

Shagufta Cheema, Iqra, ed., *The Other #MeToos* (New York: Oxford University Press, 2023)

Subhan, Ahmed, and Ayaz Akbar Yousafzai, '"Armed men" rape girl in Islamabad's F-9 park', *The News*, 4 February 2023 <https://www.thenews.com.pk/latest/1037501-armed-men-rape-girl-in-islamabads-f-9-park> [accessed 12 May 2023]

Weisman, Carrie, 'Why porn is exploding in the Middle East', *Salon*, 15 January 2015 <https://www.salon.com/2015/01/15/why_porn_is_exploding_in_the_middle_east_partner/> [accessed 12 May 2023]

Wertheimer, Alan, *Consent to Sexual Relations* (Cambridge: Cambridge University Press, 2003)

West, Robin, 'The Harms of Consensual Sex', in *The Philosophy of Sex: Contemporary Readings*, ed. by Alan Soble, Jacob M. Held, and Raja Halwani (Lanham, MD: Rowman and Littlefield, 2002), pp. 317–22

Zia, Afiya Shehrbano, '"My Body, Allah's Choice": Islamic Laws and Sexual Autonomies in Pakistan', *Australian Journal of Asian Law*, 23.2 (2022), 95–110

Zia, Afiya Shehrbano, 'New Directions in the Pakistani Women's Movement', in *Gender, Governance and Islam*, ed. by Deniz Kandiyoti (Edinburgh: Edinburgh University Press, 2019), pp. 165–85

Zubair, Shirin, '*Mera Jism Meri Marzi*: Framing the Contestations of Women's Rights in Pakistan', in *Global Contestations of Gender Rights*, ed. by A. Scheele, J. Roth, and H. Winkel (Bielefeld: Bielefeld University Press, 2022), pp. 307–26

5 Do to Me What I Could Never Ask of You

Consensual Non-Consent in BDSM and the Limits of Affirmative Consent

Jay Szpilka

Content Notes: This chapter contains detailed descriptions of sexual practices which purposefully flaunt principles of affirmative consent and which often seek to enact sexual fantasies of violation.

Can there be such a thing as non-consensual sex that is also non-abusive? The question may seem strange at first, and the answer to it is obvious. Consent is a concept that is, arguably, at the bedrock of contemporary thinking about sexual ethics, which is not to say that it is without its critiques. Many – chiefly feminist – scholars have for several decades pointed out that consent alone is insufficient when it comes to ensuring that a sexual encounter is free of abuse, violence, and coercion;[1] that its popular imagination as a yes-or-no binary does not reflect the ambiguity of sexual desire;[2] and that it is badly entangled in a liberal mythology of self-possessed, individual subjects.[3] But however sharp those critiques may be, they seem to tacitly agree on one common point: that while consent itself may not be enough, it is also a necessary foundation for ethical sex. Sex that is non-consensual lies in the realm of abuse, violence, and rape.

The centrality of clearly expressed consent to our visions of ethical sex is, in many ways, a reaction to a number of pernicious and persistent cultural myths that Nicola Gavey calls the 'cultural scaffolding of rape'.[4] Excusing rape as sex that might not have been consensual, but was nonetheless wanted ('it's not rape if she enjoyed it') remains common, just as implying that women who do not consent to sex, while presenting 'sexily' in their clothing or behaviour are, in fact, 'asking for it', even if they do not admit it. Indeed, on the face of it, even suggesting that there may be sex that is both non-consensual and non-abusive can only ever serve to buttress up rape culture.

However, in this chapter I want to take a closer look at a set of sexual practices which trouble this apparent obviousness. I am referring to the idea of consensual non-consent present within the world of BDSM (bondage/discipline, dominance/submission, sadism/masochism). It refers to a set of practices in which the submissive partner agrees to a sexual situation where their ability to withdraw consent will be limited or fully eliminated, and/or which intentionally goes beyond the conditions which, according to the framework of affirmative (let alone enthusiastic) consent, are required for consent to be meaningful. To

DOI: 10.4324/9781003365082-6

provide just one possible example: a person may agree to being flogged, while also accepting (and perhaps expecting!) that if, under the whip, they ask for the beating to stop, this will then be ignored by their dominant partner, and the flogging will continue. My core argument is that cases like that – and the culture that arises around them – not only expose the limitations of affirmative consent's promise of safeguarding the borders of ethical sex, but also hint at alternatives to it which, crucially, are not built around purposefully legible forms of mutual consent.

In extant literature on BDSM, consensual non-consent has not yet been given a broad consideration. The few studies that focus on it either treat it as a sexual fantasy,[5] or skirt around the 'non-consent' aspect, foregrounding the negotiated nature of most consensual non-consent practices.[6] I do not think these approaches are necessarily invalid, though they sometimes verge on apologetics; I believe that doing consensual non-consent justice requires paying no less attention to the violations of consent it entails than to the consensual aspects of it. While an argument could be made that the 'non-consensual' part of the term is overridden by the 'consensual' one, the problem here is apparent. Contemporary standards of sexual ethics – and legislation that increasingly (and problematically) draws from them[7] – are clear on the fact that sexual consent is not a one-and-done thing. If a person consents to sex, and then midway through changes their mind and withdraws it, then the sexual encounter should be terminated; if the other party continues it, we enter the realm of sexual abuse. This idea, contained within notions of 'affirmative' and 'enthusiastic' consent, is vitally important for how sexual consent is understood today.[8] In legal systems that adopt such understanding, consent must be both continuous and continuously given. In a 2011 case, the Supreme Court of Canada ruled that a man having a BDSM scene with his wife, which included strangling her to a point of momentary loss of consciousness, qualified as sexual assault, despite the couple's previous agreement to the broad parameters of the encounter.[9] Clearly then, consensual non-consent practices are not legally consensual, at least according to some highly influential understandings of this term, even if calling them fully non-consensual is similarly problematic. Perhaps most surprisingly, however, it seems that even when a practice of non-consensual sex goes awry and leaves the submissive partner hurt, this hurt is not necessarily interpreted as abuse by the 'wronged' party.

Here, relying on material gathered during my ethnographic fieldwork among Polish BDSM practitioners, I want to ask the chapter's leading question: how can sex be both consensual and non-consensual at the same time? What is the use of consensual non-consent and why do people insist on practising it? And, finally, in the absence of strict frameworks of consent and other safety tools (like safewords), how do the practitioners of consensual non-consent protect each other from sexual abuse and violence?

Before I move on to sketching out some potential answers, an important caveat needs to be made. Though consensual non-consent is the focus of this chapter, and though I adopt a purposefully broad definition of it, I do not mean to imply that it is a common occurrence within the world of BDSM practices. While it is a common object of fantasy among kinksters, its actual enactment is rare. Practices of consensual non-consent are an example of 'edge play'; that is, practices that exist at the periphery of what is and should be permissible within the world of BDSM, and which are sometimes controversial even within the communities of the practitioners.[10] The cause for that controversy – and an important context for the epistemological difficulty we are faced with when discussing consensual non-consent – is related to the broader discourse on the importance of consent for BDSM in general.

Safe, Sane… Consensual?

'Regardless of appearance', writes Stacey May Fowles, 'by its very nature BDSM is constantly about consent'.[11] Whether this is really what BDSM is all about (I would suggest that it is about many things, consent being merely one of them), this statement certainly applies to the discourse surrounding BDSM. Outside of highly tendentious critiques of such practices,[12] it is difficult to find a public-facing, either scholarly or popular, discussion of BDSM that does not foreground the fact that those practices are both consensual, and that securing consent is a key concern of BDSM practitioners.[13] This forms the basis of common knowledge which allows the BDSM scholar Margot Weiss to confidently state that 'unlike torture, consensual BDSM is of limited duration, bracketed, controlled, chosen and consensual', and then leave the importance of consent to this declaration unexplored.[14]

And this is why when I say that this focus is public-facing, I mean to say that – regardless of what discussions surrounding BDSM are constantly about – stressing consent as the backbone of those practices serves an important political function. By drawing attention to safety tools (such as safewords) that are meant to provide an 'out' for a submissive partner overwhelmed by a particular scene, or to pithy formulations of overriding principles of kink like SSC (safe, sane, consensual), RACK (risk aware consensual kink), and 4C (caring, communication, consent, caution), the appearance of danger and violence can be stripped away from the popular stereotypes of BDSM.[15] Such discursive tactics emerged in the late 1970s and 1980s as an attempt to demystify and depathologise BDSM in the public eye, and to contest the openly phobic descriptions of it that dominated the media landscape of the time.[16] In fact, some scholars even suggest that the models of affirmative consent being developed across US campuses in the 1990s were inspired by ideas and safety practices of consensual sadomasochism that were then filtering into popular consciousness.[17]

Such an image of BDSM can feel almost utopian, and certainly is apologetic in nature. There is nothing wrong about it, *per se*, but two things need to be taken into account. The first is that there is plenty of ethnographic research that points to a disjunction between the way an image of 'being always about consent' is projected to the public, and the actual practices of consent within certain BDSM communities.[18] It would be too easy to believe that practising kinky sex makes one inherently less likely to violate consent, or imply its presence where there is none. As one of my own respondents – a young woman who preferred to take on the submissive role – attested, often presenting as a female submissive during a kinky party can be interpreted by other attendees as an invitation to 'do things to her', reproducing one of the classic ideas from the 'cultural scaffolding of rape' about women's self-presentation and their availability for sex.

More pertinently for this chapter, however, there is also the other issue regarding consent in BDSM. To return to Stacey May Fowles – earlier in her essay, she noted that 'the idea of a woman consenting to be violated via play not only is difficult terrain to negotiate politically, but also is rarely discussed beyond BDSM practitioners themselves', following it up with the observation that 'the opportunity to articulate the political ramifications of rape fantasy happens rarely, if at all'.[19] Both parts of this statement find ample support in my own field material, but Fowles does not extend her own analysis to those full ramifications because she refuses to entertain the possibility that consensual non-consent may also be *non-consensual* in more than play-acting.

Fowles does not consider the possibility that having to consent to a violation can make the entire fantasy – and the practice rooted in it – end up feeling impoverished. Ingrid Olson addresses this indirectly in her autoethnographic account of abduction play, where she notes that her submissive partner agreed to the abduction itself, but pointedly was kept in the dark about the details of it, presumably so as not to spoil her own fun.[20] A playful violation is a violation all the same, even if it is desired and wanted. This, however, incurs risks. And there are BDSM practitioners (not just women) who are perfectly conscious of this bind: the fact that at some point they may have to choose between increased consent and increased pleasure.

On Not Wanting to Ruin Your Own Fun

Daniel,[21] a heterosexual middle-aged man with a strong preference towards assuming the submissive role, was one of the first people I interviewed while in the field, in early 2017. One of the particularities of his approach to BDSM was that he refused to use safewords, or any other safety tools that could allow him to interrupt a scene too early. This was especially important since his main partner was a self-described sadist who enjoyed administering heavy flogging. Daniel himself identified as a submissive, but not a masochist (which, by his personal logic, meant he was not a person who found the sensation of being flogged itself pleasurable) and participated in those gladly. However, he specifically denied himself an 'out', as he believed that given a chance to interrupt a whipping before it was finished, he would probably take it due to the unpleasantness of momentary pain – and, in doing so, ruin the fun for both himself and his partner.

Daniel's case represents what is probably the most widespread type of consensual non-consent. Agreeing to play without safety tools such as safewords (which are supposed to safeguard consent), while not a common occurrence, has recurred several times in my fieldwork. It is a solution to a practical problem. BDSM play often involves engaging with experiences which are not just unpleasant, but can be legitimately harrowing, both physically and emotionally. To keep with the example of whipping: while the overwhelming majority of people who practise kink will usually limit erotic spanking and flogging to strikes that are light enough to be easily bearable (even if they sting), some will nonetheless look to deliver – and more importantly, take – blows that will bruise, welt, and hurt. Sometimes, the pain itself is a reward, and is experienced as a form of physical pleasure. But other times – as with Daniel – pain is just pain, and nothing pleasant at all. Crucially, that does not necessarily mean that the experience of whipping itself is not pleasurable either. Quite the opposite. Importantly, however, for Daniel the pleasure of being whipped came not from the sensation itself, but rather from the broader context of it: from the submissive joy of fulfilling his partner's desire to *flog him*, and from a kind of pride at being able to take the beating. This is why the ability to interrupt the scene – one that is necessary for it to be considered consensual under the models of affirmative or enthusiastic consent – was something he willingly rejected. Even if, in the heat of the moment, he did not want the next strike of the whip to land on his flesh, he also wanted the scene to continue; without a safeword, he could not deprive himself of that pleasure.

Pleasure in BDSM practices does not have to be symmetrical, in spite of the suggestion of complementarity implied by the term 'sadomasochism'. If the most widespread forms of sex-positivity maintain mutual climax as the aspirational ideal of 'good sex', within BDSM what each party takes out of a particular practice can be radically dissimilar. A sadistic dominant may find satisfaction in the experience of inflicting pain, which for their partner may only be relevant insofar as a corporeal mark signifies their successful commitment to performing submissiveness. This asymmetry provides a strong case against psychoanalysis-influenced readings of sadism and masochism as complementary and mirrored;[22] and, more pertinently to this chapter, the asymmetry is important when thinking about consensual non-consent without stripping those practices of their onerous, unpleasant, and terrifying aspects. This includes potential violations of moment-to-moment consent, violations that are not role-played, but experienced as real, risky, and unpleasant – but which do not have to cease being so in order for the encounter they contain to be enjoyable.

Such violations need to be seen in a wider context. Although they are often going beyond the pale of consent, they are also parts of a relationship facilitating them – a relationship that is supposed to be carefully and closely negotiated. As I have written elsewhere, consensual non-consent could not work without a significant degree of trust in one's partner. After all, it is the belief that no matter what happens, ultimately a kind of mutual satisfaction and intimacy is the aim, which makes it possible to 'give in' without worrying that serious physical or emotional trauma will ensue.[23]

This becomes especially apparent once attention is placed on practices of consensual non-consent which extend beyond the bedroom/dungeon, and instead work themselves into the very foundations of kinky erotic relationships. The most widely discussed example of this would be Total Power Exchange (TPE) and 24/7-style relationships, sometimes referred to as consensual slavery.[24] Such relationships, which are a common object of sexual fantasies, are supposed to be ones in which the submissive party agrees to give up all the power they have to their partner, becoming in essence their 'slave', to be commanded and punished at will.[25] In practice, however, most 24/7 relationships rely more on a shared fantasy of submission and enslavement rather than the practice of it – due to practicalities of daily life, if nothing else. While in the ideal fantasy form of 24/7, the submissive partner would become a domestic slave or servant fully under the control of their dominant, outside of the fantasy the 'slave' usually has to lead their own fully independent life, only submitting to their partner when conditions for mutual BDSM play emerge. As one of my respondents put it, no matter what the fantasy is 'there comes a time when you have to put the panties on and go back to work'.

However, while 'ideal' 24/7 relationships are not really feasible, and doubt in their possibility was widespread in the field, the pull of the fantasy of sexual slavery and subsuming one's will and agency to that of a dominant partner remains strong. It is also this subsumption that makes the fantasy tick. To return to Fowles's formulation, its appeal is contained within the idea of 'violation via play'. This violation can be staged – and usually is little more than role-play – but that does not stop BDSM practitioners from looking for ways to make it feel more flesh-and-blood.

The easiest way to accomplish 'violation via play' is to find circumstances in which a more limited form of such practices can be enacted. This can be a weekend getaway where the partners use the time away from work to play at sexual slavery, or it can be just a side relationship arranged so that it does not necessarily interfere with daily and professional life. To use an example: for Ela, a bisexual woman in her 30s who preferred to play the submissive role, it took the form of allowing her dominant partner to assign her punishments – of the kind she found actively unpleasant – within their relationship. Importantly, they were not limited to the kind of kinky role-playing usually imagined as part of BDSM. They also included things like offering Ela a punishment-and-reward scheme for quotidian tasks she would otherwise struggle with, like visiting the post office on schedule despite her social anxieties. The entire framework, then, served a double function: not only did it motivate her to work towards being her 'best self', but also allowed the punishment itself to fit into the fantasy of having her will violated. However, even if the boundaries of this violation were not fully under her control, they nonetheless remained buttressed by mutual trust and attraction.

When Things Go Wrong

But what happens if this trust is betrayed? It is the likeliest failure point for practices of consensual non-consent, and the consequences of its breach are illuminating. Let's consider the case of Anka, a heterosexual woman in her 20s with a submissive preference. Here, I would like to quote at length from an interview with her:

> ANKA: [With my boyfriend] we used to play in our daily life. [It was] the kind of mixing of sexual practices with me cleaning and cooking. But later on, I started getting warning signs, and wondered if the other side really treats this as a game, or me as a housemaid. So, we were playing as if I was his private slave in every sphere, so for example I would wait naked and kneeling for him to come back home from work, welcomed him with a dinner, and knelt naked while he was eating. And then, when we'd watch TV, he'd sit on a couch, and I'd kneel by him on the floor. Only in time I realised that for him, it stopped being play, and became a very convenient reality. And then, I ended the relationship.

It is important to note that, for Anka, the reason to remove herself from the relationship did not lie in the potentially non-consensual aspects of her kinky play. In fact, playing a 'private slave in every sphere' remained appealing for her throughout. What changed, however, was the way her partner framed the relationship. When it stopped being play, and became a fact of life, the scaffolding of consensual non-consent began to deteriorate. While such practices can (and often do) blur the boundary between sexual practices and daily life, and help to build relationships in which such distinctions are permeable, the end goal remains erotic and emotional gratification. For Anka, the appeal of service to her boyfriend lay in being seen sexually, and not in the act of service itself. In a way, this is similar to the case of a submissive enduring a painful flogging not for the love of the practice itself, but rather for the sake of the emotional satisfaction of fulfilling their partner.

Just as importantly, Anka opted to portray this situation not through the lens of abuse or exploitation, stressing her agency in quitting the relationship once it ceased to be fulfilling. Such self-awareness is key for practitioners of consensual non-consent who, after all, play not only with their partners, but also with risk. In fact, one of the few cases of an unambiguously abusive relationship of this type I have heard of while in the field persisted precisely because the submissive partner was too inexperienced to recognise signs of emotional and sexual manipulation from her partners who, like in Anka's case, used the framework of consensual non-consent for purely egoistical gratification.

By the same token, however, understanding oneself as self-aware and self-possessed may provide a buffer against failures of trust within practices of consensual non-consent. Here is an exchange from an interview I conducted with Andrzej, a heteroflexible man in his 40s who took on submissive roles:

ANDRZEJ: Once during bondage my hands got tied so tightly that the arm nerves got paralysed and for good two days I was unable to raise my hands. They just tied them too tightly.

J. S.: Were you angry at your partner for that?

ANDRZEJ: No, it was an accident. I don't blame her. It was unpleasant for me afterwards, very unpleasant. It's hard when you can't raise a glass and it falls out of your hand. That happens often after bondage, when arms were too tightly bound. It's a common side effect. Usually it goes away, but not instantly. Sometimes after a few hours, sometimes after a few days. In that case, it stayed with me for two days.

When taking the interview, I was shocked by Andrzej not taking what I perceived to be an obvious violation of common BDSM safety practices more seriously, and especially not begrudging his partner for what seemed to me a clear violation of a submissive's trust. And yet, while I still do believe that, and by no means seek to endorse a potentially dangerous way of practising BDSM, his reaction becomes more legible once the scene is viewed through the lens of consensual non-consent.

From this perspective, the key issue is not whether a practice ticks boxes like 'safe' or 'consensual', but if the risks of entering it are properly managed. Andrzej refused to blame his partner, because he understood the risks of the practice as inherent to the act of violation itself. This does not mean that he wanted the danger – the memory was an unpleasant one. Consensual non-consent functions through the loss of control present in such scenes, loss which is always an exposure to risk (even more so than sex in general is, as Katherine Angel argues),[26] but also to potential pleasures not available in more tightly controlled circumstances. There is no guarantee that the pleasures will offset the hurt, because they do not negate it, only arise through it. A wanted violation must remain something that at least a part of you wants to refuse.

Unwanted Wanted Things

The risk factor in consensual non-consent, even if it ultimately spoils the practice itself, provides a crucial element of uncertainty and danger. If the fantasy of violation is to work, it must remain a violation, at least to a degree. The scheme of punishment and discipline it entails needs to retain at least some element of unwantedness for it to keep its erotic appeal. A punishment one consents to eagerly lacks such an edge, even if one secretly desires to suffer it. The logic here is not too dissimilar from the way that Arielle Zibrak describes the 'guilty pleasure' of scenes of sexual 'ravishment' in romance fiction. She suggests that a significant part of their appeal is how they allow one to imagine getting 'what they want without having to admit they want it' but, crucially, 'without the guilt excised'.[27] The point then is not that, say, Daniel secretly enjoys the pain of a flogging, but rather that his pleasure of fulfilling his partner's desire hinges around being *made* to suffer that pain, regardless of whether he finds it enjoyable or not.

Similarly, consensual non-consent can provide a way to explore outside of one's sexual comfort zones. The desire for overcoming personal barriers in the erotic sphere, and for experimenting with new pleasures was a recurring theme in the interviews collected during my research, as were statements of wanting to experiment with something (be it breath play, cutting, or electroshocks), but lacking the courage to do so – of *their own volition*.

Split will – the possibility to want a thing, and yet not want it at the same time – is a problem for discussions of consent, and the supposed clarity of its yes-or-no binary. Such clarity, in practice, is less about reflecting on the complexities of sexual desire, and more about legally defining what actions constitute offenses, and which do not.[28] As Sarah Schulman and Katherine Angel both state, it is difficult to expect people (their arguments focus on women, but I think it is important to extend it) to be perfectly cognisant of their own sexual needs and desires.[29] 'Why should we know what we want?' asks Angel, who suggests that 'the fixation on yes and no doesn't help us navigate these waters; it's precisely the uncertain, unclear space between yes and no that we need to learn to navigate'.[30]

Consensual non-consent makes us approach this question from a different angle. Assuming we know what we want, how do we make ourselves act on that desire? One of the most salient critiques of consent is that it often presupposes a self-possessed subject that exists outside of coercion, both by individuals and the social structures of domination. Sex happens within the field of power, and is not free from the uneven power hierarchies that undergird the Western culture, and individuals who consent to sex may not be acting out of their free and unrestrained will. If consent, to be valid, requires freedom from coercion, there may well not be such a thing as consensual sex.[31] However, by focusing so much on whether consent can ever fulfil its promise of securing ethical sex, attention can easily slip from the other way that consent falls short as a concept: the case of people who want to consent, but remain unable to act on such needs. To acknowledge them is, in itself, a thorny notion. It lies dangerously close to a number of myths surrounding sexual abuse and rape, which posit that the victim was 'secretly asking for it all along', and which present rape as just a particularly forward form of flirting gone awry. This makes it difficult to frame such people through a feminist critique. Both the radical feminist quest to demystify rape myths as a tool for the subjugation of women and liberal feminist attempts to establish clear legal norms for ethical sex fail to address the question of what happens when there seems to be a desire to consent that is not backed by the will to do so. This failure is not hard to understand: even accepting the notion that such people may exist may feel like giving undue credence to deeply harmful ideas of what sex should and could be.

Queer theory, likewise, does not provide much help. While the ambivalence of desire is an important theme in a lot of queer theorising on sexuality,[32] it has thus far lacked a more robust account of desires that go unfulfilled, and not for the lack of opportunity or ability, but for the lack of trying and courage. Even works that focus on queer negativity and reticence tend to foreground desire that is *stymied*, but nonetheless *expressed*.[33] To use Sara Ahmed's metaphor, desires that are not used often end up seeming like they are not usable at all.[34] And yet, we should all be aware of how desire can be just as appealing as it is terrifying, and quite often it is the terror that tilts the scales towards inaction.

Interestingly, however, trans studies offer a helpful point of reference here, as they can give an account of sexualities in tension between the (potentially) pleasurable submission to a coercive force of gender and the feminist demand that this coercion should be resisted. Trans sexual practices, like forced feminisation, are distant from an utopian hope for gender (and sex) that is free of coercion. Instead, they make coercion itself into a vehicle of pleasure, even though it remains a kind of violence nonetheless. In this sense, it is perhaps within the accounts of trans sexuality, like the writings of Andrea Long Chu or Hil Malatino,[35] that we can find a hint on how to approach consensual non-consent as a form of erotic play with the awful complexity of identification and desire that does not seek to resolve it, instead offering a way of thriving within it. This is, however, always easier said than done.

Uses of Non-consent

The examples of consensual non-consent I have presented show a range of practices which do not easily fit into the most common models of affirmative and enthusiastic consent. They occupy an ambivalent neither-nor position between consent and non-consent. As such, it is easy to either dismiss them as a cover for sexual abuse (as anti-SM feminists have long maintained) or, as most pro-BDSM scholars hold, frame them primarily through the 'consensual part'. Although the latter approach is clearly closer to mine, I believe that both ultimately come short.

In practices of consensual non-consent, *consent is violated purposefully and desirably.* This is risky, but the practitioners who engage in it are cognisant of those risks and attempt to manage them. Furthermore, such violations are enabled by a broader framework of trust, desire, and personal emotional ability and inability; as Angel reminds us, consent is not the be all and end all,[36] and within consensual non-consent, its partial absence can be fulfilled by other factors.

This is a fraught proposal on many grounds, and cannot ever serve the legal function that politics of consent usually offer. It is also dangerous because of its similarity to rhetorics supportive of rape culture. But, ultimately, consensual non-consent is neither a model to emulate, nor a dangerous practice to reject. If anything, it should be seen similarly to how Milena Popova traces out the concept of 'dubious consent' in fanfiction. For her, 'dubcon' is a fantasy that exists not just to titillate, but also to open up a way of thinking through the complexities of consent and desire in situations where neither is ever fully transparent, and where liberation from hierarchies of power and oppression that undergird both of them is not possible.[37] Crucially, according to Popova, it is in the acknowledgment of such complexity and the willingness to work with it that 'dubcon' fanfiction offers grounds for a new praxis of consent, attentive not only to what it secures, but also to where it becomes a stumbling block.[38]

Seen in a similar light, practices of consensual non-consent are an attempt at attending to the many ambivalences of will and desire. They are purposefully risky, always in danger of sliding towards hurt and abuse – but so is sex. If one of the standard critiques of consent is that it is irrevocably tied to the idea of a self-governing, self-possessed subject, and we are presently living through a time defined by an increasing recognition not of our individuality, but interdependence, it behoves us to accommodate erotics that do not yield to the liberal myth of singularity. Our desires exceed us – as so many feminist writers cited here attest to – and also exceed our ability to ever fully master them. What is left remains open to question. Writers like Amia Srinivasan argue that we are nonetheless obliged to seek to try to master our desires anyway,[39] while others, like Andrea Long Chu, would rather have us stay with the trouble of being unable to 'consent to oneself'.[40] No matter, however, which answer we ultimately choose, in the end we are left with the lesson of consensual non-consent: sometimes, it is possible to want having things done to you which you would never want to suffer; and this contradiction is laden with erotic potential.

Notes

1 See Linda Martín Alcoff, *Rape and Resistance* (Cambridge, MA: Polity, 2018); Nancy Tuana, 'Sexual Harassment: Offers and Coercion', *Social Philosophy*, 19 (1988), 30–42.

2 See Katherine Angel, *Tomorrow Sex Will Be Good Again: Women and Desire in the Age of Consent* (London: Verso, 2021); Sarah Schulman, *Conflict is Not Abuse: Overstating Harm, Community Responsibility, and the Duty of Repair* (Vancouver: Arsenal Pulp Press, 2016), pp. 38–73.

3 See Daniel Loick, '"... as if it were a thing." A feminist critique of consent', *Constellations*, 23 (2020), 412–22.

4 Nicola Gavey, *Just Sex? The Cultural Scaffolding of Rape* (New York: Routledge, 2019).

5 See Angelika Tsaros, 'Consensual Non-Consent: Comparing EL James's *Fifty Shades of Grey* and Pauline Réage's *Story of O*', *Sexualities*, 16 (2013), 864–79.

6 See Ingrid Olson, 'Asking for it: Erotic Asphyxiation and the Limitations of Sexual Consent', *Jindal Global Law Review*, 4 (2012), 171–200; Ingrid Olson, 'Abduction in the Public Sphere: Sadomasochism, Surveillance, and Counterpublics', *Sexuality and Culture*, 21 (2017), 795–812.

7 Jill Weinberg, *Consensual Violence: Sex, Sports and the Politics of Injury* (Oakland: University of California Press, 2016), pp. 13–16.

8 Milena Popova, *Consent* (Cambridge, MA: MIT Press, 2019), p. 17.

9 Olson, 'Asking for it', pp. 172–73.

10 Staci Newmahr, *Playing on the Edge: Sadomasochism, Risk and Intimacy* (Bloomington: Indiana University Press, 2011), pp. 147–54.

11 Stacey May Fowles, 'The Fantasy of Acceptable "Non-Consent": Why the Female Sexual Submissive Scares Us (and Why She Shouldn't)', in *Yes Means Yes! Visions*

of Female Sexual Power and a World Without Rape, ed. by Jaclyn Friedman and Jessica Valenti (Berkeley, CA: Seal Press, 2008), pp. 117–26 (p. 117).

12 A thorough analysis and critique of such approaches can be found in Ummi Khan, *Vicarious Kinks: S/M in the Socio-Legal Imaginary* (Toronto: Toronto University Press, 2014), pp. 54–117.

13 See Andrea Beckmann, *The Social Construction of Sexuality and Perversion: Deconstructing Sadomasochism* (New York: Palgrave MacMillan, 2009); Lewis Call, *BDSM in American Science Fiction and Fantasy* (New York: Palgrave MacMillan, 2013).

14 Margot Weiss, 'Rumsfeld!: Consensual BDSM and "Sadomasochistic" Torture at Abu Ghraib', in *Out in Public: Reinventing Lesbian/Gay Anthropology in a Globalizing World*, ed. by Ellen Lewin and William Leap (Chichester: Wiley-Blackwell, 2009), pp. 180–201 (p. 182).

15 D. J. Williams, et al., 'From "SSC" and "RACK" to the "4Cs": Introducing a New Framework for Negotiating BDSM Participation', *Electronic Journal of Human Sexuality*, 17 (2014) <http://www.ejhs.org/volume17/BDSM.html> [accessed 10 May 2023].

16 Stephen K. Stein, *Sadomasochism and the BDSM Community in the United States: Kinky People Unite* (New York: Routledge, 2021), p. 117.

17 John K. Noyes, *The Mastery of Submission: Inventions of Masochism* (Ithaca, NY: Cornell University Press, 1997), pp. iii–iv.

18 Alexandra Fanghanel, 'Asking for It: BDSM Sexual Practice and the Trouble of Consent', *Sexualities*, 23 (2020), 269–86.

19 Fowles, p. 118.

20 Olson, 'Abduction in the Public Sphere', pp. 806–07.

21 All my interview partners were Polish nationals based in major Polish urban centres. The interviews were conducted in private, but not play, spaces. All names have been changed to preserve anonymity.

22 Allison M. Moore, *Sexual Myths of Modernity: Sadism, Masochism, and Historical Teleology* (London: Lexington Books, 2016), pp. 137–66.

23 Jay Szpilka, 'Waterboard Me Real Good: Torture, Consent, and Trust in BDSM', in *The Routledge Companion to Gender, Sexuality, and Culture*, ed. by Emma Rees (London: Routledge, 2022), pp. 282–92 (pp. 288–89).

24 See Angel M. Butts, '"Signed, Sealed, Delivered … I'm Yours": Calibrating Body Ownership through the Consensual Mastery/Slavery Dynamic', *Sexuality and Culture*, 11 (2007), 62–76.

25 Tsaros, p. 871.

26 Angel, pp. 23–27.

27 Arielle Zibrak, *Guilty Pleasures* (New York: New York University Press, 2021), p. 73.

28 Weinberg, pp. 42–62.

29 Schulman, p. 51.

30 Angel, p. 110.

31 Mairead Sullivan, *Lesbian Death* (Minneapolis, MA: University of Minnesota Press, 2022), pp. 108–12.

32 See, for example, Jack Halberstam, *Wild Things* (Durham, NC: Duke University Press, 2020).

33 See, for example, Ann Cvetkovich, *An Archive of Feelings: Trauma, Sexuality, and Lesbian Public Cultures* (Durham, NC: Duke University Press, 2003).

34 Sara Ahmed, *What's the Use? On the Use of Use* (Durham, NC: Duke University Press, 2019).

35 See Andrea Long Chu, *Females* (London: Verso, 2019); Hil Malatino, *Side Affects: On Being Trans and Feeling Bad* (Minneapolis: University of Minnesota Press, 2022), pp. 69–73.

36 Angel, pp. 13–14.

37 Milena Popova, *Dubcon: Fanfiction, Power, and Sexual Consent* (Cambridge, MA: MIT Press, 2021), pp. 15–30.
38 Ibid., pp. 141–64.
39 See Amia Srinivasan, *The Right to Sex: Feminism in the Twenty-First Century* (London: Bloomsbury, 2021), pp. 93–122.
40 Chu, p. 38.

Bibliography

Ahmed, Sara, *What's the Use? On the Use of Use* (Durham, NC: Duke University Press, 2019)

Alcoff, Linda Martín, *Rape and Resistance* (Cambridge, MA: Polity, 2018)

Angel, Katherine, *Tomorrow Sex Will Be Good Again: Women and Desire in the Age of Consent* (London: Verso, 2021)

Beckmann, Andrea, *The Social Construction of Sexuality and Perversion: Deconstructing Sadomasochism* (New York: Palgrave MacMillan, 2009)

Butts, Angel M., '"Signed, Sealed, Delivered … I'm Yours": Calibrating Body Ownership through the Consensual Mastery/Slavery Dynamic', *Sexuality and Culture*, 11 (2007), 62–76

Call, Lewis, *BDSM in American Science Fiction and Fantasy* (New York: Palgrave MacMillan, 2013)

Chu, Andrea Long, *Females* (London: Verso, 2019)

Cvetkovich, Ann, *An Archive of Feelings: Trauma, Sexuality, and Lesbian Public Cultures* (Durham, NC: Duke University Press, 2003)

Fanghanel, Alexandra, 'Asking for It: BDSM Sexual Practice and the Trouble of Consent', *Sexualities*, 23 (2020), 269–86

Fowles, Stacey May, 'The Fantasy of Acceptable "Non-Consent": Why the Female Sexual Submissive Scares Us (and Why She Shouldn't)', in *Yes Means Yes! Visions of Female Sexual Power and a World Without Rape*, ed. by Jaclyn Friedman and Jessica Valenti (Berkeley, CA: Seal Press, 2008), pp. 117–26

Gavey, Nicola, *Just Sex? The Cultural Scaffolding of Rape* (New York: Routledge, 2019)

Halberstam, Jack, *Wild Things* (Durham, NC: Duke University Press, 2020)

Khan, Ummi, *Vicarious Kinks: S/M in the Socio-Legal Imaginary* (Toronto: Toronto University Press, 2014)

Loick, Daniel, '"… as if it were a thing." Feminist Critique of Consent', *Constellations*, 23 (2020), 412–22

Malatino, Hil, *Side Affects: On Being Trans and Feeling Bad* (Minneapolis: University of Minnesota Press, 2022)

Moore, Allison M., *Sexual Myths of Modernity: Sadism, Masochism, and Historical Teleology* (London: Lexington Books, 2016)

Newmahr, Staci, *Playing on the Edge: Sadomasochism, Risk and Intimacy* (Bloomington: Indiana University Press, 2011)

Noyes, John K., *The Mastery of Submission: Inventions of Masochism* (Ithaca, NY: Cornell University Press, 1997)

Olson, Ingrid, 'Abduction in the Public Sphere: Sadomasochism, Surveillance, and Counterpublics', *Sexuality and Culture*, 21 (2017), 795–812

Olson, Ingrid, 'Asking for it: Erotic Asphyxiation and the Limitations of Sexual Consent', *Jindal Global Law Rewiew*, 4 (2012), 171–200

Popova, Milena, *Consent* (Cambridge, MA: MIT Press, 2019)

Popova, Milena, *Dubcon: Fanfiction, Power, and Sexual Consent* (Cambridge, MA: MIT Press, 2021)

Schulman, Sarah, *Conflict is Not Abuse: Overstating Harm, Community Responsibility, and the Duty of Repair* (Vancouver: Arsenal Pulp Press, 2016)

Srinivasan, Amia, *The Right to Sex: Feminism in the Twenty-First Century* (London: Bloomsbury, 2021)

Stein, Stephen K., *Sadomasochism and the BDSM Community in the United States: Kinky People Unite* (New York: Routledge, 2021)

Sullivan, Mairead, *Lesbian Death* (Minneapolis, MA: University of Minnesota Press, 2022)

Szpilka, Jay, 'Waterboard Me Real Good: Torture, Consent, and Trust in BDSM', in *The Routledge Companion to Gender, Sexuality, and Culture*, ed. by Emma Rees (London: Routledge, 2022), pp. 282–92

Weinberg, Jill, *Consensual Violence: Sex, Sports and the Politics of Injury* (Oakland: University of California Press, 2016)

Weiss, Margot, 'Rumsfeld!: Consensual BDSM and "Sadomasochistic" Torture at Abu Ghraib', in *Out in Public: Reinventing Lesbian/ Gay Anthropology in a Globalizing World*, ed. by Ellen Lewin and William Leap (Chichester: Wiley-Blackwell, 2009), pp. 180–201

Williams, D. J., Jeremy N. Thomas, Emily E. Prior, and M. Candace Christensen, 'From "SSC" and "RACK" to the "4Cs": Introducing a New Framework for Negotiating BDSM Participation', *Electronic Journal of Human Sexuality*, 17 (2014) <http://www.ejhs.org/volume17/BDSM.html> [accessed 10 May 2023]

Tsaros, Angelika, 'Consensual Non-consent: Comparing EL James's *Fifty Shades of Grey* and Pauline Réage's *Story of O*', *Sexualities*, 16 (2013), 864–79

Tuana, Nancy, 'Sexual Harassment: Offers and Coercion', *Social Philosophy*, 19 (1988), 30–42

Zibrak, Arielle, *Guilty Pleasures* (New York: New York University Press, 2021)

Part II

Consent on Stage and Screen

6 'You Have No Right to Do What You Like with Me'[1]

Rape, Sexual Abuse, and Consent in African American Enslavement and its Afterlives

Rebecca White

Content Notice: This chapter contains reference to enslavement, rape, sexual abuse, abortion, and racism.

In 1962, Malcolm X declared that 'the most disrespected person in America is the black woman. The most unprotected person in America is the black woman.'[2] His comments point to the long history of rape and sexual trauma experienced by black women, rooted in historical enslavement and reinforced by its ongoing legacies. As a 'flesh and blood commodity', enslaved women were denied bodily ownership and, therefore, the right to (refuse) consent, shackled to the dual role of 'breeding wench' and sexual plaything.[3] From the Middle Passage onwards, enslaved women possessed 'no rights that white men [were] bound to respect'; consequently, rape was not recognised in relation to the enslaved.[4] While Emancipation (1863) nominally unfettered person from property, Reconstruction Era (1865–1877) prejudices subsequently wielded metaphorical – rather than metal – chains, shaping discourses which enforced new forms of subjugation; (white) male-imposed (sexual) injustice targeted at black women became reconfigured as female-driven immorality, consolidating the myth of the ('always consenting') 'black Jezebel' that was born out of the enslaved past and remains entrenched in twenty-first-century America.[5] As Estelle Freedman concludes, 'the centrality of race to the political history of rape' – and, by extension, of consent – in the United States is clear.[6]

This history, however, has been persistently silenced – a tradition stemming from the nineteenth-century abolitionists themselves, with Frederick Douglass's assertion that the plight of enslaved women 'may be safely left to conjecture'.[7] Certainly, in the published testimonies of formerly enslaved women – such as Harriet Jacobs's *Incidents in the Life of a Slave Girl* (1861) – conjecture is harnessed as a reclamation of control, the suggestion of abuse implicitly exposing and excoriating white male violence and thereby (re)establishing female bodily ownership and the right to consent. However, while such narratives voice suffering out of silence, screen portrayals of enslavement blur elision and evasion, perpetuating antebellum denials of black abuse and omitting or mitigating the

DOI: 10.4324/9781003365082-8

reality of sexual coercion in enslavement. Yet films which explore sexual abuse more overtly risk countering Deirdre Cooper-Owens's recommendation to 'not recreate the trauma and oppressive gaze that historical actors experienced', where voyeurism becomes another form of violation.[8] This troubling tension is especially pronounced in slavery's (ever-evolving) online afterlives, as YouTube uploads – such as *Harriet Tubman: The Sexiest Abolitionist* (2010) and *The Harriet Tubman Sex Tape* (2013) – sustain narratives freighted with historical discrimination, ultimately reasserting (white) male ownership of black female bodies in bondage and reawakening the central plight of the enslaved woman, denied the ability to control or consent: 'I didn't want him, but I couldn't do nothin''.[9]

Historical Contexts: Enslavement and Sexual Violence

As Garrison Frazier maintained in 1865, 'slavery is receiving by [...] irresistible power the work of another', and 'not by [...] consent'.[10] As Jacobs reflected, however, 'Slavery is terrible for men; but it is far more terrible for women'.[11] On the Middle Passage, it was 'common for the dirty filthy sailors to take the African women and lie upon their bodies', their violation a spectacle 'in the presence of all the assembly'.[12] Sexual slavery at sea was perpetuated on land, embedded in the very culture of Colonial America; as Josiah Quincy noted in 1773, 'the enjoyment of a Negro or Mulatto woman is spoken of as quite a common thing'.[13] Subsequently, and especially after the prohibition of the slave trade into the US in 1808, 'slave stock' was sustained by internal 'breeding'; female sexual violation became not only a part of enslavement but a means of continuing its very existence, supported by early seventeenth-century Virginian law which dictated that offspring follow the condition of the mother. Consequently, women 'suffered a peculiar form of violence as slaveholders and doctors exploited female anatomy for their own purposes'.[14] This 'peculiarity' commenced upon the auction block, a medical marketplace which saw woman 'stripped to a nude condition and [...] careful examination [...] made of all parts of her body' to ascertain fertility.[15] Thereafter, as Mary Church Terrell recollected, 'throughout their entire period of bondage [...] colored women were debauched by their masters'.[16]

Such abuse assumed multiple guises and intersected complex issues surrounding consent. As Douglass observed, his 'master' was 'only able to buy one slave' and 'he bought her [...] for a breeder'.[17] Later, an enslaved man was purchased 'to fasten up with her every night', resonating with the testimony of Sarah Ford, an enslaved woman: 'dey jus puts a man and breedin woman together like mules. Iffen the woman don't like the man it don't make no diff'rence'.[18] In these 'unions', enslaved women were compelled to submit to enslaved men, who had themselves been compelled to rape them; the institution of slavery was sustained by the paradox of 'consent' that is commanded, as 'women [and men] were literally forced to offer themselves willingly'.[19]

Such coerced 'consent' between the enslaved sustained 'breeding' practices in the antebellum South, driven also by direct white male violence. As Angelina Grimké-Weld noted in her record of enslaved testimony, a 'master [...] took pains to breed from his best stock – the *whiter the progeny, the higher they would sell*' (my italics); fuelled by eugenics as much as eroticism, white male enslavers profiteered from black women as their own sexual property: they 'both took her – the father showing the son what it was all about – and she couldn't do nothing 'bout it'.[20] Popular Southern songs testify to the ubiquity of such sexual assault ('Massa Had a Yaller Gal', c. 1860), the bodies of 'mulatto', 'quadroon', and 'octoroon' individuals literally testifying to generations of white male sexual assault.[21]

'Breeding' for profit blurred into 'breeding' for the white man's pleasure, sexualising the black female body within the everyday culture of enslavement and, in deliberately lascivious 'slave bills', frequently encompassing a pornography of pain and punishment. Intersecting sexuality and economics, black women became further commodified through the (re)production of mass images of their bodies in bondage, the consumption of such images both perpetuating abuse and anticipating the screen's troubling voyeurism. As James Pennington reflected, 'the finest specimens of coloured females are reared [...] for the express purpose of supplying the market [to] a class of [...] gentlemen'; such women, bartered within the 'Fancy Girl Trade', were, 'on account of their attractions, exposed to the most shameful degradation' – an enslaved woman recalled being 'up on dat stand wid all dem men standin' dere lookin' at em wid what dey had on dey minds shinin' in they eyes'.[22] Those who sought to escape – to express and embody their right to (non) consent – remained framed by the (white) male gaze, their images incarcerated within 'slave bills' which perpetuated the exposure of the female body as spectacle; as announced in one such Bill, an enslaved woman 'Eloped from my residence', bearing 'a very singular mark' covering 'her breasts, body, and limbs'.[23] Such bills both record and reinforce abuse, imagining its performance in reading and inviting its actualisation in reality: 'Celia is a [...] fine figure' – '*on examining her back, you will find* marks caused by the whip'. Recaptured women were then subjected to punishment imbued with a predatory eroticism, deliberately stripped naked; as Sarah Grimké observed, whipped women were doubly violated, forced to endure simultaneously the physical pain of the lash and mentally 'the shocking exposure of her person to the eyes of brutal and licentious men'.[24]

Certainly, there were shifts during Reconstruction which enabled formerly enslaved women, such as Lucy Stone, to testify to their abuse – yet this was largely born out of the Unionist government's vested interest in discrediting the South. The postbellum period circulated 'a flood of racist rhetoric' in order to counter African-American claims to citizenship, to recast slavery in new forms. 'White-on-black rape' became endemic in the Reconstruction South as it served a dual purpose – it was supported by, and sustained, antebellum prejudices against 'hypersexual' ('immoral') black women, and it metaphorically subjugated black men unable to protect their womenfolk; rape therefore became an emblem of racial power, the mastered South searching to become 'master' once more.[25]

Enslavement thus facilitated the myth of the 'black Jezebel', 'always consenting' to – and therefore always perpetuating – her sexual role. As the white, male-authored *Directory of Medical Science* (1819) pronounced, black women possessed 'voluptuousness' and a 'degree of lascivity' beyond white women.[26] Volitive rather than violated, such discourses mitigated the actuality of abuse, and intersected with black women's wider inability to consent – simultaneously forced into motherhood and medical experimentation, for example. Although a line exists between sexual and medical consent, it remains significant, as Harriet Washington notes, that disproportionately high numbers of experimental gynaecological procedures have historically been performed on black women in the US, 'mastered' into submission in the antebellum era and misled into compliance post-Emancipation. From 1822 to 1831, François Prévost enacted experimental caesareans on Louisiana's enslaved women, his subjects drawn from a marketplace of expendable bodies that occluded the very notion of informed medical consent: 'Wanted: Fifty Negroes. Any person having sick negroes [...] and willing to dispose of them'.[27] Although James Marion Sims is celebrated as a medical benefactor of (white) women, his intimate gynaecological experiments on the enslaved – their names, tellingly, lost from a (white) historical record which has suppressed his abuse – were pursued 'whether the patient is willing or not', aligning research with rape. Just as punishment and pornography blurred in relation to enslaved women, medical abuse subjected them to a violating voyeurism: 'I saw everything as no man had seen before'.[28]

As Washington asserts, 'the culture of American medicine has mirrored the larger culture that encompassed enslavement', their legacies enduring into the twentieth century and beyond (not least in the context of the inequalities exposed by COVID-19, for instance).[29] Black female sterilisations without consent during the 1960s and 1970s recall forced terminations of pregnancy a century earlier; just as Grimké-Weld recorded that an enslaved woman was carried 'to the house, where an abortion occurred', in the mid-twentieth century, 'rendering black women infertile without their knowledge during other surgery was so common that the procedure was called a "Mississippi Appendectomy"'.[30] Reproductive coercion for black women pivoted from antebellum procreation to postbellum sterility: the 'consistent factor was white control', in place of black consent.[31]

The health inequalities faced by African Americans are part of a narrative that literally writes out black agency and consent; as Washington notes, the coercion of signatures and the falsification of medical records commonly affect black patients.[32] Such rewriting reaches back into the antebellum past, in which enslavers sought to silence the suffering of the enslaved. Certainly, at times, white abolitionist texts seek to 're-master' the 'master narrative', destabilising the language of enslavement: 'Look at the phraseology. Nothing is said of maimings, dismemberments'.[33] Yet there exists a deliberate and 'ongoing amnesia' about the nation's heritage.[34] While viewers of *Southern Slave Breeding Farms* (2021) note 'this is the first time hearing of specific breeding farms', for example, the production simultaneously adheres to a sanitising narrative: as a viewer exorted, 'The slave owners didn't "fornicate" with the slaves, they raped them. Don't belittle [through] diplomatic language'.[35]

Such diplomatic language has 'confused notions of consent'. As Michaela Kleppinger remarks, there have been 'considerable efforts in the post-slavery years to label enslaved women who had sexual relationships with their owners as "mistresses"'.[36] However, where the term 'mistress' 'implies mutual consent, [...] any form of sexual contact within [...] slavery was, if not assault, at least extremely exploitative'; although sexual agency is debated as 'a viable form of resistance', it is 'important that we not misconstrue it for consent' – and even 'consensual' relationships have to be 'viewed through the lens of enslavement'.[37]

Nineteenth-Century Female Slave Narratives

Nineteenth-century female 'slave narratives' provide a corrective to mediated and mitigated (white) accounts of enslavement, addressing also the occlusion of female figures from the historical record ('Mr Weedon owned [...] a woman slave, *whose name I have forgotten*').[38] In their narratives, voice becomes volition, wrought with 'a pen of burning steel'.[39] Although Saidiya Hartman contends that 'every attempt to emplot the slave' ultimately results in 'her obliteration', their testimonies become 'rebellion against [woman's] lot', echoing the songs of the enslaved: 'white man, let me go'.[40] Although perhaps the most celebrated 'slave narrator', Harriet Jacobs's stylisation as '*a* slave girl' (my emphasis) intimates the universality of enslaved female experience, echoing the accounts of fellow bondswomen Louisa Picquet, Elizabeth Keckley, and Sojourner Truth. Their motivating principle – 'I want to add my testimony' – counters Douglass's cautioning ('a still tongue makes a wise head') and addresses the fracturing of the abused female voice apparent in Keckley's testimony: 'he persecuted me [...], and *I* – *I* – became a mother' (my italics); a 'sisterhood' of women's voices instead resonates in resistance.[41] Although Karen Sánchez-Eppler argues that 'slave narratives' 'conform to [white] language', they deconstruct coded discourses of sexual enslavement, exposing the words that weld together metaphorical chains: 'we find [...] Elizabeth [Keckley] a *"seamstress" or concubine*' (my italics).[42] 'White' language is instead wielded against white men in counter-resistance, through cynical euphemism – 'We have the *very "gentlemanly" conduct* of Mr Cook, a married man, toward Louisa [Picquet]. What, we ask, must be the moral atmosphere in which such masters can live and breathe?' – and white male power is challenged: as Picquet reveals, 'I did not mean to go to his room, but only [said] so he would stop whippin' me'.[43]

Picquet's re-establishment of agency – 'did it so he would stop whippin' me' – points to the complex dynamics of 'consent' within enslavement. Punishment, for example, becomes a marker of self-assertion: '*I'd made up my mind* to take the whippin" (my emphasis).[44] Moreover, although Yogita Goyal argues that the 'slave narrative too often drew a veil over the scene of sexual violation, resorting to euphemism', such euphemism can be read as empowerment; rather than repeating the 'scene of sexual abuse', intimation becomes a form of indictment: in Jacobs's account, her 'master's' 'offspring are unblushingly reared for the market. If they are girls, I have indicated plainly enough what will be their inevitable destiny'.[45] In denying white male abusers explicit voices, female narratives exert 'mastery' over 'masters', (re)asserting their right to consent through the silencing of their control: 'he order me, in a […] commanding way (*I don't want to* tell you what he said)' (my italics).[46]

While 'consent' could be compelled through deception – he inquired 'if she would like to […] live with him. She eagerly answered "yes", […] nothing doubting that he was sent in answer to her prayer' – enslavers could themselves be deceived.[47] As Jacobs declares, 'I will not try to screen myself behind the plea of compulsion from a master […]. *I knew what I did, and I did it with deliberate calculation*' (my italics), agreeing to a sexual liaison with 'a white unmarried gentleman' as a means of enforcing her non-consent to the advances of her 'master', Flint.[48] Acknowledging herself as person rather than property, it 'seems less degrading to give oneself, than to submit to compulsion. There is something akin to freedom'.[49]

However, Jacobs's 'deliberate calculation' in taking a white lover constructs her as both coerced and 'consenting', a tension embodied by female 'slave narratives' themselves. Such texts navigate a complex confrontation between expressing feeling and adhering to expected form, framing the narratives of the enslaved within the sensibilities of white abolitionism and the generic conventions of sentimental fiction. As Toni Morrison reflects, 'the slave's own narrative, while freeing the narrator in many ways, did not destroy the master narrative'; tellingly, the enslaved Sethe makes Schoolteacher's ink in Morrison's neo-slave narrative *Beloved*, forced into inscribing the white male story.[50] 'Slave narratives' embody and exemplify the enslaved's liberation, establishing and asserting their right to not consent to bondage; voice becomes volition, speech becomes self. Yet they also pose questions about authorial agency and consent, which intersect with wider issues of subjugation. Certainly, Keckley equates authorship with the right to consent: 'I have often been asked to write my life' – 'I have acceded to the importunities of my friends'.[51] However, white revisionary frames remain, construing black voices through all-encompassing editorial presences. Although Truth's longest direct speech castigates enslavers, her white editor, Olive Gilbert, mitigatingly directs control of the 'proper' narrative: 'to return from our *digression*' (my italics).[52] Picquet's life is similarly deconstructed through summary chapter titles, while Lydia Maria Child likewise edits (silences) Jacobs's voice: 'such changes as I have made have been mainly for purposes of condensation'.[53]

While Jacobs invokes yet also inverts the sentimental genre – 'I feel that the slave woman ought not to be judged by the same standard as others' – Truth is shaped as a sentimental figure, implicitly placing her narrative as fiction rather than fact: 'A long series of trials in the life of *our heroine*, which we must pass over' from 'delicacy' (my italics).[54] The undermining of Truth's account as *truth* is compounded by the white and often male-authored 'Certificates of Character' which conclude the narrative; veracity is only granted through white validation. Moreover, such 'validation' could blur uneasily with violation; as Xiomara Santamarina argues, the dynamic between Picquet's narrative and its white, male editorial frame enacts an 'often salacious rendering of details', Hiram Mattison's focus on her 'fair complexion and rosy cheeks' 'totally sexualising Picquet and all slave women'.[55]

Slavery on Screen

This sexualisation becomes especially problematic on screen. In the nineteenth century, white abolitionist narratives described female nakedness as a form of shocking emotive appeal, ironically subjecting the black female body to the very gaze that such texts sought to dismantle. Similarly, for survivors such as Keckley and Jacobs, the 'excruciating agony' of enslavement intermingles remembrance with re-enactment: 'I am still pained by the retrospect'.[56] As Rudyard Alcocer asserts, however, 'Slavery films take us back to the scene of the crime [...] in a way that is closer to a real-life experience', 'literalising' that 'feeling recollection of the effect of the whip'.[57] In screening slavery, therefore, 'the sight of black bodies in pain' arguably 'serves rather than defies existing racial regimes'.[58]

Certainly, films can emancipate rather than exploit, interrogating the very processes of viewing which have violated the black (female) body. Mainstream, large-budget film and television portrayals of enslavement, such as *The Birth of a Nation* (2016), *Roots* (2016), and *The Underground Railroad* (2021), force the audience to gaze, but also to scrutinise that gaze. The trailer for *Birth of a Nation*, for instance, embodies this duality.[59] Its biblical voiceover – 'slaves, *submit yourselves* to your masters' – is overlaid with images not of agency, but of white male violence against a black woman: chained – rather than consenting – to her 'submission', the tension between ideology and image undercuts white amelioratory rhetoric. The film subsequently raises an implicitly sexualised voyeurism, including close-ups of women's breasts; the intimacy of the camera not only emulates predatory male presence, but implicates the viewer in consuming non-consenting female flesh. Such dynamics are thrown into relief, however, by scenes which markedly refuse voyeurism, aligning instead with black perspectives; the camera pans away from Cherry and Nat's consensual union – upholding them as private persons rather than public property – while the tears of a female 'houseslave' leaving a party of white men expose their violence rather than re-enact her violation.

Roots is similarly invested in privileging black perspectives, granting agency within non-agency; although Kunta declares white men 'rape slave women and pay no price', the film visualises violence in order to hold it to account. The sexual abuse of the Middle Passage is portrayed starkly, yet visual intricacies pronounce, rather than perpetuate, iniquity. White dominance is established through low-angled shots which accentuate the captain's stature as he exclaims 'Bring me the girl I like'; intersecting sex and violence, his voice is overlaid with a perspective shot over a gun. Jinna is engulfed by white men, who crowd the foreground of the frame, visually dispossessing her of agency. Denied perspective shots, her inability to (non)consent is exposed in order to be excoriated; the camera settles on the faces of other black women – tellingly filmed through imprisoning bars – emphasising (like Jacobs) the universality of enslaved female experience.

This universality of experience endures beyond the Middle Passage. Women (and men) in a Maryland 'slave market' are imprisoned as 'natural breeders' (as described by the auctioneer) behind black metal bars; Honor's death in childbirth subsequently literalises the violence of female sexual abuse. Kizzy's subjection to male authority culminates in 'Master' Tom's attack (his simultaneous recitation of the nursery rhyme – 'this is the man, all tattered and torn, who kissed the maiden all forlorn' – marking the fact that sexual abuse is written into white male narratives from infancy to adulthood). The explicit visualisation of Tom's rape of Kizzy speaks to the problem of re-enactment as reinforcing abuse. Yet the sequence visually destabilises white male control, unsettling voyeurism and, in its dialogue with Jinna's earlier rape, it both exposes the universality of abuse and addresses it – like the 'slave narratives' – through the assertion of black female perspectives. Rapid and disorientating 'breathing camera' disrupts the viewer's gaze, channelling not an objectification of the female body but an intimation of female trauma. In contrast to Jinna, Kizzy is foregrounded and granted perspective shots, both upholding her agency and focalising her inability to (non)consent. In its own visual reworking of rape, the production *itself* embodies a corrective narrative, forcing viewers to confront enslavement not only in terms of the violations of the past but the voyeurism of the present.

The Underground Railroad likewise both embodies and exposes the complex dynamics of screening slavery. In a sequence depicting white abolitionist 'performances' of enslavement (the 'actor-overseer' rehearsing brandishing the whip), the production meta-filmically layers its scrutiny of the visual as violative. Following her escape from enslavement, Cora is caged in an abolitionist exhibition cabinet picking cotton, partially obscured by bars and subjected to the gaze of white tourists, their shadow-like reflections overlaying her image on the glass; like Jacobs and Picquet, she is placed in a white frame. The camera's medium long shot, however, implicates the viewer in this voyeurism; although Cora 'consents' to being placed in the abolitionist costume of slavery, her performance perpetuates her status as property rather than person.

Recalling the 'slave narratives', the production exposes racial prejudices. Cora is granted a perspective shot, for example, yet she is revealed to be looking down a white man's camera lens; the audience is forced to view voyeurism. The confining composition of shots likewise embodies stolen agency in order to expose it, as does replaying frames in reverse, the camera pulled back towards the white man at the centre of power. The interlocking of white male sexuality and black female trauma is made explicit as 'Master' Randall lifts Cora's face to his, caressing her still-bleeding scar; extreme close-ups visualise his imprisoning presence, precluding any ability to non-consent. This disempowerment is perpetuated post-escape, as Cora undergoes a forced gynaecological examination (as part of a eugenics programme that subsequently nominates her for sterilisation without consent); intercut with memories of rape, her present 'care' blurs with past cruelties, visualising the continued aftershocks of enslavement.

The production's confused chronology intercuts past and present, evoking enslavement as both remembered and re-purposed, as enduring rather than ended. The setting of the museum as an abolitionist platform similarly invokes cultural memory, raising the question of how enslavement is recounted in the US historical record. Douglass himself was sensitive to both posterity and prophecy in reflecting upon enslavement: 'Slavery has been fruitful in giving itself names and it will call itself by yet another name; and [...] all of us had better wait and see what new form this old monster will assume'.[60] Douglass's proclaimed 'Need for Continuing Anti-Slavery Work' is, in many ways, taken up by screen portrayals of enslavement. Yet films have also *become* that old monster's 'new form', drawing on, entrenching, and further fashioning the discriminatory discourses of the antebellum past.

12 Years a Slave (2013) embodies this problematic. Full nudity at the 'slave auction' and the explicit screening of Patsy's rape and whipping exposes in order to excoriate the practices of enslavement. Yet, like abolitionist tracts designed to shock through illustrations of bare flesh, the explicitness of such scenes, shot in close-up, also perpetuates the inspection, 'at leisure', of the (non-consenting) black body. Equally, like nineteenth-century white exculpatory narratives, films mitigate or evade abuse. *The Abolitionists* (2013) omits Henry Grimké's sexual abuse of enslaved Nancy Weston, its overwriting of black female stories seen also in its focus on white abolitionists. *Freedom* (2015) mitigates white culpability; resolving past iniquities rather than resisting ongoing discriminations, the 'slavecatcher' simply repents and grants the enslaved their freedom.

Although *Underground* (2016) is professedly 'about not letting white folk buy [black] stor[ies]', it ultimately confuses its revisionary agenda, romanticising interactions between white men and enslaved women.[61] Male physical violence towards Ernestine cuts to sensuously filmed love-making, while Clara and Matthew's passionate kiss on a sunlit shoreline, accompanied by pop lyrics 'I want you to be with me', undercuts her desire to resist his 'ownership'. Abuse is pushed 'underground', reconstruing male coercion as female control and consent. This is compounded by the series' paratexts. Ernestine makes herself literally consumable to Macon, pouring red wine over her body and manipulating her sexuality for gain: 'I don't want James out in the field'. Her pained expression implies her sacrificial act; prompted to entice Macon to protect Rosalee, her 'consent' is coerced, her out-of-focus image framed by her enslaver undressing. Yet the dynamics of this scene are simplified in the production's trailer, which edits the sequence to depict Ernestine simply as seductress, reinforcing the romantic, candle-lit *mise-en-scène* and extradiegetic music ('Walking in the Light').

Slavery's Online Afterlives

In its explicit seductiveness, *Underground* emulates YouTube 'slavery sex tapes', which centre upon Harriet Tubman (1822–1913), who fled enslavement and proceeded to conduct others out of bondage via the Underground Railroad (an escape network from the Southern to the Northern states). Their voyeurism is rooted in the antebellum past, recalling a Virginian enslaver 'more interested in watching [Louisa and Sam] engage in sex at his bidding than in increasing his human property'.[62] Tubman herself recognised the violations of enslavement as spectacle: 'I got no heart' to 'see the sufferings of my people played on de stage'; 'I've seen de real ting'.[63] As Hartman notes, from coerced physical displays at auction to minstrelsy, 'blacks were envisioned fundamentally as vehicles for white enjoyment'.[64] This is scrutinised in *Roots* and *12 Years a Slave*, implicating viewers in the viewing of enforced entertainment, as the enslaved 'sing' on 'slave-ships' and 'dance' in drawing-rooms. In *The Underground Railroad*, 'entertainment' is likewise constructed in order to be deconstructed. Caesar is coerced to 'breed' with a naked woman; both are blurred in the foreground, as the camera concentrates on Randall watching them: the shot then pans back to them, in full focus. The production actively navigates voyeurism as violative, the shift from blurred to focused image aligning the viewer with the white man's gaze on non-consenting black bodies.

Both *The Harriet Tubman Sex Tape* and *Harriet Tubman: The Sexiest Abolitionist* likewise professedly counter the discriminations they enact; as the *Sex Tape* declares, 'racial inequalities' remain pervasive. Director Russell Simmons indeed maintained that Tubman's 'outwitting the slavemaster' is 'politically correct' (her 'sex tape' is 'leverage' against her enslaver).[65] Similarly, as the 'Sexiest Abolitionist', Tubman manipulates a white man, stealing not only his 'property' but his pride. However, such intentions unsettlingly reawaken perceptions of black 'theatricality' and hyper-sexuality, their 'humour' framed by the 'violence [that] undergirded the comic moment in minstrelsy'.[66] Both present Tubman as complicit in, or consenting to, 'the exchange of power' – 'I'm the master, you're the slave, but we can roleplay' (*The Sexiest Abolitionist*) – but elide the fundamental nature of bondage as acknowledged by Jacobs: 'he was my master. I was compelled'.[67]

In *The Sexiest Abolitionist*, the white man is ostensibly deflated; dancing to his proclamation 'I'm a Harriet Tubman man', he is an object of ridiculed display, reinforced by his demand, 'Now whip me, I've been a bad boy'. Significantly, Tubman refuses expletively, and resumes liberating his 'property'; although he consents to Tubman tying him up, he loses control of both 'sex game' and 'slaveholding' – the enslaver remains bound as the enslaved break free. However, the video re-enacts – even as it seeks to redress – abuse. The close-up of Tubman's breasts (from his perspective) as she throws the rope around him undercuts his disempowerment, embedding her placement as eroticised object, directed to perform in a 'musical' troublingly reminiscent of minstrelsy.

While the enslaver declares Tubman a 'sexy abolitionist', the video presents her as 'The *Sexiest* Abolitionist', its titling further entrenching ante/post-bellum perceptions of black female hyper-sexuality; the video, ultimately, enacts its own (prejudicial) gaze. This problematic gaze also underpins the *Sex Tape*. Tubman ostensibly directs the intradiegetic camera: 'make sure you catch it all'. However, her assertion that the tape is the 'only chance to gain freedom' exemplifies the fact that her consent is coerced. The video's extra-diegetic camera compounds this lack of control, further layering the voyeurism of a sequence in which Tubman is seen simultaneously through the eyes of a black man and his camera lens. While she instructs her *accomplice* to film her, her initial seduction of 'massa' is shot through an external camera over which she has no direction; she becomes the voyeured object alongside the sex tape itself. Moreover, her performed sexual dominance works not so much to deflate white masculinity but to reinforce black 'theatricality' and 'hyper-sexuality'. Both tapes perpetuate the 'racial inequalities' they nominally confront, the intradiegetic period camera literally – and metaphorically – distorting the actuality of the antebellum past.

Tubman's afterlives undermine the final plea of Sarah Bradford's biography, that 'the people to whom the story of this woman shall come' possess 'a like charity'. The videos' 'humour' instead touches uncomfortably upon a 'sneer' at making 'a heroine of a black woman, and a slave'.[68] Certainly, such 'sketches' have roots in the nineteenth century (*Behind the Seams*, 1868, a parody of Keckley). Yet Tubman's online adaptations trouble the question of agency, highlighting her posthumous inability to control or consent to her memory and memorialisation. Recalling the nineteenth-century literary conventions which framed and commodified 'slave narratives', the endlessly evolving internet becomes another form of 'marketplace', disempowering the image of the enslaved woman through its own forms of control; ironically, a YouTube playlist (accessed 10th August 2021) automatically followed *The Abolitionists* with *The Sexiest Abolitionist* – perpetuating the prejudices against black women the documentary avowedly disassembles.

Conclusion

At a Southern auction, white men force a young black woman 'on de block'. To their surprise, however, 'Sukie got awful mad' – 'she pullt up her dress an' tole [the] traders to look an' see if dey could fin' any teef down dere […] Massa never did bother slave gals no mor''.[69] Sukie's story illustrates the complex matrix of enslavement, consent, and coercion that marked the past and continues to resonate in the present. Like Sukie, nineteenth-century 'slave narratives' counter violation with volition, asserting selfhood out of submission. Their emancipatory voices have been met by twenty-first-century activism, including The Celia Project, uncovering enslaved female testimony. Yet, just as Sethe is haunted by the past in *Beloved*, enslavement holds its own afterlives. Sethe gives her body to a white man in payment for the engraving on Beloved's grave; her coerced consent literally and metaphorically inscribes the death of the female self – a death that remains unburied. Both *Underground* and *The Underground Railroad* re-assert, through their contemporary music and visuals, a blurring of past and present, affirming Douglass's 'Need for Continuing Anti-Slavery Work'. Yet screening slavery also perpetuates ante/postbellum definitions of black women as both (white) male sexual property and as sexuality's slave; both always denied and always giving, consent, for black US women, becomes a contradiction. As the #MeToo and Black Lives Matter campaigns have demonstrated, however, the confrontation of black abuse *is* 'a story to pass on', upholding the right to (refuse) consent and vindicating the voices of women who, like Rose Williams, were forced 'gainst [their] wants'.[70]

Notes

1 Harriet Jacobs, *Incidents in the Life of a Slave Girl* (Boston, 1861), p. 62.
2 Malcolm X, 'Who Taught You to Hate Yourself?' (1962) <https://speakola.com/political/malcolm-x-speech-to-black-women-1962> [accessed 31 May 2023].
3 Lucy Delaney, *From the Darkness Cometh the Light* (Washington: Library of Congress, 2001), p. 10.
4 H. Mattison, *Louisa Picquet, the Octoroon* (New York, 1861), p. 6.
5 The Emancipation Proclamation heralded freedom for all enslaved in the US; Reconstruction defines the period following the Civil War (1861–65).
6 Estelle Freedman, *Redefining Rape: Sexual Violence in the Era of Suffrage and Segregation* (Cambridge: Harvard University Press, 2013) <books.google.co.uk> [accessed 31 May 2023].
7 Frederick Douglass, *Narrative of the Life of Frederick Douglass, An American Slave, Written by Himself* (Boston: Cornhill, 1845), p. 5.
8 Deirdre Cooper-Owens, *Medical Bondage* (Athens: University of Georgia Press, 2017), p. 6.
9 Brenda Stevenson, '"What's Love Got to Do with It?": Concubinage and Enslaved Women and Girls in the Antebellum South', *Journal of African American History*, 98 (2013), 99–125 (p. 115).
10 As cited in Freedman, <books.google.co.uk>.
11 Jacobs, p. 119.
12 Quobna Ottobah Cugoano and Boyrereau Brinch (1810), as cited in Stevenson, p. 174.
13 Josiah Quincy, *Journal* (1773), as cited in Hazel Carby, *Reconstructing Womanhood* (Oxford: Oxford University Press, 1987), p. 30.
14 Marie Jenkins Schwartz, *Birthing a Slave: Motherhood and Medicine in the Antebellum South* (London: Harvard University Press, 2006), p. 5. Enslaved men were also subjected to sexual abuse, their right to (non)consent non-existent. Like women, they were subjected to violating, intimate examinations on the auction block to assess their fecundity. Subsequently, as 'bucks', 'stockmen', or 'studs',

men could be forced into sexual unions with enslaved women for the purposes of 'breeding' – 'commanded … to take a wife': Olive Gilbert, *The Narrative of Sojourner Truth* (Project Gutenberg, 1999), p. 86.

15 Harriet Washington, *Medical Apartheid* (New York: Broadway, 2017), pp. 94–95.

16 Mary Church Terrell, 'Lynching from a Negro's Point of View' (1904), as cited in Michaela Kleppinger, 'Denial of Consent: The Modern Heir of Sexual Violence within Slavery', *Edukacja Etyczna*, 16 (2019), 43–59 (p. 44). The terms 'black' and 'African American' are used throughout this chapter; terms such as 'colored' are only used as they occur in original quotations.

17 Douglass, p. 54.

18 Douglass, p. 55; *Remembering Slavery*, ed. by Ira Berlin, Marc Favreau, and Steven Miller (New York: The New Press, 2007), pp. 26–27.

19 John Blassingame, *The Slave Community* (New York: Oxford University Press, 1979), p. 154.

20 Angelina Grimké-Weld, *American Slavery As It Is* (New York: American Anti-Slavery Society, 1839), p. 85; Stevenson, p. 109.

21 Songs, like 'slave narratives', are both record and resistance, implicitly undercutting white male abuse through its exposure.

22 James Pennington, as cited in Stevenson, p. 105; Edward Lycurgas, as cited in Saidiya Hartman, *Scenes of Subjection: Terror, Slavery, and Self-Making in Nineteenth-Century America* (Oxford: Oxford University Press, 1997), p. 38.

23 William Robinson, *National Intelligencer* (1837), in Grimké-Weld, p. 154.

24 Grimké-Weld, p. 154; p. 24.

25 Rosen, p. 5; p. 8.

26 Washington, p. 301.

27 Washington, p. 210; p. 256; p. 369.

28 James Marion Sims, as cited in Washington, p. 367; p. 224.

29 Washington, p. 42.

30 Grimké-Weld, p. 106; Washington, p. 727.

31 Washington, p. 731.

32 Ibid., p. 729.

33 Grimké-Weld, p. 148.

34 Yogita Goyal, *Runaway Genres* (New York: New York University Press, 2019), p. 7.

35 Viewer Comments <youtube.com/watch?v=RWRKTahK7TO> [accessed 3 September 2022].

36 Kleppinger, p. 51.

37 Kleppinger, p. 51; Clint Smith, *Women's Experience Under Slavery*, online video recording, YouTube, 2021 <http://www.youtube.com/watch?v=eAe7ETfQaA> [accessed 3 September 2022]; Washington, p. 169.

38 Douglass, p. 67.

39 Gilbert, p. 63.

40 Saidiya Hartman, 'The Position of the Unthought', *Qui Parle*, 13 (2003), 183–201 (p. 184); Delaney, p. 39; Gilbert, p. 198.

41 Jacobs, p. 6; Douglass, p. 16; Elizabeth Keckley, *Behind the Scenes, Or, Thirty Years a Slave, and Four Years in the White House* (New York: Carleton, 1868), p. 16.

42 Karen Sánchez-Eppler, *Touching Liberty* (Los Angeles: University of California Press, 1993), p. 96; Mattison, p. 50.

43 Mattison, p. 50; p.12.

44 Ibid., p. 14.

45 Goyal, p. 22; Sánchez-Eppler, p. 95; Jacobs, p. 82.

46 Mattison, p. 11.

47 Gilbert, p. 70.

48 Jacobs, pp. 83–84.

49 Ibid., pp. 84–85.

50 Toni Morrison, *Playing in the Dark* (New York: Vintage, 1992), pp. 50–51; Toni Morrison, *Beloved* (London: Picador, 1988).
51 Keckley, p. 3.
52 Gilbert, p. 103.
53 Jacobs, p. 7. As biography, Sarah Bradford's *Scenes in the Life of Harriet Tubman* (1869) epitomises the tense interplay between black experience and white editing. It also further layers the question of consent in enslavement, pointing to *white* coercion: following the Fugitive Slave Act (1850), 'We [white individuals] were commanded by law to take part in the iniquity of slavery' (p. 19).
54 Jacobs, p. 86; Gilbert, pp. 74–75.
55 Xiomara Santamarina, 'Black Womanhood in North American Women's Slave Narratives', in *The Cambridge Companion to the African American Slave Narrative*, ed. by Audrey Fisch (Cambridge: Cambridge University Press, 2007), pp. 232–45 (p. 239); Mattison, p. 5; Santamarina, p. 240.
56 Keckley, p. 14; Jacobs, p. 45.
57 Rudyard Alcocer, Kristen Block, and Dawn Duke, *Celluloid Chains: Slavery in the Americas Through Film* (Knoxville: University of Tennessee Press, 2018), p. xxxiv; Sarah Bradford, *Scenes in the Life of Harriet Tubman* (Auburn: W. J. Moses, 1869), p. 117.
58 Goyal, p. 23.
59 <https://www.youtube.com/watch?v=C4TTbcXG1GQ> [accessed 31 May 2023].
60 Frederick Douglass, 'The Need for Continuing Anti-Slavery Work' (1865), in Laura Murphy, *The New Slave Narrative* (New York: Columbia University Press, 2019), p. xvii.
61 This is thrown into relief by *Free State of Jones* (2016), which tempers its portrayal of the union between Confederacy rebel Newton Knight and formerly enslaved Rachel through its dual narrative, which juxtaposes their love story with the Mississippi race laws which embroiled their mid-twentieth-century descendants. Indeed, their relationship remains framed by Rachel's memory of past abuse, unsettling the concept of consent between black women and white men.
62 Wilma King, '"Prematurely Knowing of Evil Things": The Sexual Abuse of African American Girls and Young Women in Slavery and Freedom', *Journal of African American History*, 99 (2014), 173–96 (p. 180).
63 Bradford, p. 22.
64 Hartman, p. 23.
65 The Young Turks, *Russell Simmons and the Harriet Tubman Sex Tape*, online video recording, YouTube, 2013 <https://www.youtube.com/watch?v=YYmQM1NAaWY> [accessed 15 February 2023].
66 Hartman, p. 43; p. 32.
67 Jacobs, pp. 44–45.
68 Bradford, p. 113; p. 3.
69 Berlin, p. 57.
70 Morrison, p. 274; Berlin, p. 129.

Bibliography

Alcocer, Rudyard, Kirsten Block, and Dawn Duke, *Celluloid Chains: Slavery in the Americas Through Film* (Knoxville: University of Tennessee Press, 2018)

Berlin, Ira, Marc Favreau, and Steven Miller, eds, *Remembering Slavery* (New York: The New Press, 2007)

Blassingame, John, *The Slave Community* (New York: Oxford University Press, 1979)

Bradford, Sarah, *Scenes in the Life of Harriet Tubman* (Auburn: W. J. Moses, 1869)

Carby, Hazel, *Reconstructing Womanhood* (Oxford: Oxford University Press, 1987)

Cooper-Owens, Deirdre, *Medical Bondage* (Athens: University of Georgia Press, 2017)

Delaney, Lucy, *From the Darkness Cometh the Light* (Washington: Library of Congress, 2001 [1891])

Douglass, Frederick, *Narrative in the Life of Frederick Douglass, An American Slave, Written by Himself* (Boston: Cornhill, 1845)

Freedman, Estelle, *Redefining Rape: Sexual Violence in the Era of Suffrage and Segregation* (Cambridge, MA: Harvard University Press, 2013)

Gilbert, Olive, *The Narrative of Sojourner Truth* (Project Gutenberg, 1999 [1850])

Goyal, Yogita, *Runaway Genres* (New York: New York University Press, 2019)

Grimké-Weld, Angelina, *American Slavery As It Is* (New York: American Anti-Slavery Society, 1839)

Hartman, Saidiya, *Scenes of Subjection: Terror, Slavery, and Self-Making in Nineteenth-Century America* (Oxford: Oxford University Press, 1997)

Hartman, Saidiya, 'The Position of the Unthought', *Qui Parle*, 13 (2003), 183–201

Jacobs, Harriet, *Incidents in the Life of a Slave Girl* (Boston, 1861)

Jenkins Schwartz, Marie, *Birthing a Slave: Motherhood and Medicine in the Antebellum South* (London: Harvard University Press, 2006)

Keckley, Elizabeth, *Behind the Scenes, Or, Thiry Years a Slave, and Four Years in the White House* (New York: Carleton, 1868)

King, Wilma, '"Prematurely Knowing of Evil Things": The Sexual Abuse of African American Girls and Young Women in Slavery and Freedom', *Journal of African American History*, 99 (2014), 173–96

Kleppinger, Michaela, 'Denial of Consent: The Modern Heir of Sexual Violence within Slavery', *Edukacja Etyczna*, 16 (2019), 43–59

Mattison, H., *Louisa Picquet, the Octoroon* (New York, 1861)

Morrison, Toni, *Beloved* (London: Picador, 1988)

Morrison, Toni, *Playing in the Dark* (New York: Vintage, 1992)

Murphy, Laura, *The New Slave Narrative* (New York: Columbia University Press, 2019)

Sánchez-Eppler, Karen, *Touching Liberty* (Los Angeles: University of California Press, 1993)

Santamarina, Xiomara, 'Black Womanhood in North American Women's Slave Narratives', in *The Cambridge Companion to the African American Slave Narrative*, ed. by Audrey Fisch (Cambridge: Cambridge University Press, 2007), pp. 232–45

Smith, Clint, *Women's Experience Under Slavery*, online video recording, YouTube, 2021 <http://www.youtube.com/watch?v=eAe7ETfQaA> [accessed 3 September 2022]

Stevenson, Brenda, '"What's Love Got to Do with It?": Concubinage and Enslaved Women and Girls in the Antebellum South', *Journal of African American History*, 98 (2013), 99–125

The Young Turks, *Russell Simmons and the Harriet Tubman Sex Tape*, online video recording, YouTube, 2013 <https://www.youtube.com/watch?v=YYmQM1NAaWY> [accessed 15 February 2023]

Washington, Harriet, *Medical Apartheid* (New York: Broadway, 2017)

X, Malcolm, 'Who Taught You to Hate Yourself?' (1962) <https://speakola.com/political/malcolm-x-speech-to-black-women-1962> [accessed 31 May 2023]

Filmography

12 Years a Slave, dir. by Steve McQueen (Fox Searchlight Pictures, 2013)

The Abolitionists, dir. by Rob Rapley (PBS, 2013)

The Birth of a Nation, dir. by Nate Parker (Fox Searchlight Pictures, 2016)

Free State of Jones, dir. by Gary Ross (STX Entertainment, 2016)

Freedom, dir. by Peter Cousens (ARC Entertainment, 2015)

Funk, Josh, *Harriet Tubman: The Sexiest Abolitionist*, online video recording, YouTube, 2010 <https://www.youtube.com/watch?v=U5tAvZ_6t_g> [accessed 15 February 2023]

Roots, dir. by Bruce Beresford, Thomas Carter, Phillip Noyce, and Mario Van Peebles (The History Channel, 2016)

Simmons, Russell, *The Harriet Tubman Sex Tape*, online video recording, YouTube, 2013 <https://www.youtube.com/watch?v=1uU55OEw8Js> [accessed 15 February 2023]

Underground, dir. by Anthony Hemingway (Sony Pictures, 2016)

The Underground Railroad, dir. by Barry Jenkins (Amazon, 2021)

7 Without Consent or Memory

Consent in Michaela Coel's *I May Destroy You*

Christina Mansueti

Content Notes: This chapter discusses topics directly related to sexual assault and rape – sometimes graphic in nature. I have tried to use appropriate language in order to not minimise the acts in any way. Please use your discretion when reading this chapter.

Consent mediates many of our social relationships, and its presence can radically transform them. As Heidi Hurd argues, in 'The Moral Magic of Consent', 'consent turns a trespass into a dinner party; a battery into a handshake; a theft into a gift; an invasion of privacy into an intimate moment; a commercial appropriation of name and likeness into a biography'.[1] Consent is one of those words whose semantics is rigorously debated by legal theorists. It is also the subject of research by academics as diverse as sociologists, psychologists, and philosophers, yet it is often misunderstood, and, as statistics confirm, frequently ignored or transgressed in practice, as it relates to sex, and, in particular, as it relates to young women. In a 2023 study, 'Sexual consent norms in a cross-sectional national sample of the UK', Malachi Willis and Tiffany L. Marcantonio conclude that 'sexual assault is a pervasive problem in the UK, and young women are disproportionately affected'.[2] An important element of this pervasive problem is the fact that a socio-cultural understanding of consent is fluid, affected differently by gender, age, and context. The study found that women 'tend to define sexual consent as a process, whereas men are more likely to perceive sexual consent as a one-time sexual event'.[3] This socio-cultural understanding of consent suggests that even within a given culture, there can be radically different understandings of consent, depending on who gives or denies it, and in what context.

The UK Sexual Offences Act of 2003 states, 'someone consents to vaginal, anal or oral penetration only if s/he agrees by choice to that penetration and has the freedom and capacity to make that choice'.[4] Using this definition as a starting point, this chapter explores the complexity of sexual consent as it is portrayed and negotiated in Michaela Coel's semi-autobiographical television series, *I May Destroy You. I May Destroy You* and her other work, *Chewing Gum*, are both derived from Coel's positionality as a Black, British woman of Ghanaian descent growing up with a Christian fundamentalist working-class

DOI: 10.4324/9781003365082-9

mother in East London. *I May Destroy You* engages with the issue of sexual consent through the use of the comedy-drama genre, utilising its capacity to share her experience with other sexual abuse survivors, as well as to provide a vehicle for education, and a critique of social attitudes towards sex and consent. It also provides an empathetic portrait of Black women,[5] and, importantly, it offers a realistic exposé into the nature and complexity of sexual consent and its transgressions. While the genre of comedy has been criticised for making light of subject matter that is contentious or taboo, it can be used to strategic effect in precisely those subject areas often evaded or ignored, focusing a critical yet comic light on them. Coel's strategic use of humour links to a long history of using the genre to focus on societal issues that goes all the way back to Aristophanes, whose play *Lysistrata* involved the women of Athens and Sparta withholding their consent to sex until the war between the two city states ended. While the focus of this chapter is not on the genre, it is important to understand how this series functions in the cultural zeitgeist, and how it achieves such impact combining comedy with serious and potentially distressing subjects.[6]

The Crown Prosecution Services (CPS), in Section 74, frame consent by asserting that 'assuming that the complainant had both the [*freedom*] and [*capacity*] to consent, the crucial question is whether the complainant agrees to the activity by choice'.[7] The Rape Crisis Centre in England and Wales also adds, 'consent happens when all people involved in any kind of sexual activity agree to take part by choice. They also need to have the freedom and capacity to make that choice'.[8] Freedom and the capacity to consent are central to defining and understanding consent in any context. Sexual consent, however, is more complex than a simple yes or no. It can be revoked at any point during a sexual encounter. To add to its complexity, just because consent was granted in the past, it should not be taken for granted as a given in all future encounters, under all future circumstances. This is illustrated in shocking detail in one of the character's (Kwame's) experiences of sexual assault, explored later in this chapter.

I May Destroy You premiered in 2020 on BBC One and focuses on the trauma of rape and its after-effects, including how the protagonist, Arabella, tries to piece her life back together after experiencing assault. The twelve-episode series is set in London where Arabella is a Twitter-personality-turned-author with her book *Chronicles of a Fed-up Millennial*. Arabella's story begins as she is trying to meet a deadline for her sequel, and she decides to take a break by meeting her friends for a drink. On this occasion, she is drugged and raped. Woven into Arabella's narrative is the story of Kwame, a queer Black man who is sexually assaulted following a date arranged on Grindr. Because there are so many scenes in this series that deal with sexual consent, I have chosen to focus on four main instances as they directly relate to Arabella and Kwame. The first, which constitutes the main plot, is when Arabella is drugged and raped by a man, David, on a night out with friends. The second involves Arabella's gay male friend Kwame, who is sexually assaulted after a Grindr meetup. The third involves Zain (the writer from Henny Publishing assigned to help Arabella with her sequel), who subjects Arabella to the non-consensual removal of his condom during a sexual encounter, an act that is classified as rape under UK law.[9] The fourth scene takes place between Kwame and Nilufer, a white heterosexual woman that he meets through another dating app. It is a scene in which Coel highlights the ease of entry into the hook-up culture and the kinds of complex situations concerning consent that arise as a result.

The main plot begins with Arabella, who, needing a break from her writing, meets her friend Simon. They go to a karaoke bar where she raps on stage and then they move to another popular site, the Ego Death Bar. Here, the audience witnesses a group of four men, Arabella, and another woman conversing. David, one of the men at the table, buys a round of tequila shots for everyone and the audience sees Arabella drink one shot. Upbeat music plays and Arabella and her company are dancing. The unfolding scene shows Arabella slowly losing consciousness. Her head gets visibly heavier; her eyes glaze over; she cannot stand up straight and, finally, falls into the bar, knocking over bar equipment, tripping over a chair, and into the door – suggesting that she has been drugged. From there, the mood abruptly shifts: the music ends, and the scene cuts to Arabella typing at her desk the next morning hurriedly preparing for a meeting with her publishers. Her phone screen is cracked, and she has a cut on her forehead. There is also a small blood stain on the collar of her shirt. Once she gets home from a meeting with her publishers, the audience views her peeing, and she has a flashback to a white man standing over her, raping her. Throughout the next episode (episode two: 'Someone Is Lying'), and the duration of the series, Arabella tries to make sense of this flashback. She then goes to the police to report it and has a forensic medical examination. When Arabella reports her rape to the police, she is met by two female officers: one a white woman, and the other a Black woman. She is treated with care and consideration over many meetings. Even though they report that they do not have sufficient DNA data to convict anyone, they believe her story.

These first two episodes detail blatant non-consensual sex, although the rape happens off screen. Episode one introduces a realistic representation of the London hook-up culture in which alcohol and drugs are used to reduce, if not eliminate, the need for consent. The subsequent episodes reveal the after-effects of rape on its victim and then widen the context to include the dynamics of the legal system, the forensic procedure to establish the rape, and the subsequent interviews with the police to establish the validity of a claim of non-consensual assault.

As a point of contrast and to broaden the complexity of the nature of consent, Arabella's friend Kwame appears in episode four, 'That Was Fun'. He is first introduced into the series as he engages in sexual activity following a matchup on Grindr. Kwame performs oral sex on a man, and, soon afterwards, the audience learns that Kwame had just met the man, a cashier, and that the consensual sex has taken place in the grocery store at which the cashier works. Problematically, with his next hook-up, what began as a consensual hook-up between Kwame, his partner, Damon, and Malik (a new person Kwame met on Grindr), ends with Malik forcing himself on Kwame. Kwame only knows Malik by his Grindr handle 'HornyMan808'. Damon is uncomfortable witnessing sex between Kwame and Malik and leaves mid-way through. When Kwame and Malik are finished, Malik urges Kwame to stay, but he declines. Kwame tries to leave, but Malik shuts the door, slamming Kwame's finger and pushing him onto the bed where Malik begins to forcefully hump him. Kwame squirms and shouts, 'get off me; get the fuck off me'.[10] When all efforts to resist fail, Kwame gives up and lies there with tears in his eyes, looking lifeless. After this assault, Malik says, 'what can I say? I'm a bad boy', and Kwame hurriedly leaves Malik's apartment.[11] The encounter begins consensually, but it does not end that way, highlighting the fact that consent should be an ongoing process that can be withdrawn or affirmed at any point during a sexual encounter. In terms of the law, consent ought to be able to be withdrawn at any point, but in Kwame's case, as he learns in his interview with the police, because he initially consented, there is no grounds to prove he was assaulted. As the officer informs Kwame, 'there's no point in us doing a DNA sample. You'd just had, um, consensual sex with him, so it wouldn't really prove anything other than that'.[12] He then tells Kwame the special unit will give him a call, and Kwame asks if he is free to leave. In comparison to Arabella, Kwame is met with one officer who is male and Black – his sexuality undisclosed. Foregrounding this scene, the camera pans to the open door of the interrogation room, which reads, 'ATTENTION: This door must be shut at all times you're putting people in danger by having it open'.[13]

Kwame's assault and the subsequent police interrogation give an indication as to why in the UK, 'In the year to September 2021, just 1.3% of rape cases recorded by police resulted in a suspect being charged (or receiving a summons)'.[14] Significantly, within these episodes, the audience witnesses that the public's misunderstanding of the law hampers the criminal justice system that enforces these laws. In response to Arabella's question of the law concerning the removal of a condom during sex, her attending police offer, Detective Beth, informs her that 'the problem is when people don't know what is a crime, and what isn't a crime, they don't report it.[15]

Importantly, in terms of victims, Kwame's experience demonstrates that while non-consensual sexual activities occur more frequently for women and girls, the issue of sexual consent affects not only women but also individuals of all genders and sexualities,[16] including gay, Black men. The lack of a cultural conversation about the sexual assault of men results in a lack of reporting on the issue, which affects gay and bisexual men more than heterosexual ones, according to Survivor's UK charity organisation's research.[17] This highlights the need to prioritise intersectional framings of consent, as I develop further later in this chapter.

Kwame's assault is shown with all of its impact registering, graphically, on his on-screen face in contrast to Arabella's off-screen rape presented in flashbacks. Despite their differences, Arabella's and Kwame's experiences provide representations of non-consensual sex, their consequences, and the hook-up culture in which they occurred. Through her sympathetic characters, Arabella and Kwame, Coel brings the topic of sexual consent into public discourse, as she places consent in the context of contemporary dating and hook-up culture in London, revealing the effects of rape and transgressions of consent through a variety of scenes, some graphically represented. Her creative efforts seek to counter the media representations of rape culture,[18] a summary of which is detailed by Anastasia Powell and Nicola Henry, in 'Framing Sexual Violence Prevention':

> In a rape culture, violence against women is eroticised in literary, cinematic and media representations; victims are routinely disbelieved or blamed for their own victimisation; and perpetrators are rarely held accountable or their behaviours are seen as excusable or understandable. These manifestly sexist attitudes and beliefs about rape, rape victims and rapists do not exist in isolation but rather are part of a broader manifestation of gender inequality, prevalent in the language, laws and institutions that are supposed to criminalise, challenge and prevent sexual violence but instead perpetuate, support, condone or reflect these values (see Smart, 1989; Temkin, 2002). Resistance to changing or challenging this rape culture can also be found in the erroneous but deeply embedded belief that rape is an inevitable and natural fact of life (Marcus, 199).

In her approach to the representation of sexual abuse and violence, Coel treats contemporary London's dating and hook-up culture as a site that has the need and the potential for change in terms of understanding and applying sexual consent.[19] Her approach to the challenge, however, is far from simple, as Coel adds another complicating factor in the fourth instance when consent involves a person having the right information before consenting to engage in sexual activity. In episode eight, 'Line Spectrum Border', Kwame has sex with Nilufer, a white heterosexual woman who he meets on another dating app. After Kwame has been raped, he no longer feels safe having sex with men. As a result of this insecurity, he meets Nilufer and has sex with her without disclosing that he is gay. She is offended, hurt, and somewhat angry when he discloses that he is gay after she makes homophobic remarks. This episode presents more of the complexities of consent as Coel's sympathetic character, a victim of rape, fails to disclose important information. If this information is considered relevant to Nilufer's ability to give full, informed consent (a topic Kyle Murray discusses in his chapter later in this volume), Coel may be problematising the victim/perpetrator binary with this scene.

Coel's efforts to intervene in London rape culture align with Afrofuturist practice, originally conceived by Mark Dery in the 1990s.[20] Afrofuturism offers a cultural lens through which to imagine a new future for people of African descent by describing the cultural experience of Black people.[21] It typically incorporates three themes: reclamation, Black liberation, and a revisioning of the past and envisioning a future through a Black cultural lens that is safer and more equitable.[22] Coel uses her traumatic experience and recovery as a form of Black joy,[23] as a survival strategy, and she encourages other Black writers to tell their stories, to share their lived experience with different representations of those cultural experiences, and to create a world that is safer for everyone.

I May Destroy You also grew out of the #MeToo era of fourth-wave feminism, which focuses on intersectionality and the ways in which the mechanisms of oppression work to further subjugate those on the margins. Intersectionality refers to Kimberlé Crenshaw's legal and theoretical explication of the lens through which power can be explored at the different convergences of identity – specifically as they relate to gender, race, and class, and, in this chapter, sexuality.[24] As Patricia Hill Collins writes,

> the events and conditions of social and political life and the self can seldom be understood as shaped by one factor. They are generally shaped by many factors in diverse and mutually influencing ways. When it comes to social inequality, people's lives, and organisation of power in a given society, are better understood as being shaped not by a single axis of social division, be it race or gender or class, but by many axes that work together and influence each other. Intersectionality as an analytic tool gives people better access to the complexity of the world and of themselves.[25]

Coel, as a young, Black, British woman of immigrant descent, living within the London hook-up culture, highlights the way that sexual consent is interpreted, assumed, or ignored in the community and culture in which she participates, maintaining the agenda of the #MeToo Movement but giving its concerns a London-based and intersectional focus. The origins of the #MeToo Movement grew elsewhere but for similar reasons to Coel's dramatisation of her experience on screen. With the failure of legal systems to adequately prosecute perpetrators of sexual violence, resonating with how neither Kwame's nor Arabella's rapists are held legally responsible, the court of public opinion took over in the form of the #MeToo Movement. #MeToo, developed by Tarana Burke in 2006, focuses on (digital) activism, protest feminism, and, importantly, intersectionality. The hashtag, #MeToo, went viral in 2016 with Alyssa Milano, who is credited with using it in response to the multitude of accusations of sexual assault levied against Harvey Weinstein, an American film producer.[26] Part of the power of the movement resides in its almost global reach through social media. Social media not only gives victims of sexual violence a platform to share their stories, as Coel does after being victimised by her book editor, Zain, but it also provides them with a global community to discuss the endemic sexual violence. #MeToo also brings awareness to women and girls who have suffered sexual assault and/or violence and offers available resources for healing. It works to share stories of assault, create a digital community, and call out perpetrators in the court of public opinion when the judicial court fails to do so. It grew out of the need to give voice to the victims of sexual assault as well as the belief that to prevent these assaults, there needed to be a change in the narratives concerning rape and its prevention. That change begins with the recognition that sexual consent is about power, bodily autonomy, and boundaries. It continues with a need to educate the public about the murky waters of certain areas of the legal parameters of consent, areas that Coel addresses in another scene that indexes a lack of understanding shared by both the perpetrator and Arabella.

In episode four, 'That Was Fun…', Arabella engages in consensual sex with Zain, a writer whom her production team thinks will help her write her next project. Prior to engaging in sex with Zain, she asks him to wear a condom, and he obliges. During sex, Zain removes the condom without her knowledge and, therefore, without her consent. At the beginning of the following episode (episode five '…It Just Came Up'), Arabella is listening to a podcast (the Tea and Two Chicks podcast episode 'Condom removal'). This podcast features two women discussing the act of non-consensually removing a condom during sex and a Reddit forum where men discuss tips and tricks for how to do so. For example, they highlight that men will say, 'I thought you knew'.[27] This is exactly what Zain said to Arabella when she realised that he removed the condom during sex without her permission or knowledge. When Arabella is at the police station in a follow-up meeting about her rape, the two female officers inform her that the non-consensual removal of a condom during a sex act, known as 'stealthing', is, in fact, illegal and classified as rape – an educational moment for both Arabella and Coel's audience. In the episode '…It Just Came Up', Arabella, in a #MeToo gesture, publicly outs Zain as a rapist at a writer's summit.

This #MeToo-style outing achieves a few dramatic effects. First, it makes Coel a spokesperson for survivors of sexual violence, prompting her followers to comment on social media with their own stories of violations of consent, fostering a sense of solidarity. Second, it educates the audience both at the writer's summit and of the television series that 'stealthing' is classified as rape under UK law. In episode six, 'The Alliance', one of Arabella's social media followers suggests that they, the victims, start leaking public information about the people who have violated them – an act of doxing, which the *Cambridge Dictionary* defines as 'the action of finding or publishing private information about someone on the internet without their permission especially in a way that reveals their name, address, etc'.[28]

This act of calling people out, and here, revealing personal information about abusers, aligns with the agenda of the #MeToo Movement. In addition, the plotline of Zain and Arabella's interaction concerning stealthing is credited with giving language to the act and having a global reach.[29]

Consent, then, covers a wide range of sexual situations. In *Sexual Consent*, Milena Popova succinctly outlines four historical approaches to consent: the radical feminist approach; 'no means no'; 'yes means yes'; the sex-critical approach. These approaches demonstrate a historically concerted effort to create greater understanding and clarity around sexual consent. The approach displayed in *I May Destroy You* is the sex-critical approach that is a more recent feminist approach to consent, which, like the radical feminist approach, looks at power imbalances; however, it pays critical attention to the nuances of power in consent negotiations. Popova argues that this approach also focuses less on the legal construction of consent and more on the cultural understanding of consent as expressed in everyday life and popular culture.[30] Here, it might be useful to turn to the concept of culture and see why this might be the case.

In Susan Brownmiller's controversial book, *Against Our Will*, she begins with the term 'culture', noting that while it is a descriptive term, it embodies a set of expectations with regards to behaviour and values. It functions, she argues, as a discourse, in the Foucauldian sense, determining what can and cannot be said about a certain subject, as well as what constitutes knowledge about that subject and the value that it holds. In contextualising rape culture, Brownmiller characterises it as 'one that normalises and excuses rape, a social context in which the desires of privileged aggressors are prioritised over the comfort, safety, and dignity of marginalised populations that are seen as targets, as prey. This context does not have to be gendered, but it typically is'.[31]

For Brownmiller, the term 'culture' is used to describe a set of beliefs, attitudes, and practices that are shared somewhat unconsciously amongst groups of people with a similar geographic location, sexuality, gender, or religion. Stuart Hall adds to this definition by stating that culture is not limited to the interests of the elite, such as the high culture of art, literature, and music, but it is 'experience lived, experience interpreted, experience defined'.[32] Importantly, in terms of Coel's work, for Hall, popular culture is also one of the sites where this struggle for and against a culture of the powerful is engaged: it is also the stake to be won or lost *in* that struggle. It is the arena of consent and resistance. It is partly where hegemony arises, and where it is secured. That is why 'popular culture' matters.[33]

If, in fact, any particular culture does involve an unconscious sense of values its people share, of what it means to be right or wrong, as Hall argues, then cultural productions, such as television, cinema, and other forms of media give language and representation to these values, indeed, reinforce these values and provide the lens through which acts such as rape are viewed. It is precisely these unconscious sets of values and the understanding of what it means to be right or wrong with regards to sexual assault that are challenged in *I May Destroy You*, as Coel grapples with the after-effects of her experience within the London culture. But *I May Destroy You* does not stop there in focusing on the current state of that culture; it also has hope for the future. The process of building that future begins with understanding the present culture, its current values, who is privileged, and at what cost.

The patriarchal systems under which Western Europe and North America operate privilege male entitlement and normalise, if not license, desires that derive from the rule of men over economic, social, and political life of any given society, argue authors Mary Daly and Emily Culpepper in their Cambridge documentary *Rape Culture.* As a result, what is referred to as rape culture is a by-product of a system that licenses and privileges male sexual fantasies, they argue.[34]

In popular culture, graphic scenes of sexual assault are routine, and rationalised through television, film, news, video games, and pornography to such a degree that we speak of 'a rape culture'. The season five finale of the popular *Outlander* offers a graphic scene in which the protagonist, Dr Claire Fraser, is beaten and gang-raped. As Lynette Rice writes, a 'shocking scene in the season 5 finale served as a sobering reminder that graphic depictions of sexual violence remain an oft-used trope in the saga'. And she might have added 'in many contemporary sagas'.[35] In an interview with the *Hollywood Reporter,* Executive Producer Mathew Roberts responded to criticism about the rape scene with the following remark:

> When a modern audience views *Outlander* through a modern lens, then yes, you can have problems with it. But if you place yourself in the period [...] and we're not saying that rape was okay in that period either [...] but how the characters view it is how we're showing it. We're not showing it how we view it, and that makes a difference.[36]

As an act of intervention into this structural violence, *I May Destroy You* takes its place at the intersection of subjectivity, gender identity, and culture. It is formative in its intervention in the politics of representation, both on and behind the screen, as it goes beyond the victim versus perpetrator binary in its attempt, in the first instance, to portray the complexity and complications of consent in sexual acts. Coel adds another complicating factor in the scenes between Arabella and Zain discussed above, when consent involves a person having the right information before consenting to engage in sexual activity.

The significance of this series resides in the inclusion of both the overt as well as the grey areas of sexual consent and in its uncompromising portrayal of the realities of sexual assault and its troubling aftermath. From start to finish, it never defaults to titillation or gratuitous dialogue. The conclusion is open-ended, as is the continuing process that Arabella and her group live as they work their way to recovery. In the final episode, Coel creates several fantasies that represent different responses to her rapist, from revenge to radical empathy, each offering the audience different subject positions from which to view the rapist, with each offering a different affective response.[37] Ultimately, Arabella chooses radical empathy as a way to come to terms with this life-changing experience. The ending reveals that these experiences have changed Arabella, but they leave her empowered by the choice to let go and to author her own story. Part of Arabella's healing comes from writing her own story, in her own way, and the same goes for Michaela Coel's story. Coel's semi-autobiographical work is owned, controlled, and produced by her. That, in the world of media, is as important as it is rare, for a Black, British woman has refused to give consent to a network having control over the body of her work and how it is being presented. Through this act of affirmative non-consent, she has given herself the power to tell her own story, in her own way, in all of its complexity, to own it, emotionally, financially, and legally.

Notes

1 Heidi Hurd, 'The Moral Magic of Consent', *Legal Theory*, 2 (1996), 121–46 (p. 123).

2 Malachi Willis and Tiffany L. Marcantonio, 'Sexual consent norms in a cross-sectional national sample of the UK', *Journal of Public Health*, 45 (2023), 84–90 (p. 85).

3 Ibid.

4 The Crown Prosecution Services, *What is Consent* (n.d.) <https://www.cps.gov.uk/sites/default/files/documents/publications/what_is_consent_v2.pdf> [accessed 31 May 2023].

5 Olive Pometsey, 'How Michaela Coel Transformed her Trauma Into the Year's Best TV Show', *GQ*, 10 July 2020 <https://www.gq.com/story/michaela-coel-i-may-destroy-you-interview> [accessed 31 May 2023].

6 'Incredibly, *I May Destroy You* still manages to laugh, and get laughs, thanks to Coel's undeniable knack for finding comedy in the darkest places': Lorraine Ali, 'Commentary: A new HBO series rethinks the sexual assault survivor story. It's brave and charming', *Los Angeles Times*, 14 June 2020 <www.latimes.com/entertainment-arts/tv/story/2020-06-14/hbo-i-may-destroy-you-michaela-coel-commentary> [accessed 31 May 2023].

7 Crown Prosecution Services, Rape and Sexual Offences – Chapter 6: Consent (2021) <https://www.cps.gov.uk/legal-guidance/rape-and-sexual-offences-chapter-6-consent> [accessed 31 May 2023].

8 Rape Crisis England & Wales, *What is Sexual Consent* (n.d.) <https://rapecrisis.org.uk/get-informed/about-sexual-violence/sexual-consent/> [accessed 31 May 2023].

9 Rape Crisis England & Wales, *Stealthing=Rape* (n.d.) <https://rapecrisis.org.uk/get-informed/types-of-sexual-violence/what-is-rape/#stealthing> [accessed 31 May 2023].

10 'That Was Fun', *I May Destroy You*, BBC1, Crave, 28:00–28:10.

11 Ibid., 28:27–28:32.

12 Ibid., 25:37–25:46.

13 'It Just Came Up', *I May Destroy You*, BBC1, Crave, 20:56.

14 Reality Check, 'Why do so few rape cases go to court?', BBC, 27 May 2022 <https://www.bbc.com/news/uk-48095118> [accessed 31 May 2023].

15 'That Was Fun', 8:11–8:19.

16 Rape Crisis England & Wales, *Statistics about sexual violence and abuse* (n.d.) <https://rapecrisis.org.uk/get-informed/statistics-sexual-violence/> [accessed 31 May 2023].

17 Eleanor Lawrie, 'I thought rape isn't something that happens to men', BBC, 22 July 2021 <https://www.bbc.com/news/uk-england-57892684> [accessed 31 May 2023].

18 Nicola Henry and Anastasia Powell, 'Framing Sexual Violence Prevention: What Does it Mean to Challenge a Rape Culture', in *Preventing Sexual Violence*, ed. by Nicola Henry and Anastasia Powell (London: Palgrave Macmillan, 2014), pp. 1–21.

19 Stuart Hall, 'New Ethnicities', in *Black Film British Cinema*, ed. by Erica Carter (London: Institute of Contemporary Arts, 1988), pp. 27–31. Stuart Hall identifies representation as a constitutive role in the formulation of identity and subjectivity, and the way each of these are viewed and valued within a certain culture. For Hall, 'how things are represented and the "machineries" and regimes of representation

in a culture do play a constitutive, and not merely a reflexive, after-the-event, role. This gives questions of culture and ideology, and the scenarios of representation, subjectivity, identity, politics a formative, not merely an expressive, place in the constitution of social and political life’.

20 Mark Dery, ‘Black to the Future’, in *Flame Wars: The Discourse of Cyberculture*, ed. by Mark Dery (Durham, NC: Duke University Press, 1994), pp. 179–222.

21 Ingrid Lafleur, ‘Afrofuturism’ (n.d.) <https://www.ingridlafleur.com/afrofuturism> [accessed 31 May 2023].

22 Subcultures and Sociology, *Afrofuturism* (n.d.) <https://haenfler.sites.grinnell.edu/afrofuturism/#:~:text=Though%20there%20are%20many%20definitions,black%20cultural%20lens%20in%20common> [accessed 31 May 2023].

23 Bettina L. Love, *We Want to Do More Than Survive: Abolitionist Teaching and the Pursuit of Educational Freedom* (Boston: Beacon Press, 2020).

24 Kimberlé Crenshaw, ‘Mapping the Margins: Intersectionality, Identity Politics and Violence against Women of Color’, *Stanford Law Review*, 43.6 (1991), 1241–99; Crenshaw, *On Intersectionality: Essential Writings of Kimberlé Crenshaw* (New York: The New Press, 2017).

25 Patricia Hill Collins and Sirma Bilge, *Intersectionality* (Cambridge: Polity Press, 2016), p. 2.

26 Harvey Weinstein is an American film director that was charged with sexual assault and rape. In all, 80 women in the film industry accused him, and he was sentenced, in March 2020, to 23 years in prison.

27 ‘Don’t Forget the Sea’, *I May Destroy You*, BBC1, Crave, 3:27–3:30.

28 ‘Doxing’, in *Cambridge Dictionary* [online] <https://dictionary.cambridge.org/dictionary/english/doxing> [accessed 31 May 2023].

29 Rebecca Thorn, ‘“They allow us to name something we know is wrong”: The new words defining sexual abuse’, BBC, 6 December 2022 <www.bbc.com/news/world-latin-america-63811380> [accessed 31 May 2023].

30 Milena Popova, *Sexual Consent* (London: MIT Press, 2019), pp. 28–36.

31 Cited in Tracy Nicholls, *Dismantling Rape Culture: The Peacebuilding Power of ‘Me Too’* (London: Routledge, 2021), p. 26.

32 Hua Hsu, ‘Stuart Hall and The Rise of Cultural Studies’, *New Yorker*, 17 July 2017 <www.newyorker.com/books/page-turner/stuart-hall-and-the-rise-of-cultural-studies> [accessed 31 May 2023].

33 Stuart Hall, ‘Notes on Deconstructing “The Popular”’, in *People’s History and Socialist Theory*, ed. by Raphael Samuel (London: Routledge, 1981), pp. 227–239 (p. 239).

34 Mary Daly and Emily Culpepper, *Rape Culture* (n.d./15 February 2021) <https://www.cambridgedocumentaryfilms.org/filmsPages/rapeculture.html> [accessed 31 May 2023].

35 Lynette Rice, ‘We need to talk about rape on *Outlander*’, *Entertainment Weekly*, 10 May 2020 <https://ew.com/tv/outlander-season-5-finale-claire-shocker/> [accessed 31 May 2023].

36 Ibid.

37 Alex E. Jung, ‘How Michaela Coel Wrote *I May Destroy You’s* Dreamlike Ending’, *Vulture*, 24 August 2020 <www.vulture.com/2020/08/i-may-destroy-you-ending-explained-michaela-coel.html> [accessed 31 May 2023].

Bibliography

Ali, Lorraine, ‘Commentary: A new HBO series rethinks the sexual assault survivor story. It’s brave and charming’, *Los Angeles Times*, 14 June 2020 <www.latimes.

com/entertainment-arts/tv/story/2020-06-14/hbo-i-may-destroy-you-michaela-coel-commentary> [accessed 31 May 2023]
Atler, Alexandra, 'A Crop of New Novels About Race and Racism Find Freedom in Satire', *New York Times*, 19 July 2022 <www.nytimes.com/2022/07/17/books/new-novels-race-racism-satire.html> [accessed 31 May 2023]
Aziz, Fatima, 'Warning not to walk alone after woman pulled into bushes and sexually assaulted in Burnley', *LancsLive*, 24 July 2022 <https://www.lancs.live/news/lancashire-news/warning-not-walk-alone-after-24575202> [accessed 31 May 2023]
Bodenheimer, Rebecca, 'The best and worst portrayals of sexual assault on TV', *Datebook* <https://datebook.sfchronicle.com/movies-tv/the-best-and-worst-portrayals-of-sexual-assault-on-tv> [accessed 22 May 2022]
Collins, Patricia, and Sirma Bilge, *Intersectionality* (Cambridge: Polity Press, 2016)
Coel, Michaela, *Misfits: A Personal Manifesto* (New York: Henry Holt and Company, 2021)
Crenshaw, Kimberlé, 'Mapping the Margins: Intersectionality, Identity Politics and Violence against Women of Color', *Stanford Law Review*, 43.6 (1991), 1241–99
Crenshaw, Kimberlé, *On Intersectionality: Essential Writings of Kimberlé Crenshaw* (New York: The New Press, 2017)
Crown Prosecution Services, Rape and Sexual Offences, 'Chapter 6: Consent' (2021) <https://www.cps.gov.uk/legal-guidance/rape-and-sexual-offences-chapter-6-consent> [accessed 31 May 2023]
Daly, Mary, and Emily Culpepper, *Rape Culture* (n.d./15 February 2021) <https://www.cambridgedocumentaryfilms.org/filmsPages/rapeculture.html> [accessed 31 May 2023]
Davis, Angela, *Women, Race & Class* (New York: Vintage Books, 1983)
Dery, Mark, 'Black to the Future', in *Flame Wars: The Discourse of Cyberculture*, ed. by Mark Dery (Durham, NC: Duke University Press, 1994), pp. 179–222
'Doxing', in *Cambridge Dictionary* [online] <https://dictionary.cambridge.org/dictionary/english/doxing> [accessed 31 May 2023]
Edinburgh Television Festival, 'Michaela Coel | James MacTaggart Lecture | Edinburgh TV Festival 2018', online video recording, YouTube, 23 August 2018 <www.youtube.com/watch?v=odusP8gmqsg&ab_channel=EdinburghTelevisionFestival> [accessed 31 May 2023]
Ehrlich, Susan, 'Intersections of Race and Gender in Sexual Assault Trials', *Gender and Language*, 15.3 (2021), 430–38
Hall, Stuart, 'New Ethnicities', in *Black Film British Cinema*, ed. by Erica Carter (London: Institute of Contemporary Arts, 1988), pp. 27–31
Hall, Stuart, 'Notes on Deconstructing "The Popular"', in *People's History and Socialist Theory*, ed. by Raphael Samuel (London: Routledge, 1981), pp. 227–39
Henry, Nicola, and Anastasia Powell, 'Framing Sexual Violence Prevention: What Does it Mean to Challenge a Rape Culture', in *Preventing Sexual Violence*, ed. by Nicola Henry and Anastasia Powell (London: Palgrave Macmillan, 2014), pp. 1–21
Hsu, Hua, 'Stuart Hall and The Rise of Cultural Studies', *New Yorker*, 17 July 2017 <www.newyorker.com/books/page-turner/stuart-hall-and-the-rise-of-cultural-studies> [accessed 31 May 2023]
Hurd, Heidi, 'The Moral Magic of Consent', *Legal Theory*, 2 (1996), 121–46
I May Destroy You, BBC1, Crave
Jung, Alex E., 'How Michaela Coel Wrote *I May Destroy You*'s Dreamlike Ending', *Vulture*, 24 August 2020 <www.vulture.com/2020/08/i-may-destroy-you-ending-explained-michaela-coel.html> [accessed 31 May 2023]

Lafleur, Ingrid, 'Afrofuturism' (n.d.) <https://www.ingridlafleur.com/afrofuturism> [accessed 31 May 2023]

Lawrie, Eleanor, 'I thought rape isn't something that happens to men', BBC, 22 July 2021 <https://www.bbc.com/news/uk-england-57892684> [accessed 31 May 2023]

Love, Bettina L., *We Want to Do More Than Survive: Abolitionist Teaching and the Pursuit of Educational Freedom* (Boston: Beacon Press, 2020)

Maxwell, Zerlina, 'Rape Culture Is Real', *Time*, 17 March 2014 <https://time.com/40110/rape-culture-is-real/> [accessed 31 May 2023]

Metz, Julia, Kristen Myers, and Patricia Wallace, '"Rape is a Man's Issue": Gender and Power in the Era of Affirmative Consent', *Journal of Gender Studies*, 30 (2021), 52–65

'Michaela Coel: "If you don't show it, it can be erased"', *British GQ*, online video recording, YouTube, 26 October 2020 <www.youtube.com/watch?v=SZ_0_DEe_2A&ab_channel=BritishGQ> [accessed 31 May 2023]

Nicholls, Tracey, *Dismantling Rape Culture: The Peacebuilding Power of 'Me Too'* (London: Routledge, 2021)

Pometsey, Olive, 'How Michaela Coel Transformed her Trauma Into the Year's Best TV Show', *GQ*, 10 July 2020 <https://www.gq.com/story/michaela-coel-i-may-destroy-you-interview> [accessed 31 May 2023]

Popova, Milena, *Sexual Consent* (London: MIT Press, 2019)

Projansky, Sarah, *Watching Rape: Film and Television in Postfeminist Culture* (London: New York University Press, 2001)

Rape Crisis England & Wales, 'Statistics about sexual violence and abuse' (n.d.) <https://rapecrisis.org.uk/get-informed/statistics-sexual-violence/> [accessed 31 May 2023]

Rape Crisis England & Wales, 'Stealthing=Rape' (n.d.) <https://rapecrisis.org.uk/get-informed/types-of-sexual-violence/what-is-rape/#stealthing> [accessed 31 May 2023]

Rape Crisis England & Wales, 'What is Sexual Consent' (n.d.) <https://rapecrisis.org.uk/get-informed/about-sexual-violence/sexual-consent> [accessed 31 May 2023]

Reality Check, 'Why do so few rape cases go to court?', BBC, 27 May 2022 <https://www.bbc.com/news/uk-48095118> [accessed 31 May 2023]

Rice, Lynette, 'We need to talk about rape on *Outlander*', *Entertainment Weekly*, 10 May 2020 <https://ew.com/tv/outlander-season-5-finale-claire-shocker/> [accessed 31 May 2023]

'Subcultures and Sociology', *Afrofuturism* (n.d.) <https://haenfler.sites.grinnell.edu/afrofuturism/#:~:text=Though%20there%20are%20many%20definitions,black%20cultural%20lens%20in%20common> [accessed 31 May 2023]

Talbot, Mary, *Language and Gender*, 3rd edn (Cambridge: Polity Press, 2020)

Taub, Amanda, 'Rape culture isn't a myth. It's real, and it's dangerous', *Vox*, 15 December 2014 <https://www.vox.com/2014/12/15/7371737/rape-culture-definition> [accessed 31 May 2023]

Thorn, Rebecca, '"They allow us to name something we know is wrong": The new words defining sexual abuse', BBC, 6 December 2022 <www.bbc.com/news/world-latin-america-63811380> [accessed 31 May 2023]

Willis, Malachi, and Tiffany L. Marcantonio, 'Sexual Consent Norms in a Cross-Sectional National Sample of the UK', *Journal of Public Health*, 45 (2023), 84–90

8 Beyond 'Yes, and…'

Consent in the Theatre Arts Curriculum, On-stage and Off

Natashia Lindsey and Emily A. Rollie

When discussing consent within wellness and sex curricula, 'no' is considered a complete sentence. However, for theatre artists whose work depends on collaboration and physical contact, the word 'no' is often perceived as blocking the creative process. Many theatre artists, particularly actors, are trained to respond to requests in the classroom or rehearsal with the improvisation adage 'yes, *and…*' – a response that not only presumes the artist's agreement but also not-so-subtly asks them to offer something *beyond* agreement. While a useful technique to support improvisation and building scenes, this 'yes, and' approach can, especially when considered alongside the power dynamics of director-actor or teacher-student relationships, be detrimental to emerging artists who are developing their creative tools, voices, and artistic agency.

Furthermore, some older models and philosophies of actor training, often reliant on techniques such as emotional memory and personal experience, have, in an effort toward rigour and under the auspices of professionalisation, pushed young artists in ways that do not recognise the diversity of their lived experiences or their boundaries.[1] In the preface to *Acting in the Academy*, Peter Zazzali explores the evolution of acting pedagogies and urges theatre educators to re-consider the approaches of early hierarchical models that reduced actors' agency and instead find ways to move 'towards empowering our students to become "successful" artists and individuals' – a philosophy that resonates deeply with practices in consent-based, anti-racist theatre pedagogies.[2] Considering this 'yes, and…' adage alongside contemporary training models prompts us to ask: How far can and should artists – particularly emerging artists – be asked to explore in the name of training?

In recent years, greater awareness of culturally and trauma-informed teaching practices, such as those discussed by Zaretta Hammond, have prompted further discussion surrounding expectations of students' willingness to sacrifice their boundaries and personal needs for artistic work.[3] These and related conversations surrounding equity and diversity in theatre were further ignited by the 2017 surge of #MeToo (a movement originally created by activist Tarana Burke in 2006 to support survivors of sexual violence) alongside the 'We See You, White American Theatre' demands, published in June 2020.[4] Together, they amplified the need to re-examine theatrical training models and pedagogies, prompting

DOI: 10.4324/9781003365082-10

arts educators and professionals to interrogate assumptions around what artists 'must' do to secure a role and create art.

It is into this discourse that we – activist artist-scholar-teachers who are dedicated to student-centred learning and brave spaces that support liberatory learning, as espoused by bell hooks and Paulo Freire – aim to intervene. In this essay, we explore the emergence of consent-based practices within the theatre industry and curricula, and we examine the overlap between consent-based practices and anti-racist work in theatre and performance. While many of these approaches rightfully focus on supporting actors' agency and work in performance spaces, we ultimately advocate for the inclusion of consent-based practices not only in performance classrooms but also in literature, history, and all arts classes to create more inclusive, anti-racist, and brave creative spaces.

Throughout this essay, we draw on our work and experiences as artist-scholar-teachers – Dr Rollie as an intimacy choreographer, theatre director, and scholar of gender studies and Dr Lindsey as dramaturg and activist-scholar with expertise in the intersections of race and performance. Within these areas of training and expertise, we also recognise our own lived identities and positionalities as cis, white women writing from US socio-cultural frames of reference. Our work intends to support progressive consent-based and anti-racist approaches to theatre pedagogies and artistic creation; however, we acknowledge that many existing publications and the field of intimacy itself tend to promote the voices of white artists and scholars. Thus, we aim to amplify the work of artist-scholars of the global majority and acknowledge as well as actively investigate our own whiteness and privilege as part of this work and activist pedagogy.[5]

Consent in Theatre and Performance: Surrounding Context

In the wake of the #MeToo movement and the 2016 #NotInOurHouse campaign (which began following revelations of longstanding abuse and inequity in prominent Chicago theatres), the role of the intimacy director emerged. *American Theatre*'s Carrie Purcell attributes the first published use of the term 'intimacy choreography' to Tonia Sina's MFA thesis, which outlines the need for intimacy choreography similar to fight or dance choreography on stage to support actors' safety.[6] Now a professionally recognised role and burgeoning area of artistic expertise, intimacy professionals (also called intimacy directors, choreographers, and coordinators, depending on the modality in which one works) are increasingly included on artistic production teams and theatre department faculties.

Organisations such as Theatrical Intimacy Education (TIE, US), Intimacy Directors and Coordinators (IDC, US), National Society of Intimacy Professionals (NSIP, Canada), and others offer workshops and advocate for recognition and incorporation of consent-based practices in professional theatre; regional intimacy organisations such as Pacific Northwest Theatrical Intimacy Collective have also emerged to educate local artists and organisations regarding consent-informed and consent-forward theatrical practices.[7] Additionally, intimacy professionals such as Ann James and Intimacy Coordinators of Color (ICOC, US) specifically focus on the ways that race and the experiences of artists of the global majority deeply inform consent and intimacy.

While much work happens in rehearsals, publications have also increased. Chelsea Pace's book *Staging Sex* offers practical tools to help artists articulate consent and establish boundaries that both ensure personal agency and collaborative contributions. Similarly, the *Journal of Consent-Based Performance*, launched in Spring 2022, is an open access, peer-reviewed journal dedicated to exploring, expanding, and documenting these practices.

Despite these and other emerging resources, it is essential to acknowledge that consent-based work in theatre is not new. Rather, this work has often been done under other auspices. In the introduction to a special issue of *Journal of Dramatic Theory and Criticism*, Joy Brooke Fairfield connects consent-based work to the legacies and often invisible labour of activists and communities outside theatre. While intimacy professionals and the field have begun to codify and formalise these techniques, they are 'informed by the cultural work done toward normalizing negotiation of consent within scenarios of *actual* sex, efforts that have been historically led by survivors of sexual violence, sex workers, porn performers, sexuality activists, and members of kink communities'.[8] Further, in educational contexts, activists and educators such as bell hooks have long written about 'education as the practice of freedom' and have advocated for teaching models that empower students and recognise the liberatory potential of learning and growth.[9] Our work is indebted to and in conversation with the ideas and paths forged by these forebears.

In higher education specifically, many theatre and performance departments have begun to incorporate consent-based practices into their production work and, in some cases, across their department. This cross-curricular incorporation of consent-based practices is an initiative that our Theatre Arts Department at Central Washington University has consciously and intentionally taken on over recent years – an initiative that is a central, experiential piece of this essay and shapes the strategies we offer to incorporate consent-based and anti-racist approaches across arts curricula.

Consent-based Practice in Theatre Practice and Training

Consent-based practices in theatrical classrooms often begin with and focus on the work of actors, and rightfully so, as performers are often the 'most vulnerable in the room'.[10] The power hierarchy developed as part of the emergence of the role of the contemporary director, combined with the 'yes, and' ideology that informs many actors' approaches and training, means that the power dynamics of the theatre space often place the actor literally and figuratively in the spotlight, yet minimise their creative agency. If an actor has been trained and conditioned to respond with 'yes, and' to any request made of them by a director, that actor, to be perceived as a 'good' collaborator, is unlikely to refuse the request, however supportive or approachable that director may be.

Moreover, the actor's job – to use their bodies and voices to portray a character's behaviour amid extraordinary circumstances and dramatic conflict – inherently places them in vulnerable positions. This vulnerability is exacerbated by other stressors such as financial pressures to accept artistic work and expectations around perceived 'professional' conduct. Those intertwined elements often leave actors with minimal power in artistic spaces. Further, when power dynamics and hierarchies are considered alongside the complex interplay of intersectional identities, privilege, and biases, actors of the global majority, actors who are women, transgender, or non-binary, actors who are fat or disabled, or actors who experience neurodivergence become further marginalised, are increasingly vulnerable, and have less opportunity and ability to articulate artistic agency.

In educational spaces, the power dynamics of teacher-student relationships further complicate student-artists' ability to consent. Although many arts instructors strive toward student-centred learning and democratic classrooms, educational structures continue to support discrepancies in power. As Pace writes, 'student actors are particularly vulnerable – their directors assign not only roles but grades and recommendation letters'.[11] Increasingly, instructors are adopting more accessible, equitable, and inclusive grading practices such as 'ungrading' (described by progressive educators such as Susan Blum and Jesse Stommel), which focus on the process of learning and revision rather than a singular summative assessment; however, the perception of grades as the measure of success persists, placing instructors in positions of institutional power. Further, grades are often tied to financial aid, an element extraneous to the classroom that nevertheless heightens students' focus on 'good' grades. No matter how much teachers might emphasise a shared classroom community, we cannot give our power away. However, we can recognise the power dynamics at play and strive to mitigate or decentralise them. Consent-based, anti-racist pedagogical approaches are integral parts of that process.

In addition to discussions about the relations of power by theorists such as Michel Foucault, Nancy Hartsock, and Judith Butler, numerous sociological and psychological studies outline the complex dynamics of power.[12] Most agree that power can be organised into two broad categories: formal and informal. Per John French and Betram Raven, power within these two broad categories can be delineated into five different types: referent, expert, legitimate, reward, and coercive.[13] Of the five types, referent and expert power are informal and can be held by anyone in the room; however, legitimate, reward, and coercive power are tied to formal power – in other words, the power conferred upon someone due to their position or rank in an organisation. For teachers and/or artistic mentors, we hold positions involving informal *and* formal power; we are often the more experienced in the room (expert power), we are structurally in a position as a teacher/director (legitimate power), and we have control over grades, required in some manner by universities (reward power). All can, if used negatively, funnel into coercive power.

Power also informs how young artists physically respond in the rehearsal and learning space. According to Stephen Porges's articulation of polyvagal theory, when someone is placed in stressful moments (such as being on stage), if they do not have tools to regulate their nervous system or are placed into moments of perceived trauma, they physically and neurologically respond with protective, survival instincts: the automatic, defensive responses of the brain take over, restricting executive function and critical thought.[14] Frequently, we label these survival instincts as fight, flight, or freeze; however, a fourth response, which therapist Pete Walker termed 'fawn' (agreeing quickly and automatically to anything asked), is also important to recognise, particularly for student artists.[15] None of these survival states allows fully informed consent, much less the creative or critical thought teachers and artists hope to encourage. Thus, consent-based pedagogies offer tools for students to articulate a need and to engage in open dialogue around collaborators' needs (such as utilising open questions like 'how does that work for you?' rather than closed questions implying a yes answer).

Power dynamics of consent are also tied to boundaries, the recognition of which is important for teachers, artists, and mentors. In Theatrical Intimacy Education's pedagogy, boundaries are categorised into four areas: physical, personal, professional, and cultural boundaries.[16] Other systems, such as those articulated in the *Ethics of Touch*, consider categories like physical, emotional, intellectual, sexual, and energetic boundaries.[17] Often, the first – and sometimes only – boundary considered is the physical; however, it is important for artist-educators to recognise how a variety of different boundaries intersect to impact students in the rehearsal and classroom space.

Like consent-based practices, which ask us to recognise varying contexts impacting consent, boundaries vary from person to person and within different contexts.[18] For instance, a student of the global majority might have varying boundaries around reading texts depicting racialised content versus performing and physically embodying those roles. Because of the diverse array of factors that shape and impact student-artists' boundaries, we must consider how consent and boundaries can be supported and practiced in rehearsals and classrooms *and* across the arts disciplines. For instance, in a theatre history seminar, especially one confronting and countering the white, patriarchal, Western-centric narrative of a 'canon', students need tools to explore and articulate their boundaries and, by extension, their consent to engage with the material.

But if we encourage students to voice their boundaries, what if they opt out of learning altogether? This question is often voiced by faculty – many of whom have been trained to support the 'yes, and' mentality themselves. In our experience, encouraging students to voice their boundaries has precisely the opposite effect. Once student-artists recognise their boundaries will be supported and they have space to explore them, they make bolder creative choices. Having a clear framework in which to work at their own pace, according to their needs, allows them greater freedom to explore cognitively and creatively. While perhaps counterproductive to romantic notions of complete creative freedom, consent-based practice and boundary establishment offer *more* agency to *all* collaborators. As Anne Bogart writes, 'limits are a necessary partner in the creative act as well as in the crafting of a successful life'.[19] Thus to begin 'empowering our students' as advocated by Zazzali, we must intentionally incorporate consent-based tools in *all* arts classrooms to increase access and work toward authentically inclusive art-making.[20]

Anti-racist Practice in Theatre Practice and Performance

The publication of 'We See You, White American Theatre' further heightens the need to examine inclusive practices in professional theatres and educational institutions and dovetails with the power imbalances and hierarchical training models that consent-based theatre practices combat. Penned by theatremakers of the global majority, the document illuminated inequities in theatre due to white supremacy and offered a list of demands to move the field toward an anti-racist, more inclusive environment. The creators call for the 'develop[ment] of a new social construct for our work environments that cares for and sustains our artistry and lives'.[21] The demands addressed structures, policies, and the well-being of artists of the global majority in not only professional theatre but also higher education, recognising the import training programmes have as well as their historical complicity in perpetuating coercive cultures. The anti-racist theatre practices and demands outlined by the We See You collective focus on a 'code of conduct' that aims to create a 'transformation of the theatrical ecosystem' – all deeply tied to the work of consent.[22]

Just as consent-based practices address the power dynamics in rehearsal spaces, it is imperative to name and recognise whiteness and white supremacy and the myriad ways they inform theatre work and education. As Sara Ahmed states, whiteness is often 'represented as invisible, as the unseen or the unmarked, as a non-colour, the absent presence or hidden referent, against which all other colours are measured as forms of deviance'.[23] As long as whiteness goes unmarked, it is allowed to function as a 'mythical norm' in which 'the trappings of power reside'.[24] To be clear, whiteness is only invisible to white people.[25] As the title and demands of 'We See You, White American Theatre' demonstrate, whiteness and white supremacy is 'everywhere'.[26]

Consent-based and anti-racist theatre practices must consider how whiteness goes unmarked within our curriculum and pedagogy. Kaja Dunn argues that 'a physical and cognitive dissonance occurs when nonwhite students are taught about "universal" theatre truths and "universal" stories. Universal most often equates to white-Eurocentric'.[27] This universality is neither true nor helpful in creating a welcoming space for people of the global majority who may or may not identify with the truths of these stories. Sharrell D. Luckett and Tia M. Shaffer posit, '(w)hite-ness overtly and covertly pervades the texts and linguistic structures, and those who do not share a white lineage or hue are de-centered, misaligned and exiled from a theatre history that they rightfully co-constructed'.[28] In fact, 'students of color in theatre training programmes often get the message right away that being a successful acting student will involve disappearing themselves, their experiences, their speech and culture, to become a "better trained" actor'.[29] This inequitable, white-centric approach is not limited to the acting classroom and informs the structures and learning environments across the theatrical areas, exacerbating the lack of agency student-artists of the global majority might feel.

A theatre culture that assumes whiteness as the human norm is one that upholds white supremacy on every level. Tema Okun articulates that 'white supremacy culture is the widespread ideology baked into the beliefs, values, norms, and standards of our groups (many if not most of them), our communities, our towns, our states, our nation, teaching us both overtly and covertly that whiteness holds value, whiteness is value'.[30] Edward Taylor notes that 'racism is a normal […] fact of daily life' in the US and 'the assumptions of White [sic] superiority are so ingrained in political, legal, and educational structures that they are almost unrecognizable' by its beneficiaries.[31] The white supremacist characteristics of theatre spaces are any number of 'beliefs, values, norms, and standards' that centre white ways of being, doing, and knowing.[32] Therefore, in addition to considering how consent informs artistic work, theatremakers must interrogate the ways our practices uphold white supremacist culture by marking and decentring whiteness to create a community where everyone's voice, perspective, and experience are acknowledged and incorporated.

According to Okun, paternalism is one aspect of white supremacy culture that appears in workplaces and manifests when those with power in decision-making assume 'they are qualified and entitled to define group standards'.[33] Paternalism emerges in arts classrooms and productions when teachers and directors are positioned as the source of power and knowledge. As mentioned above, teachers cannot give up power, but can manage how power plays out. For instance, we can create a more democratic space by 'always includ[ing] those most affected in the brainstorming and decision-making' by asking for and honouring students' access needs to demonstrate everyone's voice will be heard. We can also develop 'a learning community […] where the stated expectation is that everyone will make mistakes and those mistakes offer opportunities for learning'.[34] Student theatremakers often feel pressure to 'get it right' the first time due to grades, a sense of scarcity in the field, and fear of being labelled as 'hard to work with'. Reframing mistakes as learning opportunities can chip away at the pressure young artists feel due to paternalism.

Theatre also often suffers from a sense of urgency. This urgency, as Okun argues, 'reinforces the idea that we are ruled by time, deadlines, and needing to do things in a "timely" manner' – all of which limits our ability to form relationships with our collaborators and/or students and reduces time needed for intentional decision-making.[35] Furthermore, a sense of urgency can 'reinforce existing power hierarchies' when those in power make hasty decisions due to perceived lack of time. This urgency can lead 'to mental, physical, intellectual, and spiritual burnout and exhaustion'.[36]

Theatre practitioners may recognise these aspects of urgency as part of the production process, and educators may feel urgency as they try to cover all the important material in a term. To combat this, theatremakers and educators can 'learn from past experience how long things take' and create 'realistic workplans based on the lived experience' of those working on the project or taking the class. This re-focuses on the *process* that accounts for everyone in the room and their needs. Furthermore, consent-based practices create the time/space for participants to acknowledge their needs and have them met in the moment – a pause that combats the sense of urgency and allows everyone to 'deliberate with thoughtfulness and intention about the nature of the urgency and the range of options available' to participants.[37]

Unearthing and dismantling racism and white supremacy through structural, systemic means is vital in creating safer spaces for theatremakers of the global majority and, as such, also supports more authentic modes of consent and engagement. This work requires individuals to unlearn their racism and white supremacy. Per Taylor's observation, white supremacy is 'embedded in our political, legal, and educational structures', meaning everyone is susceptible to perpetuating its violence.[38] However, because 'we are not all affected in the same ways' by white supremacy, we have different forms of anti-racist work to do.[39] To this end, in this essay, we are particularly focused on the work that we must do as white theatremakers in the pursuit of anti-racist theatre culture and consent-based practice. This work requires us to listen and learn from scholars, activists, and artists of the global majority such as James Baldwin, Audre Lorde, and Resmaa Menakem, all of whom point out the work white people must do to unlearn and dismantle white supremacy.[40] As white theatremakers and teachers, we must do personal work in decentring our whiteness and unlearning white supremacy. We know this work requires everyone, white folks and people of the global majority, but we also recognise that people of the global majority have been doing the vast majority of this labour and it is time for white artists-scholars-teachers to catch up.

The individual work in recognising the racialised power dynamics at play in mentor-student relationships and examining individual biases and influences of white supremacy is particularly useful for theatre teachers and students, as it also deeply informs the body, much like the embodied work done in theatre. As Resmaa Menakem argues, 'we've tried to teach our brains to think better about race', but white supremacy 'doesn't live in our thinking brains. It lives and breathes in our bodies'.[41] Anti-racist work cannot live only in our brains because racism and racialised trauma have real, lived consequences on the bodies and lives of people of the global majority. To fully consent to and do the work of the theatre – reflecting on and embodying the human experience – we and arts students of all backgrounds must be able to be fully human.

While consent-based practices are often seen as distinct from anti-racist theatre practices, we argue they are inextricably linked. Both are tied to access, specifically access for all. If we can create access in creative spaces by addressing the inequitable, oppressive power structures that exist and embedding tools to promote dialogue, consent, and agency, we can create a holistic way of learning and structuring creative spaces that *presumes* access and offers inclusion and agency to all – a truly liberatory practice per bell hooks.

Incorporating consent-based and anti-racist practices in theatre curricula and pedagogies also offers a more ethical approach to training artists. As Kim Shivley and Susanne Shawyer argue, intimacy practices counter a long, traumatic history in actor training programmes of overlooking boundaries in the name of 'professional training'; thus these are not only more inclusive practices but also more ethical approaches that place teachers and students in a 'relationship of care toward others' – a statement that echoes tenets of care ethics.[42]

To prompt the deep, structural change necessary in both higher education and the professional theatrical industrial complex, anti-racist and consent-forward tools need to be applied *across* classes and *throughout* a department. In our work and collaborations, we have explored ways to bring consent-based and anti-racist practices to our community to create substantial, lasting change in our working structures and pedagogies. We share some of those tools here to offer tangible evidence and applications of the overlapping, interconnected methods of consent-based and anti-racist theatre work.

Consent-based, Anti-racist Practices for Performing Arts Curricula

Institutions, departments, and educational organisations function differently and have unique needs per their specific communities. We offer here best practices and recommendations based on how we incorporate these tools across curricular areas in our work. We encourage readers to consider how these might be adapted and applied in other arts curricula to foster brave learning spaces that encourage dialogue and inclusion.

First, think structurally. How can consent-based *and* anti-racist practices be utilised across disciplinary areas and in different classes, from performance to discussion-based seminars? We incorporate consent tools such as a self-care cue throughout our department to provide a shared language and technique for students and faculty alike to alert their collaborators when they have a need. In many theatrical settings, artists are familiar with terms like 'hold', a word, usually uttered by a stage manager, that pauses action in rehearsal or performance and allows the team to address a technical element of production. The self-care cue has a similar function and shared understanding; however, having a specific word not tied to other terms already in use recognises the import of self-care and articulating consent and boundaries. A common self-care cue, originated by TIE and used in many artistic spaces, is the word 'button' – an active word that encourages artists to imagine pressing a pause button, which does not halt the work but pauses it so the artist can express a need that will help them contribute effectively to the creative process.[43] (A non-verbal alternative to 'button' is a double clap or double tap on the body. This alternative further increases accessibility, as it does not depend on a verbal utterance and can be physically grounding, particularly useful for artists who are neurodivergent.)

Useful in performance classes, which often feature 'in the moment' interactions meriting a brief pause to determine consent, the self-care cue has also been effectively implemented in seminar and literature-based classes such as 'Theatre History' and 'Race and Performance', which grapple with material that can activate students' personal, cultural, or professional boundaries. For example, classes that discuss the racism and colonialism that inform history and theatremaking practices can benefit from the self-care cue. This is especially important for students of the global majority who otherwise may feel unable to pause or stop when material may activate racialised trauma.

If employed across the full department and all classes, the self-care cue becomes part of the shared culture. It can be used in collaborative planning situations (such as production meetings), which are frequently spaces that function under time constraints that lend themselves to urgency – an urgency not always conducive to fully creative or consent-based thought. We have successfully incorporated the self-care cue in our production process as part of safety protocols; all collaborators – students and faculty, actors and technicians, directors and dramaturgs – have the self-care cue and consider it part of addressing and mitigating risk throughout and across the production. By presenting the self-care cue as a professional tool for collaboration and a term understood by all collaborators, more effective, clear communication occurs, creating a more equitable, inclusive, and accessible environment.

Another specific strategy effectively employed for more equitable, anti-racist, and consent-forward structures in learning environments is creating community agreements. Community agreements, guidelines created by the students in a class for that particular term, allow students to consider their own and others' access needs, a term often used in disability justice frameworks to describe what one requires to fully participate in the work.[44] Access needs might include the ability to stand rather than sit during a long time-period, access to gender-inclusive restrooms, or use of alternative text for images on electronic documents to support screen reader use. Community agreements also articulate how this ensemble of students plans to engage with each other and the class/rehearsal content. This may include guidelines for navigating class discussions or holding each other accountable for deadlines and class engagement. Incorporating community agreements and involving student-artists in their creation allows students to articulate their boundaries and needs around content and engagement. They also offer tangible, actionable guidelines to support ambiguous expectations such as 'being respectful'. While creating community agreements can take time, it is important not to give in to the sense of urgency or perceived time scarcity. In her Antiracist Theatre training, artist-activist Nicole Brewer spends a significant amount of time establishing the anti-racist space with access needs, session agreements, and her three guiding principles to 'keep white supremacy from creeping in'.[45] If, as articulated in 'We See You, White American Theatre', we intend to create 'transformative measures guided by principles of self-determination, presence, joy, access, protection, transparency, and integrity', then this structural approach across all areas of theatrical creation is imperative.[46]

Certainly, wholesale, structural change takes time. As Ibram X. Kendi articulates, becoming anti-racist is a constant act, an on-going and active process.[47] Similarly, Theatrical Intimacy Education facilitators regularly advise, 'better is better'.[48] Inspired by Maya Angelou's 'when you know better, do better', this reminds us that any step toward change is necessary and useful.[49] The structural change of embedding consent-based and anti-racist practices in theatre pedagogies is deeply supported by the small endeavours each artist-scholar-teacher takes.[50]

One step may be attending to language used in the classroom. In intimacy direction, best practice is to 'de-load' the process, which includes being mindful of language used to refer to intimate moments as well as actors' bodies.[51] Rather than using a phrase that originates in potentially activating slang or conveys patriarchal, objectifying assumptions about gender or sexuality, intimacy choreographers might use anatomical language such as 'front of chest' or 'front of pelvis'. This attention to language and the sexist, racist, ableist connotations of phrases can be a powerful step toward inclusivity in arts classrooms. It creates opportunities to find 'alternative grammars that do not structurally erase individuals' humanity'.[52] Further, it can become a teachable moment to help students understand the origins and implications of language being brought into creative, learning spaces – the work of not only consent-based but anti-racist practice.

Related to re-framing language, the idea of 'working in draft', a strategy emerging from the work of Nicole Brewer, allows space for creative risk as well as learning and discovering one's boundaries – essential tools in consent-based and anti-racist theatre work. We utilise 'speaking in draft' across classes – from 'Theatre History' and 'Dramaturgy' to 'Acting' and 'Directing' – which mirrors the on-going, iterative process of developing creative ideas and artistic processes. 'Speaking in draft' also emphasises the importance of feedback and opportunities for growth, both necessary to unlearn and dismantle systems of theatrical creation driven by urgency, pressure to consent, and the power of paternalism.

Finally, it is important in consent-based, anti-racist arts work to hold ourselves and others accountable. Intention is not the same as impact, especially as consent and boundaries are contextual and individual. We, teachers and students, are human, and we should learn and help each other learn – especially important in a world and field where language evolves and develops quickly. By using consent tools such as a self-care cue, honouring boundaries (including cultural boundaries that relate to a student-artist's racial or ethnic background), and considering our own biases, we can encourage our students, our collaborators, and ourselves to lean into the discomfort of a challenging conversation, accept the impact of words and actions, and repair harm caused. Moreover, these strategies aid students and faculty in recognising the difference between feeling 'uncomfortable' – something inherent to theatre, for dramatic works require conflict and depict characters' discomfort – and meeting a firm boundary.

Conclusion

In the past decade there have been significant, necessary changes in the field of theatre and performance to work toward more equitable, holistic, trauma-informed modes of creating, teaching, and learning. But this work is not finished, nor should it be. Echoing this volume's call for and articulation of the ways that approaches to consent require dialogue that crosses borders, we urge readers – artists, teachers, and scholars alike – to see the ways that consent-based approaches naturally align with and amplify anti-racist practices and pedagogies. If we incorporate these consent-based practices alongside anti-racist practices, particularly in and across arts curricula, we can initiate long-standing, structural changes in higher education and the theatrical industrial complex that ultimately support all artists and truly build a more collaborative, creative community.

Notes

1 Emotional memory, or affective memory, is a somewhat controversial technique in acting theory and pedagogy. Used in early iterations of Stanislavsky's acting technique, it is most commonly associated with the work of Lee Strasberg. Emotional memory asks actors to become the character, a technique often associated with 'method acting', and draw on personal emotions to bring themselves into the emotional state of the character. Stanislavsky abandoned the use of emotional recall in his later work, recognising the blurred boundary between actor and character, and instead advocated that the actor should use their imagination and physical action to create a believable character.

2 Peter Zazzali, *Acting in the Academy: The History of Professional Actor Training in US Higher Education* (New York: Routledge, 2016), p. xiv.

3 Zaretta Hammond, *Culturally Responsive Teaching and the Brain: Promoting Authentic Engagement and Rigor Among Culturally and Linguistically Diverse Students* (Thousand Oaks: Corwin, 2015).

4 'We See You, White American Theatre' <https://www.weseeyouwat.com/> [accessed 1 August 2022].

5 We draw from the work of Rosemary Campbell-Stephens who coined the term 'Global Majority' in 'Global Majority; Decolonising the language and Reframing the Conversation about Race' (2020) <https://www.leedsbeckett.ac.uk/-/media/files/schools/school-of-education/final-leeds-beckett-1102-global-majority.pdf> [accessed 15 January 2023]. She notes the term decentres whiteness both in naming and in sheer numbers. Acronyms and titles like BIPOC, BAME, and people of colour 'situate whiteness as the norm within their respective local contexts even when the opposite is true'. The people named by these acronyms and titles make up about 80% of the world's population, 'making them the global majority'.

6 Tonia Sina Campanella, 'Intimate Encounters: Staging Intimacy and Sensuality' (unpublished master's thesis, Virginia Commonwealth University, 2006); Carrey Purcell, 'Intimate Exchanges', American Theatre (2018) <https://www.americantheatre.org/2018/10/23/intimate-exchanges/> [accessed 15 July 2022].

7 In most intimacy choreography and theatre discourse, 'consent-based' is the most commonly used term. While there has been some conversation among intimacy organisations and professionals distinguishing between the use of 'consent-based' and 'consent-forward', the terms are often used interchangeably.

8 Joy Brooke Fairfield, 'Introduction: Consent-Based Staging in the Wreckage of History', *Journal of Dramatic Theory and Criticism*, 34.1 (2019), 67–75 (p. 68).

9 bell hooks, *Teaching to Transgress: Education as the Practice of Freedom* (London: Routledge, 1994), p. 11.

10 Theatrical Intimacy Education, 'Best Practices' Workshop. Presented by Theatrical Intimacy Education faculty (Online, August 2020).

11 Chelsea Pace, *Staging Sex: Best Practices, Tools, and Techniques for Theatrical Intimacy* (New York: Routledge, 2020), p. 9.

12 See Foucault, 'The Subject and Power', *Critical Inquiry*, 8.4 (1982), 777–95; Hartsock, 'Foucault on Power: A Theory for Women?', in *Feminism/Postmodernism*, ed. by Linda Nicholson (New York: Routledge, 1990), pp. 157–75; and Butler, *The Psychic Life of Power: Theories in Subjection* (Stanford: Stanford University Press, 1997).

13 John R. B. French and Bertram Raven, 'The Bases of Social Power', in *Studies in Social Power*, ed. by Dorwin Cartwright (Ann Arbor: Institute for Social Research, 1959), pp. 150–67.

14 Stephen Porges, *The Pocket Guide to the Polyvagal Theory: The Transformative Power of Feeling Safe* (New York: Norton, 2017).

15 Pete Walker, *Complex PTSD: From Surviving to Thriving: A Guide and Map for Recovering from Childhood Trauma* (New York: Azure Coyote, 2013).

16 Theatrical Intimacy Education, 'Best Practices' Workshop (Online, August 2020).

17 Ben E. Benjamin and Cherie Sohnen-Moe, *Ethics of Touch*, 2nd edn (Tucson: Sohnen-Moe Associates, 2014), p. 28.

18 Ibid., p. 27.

19 Anne Bogart, *What's the Story?: Essays about Art, Theatre, and Storytelling* (Abingdon: Routledge, 2014), p. 54.

20 Zazzali, p. xiv.

21 'We See You, White American Theatre'.

22 Ibid.

23 Sara Ahmed, 'Declarations of Whiteness: The Non-performativity of Anti-racism', *borderlands* e-journal 3.2 (2004) <https://rbb85.wordpress.com/2014/08/24/declarations-of-whiteness/> [accessed 10 January 2023].

24 Audre Lorde, *Sister Outsider: Essays and Speeches* (New York: Crossing Press, 1984), p. 116.

25 Ahmed.

26 Ibid.

27 Kaja Dunn, 'Hidden Damage: When Uninformed Casting and Actor Training Disregard the Effect of Character Embodiment on Students of Color', *Theatre Symposium*, 27 (2019), 68–79 (p. 71).

28 Sharrell D. Luckett and Tia M. Shaffer, *Black Acting Methods: Critical Methods* (New York: Routledge, 2017), p. 1.

29 Dunn, pp. 71–72.

30 Tema Okun, 'What it is', White Supremacy Culture, 2022 <https://www.whitesupremacyculture.info/what-is-it.html> [accessed 1 August 2022].

31 Edward Taylor, 'A Critical Race Analysis of the Achievement Gap in the United States: Politics, Reality, and Hope', *Leadership and Policy in Schools*, 5.1 (2006), 71–87 (p. 73).

32 Okun, 'What it is'.
33 Tema Okun, 'One Right Way', *White Supremacy Culture*, 2022 <https://www.whitesupremacyculture.info/one-right-way.html> [accessed 1 August 2022].
34 Ibid.
35 Ibid.
36 Ibid.
37 Ibid.
38 Taylor; Okun, 'What it is?'.
39 Ibid.
40 See James Baldwin, 'Unnameable Objects, Unspeakable Crimes', *The White Problem in America*, ed. by *Ebony* editors (Chicago: Johnson, 1966), pp. 174–75; Lorde; Resmaa Menakem, *My Grandmother's Hands: Racialized Trauma and the Pathway to Mending our Hearts and Bodies* (Las Vegas: Central Recovery Press, 2017).
41 Menakem, pp. 4–5.
42 Susanne Shawyer and Kim Shivley, 'Education in Theatrical Intimacy as Ethical Practice for University Theatre', *Journal of Dramatic Theory and Criticism*, 34.1 (2019), 87–104 (p. 89).
43 Pace, p. 17.
44 Patricia Berne, Aurora Levins Morales, David Langstaff, and Sins Invalid, '10 Principles of Disability Justice', *WSQ: Women's Studies Quarterly*, 46.1–2 (2018), 227–30.
45 Nicole Brewer, 'Anti-Racist Theatre: A Foundational Course'. Presented by Nicole Brewer / Conscientious Theatre Training (Online, August 2020).
46 'We See You, White American Theatre'.
47 Ibram X. Kendi, *How to Be an Antiracist* (New York: One World, 2019), p. 23.
48 Theatrical Intimacy Education, 'Best Practices' Workshop.
49 Oprah Winfrey, *The Powerful Lesson Maya Angelou Taught Oprah*, online video, Oprah.com, 19 October 2011 <https://www.oprah.com/oprahs-lifeclass/the-powerful-lesson-maya-angelou-taught-oprah-video> [accessed 14 August 2022] (Time stamp 2:27).
50 Brewer.
51 Theatrical Intimacy Education, 'Best Practices' Workshop.
52 Kari Barclay, 'Impersonal Intimacies: Reflections on Desexualized Language in Intimacy Choreography', *Journal of Consent Based Performance*, 1.1 (2022), 24–34 (p. 30).

Bibliography

Ahmed, Sara, 'Declarations of Whiteness: The Non-performativity of Anti-racism', *borderlands e-journal*, 3.2 (2004) <https://rbb85.wordpress.com/2014/08/24/declarations-of-whiteness/> [accessed 10 January 2023]

Baldwin, James, 'Unnameable Objects, Unspeakable Crimes', in *The White Problem in America,* ed. by *Ebony* editors (Chicago: Johnson, 1966), pp. 174–75

Barclay, Kari, 'Impersonal Intimacies: Reflections on Desexualized Language in Intimacy Choreography', *Journal of Consent Based Performance*, 1.1 (January 2022), 24–34

Benjamin, Ben E., and Cherie Sohnen-Moe, *Ethics of Touch*, 2nd edn (Tucson: Sohnen-Moe Associates, 2014)

Berne, Patricia, Aurora Levins Morales, David Langstaff, and Sins Invalid, '10 Principles of Disability Justice', *WSQ: Women's Studies Quarterly*, 46.1–2 (2018), 227–30

Bogart, Anne, *What's the Story?: Essays about Art, Theatre, and Storytelling* (New York: Routledge, 2014)

Brewer, Nicole, 'Anti-Racist Theatre: A Foundational Course', presented by Nicole Brewer / Conscientious Theatre Training (Online, August 2020)

Butler, Judith, *The Psychic Life of Power: Theories in Subjection* (Stanford: Stanford University Press, 1997)

Campanella, Tonia Sina, 'Intimate Encounters: Staging Intimacy and Sensuality' (unpublished master's thesis, Virginia Commonwealth University, 2006) <https://scholarscompass.vcu.edu/cgi/viewcontent.cgi?article=2070&context=etd> [accessed 1 August 2022]

Campbell-Stephens, Rosemary, 'Global Majority; Decolonising the language and Reframing the Conversation about Race' (2020) <https://www.leedsbeckett.ac.uk/-/media/files/schools/school-of-education/final-leeds-beckett-1102-global-majority.pdf> [accessed 15 January 2023]

Dunn, Kaja, 'Hidden Damage: When Uninformed Casting and Actor Training Disregard the Effect of Character Embodiment on Students of Color', *Theatre Symposium*, 27 (2019), 68–79

Fairfield, Joy Brooke, 'Introduction: Consent-Based Staging in the Wreckage of History', *Journal of Dramatic Theory and Criticism*, 34.1 (2019), 67–75

Foucault, Michel, 'The Subject and Power', *Critical Inquiry*, 8.4 (1982), 777–95

French, John R. B., and Bertram Raven, 'The Bases of Social Power', in *Studies in Social Power*, ed. by Dorwin Cartwright (Ann Arbor: Institute for Social Research, 1959), pp. 150–67

Hammond, Zaretta, *Culturally Responsive Teaching and the Brain: Promoting Authentic Engagement and Rigor Among Culturally and Linguistically Diverse Students* (Thousand Oaks: Corwin, 2015)

Hartsock, Nancy, 'Foucault on Power: A Theory for Women?', in *Feminism/Postmodernism*, ed. by Linda Nicholson (New York: Routledge, 1990), pp. 157–75

hooks, bell, *Teaching to Transgress: Education as The Practice of Freedom* (London: Routledge, 1994)

Kendi, Ibram X., *How to Be an Antiracist* (New York: One World, 2019)

Lorde, Audre, *Sister Outsider: Essays and Speeches* (New York: Crossing Press, 1984)

Luckett, Sharrell D., and Tia M. Shaffer, *Black Acting Methods: Critical Methods* (New York: Routledge, 2017)

Menakem, Resmaa, *My Grandmother's Hands: Racialized Trauma and the Pathway to Mending our Hearts and Bodies* (Las Vegas: Central Recovery Press, 2017)

Okun, Tema, 'One Right Way', *White Supremacy Culture*, 2022 <https://www.whitesupremacyculture.info/one-right-way.html> [accessed 1 August 2022]

Okun, Tema, 'Sense of Urgency', *White Supremacy Culture*, 2022 <https://www.whitesupremacyculture.info/urgency.html> [accessed 1 August 2022]

Okun, Tema, 'What it is', *White Supremacy Culture*, 2022 <https://www.whitesupremacyculture.info/what-is-it.html> [accessed 1 August 2022]

Pace, Chelsea, *Staging Sex: Best Practices, Tools, and Techniques for Theatrical Intimacy* (New York: Routledge, 2020)

Purcell, Carrey, 'Intimate Exchanges', *American Theatre*, 2018 <https://www.americantheatre.org/2018/10/23/intimate-exchanges/> [accessed 15 July 2022]

Porges, Stephen, *The Pocket Guide to the Polyvagal Theory: The Transformative Power of Feeling Safe* (New York: Norton, 2017)

Shawyer, Susanne, and Kim Shivley, 'Education in Theatrical Intimacy as Ethical Practice for University Theatre', *Journal of Dramatic Theory and Criticism*, 34.1 (2019), 87–104

Taylor, Edward, 'A Critical Race Analysis of the Achievement Gap in the United States: Politics, Reality, and Hope', *Leadership and Policy in Schools*, 5.1 (2006), 71–87

Theatrical Intimacy Education, 'Best Practices' Workshop. Presented by Theatrical Intimacy Education faculty (Online, August 2020)

Walker, Pete, *Complex PTSD: From Surviving to Thriving: A Guide and Map for Recovering from Childhood Trauma* (New York: Azure Coyote, 2013)

'We See You, White American Theatre' <https://www.weseeyouwat.com/> [accessed 1 August 2022]

Winfrey, Oprah, *The Powerful Lesson Maya Angelou Taught Oprah*, online video, Oprah.com, 19 October 2011 <https://www.oprah.com/oprahs-lifeclass/the-powerful-lesson-maya-angelou-taught-oprah-video> [accessed 14 August 2022]

Zazzali, Peter, *Acting in the Academy: The History of Professional Actor Training in US Higher Education* (New York: Routledge, 2016)

Part III

Lived Experience and (Authorial) Expressions

9 Re-establishing Identity through Testimony

The Rape Survival Narratives of Mary Hays's *The Victim of Prejudice* (1799) and Mary Wollstonecraft's *Maria, or The Wrongs of Woman* (1798)

Megan Batterbee

Content Notes: This chapter contains references to sexual assault, rape and abortion within the eighteenth-century novel.

Dramatic shifts in the understanding of consent are reflected in the eighteenth-century novel. Seduction stories from the early part of the century frequently focused on dominant male sexual agency forcing women into sexual compliance under the guise of consensual relations. Katherine Binhammer argues that the genre 'pauses in the moment where seduction represents neither women's erotic agency nor their passive victimization but a complex in-between where anything is possible'.[1] By the end of the eighteenth century, the novel form was developed by Mary Wollstonecraft in *Maria, or the Wrongs of Woman* (1798) and Mary Hays's *The Victim of Prejudice* (1799) to present an arena in which the testimony of victimised women, regardless of social position, marital status, and financial security, can reach an audience willing to listen to their struggles.[2] Enlightenment feminist novelists built on the intervention of Samuel Richardson's novel *Clarissa, or The History of a Young Lady* (1747–48), engaging with popular notions of consent to challenge assumptions of female sexual culpability and establish a new framework of consent in public conversation. There is a dissonance between the experiences of women of all classes to sexual violence, something significant when exploring the limitations of individual consent. This study explores perceptions of consent; what is possible to assume, and what is actually depicted, in sexual encounters within eighteenth-century novels. I consider John Locke's philosophical interrogation of consent when scrutinising blurred lines between consent and coercion, or to use Paul Ricouer's words, 'what distinguishes persuasion from flattery, from seduction, from threat – that is to say, from the subtlest forms of violence?'[3]

DOI: 10.4324/9781003365082-12

The Contemporary Context of Consent

As Ellen Meiksins Wood indicates, 'consent has historically been so capacious that it has been able to accommodate everything from absolutism to democracy'.[4] It is the conflict between one person's view of consent and another's interpretation of how far that consent reaches that causes harm to vulnerable women within the eighteenth-century novel. Samuel Johnson defined consent as follows in *A Dictionary of the English Language* (1755):

> To Con'sent. *V. n.* [*consentio,* Latin.]
> 1. To be of the same mind; to agree.
> 2. To co-operate to the same end.
> 3. To yield; to give consent; to allow; to admit.[5]

The fact that the *Dictionary* offers three distinct definitions of consent is significant and not lost on eighteenth-century women novelists, who used their fiction to tease out the devastating implications of this ambiguity. This final definition of consent in Johnson's *Dictionary* depends upon, and further reinforces, a disparity of power between men and women. Without a singular definition of consent that all characters acknowledge and to which they adhere, I argue that it is impossible for any female character within the eighteenth-century novel to know what they are consenting to, as there is no way of proving the intentions of another. This allows consent to become, as Toni Bowers argues, 'little more than an intermittently useful pretence to be manipulated when it suits [and] discounted when it does not'.[6]

However, being unable to consent freely does not necessarily make these women powerless, nor their attempts to consent to their own destinies entirely futile. Locke argues that 'there may be Thought, there may be Will, there may be Volition, where there is no *Liberty*'.[7] It is the manner in which women express their thoughts, will, and volition that is important; their ability to communicate their will is often the only power that women have. As Mithu Sanyal reasons, 'consent doesn't mean free will: it *means free will under certain given social circumstances*'.[8] One of the few social circumstances in which women's consent is actively sought is in courtship; 'that women can be taught how to avoid ruin implies they have sexual agency, even if only in the negative, the will and the knowledge to say "no"'.[9] Thus, courtship within the eighteenth-century novel becomes the platform on which a woman's ability to consent is probed, analysed, and found wanting as an effective means of promoting their own interests and protecting themselves from harm.

Clarissa Harlowe and Consent

Samuel Richardson's *Clarissa,* critical in the development of the rape narrative, does not give Clarissa Harlowe the liberty to consent in the moment of her ruination, nor the knowledge of what has befallen her; unconsciousness negates any thought, will, or volition that Clarissa could hope to express to prevent Lovelace's assault. As Terry Eagleton argues, Richardson leaves the moment of violation 'wholly unrepresented [...] the hole at the centre of the novel towards which this huge mass of writing is sucked only to sheer off again'.[10] The erasure of rape from a novel entirely centred around it disconcerts the reader; the contemporary audience understood that the increase in violence towards Clarissa anticipates rape, so why exclude it from the narrative?

Clarissa Harlowe's most powerful weapon against Lovelace's continual assaults is that she is able to eloquently, passionately, and clearly refuse his advances verbally and in the letters that create this epistolary novel. Lovelace's solution to Clarissa's continual resistance is to remove Clarissa's agency by drugging and raping the unconscious heroine, which accomplishes nothing; 'why say I, *completed?* when the *will,* the *consent*, is wanting' (my emphasis).[11] Clarissa can only disclose the truth of her victimisation posthumously because, as Anna Clark asserts, the 'rape victim who tried to gain redress [...] broke the taboo on female speech about sex'.[12] Clarissa's lack of knowledge of what has happened to her is heartbreakingly depicted in Paper X. This is Clarissa's attempt to piece together her violation using literary allusions and fragments of poetry; 'Fool! to that body to return, / Where condemn'd and destin'd is to *mourn*'.[13] Clarissa mourns what is lost; her thought, her will, her volition in the moment of violation. Because she has never encountered the vocabulary to characterise her trauma, the most eloquent of women is reduced to ventriloquising the works of others. Clarissa's power returns in her testimony from beyond the grave. In her last will and testament, Clarissa declares that 'I am nobody's' and hopes that Lovelace will not have 'insisted upon viewing *her dead* whom he ONCE before saw in a manner dead'.[14] This is the most explicitly and obviously she can refute the assumptions of her complicity with Lovelace's schemes, restate her testimony, and reiterate that the singular moment of sexual violation was not consensual.

Mary Wollstonecraft's *Maria, or The Wrongs of Woman* (1798) and Mary Hays's *The Victim of Prejudice* (1799) sought to develop the rape narrative beyond Clarissa's fantastical anomaly, foregrounding the moment of violation and the knowledge of female ruin as the critical, inevitable steps in their heroines' suffering. Wollstonecraft and Hays bring the rape narrative into the world they and their first readers inhabited, a world they recognise as dangerous for all women. One contemporary reviewer of *The Victim of Prejudice* publicly stated that 'if the sad vicissitudes of this tale be founded on fact, happily they are of a very uncommon description'.[15] Yet, as Sanyal argues, 'hardly any subject is as full of contradictions as rape. What other fear lurks behind every corner yet is at the same time supposed to be as rare as being hit by lightning?'[16] Hays directly addressed the issues in Richardson's depiction of his eponymous heroine as a martyr:

> The character of Clarissa, a beautiful superstructure upon a false and airy foundation can never be regarded as a model for imitation. It is the

portrait of an ideal being, placed in circumstances equally ideal, far removed from common life and human feelings.[17]

Neither Wollstonecraft nor Hays wish to emulate a perfect archetype of virtuous femininity like Clarissa as the survivors of sexual assault in their novels. Instead, they create flawed characters from different social classes that have to learn to live with their trauma in a world that conspires to disbelieve their suffering. Hays and Wollstonecraft seek to break the taboo around disclosing sexual trauma during their heroines' lifetimes, using verbal and written testimony of suffering as proof of the social, physical, and spiritual damage they endure as a result of violated consent.

Learning and Demonstrating Consent

Hays and Wollstonecraft expose the myriad ways in which consent could be misunderstood in their novels. With this in mind, it is helpful to consider where fictional heroines learn the meaning of consent, and how to apply this practically. A woman's education defines a female character before she reaches an age where she is judged by her sexual availability, which is why the value of an appropriate female education became a priority of Enlightenment feminism.[18] As 'the practice of giving one's rational consent is something that must be learned in the context of the family', the formative years of the heroines of these novels are critical in their emotional development.[19] In Hays's *The Victim of Prejudice,* Mary Raymond's education produces a paradoxical character who believes herself independent, yet relies entirely on her guardian's judgement. Her guardian argues that the 'canker most pernicious to every virtue is *dependence*', yet this is exactly what he fosters in his ward.[20] Similarly, Wollstonecraft's Maria Venables learns that she is more valued the more she mimics her uncle's ideas: 'I grew dear to him in proportion as I imbibed his sentiments'.[21] Sandra Sherman argues that men take 'delight in [the] deferral of rational autonomy' in women; something established at home and developed in romantic relationships.[22] Women are taught that their value lies in their utility to men, both personally and as a pawn in establishing future connections.

Consent within the romantic relationships entered into by the heroines of *The Victim of Prejudice* and *Maria, or The Wrongs of Woman* deserves greater scrutiny because it depicts the shift in loyalty from one patriarchal figure to another: from guardian to lover, blood ties to marital allegiance. The abuses within this transition of power concern both the authors and modern consent scholars alike. Katie Barclay notes that, to eighteenth-century authors, 'the act of falling in love involved overcoming the female will, an inherently violent act, preparing her for the loss of her identity expected within marriage'.[23] The key problem with eighteenth-century marriage is that a woman's consent to marriage becomes seen as perpetual consent to the edicts of the husband.[24] As William Blackstone contemporarily commented on eighteenth-century legislation, particularly in regards to the practice of coverture, 'the husband and wife are one person in law: that is, the very being or legal existence of the woman is suspended during the marriage'.[25]

One way in which Wollstonecraft and Hays show the subjugation of women within romantic attachments is through coercion, contemporarily defined by Johnson as 'that which has the power of restraint [and] the authority of restraining by punishment'.[26] I see coercion and tyranny depicted within both of these novels, yet Lockean tyranny implies that men and women are valued equally within society. Coercion accurately depicts the power imbalance at play between a husband and wife within an eighteenth-century marriage. Coercion is an inescapable factor of relationships faced by both heroines, a linguistic and physical tool used by men to erode a woman's sense of independence. Eighteenth-century legal precedent not only allows but enforces this eradication of female liberty. Both Wollstonecraft and Hays confront the absurdity of the law that allows this kind of exploitation, questioning why men should be allowed to control women through legally protected 'moderate correction' when this power so regularly leads to abuse, both in courtship and marriage.[27] Wollstonecraft in particular confronts the legal precedent that 'a man cannot grant anything to his wife [...] for the grant would suppose her separate existence'.[28] Lockean tyranny is defined as the application of power beyond right, something frequently depicted within the coercive romantic relationships of Wollstonecraft's and Hays's characters. This being the case, where does a romantic partner's right over a woman begin and end? While Locke draws the distinction between those that purposefully or accidentally harm through tyranny, Wollstonecraft and Hays show that the impact is the same: women suffer.

In *The Victim of Prejudice*, William Pelham displays the controlling behaviours that are normalised and excused as proofs of love, rather than dangerous attempts to control. William continually tests Mary's faith by demanding proofs of her devotion: 'Your friendship for me is weak, since you will hazard nothing to oblige me'.[29] To William, Mary's devotion is contingent with her obedience to his will. This comes to a head when Mary considers separation. William accuses Mary of being 'a victim of control, you have tamely submitted to a tyranny that your heart disavows' because she sees reason in her guardian's advice that they separate.[30] The irony is that William is acting tyrannically by perceiving tyranny as the reason Mary no longer conforms to his demands. Mary imparts her awareness of the sacrifice she is making in refusing to bow to the pressure of William's commands: 'I dare not, will not, consent to involve in my destiny the man I love, – to become at once his misfortune and his curse'.[31] This is the most powerful statement of intent that Mary can make; proving her unwavering devotion by defying his wishes. Binhammer argues that Mary acting with integrity in this moment does not indicate a lack of emotion: rather that Hays 'suggests that women know better than men how to properly manage and control their sexual feelings'.[32] On learning the truth of her parentage from her guardian (her mother's seduction, engagement in sex work, criminal conviction for murder, and death sentence), Mary knows that she can no longer consider herself a viable romantic partner for William.

Wollstonecraft depicts the cruelty of coercion within marriage in *Maria, or The Wrongs of Woman*. Wollstonecraft explores the hopelessness of living within a marriage where a woman 'could not become the friend or the confident of [her] husband', and navigates the moral compromises necessary for women to adapt to marriage under these circumstances.[33] With conjugal relations an expected part of marriage, Maria feels that 'women ought to, and can love their husbands, because it is their duty' even when it is distasteful to her.[34] She conceives her daughter during a time in which she finds him physically repugnant; 'the greatest sacrifice of my principles in my whole life, was the allowing my husband again to be familiar with my person', yet the result brings her 'the unutterable pleasure of being a mother'.[35] Maria's initial consent to marriage becomes a perpetual consent to conjugal relations, because this is what society of the time understands marital consent to be. Maria compromising her bodily autonomy is the price she has to pay for having consented to marriage within eighteenth-century society.

Yet, Maria draws a clear line when her husband oversteps his 'right' to her body. Maria rejects propositions from a man not only aware of her marriage, but a close associate of her husband. When she discovers her husband's knowledge and active encouragement of his friend's seduction, Maria sees her marriage as over. Nowhere in her marriage vows, or within societal expectation, is Maria supposed to consent to other men's sexual advances at her husband's command. George sees Maria's compliance as inevitable for the sole reason that because they are married, she must obey his will, and has to this point. However, by commodifying Maria's sexuality into something that can be purchased rather than consensually bestowed, George goes beyond the scope of a marriage to which Maria is willing to consent. *He* may be entitled conjugally, but he has no right to compromise Maria's chastity for money. George has broken their marital vows, both by attempting to barter Maria's chastity for money, and because of his 'indulgences [...] entirely promiscuous, and of the most brutal nature'.[36] George sees the marital bed as 'the best place for husbands and wives to end their differences', yet cannot seduce Maria into compliance because she no longer considers herself his wife: 'he affected to take my silence for consent [...]. He attempted to pull me into the chamber, half joking. But I resisted.'[37]

Legally, George is completely within his right to curtail Maria for this 'pretty farce'[38] because, as a husband 'is to answer for [a wife's] misbehaviour, the law thought it reasonable to intrust him with this power of restraining her, by domestic chastisement'.[39] Maria's testimony to her daughter details her desperate quest to maintain independence from her husband until she can seek the protection of her uncle. Maria feels justified in ending her marriage because she did not consent to being a sexual pawn for her husband's advancement. Although Maria sees power in her ability to identify herself as a free woman, legally she cannot separate from him as 'Marriage had bastilled me for life'.[40] Maria consented to marriage; when she is no longer experiencing the marriage she consented to, she is unable to escape. Her testimony is documentary proof of her justifications for separation, and condemns the societal injustice that leads to her imprisonment in a mental asylum, because 'the courts of law will still permit a husband to restrain a wife of her liberty'.[41] The audience of Maria's testimony is clear: 'There may be advocates for matrimonial obedience, who, making a distinction between the duty of a wife and of a human being, may blame my conduct. – To them I write not'.[42]

Victimisation and Defiance

The privilege for consent to be acknowledged and respected is not afforded to all women: 'Eighteenth-century justice [...] made no pretence of protecting a woman from sexual assault unless she could claim the status of the sexual property of a patriarch'.[43] Where Clarissa Harlowe's vocal resistance is empowered by the threat of retribution from her family, Hays instead depicts the fruitlessness of Mary Raymond's consistent verbal non-consent when there is no risk of her perpetrator suffering repercussions. Being alone in the world, with all support systems gone, Mary Raymond is vulnerable to exploitation. Mary lives in a society where 'heavy-handed "flirtation" and pressure, especially where there were inequalities of power, was normal, blurring the dividing lines between consent and force'.[44] Verbal resistance is her only means of repelling Osborne, yet Mary is 'shocked and frightened by a brutality of manner so novel and unexpected'.[45] Because this perpetrator buys into the concept that 'rape hinges on the heroine's rather than the hero's behaviour', Osborne's actions seem not only inevitable, but actively encouraged by the woman he victimises.[46] Mary is fully conscious at the moment she 'suffered a brutal violation'.[47] However, Mary cannot publicly acknowledge the fact of her sexual ruination and plead her innocence because Osborne has planted notions of her consent in the minds of the community; 'where chastity is invisible, loss of it demanded the woman's invisibility'.[48] In an environment where 'ignorance never equals sexual innocence', society and her rapist conflate Mary's knowledge with her culpability.[49]

Mary refuses to act in any way that suggests active participation in seduction: 'abandoned to infamy and covered with shame, virtue still maintains her empire in my bosom'.[50] Therefore, she refuses to accept Osborne's money or proposals of marriage after the rape, as this would be perceived as retroactive consent. For Mary, virtue can be found seeking 'honest labour, the bread of independence'.[51] However, her attempts to create an identity outside of her perpetrator's gaze are continually thwarted by Osborne's determination to possess her, and society's reluctance to allow a compromised woman an honest means of earning a living. William Pelham's offensive offer to become his mistress compounds her suffering, only made because Mary is already 'ruined' by Osborne's assault. However, William does not anticipate the vehemence of Mary's rejection: '*it is virtue only that I love better than William Pelham*' (original emphasis).[52] Mary's supposed consent to Osborne, and the rape itself, has tarred the perception of her in society, yet it has not changed Mary's thought, her will, her volition. The knowledge that she did not consent to Osborne's attack empowers her, allowing her to maintain her internal sense of righteousness and reject the improper advances of others (who, luckily for her, prove less resolute than Osborne).

Mary Wollstonecraft first addresses the issues that are faced by lower-class victims of sexual violence through Jemima, initially the gaoler then the confidante of Maria Venables in the asylum. Jemima's story is fundamentally different to that of Maria Venables and Hays's Mary Raymond; Mary and Maria are haunted by a single determined perpetrator, whereas Jemima's life is plagued with multiple predators that take sexual advantage of her. Though Maria Venables has resources while fleeing from her husband (wealthy family and support in her quest for divorce), Jemima is thoroughly aware of the danger faced by a woman of no means.

> How often have I heard […] in conversation, and read in books, that every person willing to work may find employment? […] with respect to women, I am sure of its fallacy, unless they will submit to the most menial bodily labour; and even to be employed at hard labour is out of the reach of many, whose reputation misfortune or folly has tainted.[53]

Jemima speaks from experience. Jemima is raped in her first servant position. The brutality of the moment is viscerally described to Maria; he 'contrived to be alone in the house with me, and by blows – yes; blows and menaces, compelled me to submit to his ferocious desire; and to avoid my mistress's fury, I was obliged in future to comply'.[54] Jemima thinks herself 'a slave, a bastard, a common property' because she has been brutalised multiple times by multiple perpetrators through her life.[55] When she can no longer sustain herself as a washerwoman, there is only one option available to a woman with no family or honest means of survival. Jemima endures the full spectrum of sex work, from working the streets to becoming the kept woman of 'a worn-out votary of voluptuousness', because there is no choice but to do this to survive.[56]

There are marked similarities in the histories of Wollstonecraft's Jemima and Hays's Mary Raymond. Both are born outside of wedlock and are the children of seduction in which the mother is deserted and dies prematurely. Both face the stigma of illegitimacy, and feel the moral ramifications of the sins of the mother, assumed to possess the temperament predisposed to infamy. Both are tormented by sexually aggressive men. Both are refused entry into honest employment as a means of escaping inevitable destitution. Both are the last of their familial lines. However, while the orphaned Mary is left to die alone because her network of guardians and friends die during the course of her troubles, Jemima takes steps to actively end her line with her.

Pregnant with the product of her master's assaults and dismissed from her position, Jemima feels a sense of kinship between herself and her unborn child: 'I know not why I felt a mixed sensation of despair and tenderness, excepting that, ever called a bastard, a bastard appeared to me an object of the greatest compassion in creation'.[57] She aborts the pregnancy *because* she feels this kinship; she would not wish her situation on another as 'life had been a curse to me'.[58] The abortion allows Jemima a moment of bodily autonomy in which she has power. Jemima did not consent to the conception of her child; neither does she consent to raise the child into a life as cruel as hers. Wollstonecraft's open and frank depiction of abortion in this novel would have shocked a contemporary reader, yet Jemima's moving reasoning behind her decision justifies her choice to Maria, Darnford, and the reader, all captivated by her verbal testimony.[59] Again, Jemima is only able to consent in the negative; she can end the pregnancy, and with it, the generational trauma she has had to endure, and refuses to pass on to her child.

Conclusion: The Value of Testimony

These verbal and written testimonies of suffering, created after trauma as 'the only tool a survivor has to prove a crime has occurred is her own testimony', seek to give the contemporary eighteenth-century reader the vocabulary distinctly lacking from Clarissa Harlowe's narrative.[60] Mary Raymond's written account of her suffering, left in the prison cell where she presumably dies, denotes the inevitable struggles of a woman left friendless, penniless, and vulnerable due to sexual predation. Unable to gain respectable employment, Mary contracts debts she is incapable of paying (something that the law *can* prosecute), and is imprisoned. Here, she writes a testimony of her suffering at the hands of the world which can no longer accommodate her. Mary Raymond states that 'I *have lived in vain!* unless the story of my sorrows should kindle in the heart of man, in behalf of my oppressed sex, the sacred claims of humanity and justice' (original emphasis).[61] Her woes reveal society's prejudice towards a victimised woman trying to survive in a world designed to exile her. Maria Venables's incomplete account depicts the abuses of consent women face both inside and outside of matrimony. Wollstonecraft's novel collates the experiences of women of lower social classes that Maria encounters in her struggle to escape the clutches of her husband to create a wider impression of the universal female experience. Maria creates a memoir designed to educate her daughter in the compromises necessary to survive in a world designed to oppress womankind. Both Mary and Maria are subjected to, and learn of, horrific violations of consent (whether social, sexual, or physical), and find solace through the sharing of their life stories in an attempt to stop this pattern of abuse continuing through future generations of women.

Contemporary criticism of Hays took an apologist stance to the perpetrators within the rape survival narratives: 'unable to control his passions, he at least shews every willingness to repair the injurious consequences of *their* indulgence', again demonstrating a societal assumption of complicity between victim and perpetrator.[62] Sir Peter Osborne is not prosecuted for rape, Jemima's master has no repercussions for his actions, George Venables remains justified in incarcerating his wife: these crimes, and many others, remain largely unacknowledged and unpunished by society. Even in terms of divine retribution, the Richardsonian alternative to legal justice, there is no satisfactory conclusion; no Lovelace seeking death to punish himself, no avenging relatives ready to defend the honour of the ruined. Instead, as Colleen Fenno argues, Wollstonecraft 'anticipates the restorative value that victim testimony may offer for both the individual and the community'.[63]

Wollstonecraft's Jemima and Maria Venables, and Hays's Mary Raymond, represent a tiny proportion of the women struggling to survive in a society designed to despise their existence. In verbalising their trauma, sharing their experience in the public sphere, and documenting their experiences for the benefit of other women, these characters attempt to leave a record of their suffering so that they have made a mark on the world. In a society where 'Women could not publicly protest rape, for they were forbidden to speak about sex at all', these characters are exceptional in their dedication to finding a sympathetic audience to listen to their plights.[64] Within *The Wrongs of Woman* and *The Victim of Prejudice*, we encounter so many women beyond the principal characters who suffer from the brutality of the patriarchal world; Mary Raymond's mother, Mrs Neville's decline into insanity after the death of her husband, the landlady left financially destitute by a philandering husband, the pregnant mistress that publicly commits suicide when deserted, the washerwomen left no alternative but to toil for a pittance, and many others that lack the ability to tell their own story. While these characters hear fragments of each other's lives, there is no archive for their stories to be preserved, no repository for them to share their trauma. Wollstonecraft and Hays establish the foundation of this archive with these novels. The tragedy of *The Wrongs of Woman* is that it is incomplete, leaving the reader with 'a melancholy delight in contemplating these unfinished productions of genius' because Wollstonecraft's own story ended too soon.[65] Within the novel, rather than their testimony being concluded by the death of the heroine, as is the case within Richardson's *Clarissa,* these heroines create an ongoing manuscript, a testament to their continual suffering, first from personal violation, then from the repercussions of publicly voicing their own distress and the collective trauma that women suffer. Mary Wollstonecraft and Mary Hays create this space in which women can tell their stories, complete or incomplete, testimonies of experience and life. Mary Hays wrote that the novel should have a similar effect in the real world as the testimony of her heroine had in the fictional world:

> Fictitious histories, in the hands of persons of talents and observation, might be made productive of incalculable benefit; by interesting curiosity, and addressing the common sympathies of nature, they pervade all ranks; and, judiciously conducted, would become a powerful and effective engine of truth and reform.[66]

The intervention of *The Wrongs of Woman* and *The Victim of Prejudice* in consent studies is that they become the first novels of their kind, in which collective experience of violations of consent, of trauma, of rape, have an audience willing to learn from their characters' sorrows and apply those lessons to the society in which they themselves live. Hays and Wollstonecraft become the advocates they themselves see as necessary to create change. The message within their novels, that these stories need an audience, becomes a metatextual cry to the readership of the Enlightenment feminist novel of the late eighteenth-century. *We*, the reader, should strive to make the change that these novels show is so desperately needed in society. We become the next inmate of Mary Raymond's prison cell, finding her testimony, desperate for the legal system to recognise its own incompetence. We become the asylum dweller listening to Jemima's history. We become Maria's daughter, learning from her mother 'to gather the instruction, the counsel, which is meant rather to exercise than influence your mind'.[67] By that same logic, Wollstonecraft and Hays imagine their testimony presented in an arena which surpasses any established law of man because their testimony is indisputable; creating a court that could not exist in the eighteenth century, one that is worthy of their testimony. Here, both the contemporary and modern readership receive the testimony of persecution in the form of the novel, evaluate criminality for ourselves as it is experienced, and pass judgement when we close the book. Today, we still possess a legal system that rarely effectively prosecutes sex crimes: the criminal system of the twenty-first century is 'a very blunt instrument for a very intricate operation'.[68] As individuals, there is little we can do to instigate systemic change, but, as a readership, we can believe testimony; something more meaningful to a survivor of trauma.

Notes

1 Katherine Binhammer, *The Seduction Narrative in Britain, 1747–1800* (Cambridge: Cambridge University Press, 2009), p. 8.

2 The Enlightenment feminist movement centred marriage reform and the improvement of female education as critical issues which needed to be addressed for the improvement of women's status in society. Revolutionary works in this field include Wollstonecraft's *A Vindication of the Rights of Woman with Strictures on Moral and Political Subjects* (1792) and Hays's *Appeal to the Men of Great Britain in Behalf of Women* (1797), building on the works of earlier (proto-)feminist writers such as Mary Astell and Catharine Macaulay.

3 Paul Ricoeur, *The Rule of the Metaphor: The Creation of Meaning in Language* (London: Routledge, 2003 [1977]), p. 11.

4 Ellen Meiksins Wood, 'Locke against Democracy: Consent, Representation and Suffrage in the Two Treatises', *History of Political Thought*, 13.4 (1992), 657–89 (p. 663).

5 Samuel Johnson, *A Dictionary of the English Language* (London: printed by W. Strahan, for J. and P. Knaptor; T. and T. Longman; C. Hitch and L. Hawes; A. Millar; and R. and J. Dodsley, 1755), 'consent'.

6 Toni Bowers, *Force or Fraud: British Seduction Stories and the Problem of Resistance, 1660–1760* (Oxford: Oxford University Press, 2011), p. 266.

7 John Locke, *An Essay Concerning Human Understanding* (Oxford: Clarendon Press, 1975 [1689]), p. 238.
8 Mithu Sanyal, *Rape: From Lucretia to #MeToo* (London: Verso, 2019), p. 160.
9 Binhammer, *The Seduction Narrative*, p. 23.
10 Terry Eagleton, *The Rape of Clarissa* (Oxford: Blackwell, 1982), p. 61.
11 Samuel Richardson, *Clarissa, or The History of a Young Woman* (London: Penguin, 1985 [17487–49]), p. 888 (Letter 261).
12 Anna Clark, *Women's Silence, Men's Violence: Sexual Assault in England, 1770–1845* (London: Pandora Press, 1987), p. 59.
13 Abraham Cowley, *The Mistress*, 'The Despair', L32–33, in Samuel Richardson, *Clarissa*, p. 893 (Paper X).
14 Richardson, *Clarissa*, p. 1413 (Letter 507).
15 *Critical Review, or Annals of Literature*, 26 (May–August 1799), 450–52 (p. 452).
16 Sanyal, *Rape*, p. 3.
17 Mary Hays, 'On Novel Writing', *Monthly Magazine* (Sept. 1797), 180–81 (p. 180).
18 Mary Wollstonecraft and Mary Hays write extensively about the need for adequate and appropriate education for women beyond the two novels that are the focus of this study. Other works include Wollstonecraft's *Thoughts on the Education of Daughters: With Reflections on Female Conduct, in the More Important Duties of Life* (1787) and Hays's 'Improvements Suggested in Female Education', *Monthly Magazine*, 3 (March 1797), 193–95.
19 Richard Ashcraft, *Locke's Two Treatises of Government* (London: Allen & Unwin, 1987), p. 158.
20 Mary Hays, *The Victim of Prejudice* (Letchworth: Broadview Literary Texts, 1998 [1799]), p. 38.
21 Mary Wollstonecraft, *Maria, or The Wrongs of Woman* (Oxford: Oxford University Press, 2009 [1798]), p. 114.
22 Sandra Sherman, 'Feminization of Reason', *Centennial Review*, 41.1 (1997), 143–72 (p. 156).
23 Katie Barclay, 'From Rape to Marriage: Questions of Consent in Eighteenth-Century Britain', in *Interpreting Sexual Violence, 1660–1800*, ed. by Anne Greenfield (New York: Routledge, 2016), 35–44 (p. 36).
24 Something that did not end in the eighteenth century; marital rape was only criminalised in 1991 in England, Scotland, and Wales.
25 William Blackstone, *Commentaries on the Laws of England, Book the First* (Dublin: printed for John Exshaw, Henry Saunders, Samuel Watson, and James Williams, 1766), p. 430.
26 Johnson, *Dictionary*, 'coercion'.
27 Blackstone, p. 432.
28 Ibid., p. 430.
29 *The Victim of Prejudice*, pp. 12–13.
30 Ibid., p. 52.
31 Ibid., p. 79.
32 Katherine Binhammer, 'Thinking Gender with Sexuality in 1790s' Feminist Thought', *Feminist Studies*, 28.3 (2002), 667–90 (p. 673).
33 *The Wrongs of Woman*, p. 129.
34 Ibid., p. 135.
35 Ibid., p. 136.
36 Ibid., p. 129.
37 Ibid., p. 146.
38 Ibid., p. 147.
39 Blackstone, p. 430.
40 *The Wrongs of Woman*, p. 137.
41 Blackstone, p. 433.

42 *The Wrongs of Woman*, p. 144.
43 Clark, p. 58.
44 Greg Durston, 'Rape in the Eighteenth-Century Metropolis: Part 2', *British Journal for Eighteenth-Century Studies*, 29.1 (2006), 15–31 (p. 23).
45 *The Victim of Prejudice*, p. 14.
46 Sarah Purdie and Sarah Oliver, 'William Frend and Mary Hays', *Women's Writing*, 17.1 (2010), 93–110 (p. 101).
47 *The Victim of Prejudice*, p. 117.
48 Marilyn L. Brooks, 'Mary Hays's *The Victim of Prejudice*: Chastity Re-Negotiated', *Women's Writing*, 15.1 (2008), 13–31 (p. 22).
49 Laurie Langbauer, *Women and Romance: The Consolations of Gender in the English Novel* (Ithaca, NY: Cornell University Press, 1990), p. 97.
50 *The Victim of Prejudice*, p. 127.
51 Ibid., pp. 119–20.
52 Ibid., p. 127.
53 *The Wrongs of Woman*, p. 102.
54 Ibid., p. 96.
55 Ibid., p. 98.
56 Ibid., p. 99.
57 Ibid., p. 96.
58 Ibid., p. 97.
59 Although Jemima's master is the one to procure the abortive solution, Jemima chooses to take it in this moment, and not when under pressure earlier in the novel.
60 Camille Haisell, '"Imprudent Sluts" & "Sober Gentlemen": Testimonial Injustice in Rape Trials at the Old Bailey, 1720–1742', *Ascendant Historian*, 6.1 (2019), 76–89 (p. 78).
61 *The Victim of Prejudice*, p. 174.
62 *Analytical Review*, N.S.I (January–June 1799), p. 328 [my emphasis].
63 Colleen Fenno, 'Testimony, Trauma, and a Space for Victims: Mary Wollstonecraft's *Maria: Or the Wrongs of Woman*', *Nineteenth-Century Gender Studies*, 8.2 (2012) <https://www.ncgsjournal.com/issue82/fenno.html> [accessed 31 May 2023].
64 Clark, p. 130.
65 William Godwin, 'Preface', in Wollstonecraft, *The Wrongs of Woman*, p. 65.
66 Hays, 'On Novel Writing', p. 181.
67 *The Wrongs of Woman*, p. 111.
68 Sanyal, *Rape*, p. 167.

Bibliography

Anonymous, *Analytical Review*, N.S.I (January–June 1799), 326–29

Anonymous, *Critical Review, or Annals of Literature*, 26 (May–August 1799), 450–52

Ashcraft, Richard, *Locke's Two Treatises of Government* (London: Allen & Unwin, 1987)

Barclay, Katie, 'From Rape to Marriage: Questions of Consent in Eighteenth-Century Britain', in *Interpreting Sexual Violence, 1660–1800*, ed. by Anne Greenfield (New York: Routledge, 2016), pp. 35–44

Binhammer, Katherine, *The Seduction Narrative in Britain, 1747–1800* (Cambridge: Cambridge University Press, 2009)

Binhammer, Katherine, 'Thinking Gender with Sexuality in 1790s' Feminist Thought', *Feminist Studies*, 28.3 (Fall 2002), 667–90

Blackstone, William, *Commentaries on the Laws of England, Book the First* (Dublin: printed for John Exshaw, Henry Saunders, Samuel Watson, and James Williams, 1766)

Bowers, Toni, *Force or Fraud: British Seduction Stories and the Problem of Resistance, 1660–1760* (Oxford: Oxford University Press, 2011)
Brooks, Marilyn L., 'Mary Hays's *The Victim of Prejudice*: Chastity Re-Negotiated', *Women's Writing*, 15.1 (2008), 13–31
Clark, Anna, *Women's Silence, Men's Violence: Sexual Assault in England, 1770–1845* (London: Pandora Press, 1987)
Durston, Greg, 'Rape in the Eighteenth-Century Metropolis: Part 2', *British Journal for Eighteenth-Century Studies*, 29.1 (2006), 15–31
Eagleton, Terry, *The Rape of Clarissa* (Oxford: Blackwell, 1982)
Fenno, Colleen, 'Testimony, Trauma, and a Space for Victims: Mary Wollstonecraft's *Maria: Or the Wrongs of Woman*', *Nineteenth-Century Gender Studies*, 8.2 (2012) <https://www.ncgsjournal.com/issue82/fenno.html> [accessed 31 May 2023]
Godwin, William, 'Preface', in Mary Wollstonecraft, *Maria, or The Wrongs of Woman* (Oxford: Oxford University Press, 2009 [1798])
Haisell, Camille, '"Imprudent Sluts" & "Sober Gentlemen": Testimonial Injustice in Rape Trials at the Old Bailey, 1720–1742', *Ascendant Historian*, 6.1 (2019), 76–89
Hays, Mary, 'On Novel Writing', *Monthly Magazine* [September 1797]
Hays, Mary, *The Victim of Prejudice* (Letchworth: Broadview Literary Texts, 1998 [1799])
Johnson, Samuel, A Dictionary of the English Language; in Which the Words Are Deduced From Their Originals and Illustrated in Their Different Significations by Examples From the Best Writers. To Which Are Prefixed, a History of the Language, and an English Grammar, 2 vols (London: printed by W. Strahan, for J. and P. Knaptor; T. and T. Longman; C. Hitch and L. Hawes; A. Millar; and R. and J. Dodsley, 1755)
Langbauer, Laurie, *Women and Romance: The Consolations of Gender in the English Novel* (Ithaca, NY: Cornell University Press, 1990)
Locke, John, *An Essay Concerning Human Understanding* (Oxford: Clarendon Press, 1975 [1689])
Purdie, Sarah, and Sarah Oliver, 'William Frend and Mary Hays', *Women's Writing*, 17.1 (2010), 93–110
Richardson, Samuel, *Clarissa, or The History of a Young Woman* (London: Penguin, 1985 [1747–1748])
Ricoeur, Paul, *The Rule of the Metaphor: The Creation of Meaning in Language* (London: Routledge, 2003 [1977])
Sanyal, Mithu, *Rape: From Lucretia to #MeToo* (London: Verso, 2019)
Sherman, Sandra, 'Feminization of Reason', *Centennial Review*, 41.1 (1997), 143–72
Wollstonecraft, Mary, *Maria, or The Wrongs of Woman* (Oxford: Oxford University Press, 2009 [1798])
Wood, Ellen Meiksins, 'Locke against Democracy: Consent, Representation and Suffrage in the Two Treatises', *History of Political Thought*, 13.4 (1992), 657–89

10 'A Skin of One's Own'

Decolonising Traumatic Testimony and the Poetics of Wholeness

Arya Thampuran

Content Notes: This chapter contains references to practices of skin cutting and references to blood.

> First they made the whole skin area numb, then they took this very long, thin cylinder, like a stick, sharp on one end, and they kind of drilled it into my arm to cut the skin. They took the skin off, it was at the end of this little cylinder thing. It was all inside. They did that twice. Once they took the two pieces of skin off my arm, they put in skin from my sister Oopah and my brother Jake's arm. I got their skin, Jake got my skin and Oopah's, Oopah got Jake's and mine. I think my mom was there. Of course we were her children, so she had to be there, maybe to consent or something like that. But I don't think it was a matter of her consenting, I don't think she thought of it that way.[1]

This is the striking, sobering testimony of Rhoda Katsak, a former subject of colonial medical experimentation on the Inuit people of Canada during the 1950s–70s. In 2019, a group of Inuit filed a lawsuit against the Canadian federal government as subjects of these non-consensual practices, which ranged from blood sampling and cardiac and dental testing to skin grafting and cold exposure.[2] Much of this experimentation operated within questionable bioethical territory: while Canadian assimilationist policy of the time targeted some of these practices at enhancing Inuit health, experiments like cold acclimatisation studies reproduced asymmetrical colonial power dynamics through what Matthew Wiseman dubs 'biological appropriation'. Wiseman defines this as 'the attempted use of Inuit biology for a non-Inuit purpose', predominantly to enhance Canadian professional and military capabilities in the Arctic and develop a body of medical knowledge.[3] This treatment of the vulnerable body, and the production of an extractive body of knowledge, are exposed in Katsak's account of family bound skin grafting; this practice involves the laceration of the individual's skin which was then grafted onto that of a family member.

It is noteworthy that the issue of consent – as pervasive as it is in the contemporary Western legal lexicon and common cultural parlance – lies outside the realm of discursive and medico-legal possibility for Katsak and her

DOI: 10.4324/9781003365082-13

family: 'I don't think it was a matter of [my mother] consenting. I don't think she thought of it that way'. For skin implicated in a social life inscribed by the violently exclusionary borders of coloniality and citizenship, the question of consent – mired as it is in the notion of embodied boundaries – becomes culturally unimaginable and politically inaccessible. Elaine Scarry potently argues that citizenship has been positioned as a means to protect personhood, a formulation that is far from benign: the 'centering of the body in citizenship provides a doorway for the continual entry of political philosophy into medicine', with this social contract and the consensual act underpinned by a particular logic of the 'protection of persons, the prevention of injury'.[4] As Scarry notes, 'injury' has a particular conceptual stronghold in the Western intellectual tradition, prevalent in the writings of Immanuel Kant, Thomas Hobbes, John Locke, and Jean-Jacques Rousseau.

But how do we express consent when it is the very terms of citizenship and participation that deny access to its fundamental premises and the protective sociality of this constructed contract – a contract which, as I seek to demonstrate, is an asymmetrically endowed privilege with particular conditions of access. I am interested here in how these boundaries of consent are mapped through geopolitical borders, how the body reduced to a test subject becomes an unquestioning subject to – and a subject of – this trespassing of biological boundaries. The biological construction of the colonial Other in the Western scientific imaginary is instrumentalised as a justificatory basis for its claims to epistemic and political hegemony; fundamentally, it becomes a bulwark against questionable ethical encroachment into the boundaries of the colonised Other. Indeed, in Inuit testimonies, there is an acknowledgment of the unquestioned intellectual authority of the Qallunaat ('white'). Paul Quassa, one of the Nunavut claimants in the lawsuit, states that he never consented to being experimented on, and that Inuit were compliant and trusting, doing what they were told.[5] The collective statement testifies to this exploitation of asymmetrical power and knowledge structures: 'Canada intentionally instilled in Nunavummit the perception that they must do, without question, as they were told by Canada'. It goes on to state that 'the experiments could not have taken place without the concurrence, consent or collaboration of Canada and Canada took no or inadequate steps to prevent the experiences'.[6]

The colonised body is variously reimagined here: figured as an experimental 'guinea pig' and 'monkey', as these testimonies potently express, a text mined to enhance a body of Western medical knowledge. In its transformation into a medicalised subject and spectacle of technological mediation, the body is denied human status, and by extension, privileged access to the legal standards and social contracts of consent. This underscores a fundamental denial of subjectivity: what is anaesthesised, just like Katsak's 'numb' skin, is the capacity for both self-expression and representation.[7] The question of consent exceeds the possibilities of expression in this context: it is not simply that consent is unsolicited, but that its very premises exceed the parameters – and possibilities – of imagination.

Re-Situating Consent in Reading Practice: A Decolonial and Intersectional Approach

I opened this chapter with Katsak's testimony to reflect the decolonial reading practice for engaging with expressions of embodied distress that I seek to develop in this chapter. If the body becomes a text to be exploitatively mined on the basis of Western rationality, and to enhance a Western epistemic body, then how might the relationship between the textual and corporeal be radically reimagined, such that consent is re-centered as a critical consideration? I situate this intervention within the paradigm of the critical medical humanities, considering what the literary textual encounter might offer by way of a contextually salient account of consent. If the skin has historically been a site where difference is inscribed and the boundaries of the human – and humanity – are constructed, then the skin is also a zone of contestation, where the possibilities and parameters of expression are negotiated. This chapter draws on a body of Western intellectual tradition – philosophical, psychoanalytic, and psychiatric – which has variously defined the healthy biological body, and by extension, regulated the boundaries of a consensual clinical encounter. By prefacing this discussion of colonial experimentation with testimonies from within the Inuit community, the reading practice here fundamentally re-orients the narrative power and representational position from which colonial agents and scripts have historically privileged, and re-invests this agency where it has been forcibly foreclosed. These testimonies become a counter-hegemonic narrative against prevailing epistemic authority, a means of surfacing a suppressed narrative and redressing erasure; principally, it is a means of demanding participation in a national historical narrative dominated by a singular, totalising perspective.

I take skin as a landscape on which to develop this practice because of its multivalent significance and the plural possibilities for reading this affords: the skin has historically been a political signifier of difference, visibly marked as it is by colour, age, hair(lessness), to highlight a few prominent features. The skin has also acquired a particular stronghold in psychoanalytic and psychological theorisations of healthy selfhood: in particular, the *bounded*, 'whole' self. As Claire Stocks notes, Western trauma models equate the whole self with the healthy self.[8] This conception of selfhood interacts in significant ways with contemporary conceptions of consent in legal discourse, rooted in Enlightenment rationality. But if this epistemic mode has historically been instrumentalised to deny human status – and disavow the fundamental humanity – of those who have historically and politically been designated the Other, how might this asymmetrical dynamic be remedied through the textual encounter with the body in distress? What does it mean to read the visibly marked Other on their own terms, to relate to another while being attentive of difference? How do our positionalities as readers inflect this encounter, and how might the boundaries we inscribe between self and other be actively reconfigured? How do we engage with experiences that might lie outside our intelligible or familiar frames of reference?

This chapter explores the epistemic cost – and violence – of containing experiences through frames of reference culturally consonant within a canonical Western intellectual tradition and for a Euro-American audience, but fundamentally discordant with the experiencer and expressor. In this chapter, I consider the colonial testimonies within the Inuit community and in an Igbo literary landscape. This might seem like an unlikely pairing of contexts, but what this comparative analysis hopes to legitimise is the validity of a variety of different testimonial possibilities, ones that might exceed the formal verbal or textual apparatus we are equipped with as literary scholars educated in, and operating within, Euro-American contexts, as I presently am. While I have taken terms like 'West', 'Other', and 'culture' as taxonomic shorthands, these are by no means conceptually conclusive paradigms, and are themselves susceptible to terminological inadequacies; these aggregated, generalised terms do not capture the experiential diversity produced by complex, intersecting metrics of race, sex, class, and socioeconomic status. This contextual pairing, in foregrounding a variety of testimonial forms and expressions of selfhood, seeks to demonstrate the heterogeneity of what I have designated as cultural counter-expressions. It is profoundly committed to a methodological practice of disrupting the binary mode entrenched in Western intellectual tradition – from the Cartesian mind-body dualism that dominates health discourses to the geopolitical constructions of West and Non-West, self and Other. What this approach seeks to further underscore is how culture mediates consent, and to generate the kind of methodological competences in cultural sensitivity necessary for a consensual clinical encounter. I argue that a decolonial and intersectional prism for reading embodied expressions is both a pedagogically and politically urgent issue of consent. An intersectional lens enables us to visualise how structures of oppression operate through and across race, sex, and class (to name but a few identity markers), to produce distinct healthcare asymmetries within marginalised populations. The value – and dire urgency – of such an approach has been sharply registered in the healthcare inequalities that have surfaced during the COVID-19 pandemic; one need only consider the disparities in vaccination uptake amongst black and minority groups. But this is not a new phenomenon; the pandemic simply exposed the entrenched vestiges, and enduring legacies, of medical mistrust in the wake of colonial medical malpractice, from gynaecological experimentation on enslaved black women to the Tuskegee syphilis study on black men.[9]

In *Beyond the Hippocratic Oath: A Memoir on the Rise of Modern Medical Ethics* (2005), Dr John B. Dosseter unpacks the treatment of consent amongst the Inuit community, from his vantage point of a medical practitioner involved in the 1970s experiments. Dossetor sought the help of an intermediary, Dr Otto Shaeffer, a medical practitioner 'trusted' by the Inuit community, to communicate with them in Igloolik and seek 'informed consent'.[10] Kristina Cordasco defines informed consent as a discussion between patient and practitioner, where 'proposed medical treatment, its anticipated consequences, potential risks and benefits, and alternatives' are made transparent.[11] Dosseter notes that in his context, consent was primarily figured as 'community consent', and that this, along with 'individual consent', was solicited from the elders and experiment subjects.[12] But Dosseter expresses a disconcerting ambivalence towards Katsak's testimony, which he includes in his book; this is ambiguity, or perhaps even defensiveness, over the inconsistencies between Katsak's account of unexplained, non-consensual experimentation and his own recollections of research practice. He goes on to retrospectively reflect that 'community consent' is an inadequate basis for medical research ethics, and that more care should be taken in explaining the procedure for informed individual consent instead of relying on the respected elders as an intermediary.

It is worth dwelling on the role of communication in consent discourse here; as Cordasco notes, it is the *dialogue* that constitutes this process, one which purportedly circumvents medical risk and enhances 'patient empowerment'.[13] It would appear that the ambiguities over consent, in Dosseter's estimation, are at least partly attributable to communicative gaps – a fundamental gulf of cultural translation that exceeds linguistic barriers. But it would be remiss, and politically irresponsible, to attribute medical malpractice exclusively to issues of incomprehension and intelligibility; to do so would be to efface a necessary confrontation with the entrenched roots of colonial biological racism that mediates the clinical encounter and its construction of the healthy, consenting subject – and its enduring physical and psychosocial impacts, as the testimonies of these communities express. The interplay between community and individual consent highlights a fundamental organisation of kinship and leadership across the Inuit population, where the individual body is situated within a networked communal body; this is distinct from Western forms of sociality. If the question of consent is largely an individual conception in Western discourse, how do we conceptualise a more contextually meaningful definition sensitive to non-Western modes of understanding selfhood and sociality? This individualism has shaped Western political discourse and its construction of the boundaries of consent; philosophically underpinned by Enlightenment rationality and Hobbesian social contract tradition, 'the conception of consent prioritised today continues to be one which assumes consent to be a medium for the communication of agreement between mutually distinct and disinterested human agents'.[14] This notion of the bounded, healthy self and the existing parameters of consent, however, delimits the possibilities of accessing and engaging with multivalent forms of self-expression and representation that exceed institutionally endorsed forms of hegemonic Western epistemes. This chapter further elaborates the cost of containing consent – as philosophical concept and contemporary liberal practice – within certain institutionalised definitional boundaries.

Consent is treated here as both an embodied and epistemic issue. If the violated boundaries of the body have been the critical linchpin of contemporary sexual consent discourse, then the epistemic violence of possessing bodies within a singular Eurocentric frame must also enter this urgent conversation. How does colonial power permeate and prescribe the body's boundaries, enacting this epistemic violence by silencing indigenous knowledges? And how might epidermal expressions of trauma – sexual and colonial – occupy grey spaces that resist singular claims to explanatory ownership? Consent here is framed through an ethics of reading: I am interested in what testimony can teach us, and how we, as readers, might actively address and redress the issues that plague medical practice in reading expressions of distress. I approach this reading practice as a relational contract: a set of affective commitments underpinning certain political investments. I argue that a decolonial and intersectional approach to engaging with embodied expressions of distress is critical in redressing the epistemic violence of erasure and denial of representational power, rooted in persistent (neo)colonial power structures. As Quassa, one of the claimants in the suit, forcefully articulates, they too deserve 'respect'.[15] How then do we acquire access to a text, engaging with it on terms that are respectful, to borrow Quassa's term? How do we re-dignify these experiences in our reading, when such affective commitments have been foreclosed from the legal and relational considerations that marginalised communities have historically been excluded from? In this chapter, I adopt an approach that is guided by the testifying subject; it reinvests the expressor with the epistemic authority – and perhaps more profoundly, the rights of (self) representation historically foreclosed to *some* bodies. This is a relational dynamic that seeks to redress said power imbalances by radically reconfiguring the subject-object position. In my reading, the skin becomes a site where the politics of possession and place are mapped on both spatial and ontological terms. This practice affirms the right to express – and be read – on one's own terms.

The Skin and the Self: A Psychoanalytic Reading

Psychoanalyst Didier Anzieu theorised that the phantasy of 'having a skin of one's own' is indispensable to psychic autonomy.[16] Anzieu is best known for his seminal work on the Skin-ego, a literalisation of the Freudian 'surface' as the body's surface (or skin itself). Anzieu defines the 'Skin-ego' as a mental image used by the child's Ego during its early stages of development to represent itself as an Ego containing psychical contents, based on its experience of the surface of the body. Anzieu re-centralises the body in psychoanalysis, and psychical functioning more broadly, with his principle that all psychical functions rest anaclitically on the body. Anzieu's relational model, though not without its limitations, is valuable to this discussion because it deconstructs certain dualisms and deterministic qualities entrenched in Western thought. By co-implicating psyche and soma, Anzieu usefully deconstructs a paradigm of mind-body dualism. For Anzieu, the skin has manifold functions which in turn correspond to the Ego's functions; he outlines how a defect in each function manifests as identifiable psychological disorders. In forming the Skin-ego, an infant first perceives a phantasy of common skin with its mother, and the subsequent 'flaying' of shared skin is necessary for individuation. Deficiencies in this tactile 'mothering environment' (caressing, washing, feeding, etc.), as Anzieu terms it, result in a defective Skin-ego and the development of pathologies – this might manifest through the formation of 'second skins' like tattooing, drugs, sado-masochistic sex.[17] A failure of Skin-ego development can result in two possible anxieties. In the more contextually salient instance here, the wrapping exists but is 'pitted with holes' – this is formalised as the 'sieve Skin-ego', in which the individual fears 'leaking away' or being drained out.[18] What is striking about Anzieu and his contemporaries' conceptualisations of the skin, is a common anxiety over the uncontained self. Indeed, Anzieu diagnoses his contemporary twentieth-century condition as a lack of boundaries – figured through arms races, population expansion, ecological crisis, technological mediation. But how might containment be compromised not simply by developmental caregiving trauma, but by sociopolitical signifiers – like colour – inscribed on skin? How might the 'leaking' container, or skin, as it were, have a productive function of exposing such institutional violence and articulating silenced indigenous epistemologies?

Katsak's skin testimony interacts in several noteworthy ways with the psychoanalytic notion of cohesive, coherent subjectivity – or the imposed lack thereof, in her case. In a perverse reformulation of the skin's surface relationality, she watches her skin being incorporated first into the technical implement of a cylinder and later transposed onto the skin of another. This is a dissolution of the interior-exterior, self-other boundary extrapolated to ethically murky extremes through this technological mediation. The mechanical 'drill[ing]' of the skin further effects this dehumanised reduction of the Inuit child, and this has significant implications for how bioethical considerations operate on the basis of fundamental human rights. This becomes apparent in the unsolicited and silenced discourse of consent in this asymmetrical exchange. If the individuated self is the contained, continuous self in Western thought, then the anaesthetic silencing and rupture of Inuit skin exposes the asymmetrical valuation of certain lives and their potential for integrated selfhood. Containment itself, then, becomes an asymmetrically valued good, a privilege with rights of access regulated through colonial power dynamics and the boundaries of national participation. There is also an uncanny confrontation here with the anaesthesised, 'numb' self as a passive observer and not active participant of somatic, and hence, psychic life.

It is significant to note that Katsak is not, as yet, one of the claimants in the lawsuit. But where experience lies beyond the scope of verbal expression and cultural translation, however, the skin performs a powerful, remedial testifying function. Epidermal expressions become a potent demand for witnessing the (silenced) spectacle of colonial violence. That Katsak has lifelong scars from this procedure underscores a certain indelible marking of the Other. The skin's particular form of cyclical, regenerative temporality – in its scarring and scabbing – profoundly rejects the sense of temporal closure implied by the term 'postcolonial' and calls attention to the persistence of trauma as an endemic state, rather than temporally isolated event. The visibly scarred skin demands witnessing of the oft-buried legacies, and endurance, of colonial violence – but also, in its regeneration, the capacity for agentive, and resistive, self-expression on one's own terms. Katsak expresses a sense of satisfaction in her scarring, which is connotative of the skin's rejection of the transplanted skin. Though the 'holes' from the grafted skin heal over, the scars for Katsak signal a deeper rejection of selfhood or individuation in terms of wholeness or the very containment that had been politically foreclosed to her. There is also a curious inversion of power from the medicalised subject position here. Katsak remarks that she was 'happy' when her siblings' skin grafts fell off her arm: she was 'happy that I disproved their theory', and curiously takes pride in the permanence of these scars.[19] The metaphorical leaking of this skin graft signals a failure of scientific mediation into the somatic. The reversal of power here lies in the skin's visible refusal to epidermally reintegrate – and politically, then, to assimilate – within colonially defined boundaries. The scars bear testimony, exposing and refusing to contain the suppressed vestiges of colonial violence and its violation – as well as explicit denial – of issues of consent.

While Anzieu does make explicit mention of the distinctive social and biological realities of skin, there is a generalising or universalising tendency in his depiction of skin. The very ability to generalise and hence efface the social signifiers of skin, however, is itself not a universal privilege. Anzieu's model does not interrogate how pre-inscribed markers of race, sex, or culture are implicated in the fracturing of the Skin-ego beyond caregiver deficiencies – or indeed, whether such a linear causative relationship between developmental trauma, psychic (mal)functioning, and pathology is a given. What is necessary to layer with Anzieu's model are the cultural and political inscriptions etched on skin – and how these structure the experience of inhabiting one's skin (or skins). This demands a decolonial reading practice that allows us to meaningfully access and apprehend these ethical and epistemic grey spaces. In its very leakage, the skin's somatic idiom testifies to realities that cannot be contained within the bounds of a singular Western narrative frame.

Broadening Conceptions of Consent through Igbo Ontology

Having explored how the temporalities of violence might be restructured through the skin, I would like to turn to a text that demands a fundamental confrontation – and reconfiguration – of the basic ontological principles that frame our reading practice. Nigerian Igbo writer Akwaeke Emezi's debut novel, *Freshwater* (2018), offers a generative starting point for this discussion. Mining from their own experience, Emezi animates the discordance engendered by inhabiting inhospitable spaces, where one's realit(ies) are not just denied, but read and pathologised in ways they do not resonate with, and fundamentally do not consent to. Protagonist Ada grows up hearing multiple voices in her head. She engages in clinically self-destructive behaviour like cutting, starvation, and eventually undergoes sex reassignment surgery.[20] After an incident of rape whilst at college, the voices in her head come into distinction and struggle for possession over her body, and, on a fictional level, narrative perspective, as the text becomes a composite of vignettes narrated from the perspective of the individuated beings. There is much that can be said about sexual consent and embodied boundaries from this episode. In this chapter, however, I wish to unpack the boundaries of embodiment through a different prism of consent: the violence of classification, of confining consent within certain contractual schemas that are alien to, and constrain the realities of, the expressor.

The textual depiction of Ada's experiences can be quite convincingly read through the American Psychiatric Association's *Diagnostic and Statistical Manual*, a classificatory schema that occupies a stronghold in Euro-American psychiatric practice – a hegemonic text for understanding and organising psychic reality. Within its diagnostic framework, Ada might be diagnosed with possession-form dissociative identity disorder, comorbid with self-harm, and restriction sub-type eating disorder. However, Ada's experiences are instead framed through the prism of Nigerian Igbo *ogbanje* mythology. *Ogbanje* are born-to-die spirit children who engage in a cycle of premature death and rebirth to torment their biological human mother. I suggest here that Emezi draws on Igbo *ogbanje* mythology to disrupt the totalising epistemic claim of clinical readings of Ada's practices of skin mutilation. Caught between human and spirit worlds, *ogbanje* are bound by a spirit contract to return to the spirit world, through this premature death. *Ogbanje* are fundamentally anxious about the entrapment of human embodiment, because their spirit contract is threatened if the *ogbanje* child survives past puberty and has the potential to reproduce, and consequently become involved in human kinship and patrilineage. To this end, human kin might 'cut' the *ogbanje* through somatic practices like ritual scarring, tattooing, food offerings, etc. to mark the *ogbanje* child and sever ties to the spirit world.[21]

Through the multiple valences of cutting in the text, we might unpack some of the embodied and epistemic issues enmeshed in the novel's treatment of sexuality, rape, and reproduction. The term 'mutilation' is preferred in my discussion over 'self-harm' (except where the latter term is deployed in critical material) to reference episodes where Ada cuts her own skin. In their memoir, *Dear Senthuran* (2021), Emezi writes, 'I've come to think of mutilation as a shift from wrongness to alignment, and of scars as a form of adornment that celebrates this shift'.[22] Emezi imagines these marks as 'reminders' of how they 'continue choosing to move toward [themselves]'.[23] The violence, then, lies instead in forcibly aligning the body with the 'wrongness' – or incommensurability – of normative modes of being. This strikingly demands a reorientation of the way we encounter and read these practices, which are typically perceived as pathological through a Western psychiatric lens. What Emezi is 'mov[ing] toward', through these practices, is a version of selfhood that maintains the integrity of their lived experiences, movement that runs counter to the mandated momentum towards integration or wholeness, at least as these terms circulate within a psychiatric lexicon. The *ogbanje* in *Freshwater* engage in practices such as tattooing, cutting, and breast removal, to test and stretch the very limits of this embodiment, but also to find self-expression through it.

It is worth interrogating here the discordance between Ada's psychic experience and the psychiatric vernacular used to read and interpret said experience in both Western medical and scholarly circles, shaped as they are by dominant biomedical understandings of embodied experience. The current iteration of the diagnostic manual, *DSM-5*, has made attempts to inflect its diagnostic classifications with culture-specific considerations. This has largely been motivated by the goal of enhancing communication in the context of culturally dissimilar professional-patient dynamics. This iteration includes a new sub-section of 'culture-related diagnostic issues' within most of its primary classifications, and additionally features a glossary of 'Cultural Concepts of Distress'. This is defined as 'ways that cultural groups *experience, understand,* and *communicate* suffering, behavioural problems, or troubling thoughts and emotions' (emphasis added).[24] These concepts offer an alternative schema for reading distress in particular indigenous communities – though the placement of this glossary in the appendix itself speaks to a certain spatial politics of epistemic value and (in)visibility. One notable term in the *DSM-5*'s psychiatric lexicon for dissociation and its cultural variants is 'possession' or being 'taken over' by spirits, deities, or demons, which may be associated with cultural, religious, or spiritual practices (deemed prevalent in 'rural areas in the developing world' and 'among certain religious groups in the United States and Europe').[25] These terms have been used to distinguish dissociation from non-pathological 'normative possession' occurring in cultural or religious practice.[26] This term itself exposes the ambiguous boundary between clinically pathological and culturally normative. But what it also exposes is a more fundamental conceptual and communicative gulf even in culturally attentive psychiatric jargon. There has been a tendency in readings of *Freshwater* to designate Ada's experience as 'possession' too (which Emezi rejects for its conceptual inadequacy) – which is perhaps the most culturally intelligible translation for a Western readership. What then of experiences that are lost in translation, or evade such lexical (and by extension, conceptual) containment?

Indigenous expressions of mythology have been ideologically positioned as the antithesis, or discursively devalued Other, of Reality – a fictive, imaginative mode subordinate to Western rationality and its construction of reality through psychoanalytic and psychiatric discourses. This singular vision of reality is largely organised around Euro-American definitions of the self; in a clinical setting, this is defined within the parameters of normative 'healthy' human experience. Instead, *Freshwater* legitimises an alternative, mythological reading of Ada's experience, recuperating it from its subordinate position within a Eurocentric epistemic hierarchy. Emezi positions Mythology not as the devalued Other of Reality in a Eurocentric epistemic hierarchy, but rather as a valid ontological principle for defining one's identity and an epistemic schema for interpreting one's experiences. Ada's self-mutilation and her 'leaking' or bleeding skin, which would be read psychoanalytically as a defective Skin-ego or psychiatrically as self-harm comorbid with dissociation, is here repossessed, as it were, by mythological discourse. These episodes are described as 'self-worship' to 'feed' the 'newborn' 'gods' within her.[27] This complicates a singular interpretive lens for her cutting and by extension, its function. The timeline of Ada's cutting also complicates a linear psychiatric positioning of trauma as a fracture point, or a simple causative relationship between trauma and injury. Ada engages in such behaviour before and after college rape: there are episodes of self-mutilation at age 16 and subsequently a hormonal medication-induced episode of cutting. In its 'greedy' cannibalism, the plural voices that constitute Ada's identity gain voice and narrative life through this blood, refusing to be contained by either spirit or embodied human world exclusively. What it also tests is the skin's self-regenerative, healing potential – a resistive potential also registered in Katsak's testimony.

Consent in Relation: The Reader-Author-Text Relationship

The struggle over bodily boundaries staged here, then, is primarily one of narrative ownership, a struggle for the skin's inscriptions to articulate and be read beyond a pathologising psychiatric register. Anzieu suggests that for a subject who perceives himself with broken skin, and by extension, compromised boundaries, self-mutilation becomes a means of re-imposing limits. This, however, is vexed by an Igbo orientation where individual subjectivity is defined by a certain plurality; in Ada's case, her 'bag of skin' must stretch to accommodate the plural 'we' voices of the *ogbanje*, and, on a theoretical level, multiple interpretive mediums for her experiences. In Igbo ontology, *ogbanje* occupy a liminal space between human and spirit worlds. These beings exceed not just the ontological frameworks available to a Western imaginary, but its discursive capacities as well. The question of sexual and gender expression is a salient example: *Ogbanje* lie outside the binary gender classifications grounded in Western cultural consciousness; Misty Bastian notes that the *ogbanje* occupy a 'third category of gender'.[28] It is this very liminality, this resistance to neat classification, that has been a source of confoundment for Ada in *Freshwater*, and for Emezi's audience itself, rendering both body and text susceptible to misreading – a misreading that, in its evasion and forcible erasure of Emezi's reality, becomes an act of epistemic violence. Indeed, Emezi, who self-identifies as *ogbanje*, has themselves been susceptible to misgendering in media coverage of their work; they identify as trans non-binary, which is the only available, albeit inadequate, discursive framework for an experience that exceeds translation, a self-positioning that has attracted vitriolic debates over their rights of representation and the politics of inclusion in women's literary spaces. There has been a highly publicised feud between acclaimed Nigerian writer Chimamanda Ngozi Adichie and Emezi, with Emezi charging Adichie with 'transphobia'[29] for expressing the sentiment that 'trans women are trans women', and that we should consider women's issues as being distinct from those of trans women.[30] There has also been much controversy centering on *Freshwater*'s longlisting for the 2019 Women's Prize given their terms of self-identification.[31]

But as Emezi forcefully argues, 'to self-name as an entity breaks the rules, because then it means we've taken the naming and storytelling power, to wield it for ourselves'.[32] Katsak's testimony flags up several experiential parallels with Ada's epidermal expressions in *Freshwater*. Both Katsak and Ada are vulnerable to an encroachment of embodied boundaries, or borders, by virtue of social positioning. Occupying margins of Otherness – colonial, racial, and sexual – the very possibility of the integrated self or bodily integrity is foreclosed. Yet, the compromised skin – scarred for Katsak, mutilated for Ada – draws on the compromised position of such marginal Otherness, but rescripts this institutional vulnerability into an expression of durability or tenacity, one that affirms the agentive, generative potential of the dehumanised subject denied subjectivity. Mutilated skin here testifies to a particular social reality, and in so doing, becomes an act of resistance. If colonial trauma threatens the boundedness of the self, and implicates the other in its fluid leakage, then the visibility of skin-bound traumatic testimony projects private experience, forcibly suppressed, into public purview. Where politico-legal definitions of consent have failed to accommodate, and violently erased, certain experiential realities, these expressions demand that we elasticise the conceptual boundaries of consent. In elasticising the imaginative parameters of self-representation, consent is configured here as an affective contract between reader and body-as-text. Perhaps these affective, ethical principles for structuring reading practice, such as cultural sensitivity and respect for representational heterogeneity, might become a way of mediating certain communicative gaps. Strikingly in both accounts, the seemingly de-formed skin becomes a site where the political possibilities of self-representation and relationality are agentively asserted and radically reformed, where the question of consent in our encounter with embodied distress – within and beyond the written text – becomes a structuring principle and practice.

Notes

1 Rhoda Katsak, in *Saqiyuk: Stories from the Lives of Three Inuit Women*, ed. by Nancy Wachowick, Apphia Agalakti Awa, Rhoda Kaukjak Katsak, and Sandra Pikujak Katsak (Montreal: McGill-Queen's University Press, 1999), p. 175.

2 The other claimants include Zacharias Kunuk, Madeline Ivalu, Lazarie Uttak, and Lydia Inooya. Katsak is not, as yet, a claimant.

3 Matthew S. Wiseman, 'Unlocking the "Eskimo Secret": Defence Science in the Cold War Canadian Arctic, 1947–1954', *Journal of the Canadian Historical Association / Revue de la Société historique du Canada*, 26 (2015) <https://doi.org/10.7202/1037202ar> 191–223 (p. 194).

4 Elaine Scarry, 'Consent and the Body: Injury, Departure, and Desire', *New Literary History*, 21 (1990), 867–96 (pp. 871–72).

5 Kieran Oudshoorn, '"We are not monkeys": Inuit speak out about skin grafts done without consent in 1970s', CBC News, 13 May 2019 <https://www.cbc.ca/news/canada/north/inuit-skin-grafts-nunavut-experiment-1.5128279> [accessed 31 May 2023].
6 Jane George, 'Igloolik Inuit sue feds over medical experiments that they say saw them treated like "monkeys"', *Nunatsiaq News*, 21 June 2019 <https://nunatsiaq.com/stories/article/igloolik-inuit-sue-feds-over-medical-experiments-that-they-say-saw-them-treated-like-monkeys/> [accessed 31 May 2023].
7 Ibid.
8 Claire Stocks, 'Trauma Theory and the Singular Self: Rethinking Extreme Experiences in the Light of Cross Cultural Identity', *Textual Practice*, 21 (2007), 71–92 (p. 74).
9 See Karla F. C. Holloway, *Private Bodies, Public Texts: Race, Gender, and a Cultural Bioethics* (Durham, NC: Duke University Press, 2011); Ayah Nuriddin, Graham Mooney, and Alexandre White, 'Reckoning with histories of medical racism and violence in the USA', *The Lancet*, 396 (2020), 949–51.
10 John B. Dossetor, *Beyond the Hippocratic Oath: A Memoir on the Rise of Modern Medical Ethics* (Edmonton: University of Alberta Press, 2005), p. 119.
11 Kristina Cordasco, 'Obtaining informed consent from patients: brief update review', *Making Health Care Safer II: An Updated Critical Analysis of the Evidence for Patient Safety Practices*, Agency for Healthcare Research and Quality (US), 2013.
12 Dossetor, p. 119.
13 Cordasco.
14 Vanessa E. Munro, 'The ideal and the real – at the boundaries of the possibility of female consent' (unpublished doctoral thesis, University of Glasgow, 2000) <http://theses.gla.ac.uk/id/eprint/3935> [accessed 31 May 2023], p. 10.
15 Oudshoorn.
16 Didier Anzieu, *The Skin-ego*, trans. by Naomi Segal (London: Karnac Books, 2016), p. 120.
17 Ibid., p. 40.
18 Ibid., p. 10.
19 Katsak, in *Saqiyuk: Stories from the Lives of Three Inuit Women*, p. 177.
20 I deploy the term 'sex reassignment' here, rather than the more politically sensitive and accepted term in common parlance, 'gender affirmation' surgery, to indicate that within this specific cultural context, what is being undertaken is purely a set of bodily procedures to deny a particular biological, sex-driven classification of the corporeal state; this is not undertaken to affirm an alternative gender identity or expression. *Ogbanje*, in Igbo mythology, exist beyond Western constructions and conceptions of sex and gender – to designate this as 'gender affirmation', then, would be to run the representational risk of suggesting that there is a desire to assume a particular expression, when the surgery is sought to in fact, exceed it.
21 Misty L. Bastian, 'Married in the Water: Spirit Kin and Other Afflictions of Modernity in Southeastern Nigeria', *Journal of Religion in Africa*, 27 (1997), 116–34 (pp. 120–22). See also Chinwe Achebe's comprehensive study in *The World of the Ogbanje* and its elaboration on the ritual cut, quoted in Christopher N. Okonkwo, *A Spirit of Dialogue: Incarnations of Ọgbañje, the Born-To-Die* (Knoxville: University of Tennessee Press, 2008), p. 11.
22 Akwaeke Emezi, *Dear Senthuran* (London: Faber & Faber, 2021), p. 20.
23 Ibid. For Emezi's specific elaborations on 'mutilation', see pp. 11–20; on 'marking', pp. 197–200.
24 American Psychiatric Association, *Diagnostic and Statistical Manual of Mental Disorders*, 5th edn (Washington, DC: APA, 2013), p. 758. Hereafter *DSM-5*.
25 Ibid., p. 295.
26 Ibid.

27 Akwaeke Emezi, *Freshwater* (London: Faber & Faber, 2018), pp. 41–42.
28 Misty L. Bastian, 'Irregular Visitors: Narratives about *Ogbaanje* (Spirit Children) in Southern Nigerian Popular Writing', in *Readings in African Popular Fiction*, ed. by Stephanie Newell (London: James Currey, 2002), pp. 59–66 (p. 59).
29 See Emezi's Twitter thread, where they express their views on Adichie's (and later, J.K. Rowling's) 'transphobic' comments: @azemezi, *Twitter* (2020–2021) <https://twitter.com/azemezi/status/1346268453221658624> [accessed 31 May 2023].
30 Chimamanda Ngozi Adichie, interviewed by Cathy Newman, 'Chimamanda Ngozi Adichie on feminism', BBC Channel 4 (10 March 2017) <https://www.channel4.com/news/chimamanda-ngozi-adichie-on-feminism> [accessed 31 May 2023]. Adichie has since continued to express and clarify her views on trans politics and 'cancel culture', particularly in the wake of similar criticism against author J.K. Rowling in 2020. See Chimamanda Ngozi Adichie, 'IT IS OBSCENE: A TRUE REFLECTION IN THREE PARTS', Chimamanda.com (15 June 2021) <https://www.chimamanda.com/news_items/it-is-obscene-a-true-reflection-in-three-parts/> [accessed 31 May 2023].
31 For an example of controversial coverage on Emezi's inclusion in the Women's Prize longlist, see David Sanderson's article for *The Times*: 'Bearded, non-binary authors have eyes on women's prize', *The Times* (11 March 2019) <https://www.thetimes.co.uk/article/bearded-non-binary-authors-have-eyes-on-womens-prize-08n77tkjs> [accessed 31 May 2023]. Emezi has since publicly condemned and disassociated their future work from the prize, after the awarding committee requested information about Emezi's 'sex as defined by law' to submit their second novel for consideration. See Emezi's Twitter thread: @azemezi, *Twitter* (5 October 2020) <https:-//twitter.com/azemezi/status/1313003555608047616> [accessed 22 June 2022].
32 Akwaeke Emezi, *Dear Senthuran*, p. 154.

Bibliography

Adichie, Chimamanda Ngozi, interviewed by Cathy Newman, 'Chimamanda Ngozi Adichie on feminism', BBC Channel 4 (10 March 2017) <https://www.channel4.com/news/chimamanda-ngozi-adichie-on-feminism> [accessed 31 May 2023]

Adichie, Chimamanda Ngozi, 'IT IS OBSCENE: A TRUE REFLECTION IN THREE PARTS', *Chimamanda.com* (15 June 2021) <https://www.chimamanda.com/news_items/it-is-obscene-a-true-reflection-in-three-parts/> [accessed 31 May 2023]

American Psychiatric Association, *Diagnostic and Statistical Manual of Mental Disorders*, 5th edn (Washington, DC: APA, 2013)

Anzieu, Didier, *The Skin-ego*, trans. by Naomi Segal (London: Karnac Books, 2016)

Bastian, Misty L., 'Irregular Visitors: Narratives about Ogbaanje (Spirit Children) in Southern Nigerian Popular Writing', in *Readings in African Popular Fiction*, ed. by Stephanie Newell (London: James Currey, 2002), pp. 59–66

Bastian, Misty L., 'Married in the Water: Spirit Kin and Other Afflictions of Modernity in Southeastern Nigeria', *Journal of Religion in Africa*, 27 (1997), 116–34

Cordasco, Kristina, 'Obtaining Informed Consent from Patients: Brief Update Review', in *Making Health Care Safer II: An Updated Critical Analysis of the Evidence for Patient Safety Practices*, Agency for Healthcare Research and Quality (US), 2013

Dossetor, John B., *Beyond the Hippocratic Oath: A Memoir on the Rise of Modern Medical Ethics* (Edmonton, Alberta: University of Alberta Press, 2005)

Emezi, Akwaeke, *Dear Senthuran* (London: Faber & Faber, 2021)

Emezi, Akwaeke, *Freshwater* (London: Faber & Faber, 2018)

Emezi, Akwaeke, Twitter (5 October 2020) <https://twitter.com/azemezi/status/1313003555608047616> [accessed 31 May 2023]

Emezi, Akwaeke, Twitter (2020–2021) <https://twitter.com/azemezi/status/1346268453221658624> [accessed 22 June 2022]

George, Jane, 'Igloolik Inuit sue feds over medical experiments that they say saw them treated like "monkeys"', *Nunatsiaq News*, 21 June 2019 <https://nunatsiaq.com/stories/article/igloolik-inuit-sue-feds-over-medical-experiments-that-they-say-saw-them-treated-like-monkeys/> [accessed 31 May 2023]

Holloway, Karla F. C., *Private Bodies, Public Texts: Race, Gender, and a Cultural Bioethics* (Durham, NC: Duke University Press, 2011)

Munro, Vanessa E., 'The ideal and the real – at the boundaries of the possibility of female consent' (unpublished doctoral thesis, University of Glasgow, 2000) <http://theses.gla.ac.uk/id/eprint/3935> [accessed 31 May 2023]

Nuriddin, Ayah, Graham Mooney, and Alexandre White, 'Reckoning With Histories of Medical Racism and Violence in the USA', *The Lancet*, 396 (2020), 949–51

Okonkwo, Christopher N., *A Spirit of Dialogue: Incarnations of Ọgbañje, the Born-To-Die* (Knoxville: University of Tennessee Press, 2008)

Oudshoorn, Kieran, '"We are not monkeys": Inuit speak out about skin grafts done without consent in 1970s', *CBC News*, 13 May 2019 <https://www.cbc.ca/news/canada/north/inuit-skin-grafts-nunavut-experiment-1.5128279> [accessed 31 May 2023]

Sanderson, David, 'Bearded, non-binary authors have eyes on women's prize', *The Times* (11 March 2019) <https://www.thetimes.co.uk/article/bearded-non-binary-authors-have-eyes-on-womens-prize-08n77tkjs> [accessed 31 May 2023]

Scarry, Elaine, 'Consent and the Body: Injury, Departure, and Desire', *New Literary History*, 21 (1990), 867–96

Stocks, Claire, 'Trauma Theory and the Singular Self: Rethinking Extreme Experiences in the Light of Cross Cultural Identity', *Textual Practice*, 21 (2007), 71–92

Wachowick, Nancy, Apphia Agalakti Awa, Rhoda Kaukjak Katsak, and Sandra Pikujak Katsak, eds, *Saqiyuk: Stories from the Lives of Three Inuit Women* (Montreal: McGill-Queen's University Press, 1999)

Wiseman, Matthew S., 'Unlocking the "Eskimo Secret": Defence Science in the Cold War Canadian Arctic, 1947–1954', *Journal of the Canadian Historical Association / Revue de la Société historique du Canada*, 26 (2015) <https://doi.org/10.7202/1037202ar>, 191–223

11 'I wasn't aware at the time, I could actually say "no"'

Intimacy, Expectations, and Consent in Queer Relationships

Catherine Donovan, Kate Butterby and Rebecca Barnes

Introduction

While there is an emerging body of research exploring the sexual violence perpetrated against lesbians, gay and bisexual men and women, and/or trans women and men, and/or non-binary folk (LGB and/or T+),[1] much of this literature approaches sexual violence as an isolated incident. Prevalence studies based on quantitative surveys ask whether and how many times non-consensual sexual touching or sexual behaviour has occurred and, typically, are focused on the end of the continuum of sexual violence most readily regarded as criminal: rape, sexual assault, sexual harassment.[2] This approach reflects and reinforces a criminal justice system lens for describing and explicating sexual violence, and a wider societal consensus about 'what counts' as sexual violence, with rape (defined legally in the UK as forced penetration of any bodily orifice with a penis)[3] as the defining incident/crime with the most devastating impacts. The reduction of sexual violence to a discrete, material experience frames it as a physical act which takes place in a vacuum, rather than – critically – a social process, embedded in social interactions and relationships. This is particularly pertinent when sexual violence in intimate relationships becomes the focus, as in this chapter. What 'counts' as sexual violence can then extend to the web of verbal comments and coercive behaviours that can cumulatively sexually victimise an intimate partner and devastate all aspects of their sexuality and/or gender identity.

This chapter explores the social processes by which sexual violence might occur in the relationships of LGB and/or T+ folk. Our focus on relationships addresses a gap in the literature about how sexual violence can be understood and named – or not – in queer intimate relationships. This marks a deliberate shift away from the incident-based, physical violence-focused approach to understanding sexual violence, in order to include how victimisation can result from a relationship 'demeanour' of perpetrators who control the nature, dynamics, timing, and meaning of sex in intimate relationships. We adopt a sociological analysis to examine the social processes through which sexual

DOI: 10.4324/9781003365082-14

victimisation is transmitted, communicated, perpetrated, and, centrally, how consent is best viewed as a social process shaped by cis-heteronormative assumptions about gender and sexuality.

This chapter is divided into five sections. First, we consider some of the key feminist theoretical tools for conceptualising sexual violence in cis-heterosexual relationships, and question whether any of these tools are useful for our work. Second, we summarise some of the research on domestic and sexual violence in LGB and/or T+ people's relationships, including in relation to consent, to show how queering our knowledge about sexual violence might produce more nuanced insights about sexual violence that victimises queer people. Third, we discuss our methodology. In the fourth section, we discuss our data in light of the theoretical tools set out earlier, focusing on sexual scripts that shape and inform queer folk's expectations about sexual intimacy, the sexual contract in queer relationships, and how relationship rules in abusive queer relationships regulate sex and expressions of sexuality. We conclude by calling for more research in this area that focuses on the social processes that produce understandings and enactment of consent.

Broader Societal Beliefs about Sex, Gender, Sexuality, and Adult Intimacy

Catherine Donovan and Rebecca Barnes have argued that a theoretical understanding of the intimate and sexual lives of LGB and/or T+ folk cannot be divorced from the societal context of compulsory heterosexuality in which they live.[4] Dominant cis-heteronormative constructions of sexuality produce understandings of men's and women's sexuality that are binary, oppositional, and assumptive of 'real' (penile-vaginal) sex that is driven by biological imperatives to reproduce.[5] Thus, men's sexuality is believed to be driven to 'spread their oats' with as many partners as possible to secure reproduction of the self and species. This construction underpins assumptions that men, once aroused, cannot control themselves, must be satisfied, and are able to separate sex from love/emotion.[6] Women's sexuality is believed to be driven by biological maternity, and then the need to protect and nurture their children.[7]

Consequently, women are charged with regulating men's sexuality so that children are born into the 'correct' social/legal family unit, and men can be regulated with the responsibility of their provider and father roles.[8] Vaginal penetration, male orgasm, and delivery of sperm provide a particular biologically essentialist account that underpins the social adaptations developed historically to protect and reinforce the cis-heteronormative account of sex, sexuality, gender, and adult intimacy.

Marriage – as a socio-legal contract to impose relationships with ideals of dependency, responsibility, and inheritance – can be seen as one of society's attempts to manage some of the perceived problematic consequences of men's unregulated sexuality. However, historically, the marriage contract has been based on an inherently unequal relationship between men and women because women had no legal existence in their own right. Women's positioning as subordinate to their husband in marriage is evidenced in what Carole Pateman calls the sexual contract,[9] which, on marriage, gives men sexual access to women – 'conjugal rights' – and makes irrelevant women's absence of desire or consent. Rape in marriage was criminalised in 1991 in England and Wales, yet there remains a belief that consenting to be in a relationship – not just a marriage – is equivalent to consenting to sex, and that sex is a natural entitlement of men in intimate relationships. Importantly, the dominant construction of cis-heterosexuality is based on those of white, cis-heterosexual women and men, leaving, for example, racially minoritised women's sexualities simultaneously invisible and problematically othered.[10] Generally, however, there is a similarity in the belief that, regardless of their racialised identities, women's role is one of deferring to and satisfying their men's desires.

Unlike in cis-heterosexual relationships which are patriarchally produced to ensure gender inequality between men and women, assumptions are made that the relationships of LGB and/or T+ people lack these gendered power differentials and must therefore be more equal (see Donovan and Barnes for a discussion of this).[11] Yet, these assumptions do not apply to bisexual or trans people in heterosexual relationships, and non-binary people have seldom been considered at all. Setting aside the omissions, these assumptions about queer relationships are flawed since the evidence is clear that domestic abuse and sexual violence do take place.[12] Bisexual women are disproportionately more likely to report having experienced partner abuse and sexual violence than heterosexual women, and rates of sexual violence reported by trans and non-binary people are disproportionately high.[13] As Kimberlé Crenshaw argues in relation to the intersection of race, and gender, and Donovan and Barnes and Janice Ristock in relation to the intersection of sexuality and gender, patriarchal, cis-heteronormative dynamics of power do not adequately explain the multiple ways in which individuals are marginalised and rendered more vulnerable to sexual violence.[14]

Our research finds evidence that the sexual contract exists in relationships regardless of participants' sexuality and/or gender identities. Nicola Gavey contends that heteronormative discourses shape the types of sex that women often agree to, such that they may consent to unwanted sex to conform to social norms and expectations about what happens in a relationship.[15] This, Melanie A. Beres argues, blurs the distinction between 'willing to have sex' and 'wanting to have sex'.[16] Whilst willingness leads – legally, at least – to consensual sex, having sex out of a sense of duty or obligation offers a low bar for consent, and has negative impacts on one's sense of self as a sexual being.[17] In a relationship with 'relationship rules' (see below) that allow an abusive partner to insist on, coerce, or merely 'expect' sex on their terms, the victimised partner might not want, but feel unable to refuse, sex and blame themselves for falling short of the sexual contract.

Theorising Intimate Partner Sexual Violence in the Relationships of LGB and/or T+ Folk

In 2004, Catherine Donovan and Marianne Hester conducted a mixed-methods study which compared love and violence in 'same-sex' and heterosexual relationships.[18] They found that, regardless of gender and sexuality, there were similarities in how abusive partners are able to exert power and control. A key similarity is the impact on victims/survivors: erosion of self and social isolation. Another similarity concerns the relationship rules that underpin domestically abusive relationships. The first relationship rule is that the relationship is for the abusive partner, and on their terms. They make all key decisions, and define the relationship in relation to their needs/wants/demands. The second relationship rule is that the victimised partner is responsible for the partner's abusive behaviour, the relationship, for the abusive partner, the household if they share one, and children if they have them.[19] This relationship rule would include responsibility for meeting the abusive partner's sexual needs. This, Donovan and Hester argue, explains why those victimised often do not recognise their victimisation, because they do not recognise themselves as the ideal victim[20]: they are neither passive nor weak. Rather, they often understand themselves as emotionally stronger than their abusive partner who they perceive as emotionally needy and requiring support and protection.[21] Establishing the relationship rules can happen abruptly when an abusive partner uses physical violence or sexual violence in an incident that warns or punishes the victimised partner for straying from the terms of the relationship. Alternatively, the rules may be established more incrementally through emotional and verbal abuse that undermines the victimised partner's self-confidence and their sense of self and reality.

Identity abuse and experiential power are under-researched in heterosexual relationships but are important in the relationships of LGB and/or T+ folk. Experiential power can be exerted when a more established 'out' abusive partner plays on their victimised partner's lack of knowledge and/or confidence in their identities of sexuality and/or gender.[22] This is facilitated by the relative social and cultural invisibility of queer people's intimate and sexual lives. Identity abuse can underpin experiential power, whereby an abusive partner sets the terms for the 'sexual' relationship by imposing and normalising their own sexual behaviours and/or demands as representative of, for example, how 'real' gay men behave.

Methodology

The authors of this chapter have between them conducted three qualitative studies that have explored abuse in LGB and/or T+ people's relationships: the Coral Project,[23] Comparing Heterosexual and Same sex Abuse in Relationships (COHSAR) Project,[24] and the Speaking Out Project. Each study explores domestic abuse by framing the question as: 'what happens/what do you do when things go wrong in your relationships?' The COHSAR project was interested in anybody who had experience of a 'same-sex' relationship, regardless of how they identified their gender or sexuality. The Coral Project recruited those who identified as lesbian, gay, bisexual and/or trans+ to more explicitly invite participation from trans and non-binary respondents. The Speaking Out Project followed up nine trans participants from the Coral Project survey to focus on their experiences of violence and abuse in intimate relationships.

For this chapter, we have combined those nine interview transcripts with the 36 transcripts from the Coral Project and the 67 transcripts from the COHSAR Project. The combined data set improves the diversity of the sample with regard to gender and sexuality. However, there is limited ethnic diversity, with the vast majority of respondents being white British. In addition, whilst there are accounts from disabled respondents and respondents from working-class backgrounds, these aspects of their identities do not form part of the analysis. This does not mean that respondents' experiences are not integrally shaped by their race, disability, or social class. They undoubtedly are. However, in the analysis undertaken for this chapter, the intersecting ways that these aspects of respondents' identities have shaped their lives are not overtly visible. This is a limitation of the study.

Of the 112 interviews available for this analysis, 55 included accounts of sexual violence. Of these 55 participants, seven identified as trans or non-binary, one as gender-fluid, 29 as women, and 18 as men. Most of the group identified as lesbian/gay woman (25), followed by gay men (17), bisexual (seven), pansexual (three), queer (three), genderqueer (one) and heterosexual (one). Some respondents identified their sexuality in multiple ways.

Dominant Cis-Heteronormative Beliefs About Gender, Sex, Sexuality and Adult Intimacy

Many respondents' accounts reflect broader cis-heteronormative public stories[25] about romantic intimacy, highlighting qualities such as fidelity, monogamy, and the centrality of love for an enduring relationship. Yet, respondents were not straightforwardly showing allegiance to these public stories through their own intimate lives. Rather, they are referenced as a starting point for how they make sense of their experiences. The extent to which the public stories are presented or internalised as non-negotiable underpins the compromises people make in their intimate relationships and their enactment of consent. These public stories echo dominant cis-heteronormative sexual scripts which assume male initiation and female passivity,[26] and which juxtapose the different ways men and women (supposedly) approach love and sex: that men are more able to separate love from sex, are biologically driven to desire sex for its own sake, pursue a range of sexual partners, and are 'naturally' non-monogamous. This presentation of male sexuality is given by participants regardless of their own gender identity, sexuality, or behaviour:

> I would assume that any man has sexual urges, whether they're in a gay relationship or a heterosexual relationship. And I think ultimately gay men are more open about that, in general, and willing to accept that maybe sex is different to love [...] if you think about biology [...] men are designed to spread their oats. [*laughs*] [...] So that, that will always be inborn.
>
> (Edward, gay man)[27]

> The whole constructed idea is that lesbians go and get your cats and live together and it's all about love and the emotions and whatever, and the guys will do a lot of sex. And I think there are a fair amount of [...] lesbian and gay male couples that are doing that, both because it suits them and also because sometimes it's easier to follow those constructed pathways that are available.
>
> (Lynn, lesbian)

Public stories about how sexualities are cis-heteronormatively shaped in binaries are sedimented down into sexual scripts which mandate how men will conduct adult intimacy with men and how women will conduct adult intimacy with women. Alongside these expectations about the centrality of sex and the accommodations that include open relationships in order to secure long-term relationships, some men also talk about how particular kinds of masculinity are normalised that eschew emotionality between intimate partners. Kenneth, a gay man, for example, describes how his first gay partner did not show physical affection, and thus he 'kind of learned that gay men don't show each other physical affection'.

Women often refer to male sexuality in order to convey the oppositional differences that frame the expectations of their intimate lives:

> I think men get a lot of messages that they're supposed to be really, really sexually driven and women are supposed to be quite sexually passive [...] women are supposed to nurture and be cared for, you know, all those kinds of things.
>
> (Janet, lesbian woman)

The consequences of sexual passivity as a gender-defining characteristic might be obvious if there were not such similarities in the accounts of sexual violence from respondents across different identities of sexuality and gender. As we will show later in the chapter, experiential power can be as important as anybody's gender identity in shaping expectations around intimacy and consent in LGB and/or T+ relationships. Yet, there is also evidence amongst most women that their expectations are shaped by notions of monogamy, fidelity and longevity, and that love and sex are connected.

For bisexual people, the public stories that privilege cis-heteronormativity result in the construction of bisexuality as inherently problematic, threatening and – in abusive relationships – needing to be controlled. This renders bisexual people vulnerable to biphobic identity abuse.[28] In Clare's account, we see how her abusive partner problematised her bisexuality in two ways: first, that her sexual interest in men made her resemble a straight woman more than a lesbian, and second, that her identity was damaged by having been sexually intimate with men:

> She always used to make a comment that *[short laugh]* that I used to fuck like a straight woman, which used to kind of bemuse me [...] so you know it was, "you're only a true lesbian if you've never slept with a man" and that, that was always there as well kind of poking at my kind of, well am I?
>
> (Clare, bisexual woman)

Trans and non-binary folk can also be othered because of their perceived/actual non-conformity to public stories about existing 'natural' norms of gender and sexuality (often sexuality and gender are confused as being the same). This includes assumptions that they cannot conform to biologically essentialist norms of cis-heteronormative sexual desire and reproduction. The resulting perception of trans people as unnatural and the structural positioning of them as minoritised combine to produce their objectification in ways that reinforce a perception of them as fetishised, dehumanised, and as objects to be sexually coerced and/or undermined:

> I think that's what worries me the most that I could end up in that situation, simply because someone wants to [...] say "oh, I've done it to a trans woman".
>
> (Zara, trans heterosexual woman)

For those who are trans and have interests in bondage, discipline, submission, and sado-masochism, this combination can elicit reactions from abusive partners who justify their abuse because of the victimised partner's sexual desires being perceived as unintelligible and culturally taboo:

> He also had issues about the things I liked, like kinks and fetishes, and he told me that he thought I was too young to be that perverted.
>
> (Timothy, trans pansexual male)

There is an impact on Timothy of being called perverted which provides an example of how sexual violence in an intimate relationship can be conveyed verbally to set a tone and a dynamic that positions one partner – the one victimised – as problematic, as a threat, as in need of being controlled. This positioning legitimates a disregard for consent, with sexual violence being employed to contain, punish, and regulate the threat posed by the victimised partner's constructed otherness.

So far, we have outlined some of the ways in which respondents reference dominant public stories about sex, sexuality, gender, and adult intimacy in their explanations and descriptions of their own sexual and intimate lives. Yet, many simultaneously point to their own and others' deviation from those expected norms. For example, Patrick refers to the trope of rampant male sexuality and non-monogamy, and how gay male relationships will accommodate these needs and expectations. Yet, his final comment suggests that not every gay man is on board with these behaviours and will only tolerate them in order to maintain the relationship:

> I think there's more acceptance [in relationships between men] that [...] sexual activity will, can, can involve other parties and, and the partners will do that together or separately or sometimes will *tolerate it just for the sake of keeping the, the relationship* so that the other partner doesn't feel so bored or trapped and can indulge any, any side of them that they want to.
>
> (Patrick, gay man, our emphasis)

This excerpt also illustrates the ways in which consent might be reluctantly given and/or negotiated in a calculation of pros and cons about staying in a relationship and might be understood as one of the 'compromises' that Eddie (bisexual man), refers to as being made for the sake of love.

For others, the supposed differences between men and women are only presuppositions. Tessa exemplifies others who question whether the gendered assumptions hold up or whether the differences are individual: 'I think mostly it's about differences in people rather than differences in gender' (Tessa, lesbian woman). Yet, whilst some respondents can both articulate dominant public stories about gender, sex, sexuality, and intimacy and retain a critical view about whether these public stories always translate into predicable behaviours, respondents' accounts are more typically imbued with the broader societal influences. This is nowhere more strongly demonstrated than in how the sexual contract is assumed to exist in queer intimate relationships, as we consider next.

The Sexual Contract

For the vast majority of respondents, sex is expected in intimate relationships and it becomes problematic when one partner believes there is not enough or not good enough sex. Most accounts suggest that this results in a partner feeling pressured – from themselves and/or their partner – either to have (unwanted) sex or to end the relationship:

> As soon as you stop having sex with somebody that you've started having sex with, over a long period of time, I don't think that can work. I don't think you can be celibate and still have a relationship with somebody. I don't think that's fair on them, especially when they're a very sexual person.
>
> (Kay, lesbian)

> When we're seeing each other, say, three times a week if, say, something doesn't happen on the Monday then you know that when you see each other on the Friday something's, you would hope [something] would happen and if it doesn't then you're like "something's not right".
>
> (Eddie, bisexual man)

In these accounts, the lack of sex is understood to raise a question about the viability of the relationship and a recognition of the unfairness for one partner – typically the one who still wants to have sex – when a partner does not want as much or any sex.

For too many others, the existence of the sexual contract means that sex occurs that is unwanted yet performed to meet the other person's needs. Some respondents couch their experiences in language that reflects a sense of reluctance and 'duty', making notions of consent ambiguous. As Julie explains: 'I think I've certainly slept with women for the sake of a quiet life, yeah' (Julie, lesbian woman). Ryan speaks of his duty and Marc recalls being unable to say no to sex and using sex as a means of conflict resolution:

> I think more times than not I would have said no but I think there were times where just in my head I was thinking "well we haven't had sex in a week, I really should probably" you know, [...] it was more of a duty as a, as a, as a partner to do that.
>
> (Ryan, gay man)

> I remember like feeling like I'd had to sleep with her to keep the peace or to um [sighs], you know, dissolve the situation when it's really not what I wanted.
>
> (Marc, queer trans man)

Both Ryan and Marc's accounts conjure up contexts of non-consensual sex but also suggest that they understood and complied with (albeit reluctantly) the expectations of the sexual contract in their relationships. These accounts highlight the limitations of consent, as it is legally defined, and the tensions between the sexual contract and more explicit, affirmative understandings of consent.[29] Other respondents give accounts that more explicitly depict contexts of non-consensual sex. Here, the rationale of the sexual contract is invoked, albeit implicitly, but the unequal power relationship is more overtly recognisable as providing a context for sexual violence:

> I'd say "can we not, you know, can we not have a cuddle tonight" and stuff and he'd say "well you just lie there and I'll get on with it" kind of thing [...] I'd felt really pressured into having sex, you know, when I didn't want it at times and, you know, and he did that a lot.
>
> (Marcus, gay man)

Reflecting the first relationship rule – that the relationship is for them and on their terms – Marcus's abusive partner believed that he was entitled to sex regardless of whether Marcus wanted it. In fact, it was quickly established that Marcus was the 'passive' one in the relationship with sex being 'done to' him. Consent is not acknowledged here because the assumption is that Marcus has consented to the relationship and therefore 'owes' his partner sex.

A belief that a sexual contract exists within an intimate relationship can be operationalised in different ways depending on the partner whose demands are prioritised and the partner who feels obligated to fulfil their perceived duties. In abusive relationships, relationship rules provide a further context-setting backdrop that often leaves the victimised partner blaming themselves for their victimisation. We explore this next.

Relationship Rules and Experiential Power

The relationship rules that underpin a domestically abusive relationship govern its sexual aspects too. The abusive partner expects to have – or not have – sex on their terms. Any problems with sex are assumed to be the victimised partner's failings – not having a high enough libido; not being sexually competent; not being attractive; not being authentically, for example, gay or lesbian; being untrustworthy as a result of being bi- or pansexual; having an unreliably gendered body as a trans or non-binary person. All of these can be drawn on to establish a coercively controlling sexual relationship. Consent in these relationships is assumed through the sexual contract, yet at the same time constantly threatened by the abusive partner's perpetration of sexual violence. The victimised partner is often left deliberating over whether and how they have contributed to their own victimisation.

For many, the perceived rule that the relationship is for the abusive partner and on their terms is established early in the relationship:

> The thing with sex, it was because she'd use sex against you. [...] that was another way she'd control. It was like if she wanted she'd get it. If I didn't want it all hell will play [sic]. In fact it was always done on her terms.
>
> (Zara, trans woman, lesbian)

> I think that I just kind of went along with whatever he wanted me to do and one evening I just said no to sex and [...] I went and slept in the spare room and basically he then kind of just took advantage of me, but being drunk I wasn't able to fight it off.
>
> (Adam, gay man)

Typically, accounts of rape are given by those sexually victimised by men, though often there is difficulty with using the word 'rape', as Adam's excerpt illustrates. Kenneth's account also reflects this hesitancy:

> One time, fairly early on in our relationship, he [breathes out] and I still find I can't actually say that he raped me, cos it wasn't quite as simple as that, but he certainly forced, and forced very violent sex on me. Against my will. So it's effectively rape.
>
> (Kenneth, gay man)

Establishing the relationship rules not only through being the initiator of sex but also by rejecting the victimised partner's invitations to be sexual is a very powerful tool. It not only sets up the pattern of coercive control but also positions the victimised partner as subservient. Often, they are unable to recognise the relationship as controlling even as they describe the impacts of being sexually rejected by their partner:

> I remember trying to instigate sex but being very scared of it at the time, partially because it was my first relationship, but partially because she did seem to lead things, I suppose, in the relationship [...] when we'd fallen out, if she came to me, I might be able to go, "OK, we'll have a hug or maybe we'll have sex or whatever", if I tried it the other way, it never seemed to work [...] there wasn't an openness properly about that I suppose. And I wasn't aware at the time, I could actually say "no" to her. I mean it wasn't like I was raped or anything but it was, [pause] I wasn't aware enough to be able to say "I'm not entirely comfortable" [...] I couldn't get it to go the other direction properly.
>
> (Lynn, lesbian woman)

Lynn's account of her first relationship with another woman illustrates experiential power. The abusive partner positions themselves as having superior knowledge about how being a lesbian might be sexually expressed in a relationship. A person in their first relationship, like a woman who brings with her an understanding of her own sexuality derived from public stories that construct female sexuality as passive, deferential, and/or responsive, might feel grateful that their partner 'knows what to do' and is willing to initiate sex. However, when that pattern does not change, it becomes clearer that Lynn's abusive partner is using sex to control their partner, demanding intimacy after an argument, but not reciprocating when Lynn instigates it. Consent relies on the sexual contract, i.e. sex is to be expected, and the lack of ability to make it happen gradually begins to corrode Lynn's self-confidence.

Experiential power can be considered a form of capital, both more widely in queer communities, but critically, in how sexual power dynamics become established in intimate relationships. When young age intersects with identities of sexuality and/or gender, experiential power is more explicitly visible. Young people's naivety about both sex and adult intimacy make them situationally vulnerable to their abusive partners who groom them to believe that their victimisation is to be expected and 'normal' in queer relationships. The impacts of these initial relationships inform how people think about and enter into future relationships, in ways that are typically shaped and reinforced by experiences that reflect public stories about sex, sexuality, gender, and adult intimacy:

> [I] started a relationship with one of the boys in the group who was 17 and I was 12 and at first it was mostly that he was just controlling, so he'd want to see me all the time […] and then […] he'd be phoning me very late at night and then wanting to have sexual conversations on the phone […] At the time I didn't see that as abusive, I just thought this is normal, this is what happens in relationships [and] I was stupid for not being able to do it […] I was 13 at the time […] I skived off school […] and met him […] and he sexually assaulted me.
>
> (Allan, trans masculine, pansexual)

Experiential power is not only connected to age differences, but the comparative duration of being 'out' and the amount of existing experience with sex and adult intimacy. It is these factors that can construct an unequal relationship dynamic and allow abusive partners to exploit weaknesses in their partner's confidence and self-esteem:

> Aye, I loved her but […] [f]or a first time being with a woman, it was very bizarre, and even looking back on it now, I think, [half laughs, half does sharp outtake of breath] "wow!", you know […] I thought all lesbians were the same, but she was very dominant, very, very dominant, and there was a lot of things went on within that relationship and it took me *years* to get over […] Looking back, maybe if I'd been a bit more experienced or something, I would have said, "er no," you know, but I didn't know any different, I thought this is how it goes.
>
> (Jill, lesbian)

Respondents abused by women made more references to emotional coercion than physical force. These accounts described relationship contexts in which the victimised partner was systematically undermined so that their sense of self as a sexual person inhabiting identities of gender and/or sexuality was rendered situationally vulnerable to the expectations of abusive partners exerting relationship rules:

> Almost on a daily basis she'd say something negative about how I looked and my body, my appearance, everything […] and after sort of ten, 12 years, 13 years it does make a big dent.
>
> (Alan, bisexual, genderfluid)

> Oh she was just so sexual […] I would dread going to bed because I knew it had to be done, especially towards the end […] And it's just, whew, yeah it was too much, sexually, for me definitely.
>
> (Marie, lesbian woman)

After 12 years of sexual abuse, Marie still makes sense of what happened with reference to her own failings of not liking sex enough and to her abusive partner's and her own expectation that she should acquiesce to the sexual demands, regardless of her own lack of desire.

Refusal of an abusive partner's sexual demands constitutes a breach of the relationship rules, which is met with increasingly punitive behaviours. Punitive abusive behaviours can be seen in accounts from trans respondents who report being sexually assaulted in relation to transition, as Allan described:

> Someone I was seeing when I first transitioned, who was sexually abusive to me when I transitioned, which obviously is very difficult, and I split up with him very shortly after that […] basically they sexually assaulted me and I completely cut off the relationship […] in my view the crime […] had been committed against me because of my female body parts.
>
> (Allan, trans masculine, pansexual)

This can be read as an attack on Allan's gender non-conforming body by an abusive partner unable and/or unwilling to accept his decision to transition, and attempting to regulate his gender identity with sexual violence.

Conclusion

The role and implicit assumptions about sexual consent in the context of the abusive relationships of LGB and/or T+ folk are rarely the focus of research. Within this chapter, we offer a critical intervention in a discussion we hope to see continued. In future research, we also hope to see a more intersectional analysis that addresses the limitations of this chapter and interrogates how identities including race, social class, disability, and citizenship status intersect with gender and sexuality to produce the conditions in which sexual violence takes place.

In too many accounts, respondents are reluctant to name their experiences as rape or sexual assault, and to describe what happened as non-consensual even when they describe force, pressure, or their unwillingness to acquiesce to abusive partners' sexual demands. The broader relationship context provides insights into how individual incidents of sexual violence are contextualised by the abusive partner's demeanour towards the victimised partner: how the relationship rules have been established, the regular sexual intimidation, insults, withholding of affection to punish or humiliate the victimised partner, and ridicule of the victimised partner's body, their sexual attractiveness, and/or sexual performance. In addition, the sexual abuse is part of a range of abusive tactics adopted by the abusive partner to establish and maintain power and control over their victimised partner: economic abuse, physical threat, intimidation, physical violence, and/or coercively controlling emotional abuse. Cumulatively, these reinforce the relationship rules that the relationship is for the abusive partner and on their terms, and that the victimised partner is responsible for everything including the abusive partner's sexual satisfaction. It is in this context that conversations about consent must be understood – not only in a situational context in which incidents of sexual violence take place but in a relationship context where relationship dynamics and the demeanour of abusive partners shape the meanings and motives of sexually abusive behaviours.

Notes

1 We adopt the acronym LGB and/or T+ in order to better emphasise the diversity of identities included in the term and, especially, to draw attention to the distinctions between sexuality and gender identity, i.e. for example, a trans woman might identify as heterosexual. We also use the term 'queer' as a shorthand way of referring to this diverse range of people.

2 Emily F. Rothman, Deinera Exner, and Allyson L. Baughman, 'The Prevalence of Sexual Assault Against People Who Identify as Gay, Lesbian, or Bisexual in the United States: A Systematic Review', *Trauma, Violence & Abuse*, 12.2 (2011), 55–66 (p. 56); Jieru Chen et al., 'Sexual Violence, Stalking, and Intimate Partner Violence by Sexual Orientation, United States', *Psychology of Violence*, 10.2 (2020), 110–19 (p. 112); Loree Cook-Daniels and Michael Munson, 'Sexual Violence, Elder Abuse, and Sexuality of Transgender Adults, Age 50+: Results of Three Surveys', *Journal of GLBT Family Studies*, 6 (2010), 142–77 (pp. 145–46); Liz Kelly, 'The Continuum of Sexual Violence', in *Women, Violence and Social Control,* ed. by Jalna Hanmer and Mary Maynard (London: Palgrave MacMillan, 1987), pp. 46–60 (p. 47).

3 *Sexual Offences Act 2003* (c. 42, pt. 1).

4 Catherine Donovan and Rebecca Barnes, 'Help-Seeking among Lesbian, Gay, Bisexual and/or Transgender Victims/Survivors of Domestic Violence and Abuse: The Impacts of Cisgendered Heteronormativity and Invisibility', *Journal of Sociology*, 56.4 (2020), 554–70 (pp. 555, 567); Adrienne Rich, 'Compulsory Heterosexuality and Lesbian Existence', *Signs: Journal of Women in Culture and Society*, 5 (1980), 631–60 (p. 631).

5 Nicola Gavey, *Just sex? The cultural scaffolding of rape*, 2nd edn (London: Routledge, 2019), p. 117.

6 Ibid., p. 98.

7 Ibid., p. 100.

8 Norman Dennis and George Erdos, *Families Without Fatherhood* (IEA Health and Welfare Unit, London, 1992), p. 10.

9 Carole Pateman, *The Sexual Contract* (Redwood City: Stanford University Press, 1988), p. 5.

10 Kimberlé Crenshaw, 'Mapping the margins: Intersectionality, identity politics, and violence against women of color', *Stanford Law Review*, 43 (1991), 1241–99 (p. 1260).

11 Catherine Donovan and Rebecca Barnes, *Queering Narratives of Domestic Violence and Abuse* (London: Palgrave Macmillan, 2020), pp. 11–12.

12 Ibid.

13 Office for National Statistics (ONS), 'Women most at risk of experiencing partner abuse in England and Wales: Years ending March 2015 to 2017' (London: ONS, 2018); Chaka L. Bachmann and Becca Gooch, 'LGBT in Britain: Trans report' (London: Stonewall & YouGov, 2018), p. 15; Adam M. Messinger, *LGBTQ intimate partner violence: Lessons for policy, practice and research* (Oakland, CA: University of California Press, 2017), p. 6.

14 Crenshaw, pp. 1242–44; Donovan and Barnes (2020), pp. 11–16; Janice Ristock, *No more secrets: Violence in lesbian relationships* (London: Routledge, 2002), p. 4.

15 Gavey, pp. 73–128.

16 Melanie A. Beres, 'From ignorance to knowledge: Sexual consent and queer stories', *Feminism & Psychology*, 32.2 (2022), 137–55 (p. 140).
17 Gavey, pp. 128–30.
18 Catherine Donovan and Marianne Hester, 'Exploring emotion work in domestically abusive relationships', in *Intimate partner violence in LGBTQ lives*, ed. by Janice Ristock (New York: Routledge, 2011), pp. 81–101 (p. 87); Catherine Donovan and Marianne Hester, *Domestic Violence and Sexuality: What's love got to do with it?* (Bristol: Bristol University Press, 2014), pp. 35–55.
19 Ibid., p. 121.
20 Nils Christie, 'The Ideal Victim', in *From Crime Policy to Victim Policy*, ed. by Ezzat A. Fattah (London: Palgrave MacMillan, 1986), pp. 17–30 (p. 18).
21 Donovan and Hester (2014), p. 152.
22 Donovan and Barnes (2020), p. 16.
23 Ibid., p. 33.
24 Melanie McCarry, Marianne Hester, and Catherine Donovan, 'Researching Same Sex Domestic Violence: Constructing a Survey Methodology', *Sociological Research Online*, 13 (2008), 174–87 (p. 3).
25 Lynne Jamieson, *Intimacy and Personal Relationships in Modern Society* (Cambridge: Polity Press, 1998), p. 9.
26 Michael Wiederman, 'The Gendered Nature of Sexual Scripts', *The Family Journal*, 13.4 (2005), 496–502 (p. 499).
27 All participants' names have been changed to ensure anonymity.
28 Sarah Head and Martin Milton, 'Filling the silence: Exploring the bisexual experience of intimate partner abuse', *Journal of Bisexuality*, 14 (2014), 277–99 (p. 294).
29 Charlene Muehlenhard, Terry Humphreys, Kristen Jozkowski, et al., 'The Complexities of Sexual Consent Among College Students: A Conceptual and Empirical Review', *The Journal of Sex Research*, 53.4–5 (2016), 457–87 (p. 465).

Bibliography

Bachman, Chaka L., and Becca Gooch, 'LGBT in Britain: Trans report' (London: Stonewall & YouGov, 2018)

Beres, Melanie A., 'From Ignorance to Knowledge: Sexual Consent and Queer Stories', *Feminism & Psychology*, 32 (2022), 137–55

Chen, Jieru, Mikel L. Walters, Leah K. Gilbert, and Nimesh Patel, 'Sexual Violence, Stalking, and Intimate Partner Violence by Sexual Orientation, United States', *Psychology of Violence*, 10 (2020), 110–19

Christie, Nils, 'The Ideal Victim', in *From Crime Policy to Victim Policy*, ed. by Ezzat A. Fattah (London: Palgrave MacMillan, 1986), pp. 17–30

Cook-Daniels, Loree, and Michael Munson, 'Sexual Violence, Elder Abuse, and Sexuality of Transgender Adults, Age 50+: Results of Three Surveys', *Journal of GLBT Family Studies*, 6 (2010), 142–77

Crenshaw, Kimberlé, 'Mapping the Margins: Intersectionality, Identity Politics, and Violence Against Women of Color', *Stanford Law Review*, 43 (1991), 1241–99

Donovan, Catherine, and Rebecca Barnes, 'Help-Seeking among Lesbian, Gay, Bisexual and/or Transgender Victims/Survivors of Domestic Violence and Abuse: The Impacts of Cisgendered Heteronormativity and Invisibility', *Journal of Sociology*, 56 (2020), 554–70

Donovan, Catherine, and Rebecca Barnes, *Queering Narratives of Domestic Violence and Abuse* (London: Palgrave Macmillan, 2020)

Donovan, Catherine, and Marianne Hester, *Domestic Violence and Sexuality: What's love got to do with it?* (Bristol: Bristol University Press, 2014)

Donovan, Catherine, and Marianne Hester, 'Exploring Emotion Work in Domestically Abusive Relationships', in *Intimate Partner Violence in LGBTQ Lives*, ed. by Janice Ristock (New York: Routledge, 2011), pp. 55–76

Dennis, Norman, and George Erdos, *Families Without Fatherhood* (London: IEA Health and Welfare Unit, 1992)

Gavey, Nicola, *Just Sex? The Cultural Scaffolding of Rape*, 2nd edn (London: Routledge, 2019)

Head, Sarah, and Martin Milton, 'Filling the Silence: Exploring the Bisexual Experience of Intimate Partner Abuse', *Journal of Bisexuality*, 14 (2014), 277–99

Kelly, Liz, 'The Continuum of Sexual Violence', in *Women, Violence and Social Control*, ed. by Jalna Hanmer and Mary Maynard (London: Palgrave MacMillan, 1987), pp. 46–60

McCarry, Melanie, Marianne Hester, and Catherine Donovan, 'Researching Same Sex Domestic Violence: Constructing a Survey Methodology', *Sociological Research Online*, 13 (2008), 174–87

Messinger, Adam M., *LGBTQ Intimate Partner Violence: Lessons for Policy, Practice and Research* (Oakland, CA: University of California Press, 2017)

Muehlenhard, Charlene, Terry Humphreys, Kristen Jozkowski, and Zoe D. Peterson, 'The Complexities of Sexual Consent Among College Students: A Conceptual and Empirical Review', *The Journal of Sex Research*, 53.4–5 (2016), 457–87

Office for National Statistics (ONS), 'Women most at risk of experiencing partner abuse in England and Wales: Years ending March 2015 to 2017' (London: ONS, 2018)

Pateman, Carole, *The Sexual Contract* (Redwood City: Stanford University Press, 1988)

Rich, Adrienne, 'Compulsory Heterosexuality and Lesbian Existence', *Signs: Journal of Women in Culture and Society*, 5.4 (1980), 631–60

Ristock, Janice, *No More Secrets: Violence in Lesbian Relationships* (London: Routledge, 2002)

Rothman, Emily F., Deinera Exner, and Allyson L. Baughman, 'The Prevalence of Sexual Assault Against People Who Identify as Gay, Lesbian, or Bisexual in the United States: A Systematic Review', *Trauma, Violence & Abuse*, 12 (2011), 55–66

Wiederman, Michael, 'The Gendered Nature of Sexual Scripts', *The Family Journal*, 13 (2005), 496–502

Part IV

Futures of Consent

12 Troubling Technologies for Sexual Consent

Rosanna Bellini and Hazel Dixon

Introduction

Human intimacy and sexualities are increasingly shaped by digital technologies: from providing new ways to date and meet potential sexual partners to an intimate self-exploration of fantasy and pleasure. Indeed, discussions around sexual consent have significantly increased considering the rise in the uptake of online dating platforms and products that facilitate intimate self-exploration. However, there is still a lack of critical attention to how digital technologies might play a role in enforcing specific kinds of consent frameworks – how people understand and negotiate consent – over others, especially regarding how technology might mediate non-consensual or violent sexual experiences. Such technologies can harm people whether they use them in private, like secretly recording themselves in bedrooms and bathrooms, or in public, like taking pictures revealing their underwear.[1]

Entirely new technological innovations such as deepfake (synthetic media in which a person in an existing image or video is replaced with someone else's likeness) technologies also pose unique and explicit risks regarding the distribution of non-consensual intimate imagery or image-based sexual abuse.[2] However, other technologies may be more opaquely connected to concerns around consent that may otherwise go unnoticed. Since consent distinguishes sexual contact from sexual violence, and normative values are actively negotiated,[3] it is essential to study how consent is programmed or embodied in technology and identify ways in which it may already need to be reprogrammed.[4] As such a task can be bewildering for scholars, theorists, and designers, we explore existing ways to investigate embedding healthier interactions with technologies to elicit novel insights into designing for embodiment, flexibility, and reality. We do so to combat a troubling tendency to constrain sexual consenting practice through and with digital technologies in a manner that could subject others to harm.

In this chapter, we examine how sexual consent frameworks are constructed and sustained through two examples of digital technologies where sexual consent frameworks and technologies coalesce. We conduct an in-depth analysis on two retired technological artefacts, originally available for download

DOI: 10.4324/9781003365082-16

in 2018, and scrutinise the impact that their use may have on in-person interactions: a smartphone application LegalFling that digitally records consent in a quasi-legally binding agreement ('secured on the blockchain'); and a Dress for Respect garment that records physical interactions of how many times its wearer is non-consensually touched in nightclubs. Focusing on retired technologies can enable us to identify what consensual frameworks might be at play in digital technologies designed to mediate sexual consent. At a high-level, our analysis draws attention to how existing sexual technologies promote limited and potentially damaging conceptions of sexual consent that rely on inflexible, static, and contractual expectations of relationships between two people. For objects that seek to expose or protect against sexual violence, we problematise restricted and ill-informed notions of what constitute harms, promoting incorrect assumptions about sexual abuse.

We draw on John H. Gagnon and William Simon's sexual script theory to better understand the discursive production of sexual consent in these technologies.[5] A fundamental element to this theory is the notion that beliefs, behaviours, and attitudes about sexuality are constructed through cultural, social, and personal levels of interaction and development. Sexual script theory offers a valuable metaphor that lends significant language and reflective cognitive schemas that may be hard to pin down without inadvertently medicalising or removing the contextual nuances of sexual encounters.[6] Merely discussing sex and technology in the same chapter is no easy feat without directly evoking feelings of embarrassment, shame, or discomfort due to its cultural stigmatisation as a taboo topic. As all digital technologies by their very nature are designed by human hand, this metaphorical approach is valuable in 'opening up' what scripts are already embedded in digital technologies, and how these influence appropriate behaviours and emotions through their use.[7]

Our analysis led us to identify three distinct yet intersecting strategies for designing tools that augment sex and sexuality through and with technology: design for embodiment; design for flexibility; and design for reality. *Embodiment* argues that the body should be seen as an important site for intervention as non-verbal interactions play a large but under-appreciated role in providing, revoking, and complicating sexual consent. *Flexibility* argues that experiences of consent are rarely undergone in a binary sense of the consensual or non-consensual, and instead comprise a continuum of different experiences that should be sensitive to temporal and spatial factors. Finally, *reality* thinks of the use of technologies for consent embedded in the messiness of everyday reality, compelling a sense of responsibility on the part of designers to avoid producing and designing technologies that can easily be adapted for abuse.

Background and Related Literature

For this work, we accept Spencer A. Rathus et al.'s definition of sexuality as 'the way in which we experience and express ourselves as sexual beings [...] and the capacity we have for erotic experiences and responses'.[8] Sexuality is an integral part of a person's human existence, irrespective of their choice to participate in sexual activities, their sensation derived from these activities, or their acknowledgement of the sexed nature of human beings. This broad definition includes dimensions of human sexuality that go beyond the most common interpretation of sexual orientation, which include gender and intimacy.

Digital technologies are reportedly 'riding a golden trend in terms of innovation', facilitating new connections between people, sexuality, and technology; from facilitating sexual activity to connecting groups for in-person meetups.[9] Organisations that cultivate public health campaigns may choose to transmit information about sex through social media or broadcasting. A group of individuals may use online communities to navigate sexual orientation and expression, and a pair of individuals may use teledildonics (remote controlled electronic sex toys) to remotely stimulate each other in erotic play.[10] Tinder, Grindr, Bumble, Hinge, and Fetlife are further examples of some of the hundreds of applications used by millions of daily users to mediate sexual or romantic interactions in a physical space. Despite the millions of users that these platforms boast, it has been noted by several sources that discussing the design for technical tools to facilitate sex and technology in a healthy and curious way has not been at the forefront of the digital agenda.[11]

To understand the relationship between sexuality and technology involves looking beyond sexual pleasure as the goal and consequence. While pleasure is undoubtedly an important site of contestation (such as whose pleasure is prioritised and catered for), designing *only* for pleasure significantly restricts the types of technology imaginable.[12] For instance, sex through technology is often framed as motivation, as if sexual pleasure is something to be achieved, and with the greater the sensation of pleasure the better. In doing so, consent in existing technologies is often overlooked by going under-addressed or being positioned as 'getting in the way' of attaining pleasure.[13] As consent is influenced by culture, history, social positioning, and social interactions, we can infer what sexual consent frameworks are prioritised and imposed by designers and developers on their users.[14] This will allow us to assess the extent to which users may challenge or resist consent frameworks or repurpose them for positive or negative purposes.

This lack of engagement with consent has primarily arisen from framing the user of technologies as a *consumer* of sexual content through pornography and sex robots.[15] For instance, framing consent as sexually *appealing* to attain, rather than *necessary*, or coding a lack of consent as a sexual fantasy such as reluctant sex, forced sex, sexual assault, or rape.[16] In connection with sex robots or sexbots, such entities may be appealing as they do not possess the ability to decline, criticise, or become dissatisfied with the user.[17] Creating a digital service that facilitates a unidirectional sexual relationship may inadvertently lead to diminishing the social and legal importance of consent in sexual interactions.[18]

When sex and technologies come together, predominant approaches in digital design have been described as 'not actively ignoring [sex]' at best, and 'politely covering it up' at worst.[19] This results in a *de-sexualisation* of technology, where the presence of sex and sexuality contribute to a marginal understanding of the role of technology in day-to-day life. A reluctance to engage with sexual consent frameworks is even more concerning when we consider that 'sex is not a natural act', where Leonore Tiefer argued against the idea that sex is a biologically innate act, and the idea that there is a standardised or inbuilt sexual response such as describing sex as either natural or deviant.[20] As a result, many people may feel discouraged from identifying social differences that exist between different forms of sexual activity out of fear of being considered dirty, embarrassing, or crude. Through masking the social construction of sexual activity, conversations about consent, sexual violence, and exploitation are cast to the margins. In this regard, humans are highly dependent on what society informs them about sex, consent, and sexuality. This dependency can be highly problematic because the values that are embedded in technologies can lead people to troubling conclusions around what constitutes the 'natural' way to have sex, and what is considered deviant or unnatural.

Our Approach: Sexual Script Analysis

Gagnon and Simon's sexual script theory suggests that sexuality and sexual behaviours are social processes that are determined by a set of *scripts* used to organise and interpret sexual encounters within easily understood conventions in which people can predict who does what and when in a particular context.[21] Scripts are inherently social, whereby they can only be understood because people have internalised a certain set of values and expectations. This is especially useful when we throw in a non-human agent (i.e., digital technologies) as we can examine the interpersonal interpretations of that assumption. Through scripts, we can understand how designers enforce certain values and conventions in the digital tools they design. We have chosen to use sexual scripts as a critical lens and a metaphor – making our analysis descriptive rather than explanatory (or prescriptive). Sexual script theory draws from social constructionism where reality and human behaviour is produced by shared beliefs in a social group.[22]

The social scripts present within the core meaning of this theory are conceptualised as the mental representations that individuals construct and then purpose to make sense of their own experience, including their own and others' behaviour. Although script theory may be applied to other areas, sexual activities gain a special status because of how society ascribes them to be significant. We use scripts as they specify the appropriate objects, aims, and qualities of sexual interactions, while also providing actors with instruction around time, place, and steps in relation to sexual activity.[23]

Scholars have also used scripts to explore sex and digital technologies. For instance, Susanna Paasonen has investigated where and when scripts are played out, especially in the context of the online exploration of sexual fantasy and desire.[24] Douglas Zytko et al. and Mark Warner et al. have also explicitly used scripts to scrutinise how technology can mediate self-disclosure of different elements of status (for example, LGBTQ+ identity or HIV status) through informal mechanisms of disclosure such as free-text boxes and instant messaging.[25]

When digital technologies allow signalling one's statuses and identities, scholars cautiously suggest they may allow communication about different behaviours, sexual desires, and interests. However, this must be done appropriately and with power imbalances in mind, as Fiona Vera-Gray et al. describe how sexual violence can be easily endorsed as a sexual script through an analysis of online pornographic content.[26] Irrespective of the platform, the presence of technological mechanics trouble sexual scripts.

Choice of Case Studies

For this analysis, we selected two historic instances of consent frameworks and digital design clashing in unique and interesting ways: a smartphone application, LegalFling, and a garment Dress for Respect that captures how many times the garment and its wearer is touched. We chose these artefacts as they both received a significant amount of media attention, indicating these were valuable objects for discursive conversations about consent.[27] Additionally, LegalFling addresses miscommunication about sexual consent, while the other was used as an attempt to raise awareness about sexual contact – invited or not – in public spaces. With case studies, we also aspired to focus on how technologies can have divergent values and interpretations (also known as interpretative flexibility) that depend on the way they are models.[28] We aimed to grasp a greater understanding of how technologies are designed, their purposes, and their meanings.

Our first artefact, LegalFling, is a smartphone application designed to 'request and verify explicit consent before having sex' between two people.[29] Two users are paired through the LegalFling application and are prompted to sign a contract in-application to sexual activity. The contract can be furnished with exemptions or clauses to this consent, such as the requirement to use a condom, be free of sexually transmitted disease, or refrain from the use of Bondage, Discipline, Dominance and Submission, Sadomasochism (BDSM). To request sexual consent, a user sends a digital invitation to sign a virtual contract that appears as a notification on a receiver's smartphone. Once the user agrees to the stated conditions specified by the sender, the user is notified that they may 'accept and fling'. Each contract, by its nature of being stored on the blockchain, is immutable, verifiable, and referenceable, and is 'legally binding', with the potential to be used as evidence in court for wrongdoing or violation of the sexual contract.[30]

Our second artefact, Dress for Respect, is a collaboration between the advertising company, the São Paulo branch of Ogilvy, and the beverage company Schweppes as an experimental advertisement to raise awareness about sexual harassment or groping in nightclubs in the light of public campaigns such as #MeToo and #TimesUp.[31] Based on preliminary interviews with men who expressed that harassment was a fabricated or minor issue with women in clubs, the partnership sought to elevate this issue so that men could reflect and act upon their behaviours. Through this promotion, a touch-sensitive dress was designed to track how often, and with what degree of intensity, women were touched in a nightclub. The dress was embedded with unspecified sensors that tracked both touch and pressure within a sequinned, body-con dress, as three women were sent into a club in São Paulo, Brazil, to trial the system. The information from touch sensors was relayed back to a visual heatmap in an external location where researchers could 'essentially track harassment in real time'.[32] Across the space of just three hours and 47 minutes, three women were touched 157 times in total, many of these on the women's lower back, backside, and upper arms, reportedly more than 40 times an hour. Through this campaign, the men who expressed disbelief or doubt towards the issue of unwanted touching were invited to see the full results, 'to see what they couldn't see before'.[33]

Scripts at Work in LegalFling

There are various normative scripts imposed by the design of LegalFling on how it promotes how consent should occur between two (or more) individuals in sexual contexts. However, the predominant script that this application uses is that consent, once provided, is unable to be revoked, or interestingly even edited, as the receipt is stored on the blockchain. In LegalFling, sex is a single occurrence consisting of the following phases: a pre-arranged and pre-agreed consenting phase, a sexual act phase that occurs in accordance with approved conditions, and a completion of the sexual activity phase. Once complete, both parties have a record, or a receipt, of the sexual encounter and terms agreed within the application that can be used as evidence in any potential argument that supports or challenges a discussion about the session.

Sexual consent acts as a special form of permission that can be a complicated exchange between two or more individuals. Identifying the discomfort surrounding sexual communication before sex is an important element to alleviate, and therefore explore, digitally. While so-called consent applications, such as we-consent and the Yes to Sex dating application, have been present on App Stores since 2015, bringing the legalities of blockchain technologies into the picture significantly complicates matters around sexual consent. Indeed, the problem of sexual communication that LegalFling has posed here appears to be one of clarification and the permanence of recording what information was agreed to at what time. In fact, the designers of LegalFling suggest that they are solving the problem of sexual miscommunication around sexual activity and sexual consent. This is in contrast to another way of approaching such a problem, such as encouraging conversations surrounding preferences and requirements. The problem exists in individuals misinterpreting or misleading an individual about what is, and what is not, appropriate during sex – hence the requirement for 'getting explicit about sexual consent'.[34] This is both on behalf of the person requesting consent, ensuring that sex on their terms will not be (to borrow legal terminology) violated, and the person sending their consent, possessing evidential proof of 'consent' to engage in sex under certain conditions.

The matter that this design solves, however, is not clarity over the terms of engagement; instead, the terms of engagement need to be secured, proven, and evidenced for a speculative event within the future. This is an interesting interpretation of scripted sexual behaviour that frames sexual partners as being unaware of potential sexual partners' preferences and needs. As such, the application is used to state their needs and desires visually and explicitly through pre-selected (and arguably normative) categories that confine human behaviour to pre-recognised preferences, sexual identities, and kinks. The role of the application's proof-of-consent as a form of evidence of past activity is crucial in its move away from a focus on sexual communication. The implication embedded within this functionality is that this evidence will be valuable and crucial at a later stage where it could be useful in a different context beyond sexual activity. While demonstrating that someone violated your preferences in a sexual encounter in a legal court proceeding on sexual violence could be useful, LegalFling's designers are perhaps naive to the sociopolitical context in which it will be used. Against the backdrop of myths of false rape allegations,[35] and a severe drop in the number of charges by the criminal prosecution service,[36] this application could stand to support rather than challenge existing unequal and unjust treatment of survivors. The scripts inherent in this application might inadvertently provide potential abusers with evidence that an individual may have consented to a sexual activity that could have otherwise been revoked in-situ.

Furthermore, this application may be understood as a representation of sexual miscommunication theory at work; a theory that posits sexual violence occurs as a result of miscommunication between the parties involved.[37] This has the harmful side effect that the onus is on communicating and interpreting one's needs and understanding over more overt effects, such as a harmdoer's intent or wider structural factors. Indeed, instead of alleviating the problems of being explicit about sexual consent, this application erases the complexity inherent in sexual activities, to the potential detriment of both parties involved. This is due to its conflation of sexual consent with a legal or commercialised contract that is seemingly at odds with the fluidity, flexibility, and socially situated nature or situatedness of sex. In continuing with the theme of social contexts and how they may influence how consent is understood, we now move on to exploring Dress for Respect, an artefact that is most often used in the public realm.

Working Scripts for Dress for Respect

Dress for Respect is a thought-provoking interpretation of sexual communication, and like LegalFling, it identifies and imposes specific sexual scripts for how people coordinate and navigate sexual activity. While intended for a different end goal – to promote thinking around sexual communication in public nightclubs – the artefact holds interesting similarities to the use of LegalFling regarding scripted behaviour that we explore here in more detail. Firstly, we identify that Dress for Respect is explicitly gender-coded as being an artefact to be worn by women as they navigate sexual and non-sexual communication. While dresses inherently do not possess a gender, it is curious that the trial of the artefact involved only women in a campaign to draw attention to how often women are touched in nightclubs. The dress itself provides minimal, if any, flexibility in how consent is interpreted or negotiated. The dress exemplifies a unique sexual script where women are the passive recipients of sexual contact, and other individuals (men in this context) are the agents who impose this sexual contact on others. This ties into the script where men ask for or request sex and sexual activity from women, while women passively consent or actively provide access to sex. Indeed, there is no way for the dress itself to indicate how women wearing the dress might actively seek out to touch others sexually in this context.

Once again, this technical artefact frames the solution to the problem of sexual harassment in an interesting, yet challenging, way. The dress attempts to deploy sexual scripts through its focus on demonstrating how many times women are touched in clubs, that this should show men it is a larger problem than previously thought. Indeed, the garment does not purport to offer a pragmatic and simple 'solution' to consent through the sexual scripts it adopts, but it does pose itself as a creator of and contributor to the discourse of sexual consent. However, curiously as the dress does not have functionality built in that alerts the wearer or the individual touching the dress synchronously, the problem of certain men's dismissal of sexual groping in clubs is seemingly resolved by the collection and presentation of quantifiable data that presents evidence at a later stage. Arguably, collecting quantifiable data on a reportedly insidious and culturally entrenched problem is no doubt a valid and important task, particularly for information that may have been lost otherwise. However, the point of the artefact itself appears to be using the women wearing the artefact to generate data to present to others who may express their surprise at the startlingly high number of incidences in which they are touched. In this way, there is no intervention in real-time to either discourage the men's groping behaviors, or provide a way for the wearer to signal for assistance.

Furthermore, the data itself proves to be an interesting unknown; while the dress may record the number and intensity of touches, within the context of the study, we are left to assume that all recorded touches are non-consensual and of a sexual nature. This a very broad assumption to make when all variables are not considered; given the proximity of individuals within a club, what distinguishes a brush with another person required to move within crowds, and a deliberate grope? While intent is a standard exclusion from quantifiable data, the process in which women are unable to identify what was indeed consensual touching by two consenting parties, and what was not, presents us with a predicament. Given the complexity of sexual communication and miscommunication within nightclubs, it can demonise this way of communicating; there are several women who may appreciate being touched frequently (strictly *with* consent), to which this dress does not account for. Notably the cultural setting in which this dress is designed and used also has a large impact on notions of proxemics, that there are different expectations about the physicality of such interactions.

While an argument in favour of the dress is that it provides women with the agency to demonstrate the prevelance of these issues, it is somewhat strange that it is the researchers performing this role *on behalf* of the women wearing the dress. Apart from performing the test, the women curiously have no further part in the study beyond data collection, meaning a large proportion of the agency supposedly provided by the dress is in the hands of the researchers and their interpretations. The dress indicates that men might only realise the gravity of such a pressing concern through quantitive statistics on how many times women are groped in clubs. Except for performing the test, the women curiously have no further part in the study beyond data collection, and it is unclear if they have ownership over the data produced by the dress.

Discussion

In scrutinising the sexual scripts and consent frameworks inherent in our two digital artefacts, we reflect now on what designers, developers, or interested users could do to better facilitate systems for sexual consent and communication. Our recommendations fall under three themes: designing for embodiment; designing for flexibility in the technology; and designing for reality, requests for designers who build technologies with some element of sexual consent in mind, specifically in the realm of negotiating consent in physical spaces.

Designing for Embodiment

Sexual arousal and contact are deeply situated in the body and by attempting to efface this embodied element, technologies can often neglect the needs and autonomy of the actors. In LegalFling, it becomes clear how consent is broken down into a series of legal stipulations and how this can ignore sustained bodily needs. Consent is an embodied experience; it is impossible to give consent without having an embodied element to it, even in non-physical spaces. With Dress for Respect, we can understand the role of the body in a different way. Here, the technology is closer to the body in that it rests on it and the actions of the technology seek to expose the actions that are done to the person wearing it. However, the person in the dress does not retain autonomy over what the dress displays; such as the type of data it collects, how it is recorded, or what the data is then used for. As such, the purpose of the technology is still one step removed from the body. This autonomy of the body is especially pertinent for technologies where the needs of victim-survivors are to be kept in mind. Designers should think about bodies as they are; for example, through exciting explorations into biological signals (signals produced by a biological organism such as a person), somaesthetic (bodily perception, performance, and presentation), or wearable technologies that represent and communicate non-verbal and subtle changes in how sex is being done. For instance, thermal temperature, sensations, and movements could all be used to help communicate different levels of comfort and engagement that are immediately responsive to a specific context.

Designing for Flexibility

Another significant element of how sexual consent is understood within technologies is by considering the relative (in)flexibility of consent. When we conceptualise consent as something that is flexible, we move sex from being something that is simply attained or aspirational to something that is dialectically experienced and communicated between two or more people. Consent can and will be revoked during sexual contact, several times and in multiple different ways. The ability to remove sexual consent in a way that is supported is an essential part of sexual consent. Our scripts highlighted that neither of these artefacts had taken this flexibility into consideration and see consent or non-consent as a done deal without much negotiation taking place: LegalFling had made this impossible to revoke; and Dress for Respect had also been designed so that once consent was seen as having been revoked, it was unable to accommodate a user changing their mind. Although we argue that using legal frameworks to underpin sexual activity may not be appropriate for standard interactions, there is still potential in using these approaches in the context of sex work – only, however, if the worker is the one determining the nature of these contracts. We suggest that, instead, designers should consider how consent variables within digital systems can be modelled as a spectrum or a collection of indicators – from comfort, to excitement, to willingness, and beyond – to capture the breadth of impacting factors that influence sexual consent.

Designing for Reality

We suggest that artefacts need to be designed in consideration of the broader sociopolitical environments and contexts within which they will be used. LegalFling was positioned as a tool to evidence sexual consent. This exists against a backdrop of myths in false rape allegations and a severe drop in the number of sexual assault cases that progress to court. Within this reality, designers must not only take into consideration the environment in which a piece of technology for sexual consent will be used, but actively design *for* it. This can be as simple as considering how a piece of technology might be used against another person for malicious purposes, even if these go beyond what the designers were imagining. However, redesigning for the reality of Dress for Respect is more subtle. How might designers consider the setting of a nightclub where some physical touching may be understood as part of the social norms? Indeed, how do we allow for communication of sexual non-consent in an environment where sexual touching is common and can be consensual? We might approach this by understanding how technologies for sexual consent must be designed in consideration of the actors within the environments where it is being used and alongside those actors. For example, if sexual miscommunication has been identified as a real problem, we suggest discussing this with couples struggling to communicate, such as through research and outreach. Pausing before jumping into a design helps to develop critical thinking skills, such as how misuse can occur through thoughtless design. Consent can be complicated. Designers should embrace that complexity and the messiness that is inherent in sexual relationships.

Notes

1 Danielle Keats Citron, 'Sexual Privacy', *Yale Law Journal*, 128.7 (2018), 1870–961 (pp. 1874–76).

2 Claire McGlynn, Erika Rackley, and Ruth Houghton, 'Beyond "Revenge Porn": The Continuum of Image-Based Sexual Abuse', *Feminist Legal Studies*, 25 (2017), 25–46 (pp. 26–28).

3 John Danaher, 'The Symbolic-Consequences Argument in the Sex Robot Debate', in *Robot Sex: Social and Ethical Implications*, ed. by John Danaher and Neil McArthur (Cambridge, MA: MIT Press, 2017), pp. 1–59 (p. 3).

4 Ellen M. Kaufman, 'Reprogramming Consent: Implications of Sexual Relationships with Artificially Intelligent Partners', *Psychology & Sexuality*, 11.4 (2020), 372–83.

5 John H. Gagnon and William Simon, *Sexual Conduct: The Social Sources of Human Sexuality*, 2nd edn (New York: Routledge, 2017).

6 Michael W. Wiederman, 'Sexual Script Theory: Past, Present, and Future', in *Handbook of the Sociology of Sexualities*, ed. by John DeLamater and Rebecca F. Plante (Cham: Springer International Publishing, 2015), pp. 7–22 (pp. 7–9).

7 Ibid., p. 10.

8 Spencer A. Rathus, Jeff Nevid, and Lois Fichner-Rathus, *Human Sexuality in a Changing World*, 10th edn (New York: Pearson, 2017), p. 4.

9 Nicola Liberati, 'Teledildonics and Digital Intimacy', *Glimpse*, 18 (2017), 103–10.

10 For instance, fetlife.com and fetish.com both promote kink-positive and positive spaces that permit a user to explore their sexuality.

11 See Avery C. Edenfield, 'Queering Consent: Design and Sexual Consent Messaging', *Communication Design Quarterly*, 7.2 (2019), 50–63; Jane Im et al., 'Yes: Affirmative Consent as a Theoretical Framework for Understanding and Imagining Social Platforms', in *Proceedings of the 2021 CHI Conference on Human Factors in Computing Systems*, CHI '21 (New York: Association for Computing Machinery, 2021),

pp. 1–18; Matthew Wood, Gavin Wood, and Madeline Balaam, 'Sex Talk: Designing for Sexual Health with Adolescents', in *Proceedings of the 2017 Conference on Interaction Design and Children*, IDC '17 (New York: Association for Computing Machinery, 2017), pp. 137–47.

12 See Im et al., pp. 1–2; and Yolande Strengers et al., 'What Can HCI Learn from Sexual Consent? A Feminist Process of Embodied Consent for Interactions with Emerging Technologies', in *Proceedings of the 2021 CHI Conference on Human Factors in Computing Systems*, CHI '21 (New York: Association for Computing Machinery, 2021), pp. 1–13.

13 Joanna Demaree-Cotton and Roseanna Sommers, 'Autonomy and the Folk Concept of Valid Consent', *Cognition*, 224 (2022), 1–60.

14 Naomi B. McCormick, 'Preface to Sexual Scripts: Social and Therapeutic Implications', *Sexual and Relationship Therapy*, 25 (2010), 91–95.

15 Robert Kozinets, Anthony Patterson, and Rachel Ashman, 'Networks of Desire: How Technology Increases Our Passion to Consume', *Journal of Consumer Research*, 43.5 (2017), 659–82.

16 Malachi Willis et al., 'Sexual Consent Communication in Best-Selling Pornography Films: A Content Analysis', *Journal of Sex Research*, 57.1 (2020), 52–63.

17 Sinziana M. Gutiu, 'The Roboticization of Consent', in *Robot Law*, ed. by Ryan Calo, A. Michael Froomkin, and Ian Kerr (Cheltenham: Edward Elgar, 2016), pp. 186–212.

18 Federica Facchin, Giussy Barbara, and Vittorio Cigoli, 'Sex Robots: The Irreplaceable Value of Humanity', *BMJ: British Medical Journal (Online)*, 358 (2017), DOI: 10.1136/bmj.j3790.

19 Johanna Brewer et al., 'Sexual Interactions: Why We Should Talk about Sex in HCI', in *CHI '06 Extended Abstracts on Human Factors in Computing Systems*, CHI EA '06 (New York: Association for Computing Machinery, 2006), pp. 1695–98.

20 Leonore Tiefer, *Sex Is Not A Natural Act & Other Essays*, 2nd edn (Boulder, CO: Routledge, 2004), p. 1.

21 Gagnon and Simon, p. 16.

22 Ibid., p. 17.

23 Michael W. Wiederman, 'The Gendered Nature of Sexual Scripts', *Family Journal*, 13.4 (2005), 496–502 (pp. 498–500).

24 Susanna Paasonen, 'Many Splendored Things: Sexuality, Playfulness and Play', *Sexualities*, 21.4 (2018), 537–51.

25 See Douglas Zytko et al., 'Computer-Mediated Consent to Sex: The Context of Tinder', in *Proceedings of the ACM on Human-Computer Interaction*, 5.CSCW1 (New York: Association for Computing Machinery, 2021), 189.1–26; Mark Warner et al., 'Signal Appropriation of Explicit HIV Status Disclosure Fields in Sex-Social Apps Used by Gay and Bisexual Men', in *Proceedings of the 2019 CHI Conference on Human Factors in Computing Systems*, CHI '19 (New York: Association for Computing Machinery, 2019), pp. 1–15.

26 Fiona Vera-Gray et al., 'Sexual Violence as a Sexual Script in Mainstream Online Pornography', *British Journal of Criminology*, 61.5 (2021), 1243–60.

27 See E. J. Dickson, 'A "Smart Dress" Proves What Women Already Know: Sexual Harassment Is a Problem', *Vox*, 2018 <https://www.vox.com/the-goods/2018/11/29/18118402/ogilvy-schweppes-smart-dress-harassment> [accessed 8 May 2023]; Samantha Cole, 'Don't Fuck Anybody Who Wants to Get Your Consent Uploaded to the Blockchain', *Vox*, 16 January 2018 <https://www.vice.com/en/article/paqvn7/dont-fuck-anybody-who-wants-to-get-your-consent-uploaded-to-the-blockchain-legalfling-app> [accessed 8 May 2023].

28 Neil F. Doherty, Crispin R. Coombs, and John Loan-Clarke, 'A re-conceptualization of the interpretive flexibility of information technologies: redressing the balance between the social and the technical', *European Journal of Information Systems*, 15.6 (2006), 569–82.

29 *LegalThings*, 2018 <https://legalfling.io/> [accessed 31 January 2018].
30 Ibid.
31 *Schweppes – The Dress for Respect*, dir. by Ogilvy Brazil, YouTube, 2018 <https://www.youtube.com/watch?v=Lljf3C0KzH0> [accessed 8 May 2023].
32 'Ogilvy San Paolo', Ogilvy, 2018 <https://www.ogilvy.com/> [accessed 8 May 2023].
33 Ibid.
34 LegalThings.
35 Claire E. Ferguson and John M. Malouff, 'Assessing Police Classifications of Sexual Assault Reports: A Meta-Analysis of False Reporting Rates', *Archives of Sexual Behavior*, 45.5 (2016), 1185–93.
36 'The Criminal Justice System: Statistics | RAINN' <https://www.rainn.org/statistics/criminal-justice-system> [accessed 8 May 2023].
37 Hannah Frith and Celia Kitzinger, 'Talk about Sexual Miscommunication', *Women's Studies International Forum,* 20.4 (1997), 517–28.

Bibliography

Brewer, Johanna, Joseph 'Jofish' Kaye, Amanda Williams, and Susan Wyche, 'Sexual Interactions: Why We Should Talk about Sex in HCI', in *CHI '06 Extended Abstracts on Human Factors in Computing Systems*, CHI EA '06 (New York: Association for Computing Machinery, 2006), pp. 1695–98

Citron, Danielle Keats, 'Sexual Privacy', *Yale Law Journal*, 128.7 (2018), 1870–1961

Cole, Samantha, 'Don't Fuck Anybody Who Wants to Get Your Consent Uploaded to the Blockchain', *Vox*, 16 January 2018 <https://www.vice.com/en/article/paqvn7/dont-fuck-anybody-who-wants-to-get-your-consent-uploaded-to-the-blockchain-legalfling-app> [accessed 8 May 2023]

Danaher, John, 'The Symbolic-Consequences Argument in the Sex Robot Debate', in *Robot Sex: Social and Ethical Implications*, ed. by John Danaher and Neil McArthur (Cambridge, MA: MIT Press, 2017), pp. 1–59

Demaree-Cotton, Joanna, and Roseanna Sommers, 'Autonomy and the Folk Concept of Valid Consent', *Cognition*, 224 (2022), 1–60

Dickson, E. J., 'A "Smart Dress" Proves What Women Already Know: Sexual Harassment Is a Problem', *Vox*, 29 November 2018 <https://www.vox.com/the-goods/2018/11/29/18118402/ogilvy-schweppes-smart-dress-harassment> [accessed 8 May 2023]

Doherty, Neil F., Crispin R. Coombs, and John Loan-Clarke, 'A Re-conceptualization of the Interpretive Flexibility of Information Technologies: Redressing the Balance between the Social and the Technical', *European Journal of Information Systems*, 15.6 (2006), 569–82

Edenfield, Avery C., 'Queering Consent: Design and Sexual Consent Messaging', *Communication Design Quarterly*, 7.2 (2019), 50–63

Facchin, Federica, Giussy Barbara, and Vittorio Cigoli, 'Sex Robots: The Irreplaceable Value of Humanity', *BMJ: British Medical Journal (Online)*, 358 (2017), DOI: 10.1136/bmj.j3790

Ferguson, Claire E., and John M. Malouff, 'Assessing Police Classifications of Sexual Assault Reports: A Meta-Analysis of False Reporting Rates', *Archives of Sexual Behavior*, 45.5 (2016), 1185–93

Frith, Hannah, and Celia Kitzinger, 'Talk about Sexual Miscommunication', *Womens Studies International Forum*, 20.4 (1997), 517–28

Gagnon, John H., and William Simon, *Sexual Conduct: The Social Sources of Human Sexuality*, 2nd edn (New York: Routledge, 2017)

Gutiu, Sinziana M., 'The Roboticization of Consent', in *Robot Law*, ed. by Ryan Calo, A. Michael Froomkin, and Ian Kerr (Cheltenham: Edward Elgar, 2016), pp. 186–212

Im, Jane, Jill Dimond, Melody Berton, Una Lee, Katherine Mustelier, Mark S. Ackerman, and Eric Gilbert, 'Yes: Affirmative Consent as a Theoretical Framework for Understanding and Imagining Social Platforms', in *Proceedings of the 2021 CHI Conference on Human Factors in Computing Systems*, CHI '21 (New York: Association for Computing Machinery, 2021), pp. 1–18

Kaufman, Ellen M., 'Reprogramming Consent: Implications of Sexual Relationships with Artificially Intelligent Partners', *Psychology & Sexuality*, 11.4 (2020), 372–83

Kozinets, Robert, Anthony Patterson, and Rachel Ashman, 'Networks of Desire: How Technology Increases Our Passion to Consume', *Journal of Consumer Research*, 43.5 (2017), 659–82

LegalThings, 2018 <https://legalfling.io/> [accessed 31 January 2018]

Liberati, Nicola, 'Teledildonics and Digital Intimacy', *Glimpse*, 18 (2017), 103–10

McCormick, Naomi B., 'Preface to Sexual Scripts: Social and Therapeutic Implications', *Sexual and Relationship Therapy*, 25.1 (2010), 91–95

McGlynn, Claire, Erika Rackley, and Ruth Houghton, 'Beyond "Revenge Porn": The Continuum of Image-Based Sexual Abuse', *Feminist Legal Studies*, 25 (2017), 25–46

'Ogilvy San Paolo', *Ogilvy*, 2018 <https://www.ogilvy.com/> [accessed 8 May 2023]

Paasonen, Susanna, 'Many Splendored Things: Sexuality, Playfulness and Play', *Sexualities*, 21.4 (2018), 537–51

Rathus, Spencer A., Jeff Nevid, and Lois Fichner-Rathus, *Human Sexuality in a Changing World*, 10th edn (New York: Pearson, 2017)

Schweppes – The Dress for Respect, dir. by Ogilvy Brazil, YouTube, 2018 <https://www.youtube.com/watch?v=Lljf3C0KzH0> [accessed 8 May 2023]

Strengers, Yolande, Jathan Sadowski, ZhuyingLi, AnnaShimshak, and Florian 'Floyd' Mueller, 'What Can HCI Learn from Sexual Consent? A Feminist Process of Embodied Consent for Interactions with Emerging Technologies', in *Proceedings of the 2021 CHI Conference on Human Factors in Computing Systems*, CHI '21 (New York: Association for Computing Machinery, 2021), pp. 1–13

'The Criminal Justice System: Statistics | RAINN' <https://www.rainn.org/statistics/criminal-justice-system> [accessed 8 May 2023]

Tiefer, Leonore, *Sex Is Not A Natural Act & Other Essays*, 2nd edn (Boulder, CO: Routledge, 2004)

Vera-Gray, Fiona, Clare McGlynn, Ibad Kureshi, and Kate Butterby, 'Sexual Violence as a Sexual Script in Mainstream Online Pornography', *British Journal of Criminology*, 61.5 (2021), 1243–60

Warner, Mark, Juan F. Maestre, Jo Gibbs, Chia-Fang Chung, and Ann Blandford, 'Signal Appropriation of Explicit HIV Status Disclosure Fields in Sex-Social Apps Used by Gay and Bisexual Men', in *Proceedings of the 2019 CHI Conference on Human Factors in Computing Systems*, CHI '19 (New York: Association for Computing Machinery, 2019), pp. 1–15

Wiederman, Michael W., 'Sexual Script Theory: Past, Present, and Future', in *Handbook of the Sociology of Sexualities*, ed. by John DeLamater and Rebecca F. Plante (Cham: Springer International Publishing, 2015), pp. 7–22

Wiederman, Michael W., 'The Gendered Nature of Sexual Scripts', *Family Journal*, 13.4 (2005), 496–502

Willis, Malachi, Sasha N. Canan, Kristen N. Jozkowski, and Ana J. Bridges, 'Sexual Consent Communication in Best-Selling Pornography Films: A Content Analysis', *Journal of Sex Research*, 57.1 (2020), 52–63

Wood, Matthew, Gavin Wood, and Madeline Balaam, 'Sex Talk: Designing for Sexual Health with Adolescents', in *Proceedings of the 2017 Conference on Interaction Design and Children*, IDC '17 (New York: Association for Computing Machinery, 2017), pp. 137–47

Zytko, Douglas, Nicholas Furlo, Bailey Carlin, and Matthew Archer, 'Computer-Mediated Consent to Sex: The Context of Tinder', in *Proceedings of the ACM on Human-Computer Interaction*, 5.CSCW1 (New York: Association for Computing Machinery, 2021), 189.1–26

13 Sexual Offences and Defined Consent

Lessons from the Past and a Framework for the Future

Kyle L. Murray

Introduction

In recent years, there has been renewed public discussion of the ethical and legal issues raised by deceptive sexual encounters. This has been sparked by high profile legal cases – involving stealthing/contraceptive sabotage, so-called gender fraud, and undercover police relationships – along with representation in popular TV shows such as Michaela Coel's 2020 BBC series, *I May Destroy You* (the subject of Christina Mansueti's chapter in this collection).

When might such encounters lead to a sexual offence? When *should* they? Under the current structure of non-consensual sexual offences – defined as sexual contact without the consent of the complainant, and without a defendant's reasonable belief in consent – the legal question becomes: when does a false belief make a sexual encounter non-consensual?[1]

These are by no means new questions, however – they have troubled the law for centuries. This chapter critically examines the way the law of England and Wales has approached them, historically and today. I identify a repeated tendency to draw restrictive lines around what matters are capable of undermining consent – the legacy of a framework dating back to the nineteenth century.

My core argument is that these line-drawing approaches are unsuitable for a modern and principled law of sexual offences supposedly grounded in the value of sexual autonomy. They require judges to answer what are deeply personal and contestable questions surrounding the true 'nature' or 'essence' of a sexual encounter. If we are to respect sexual autonomy, these questions belong in the hands of the people involved. On this basis, I set out a framework of 'defined consent'. The act of consenting already necessarily involves an idea of what it is one is agreeing to. This approach holds that outside the scope of this defined encounter, there is no consent.

The argument proceeds as follows: the second and third sections trace the history of the courts' approach from the early nineteenth century to the modern day. While the courts have long recognised the principle of non-consent in cases of fraudulent/mistaken sex, in practice this has consistently been limited by their own interpretations of the nature of a sexual act.

DOI: 10.4324/9781003365082-17

In the fourth section, I draw out the harms these restrictive approaches do to the idea of sexual autonomy. Looking forward, I demonstrate how an alternative conception of these cases – an expansive approach of 'defined consent' – can work to protect sexual autonomy more fully, while avoiding the concerns that have worried the courts.

Historical Distinctions: Fraud, Vitiated Consent, and Non-consent

An early strand of case law – dating back to 1824 – applied a general rule that fraud vitiates consent. This was used to uphold non-sexual assault convictions in cases where defendants had: persuaded (and physically assisted) a woman to strip under the pretence of a medical examination;[2] induced sexual activity by impersonating a woman's husband;[3] and had intercourse while not disclosing their infection with a venereal disease.[4] As one judge explained to the jury: the key to conviction was that the complainant 'would not have consented if she had known the fact' of the matter involved, because then 'her consent is vitiated by the deceit'.[5] While one of these cases saw a conviction for indecent (in modern terms, sexual) assault through intercourse,[6] the courts repeatedly rejected that the vitiated consent could lead to a rape charge. The illogic of this distinction between what was, really, the same issue of consent about the same conduct, was later realised.[7]

For sexual offences, the logic of vitiated consent eventually came to be replaced by the different idea of non-consent. This idea was first seen in *R v Case* (1850). A medical practitioner had sexual intercourse with a young girl under the pretence that it was treatment rather than a sexual act. The court upheld the assault conviction on the basis that the complainant had 'consented to one thing' – treatment – and the defendant 'did another materially different'.[8] The issue was not that agreement was tainted by fraud, but that there was in fact *no agreement at all* to what happened. While it had not been charged, the Chief Justice further indicated that this logic could 'perhaps' ground the offence of rape.[9] This was followed up on in *Flattery* (1877), upholding a rape conviction in similar circumstances: 'the only thing she consented to was the performance of a surgical operation'.[10] The vitiated consent strand of cases was finally killed off following *Clarence* (1888), which rejected clearly the general proposition that fraud vitiates consent. The leading judgments explained the previous cases instead on the basis that 'consent [...] does not exist at all, because the act consented to is not the act done'.[11] This idea was applied to both sexual and non-sexual assault offences.[12]

The material difference view of non-consent, then, had come to apply across the spectrum of non-consensual offences. Cases of fraudulently induced consent came to be covered by the different statutory offence of procuring intercourse with a woman by 'false pretences or false representations'.[13]

Non-consent and the 'Nature' of the Act: A Legacy of Judicial Line-drawing

The idea that there is no consent when someone has agreed to something different to what happens seems intuitive.[14] Applying it, of course, requires one to determine when the act is 'materially different' to that agreed. It seems equally logical, however – given the issue is whether *the complainant* agreed to what happened – that this question should be answered by looking at exactly what it is *the person doing the agreeing* considered themselves to be agreeing to. This is the approach I will propose in this chapter.

In the century and a half which has followed the recognition of the non-consent idea, however, the courts have answered the question in a more limited way, using their own judgements about the essence of a sexual act.

The Historic Nature and Identity Categories

We saw this first in the 'nature of the act' category set out in *Clarence.* Justices Wills and Stephen were careful to limit the scope of the non-consent principle, noting that it had never been applied outside the context of ignorance of the 'nature of the act' as a sexual act *per se* – as in the medical pretence cases – or impersonation of a woman's husband.[15] This is often referred to as two categories: deception 'as to the nature of the act or the identity of the agent'.[16] In reality, however, the identity of the agent was relevant *because* it altered the nature of the act which occurred. Initially, this applied only to the husband impersonation situation, the logic being that marital and adulterous intercourse were 'wholly different in their moral nature', so that agreement to one is not agreement to the other.[17]

In the century which followed, the principle continued to be applied exclusively in these situations of surgical fraud and impersonation – although the impersonation idea was eventually updated at common law to cover impersonation of the (long term) partner of a woman, to reflect changes in societal values by the latter part of the twentieth century.[18] *Clarence* itself had rejected the relevance of venereal disease to the nature of the act. The majority dismissed the argument that the complainant had consented only to intercourse with a healthy partner – 'a natural and healthy connection', as Justice Field put it in his dissent.[19] Instead, the consent to the intercourse that happened was said to be 'as full and conscious as consent could be'.[20] In 1995, *Linekar* used the narrow approach to overturn a conviction for rape where a sex worker had intercourse on the basis that the customer would pay as agreed. Despite his never having the intention nor means of paying, the court found no relevant difference – the complainant had agreed to the 'actual act of intercourse'.[21]

What other situations could lead to a finding of non-consent remained to be decided on a case-by-case basis. As some noted at the time, the lack of clarity this brought to the scope of non-consensual sexual offences was unfortunate.[22] What was clear, however, was that the issue of whether a sexual encounter was different to that agreed to was a matter over which the courts had taken ownership.

The Modern Approach: The Closely Connected Test

The law of sexual offences was overhauled in 2003 through the Sexual Offences Act (SOA). The aim was to create a clear and coherent law, updated for the twenty-first century.[23] In particular, the reform was based on the idea that sexual offences are 'primarily crimes against the sexual autonomy' of people, defined as the 'right and the responsibility to make decisions about their sexual conduct'.[24] For the first time, the SOA 2003 introduced a statutory definition of consent. Under Section 74, 'a person consents if he agrees by choice, and has the freedom and capacity to make that choice'. This definition is relevant both for the issue of whether the complainant consented to the sexual activity, and whether the defendant lacked a reasonable belief in consent.

Although the aim was to update the law, the historic categories found their way into the SOA's use of presumptions for consent and deception, albeit with some alterations. Under Section 76, if the defendant has 'intentionally deceived the complainant as to the nature or purpose of the relevant act' (s76(2)(a)), or 'intentionally induced the complainant to consent to the relevant act by impersonating a person known personally to the complainant' (s76(2)(b)), it will be concluded that there was no consent, and no belief in consent. In these circumstances, there can be no further argument at trial. The jury will be directed to convict. For this reason, the courts have been reluctant to use the presumptions.[25] Instead, most of the consideration of mistaken/deceptive sex post-2003 has been under the general consent provision in Section 74.

Emphasising the idea of choice in Section 74, the courts found that rape could be established where complainants consented to sex on the basis that a condom be used, or that their partner withdraw before ejaculation, and the defendants had deliberately failed to do so.[26] As the Court of Appeal in *McNally* summarised these developments in 2013: 'the alleged victim had consented on the basis of a premise that, at the time of the consent, was false'.[27] Applying this logic, the Court of Appeal upheld a conviction where the defendant had – as the case was presented to it – 'falsely represented' their gender: this undermined the choice of the complainant 'to have sexual encounters with a boy'.[28]

Like the material difference view of non-consent, the choice logic also had the potential to be wide in scope. As it was put in *F v DPP*, for example, the complainant 'was deprived of choice relating to the crucial feature on which her original consent to sexual intercourse was based'.[29] There was no mention of a limit on what that feature could be. Once again, however, it was not long before the courts took a more restrictive reading. In doing so, they have come back to the familiar task of assessing for themselves the relevant nature of the sexual encounter.

In *Lawrance* (2020), the Court of Appeal stated that the test is whether the matter 'is so closely connected to the nature or purpose of sexual intercourse' to be capable of negating consent.[30] Cast in these terms, condom removal and non-withdrawal were said to be related to the physical nature of the act,[31] whereas the gender cases were explained on the basis that 'the nature of the sexual act was "on any common-sense view, different where the complainant is deliberately deceived by the defendant into believing that the latter is male"'.[32]

In *Lawrance,* the defendant assured the complainant that he had undergone a vasectomy – she had made clear she would only agree to sex on this basis. He was convicted of rape accordingly. Using the closely connected test, the Court of Appeal overturned the conviction. That the complainant would never have agreed to the sex had she known the truth about the vasectomy was, the court found, not enough to undermine consent in law because fertility did not relate to the 'physical performance of the sexual act but to risks or consequences associated with it' – pregnancy.[33]

In coming to this formulation, the courts were explicitly looking to the common law categories dating back to the nineteenth century: they rejected the idea that the SOA 2003 should be taken as having changed the law from this traditional approach.[34]

Historical Concerns: Difficult Questions and Overcriminalisation

The legacy of the historical approach is evident in another way. In resisting the idea that the current law should be interpreted less restrictively, the courts have explicitly referred back to concerns first put by the judges of the nineteenth century.

In 1888, the leading judges in *Clarence* had worried that a more expansive application of non-consent would mean that 'many seductions would be rape', given the widespread use of fraud, non-truths, or blandishments in sexual relations.[35] Flash forward to *Lawrance* in 2020, and we see the courts still worried that there would be 'many circumstances in which a complainant is deceived about a matter which is central to her choice to have sexual intercourse': lies about marital or relationship status, 'employment or wealth', 'political or religious views' were the examples given, but the court feared they could be 'multiplied'.[36]

Yet, if such overcriminalisation was to be avoided – the worry continued – courts would need to be able to draw a bright line between those frauds which are capable of negating consent, and the 'thousand kinds' which, apparently, no one had ever thought to consider assault or rape. This would require answering what Justice Wills described in 1888 as difficult and 'very subtle metaphysical questions'.[37] Today, we are told by the Lord Chief Justice, these 'conceptual and practical difficulties of where to draw the line' are yet to be successfully confronted by those arguing for a more expansive approach.[38] The irony, however, is that the courts have brought these very difficulties on themselves: drawing substantive lines based on the nature of the act, or matters closely connected to it, necessarily draws them into these subtle questions.

We saw this already in the idea from the husband impersonation cases that there is a moral difference between the nature of marital and adulterous intercourse. Judges have long been happy to endorse *this* metaphysical distinction. Indeed, it seemed obvious even to the judges in *Clarence* that 'consent to connection with a husband is not consent to adultery'.[39] When updated in 1994 to cover an unmarried partner there still appeared to be an implicit judging of the necessary quality of the relationship being impersonated, depending on how much significance one attaches to the references to 'long term' partner.[40]

Even the widely accepted medical pretence cases were based on metaphysical distinctions. The issue was not that the complainants were unaware that the acts were being done at all – it was their sexual meaning of which they were ignorant. Deeper than this, the courts' concern was not simply that the young victims were ignorant of the acts' sexual nature: the point was that they were unaware that the acts were, because of this nature, 'morally' wrong.[41] The courts accepted *this* metaphysical distinction too, apparently out of concern to preserve the moral integrity of – as one judge explicitly put it – the 'innocent girls' involved.[42]

While less openly moral in their concerns, the courts today still fail to appreciate the metaphysical and contestable nature of the distinctions they are making. For example, on their current explanation of the case law, the courts have taken the view that gender – while physically irrelevant – clearly goes to the heart of the sexual nature of an act, whereas marital status or wealth 'obviously' do not.[43] This may have been obvious to the court, but to others it reveals a narrow, heteronormative conception of sexual activity.

The courts never did avoid making the difficult and subtle metaphysical distinctions, then: it is just that the distinctions they do make *seem* straightforward because they accord with the judges' own concerns and inclinations.

Lawrance focused on the *physical* nature of the act, but the lines drawn here are not much less subtle and contestable. There have now been rape convictions in cases of condom removal/non-wearing, and at least one of sabotage.[44] Applying *Lawrance*, we might say that in these cases the physical act is altered: in the first, through the skin-on-skin contact of unprotected sex as opposed to the barrier of a condom; in the second, through bodily contact with semen through a sabotaged condom. Yet, as Beatrice Krebs points out, the court overlooked that there *is* in fact a physical difference in the vasectomy situation also: the existence or non-existence of sperm in the semen.[45]

Krebs accuses the court in *Lawrance* of misapplying its own test regarding the physicality of the act. But, more fundamentally I suggest, the fact that we have so quickly arrived at the possibility of such minuscule – in the fertility example, literally microscopic – distinctions shows once again that the courts have drawn themselves deeply into the difficult, subtle questions they have for centuries claimed to avoid. Nor does this technical hair-splitting fit with the respect which, I argue below, these important issues – and the people they are important to – warrant.

A Framework for the Future: Sexual Autonomy and Defined Consent

It is hardly satisfactory for legal certainty that the lines drawn have come to be determined largely by judges' own conceptions of sexuality, or else by the vividness of the imagination of the lawyers and judges who happen to be in the courtroom at the time. In this section, however, I argue that the main harm the restrictive approach does is to the value of sexual autonomy. The very idea of the judicial line-drawing approach should be rejected as a matter of principle. I then set out what a practical way forward more firmly grounded in the value of sexual autonomy could look like.

Sexual Autonomy and Non-consent

As noted above, the value of sexual autonomy underlying the current legislative framework of sexual offences holds that the individual has the right to make decisions about their own sexual conduct.[46] Putting this value to work requires that we are attuned to the way in which people actually make these decisions.[47] In any act of consent, the people involved will already have an understanding of the act to which they are agreeing. After all, agreement is always agreement *to something.* As Daniel Dennett explains more generally, 'one cannot want without wanting something, imagine without imagining something'.[48] This might be a clear and explicitly considered definition, such as 'I am agreeing to sex with a condom'. More often, however, it will be like what Mark Dsouza calls a 'visceral' idea – a picture in one's mind. Picturing the sexual act as sex with a specific person, for example.[49]

Yet, in turning their attention to external judgements about the nature of the act and what matters are relevant to it, we have seen the courts displace these understandings via their own, or, occasionally, wider societal standards (literal 'common sense').[50] If we are to take seriously a person's right to make decisions about their own sexual conduct, however, we ought to focus on the content of *their* decisions from the start. It is for the individual to define for themselves what the sexual encounter means to them. Doing otherwise takes the autonomy out of 'sexual *autonomy*'.

The Defined Consent Approach

I argued earlier that the reasoning behind the courts' refusal to give unfiltered attention to individuals' own definitions of what it is they are agreeing to is incoherent – self-defeating, even. However, even on an expansive approach, there is some truth to the idea that we need a clear and practical way of distinguishing those background misconceptions which do not change the nature of the encounter agreed to, from those central ones which do. It is surely not the case that every single matter *whatsoever* about which someone might be mistaken at any time (probably a lot!) would make their sexual encounters non-consensual – it is difficult to see how we could consent to *anything* in that case. The point is that the relevant scope of the sexual encounter is that set by the complainant's own characterisation.

The dominant test among those who accept that at least *some* mistaken beliefs can undermine consent limits these to so-called dealbreakers. For example, on Jonathan Herring's much-discussed 'Mistaken Sex' proposal, if, at the time of the sexual activity, a person is mistaken about a fact (any fact), and 'had s/he known the truth about that fact would not have consented' to the sexual act, there is no consent.[51] On the courts' current restrictive approach, it also appears to be this 'but for' test that is mediated by the closely connected standard.[52] However, the counterfactual nature of this test risks missing the point of non-consensual offences. The point is, as Emily C. R. Tilton and Jonathan Jenkins Ichikawa put it, 'what one *does* agree to, not what one *would have* agreed to in counterfactual circumstances'.[53]

Also rejecting this counterfactual, Dsouza emphasises the need to look to the state of mind of the complainant at the time of the consent. In his Refined Model, a belief may play a part in a person's consent in two ways: they may impose a specific precondition on their agreement, or the matter might form part of 'the parameters of the object of [their] consent'.[54] The second maps onto the idea above that agreement is, by definition, agreement *to something* in particular. However, the first – the preconditions category – extends beyond that. As Dsouza sees it, even in cases where the precondition does not go to the content of the encounter as envisaged by the complainant, the fact that this condition is unfulfilled would still negate their consent. He gives the example of it being highly unlikely one would frame a precondition that their partner washes the dishes before sex as consent to 'post-dishwashing sex'.[55] Even if not, for Dsouza, as long as the person actually had in mind this precondition of consent at the time they gave their agreement, the act would be non-consensual.

But this also seems overinclusive. Like the counterfactual, in this instance the precondition does not, even in the complainant's own mind, go to the issue of what was agreed to *as part of the sexual encounter at the time.* As Dsouza explains, its relevance is that the fulfilment of the prior condition was set by the complainant as necessary for the consent's 'validity' – necessary for the consent 'to arise'.[56] In focusing on how the validity of consent may be triggered, this looks more like an approach of tainted or induced consent than non-consent which, as this chapter has traced, is concerned with the content of the sexual encounter agreed to rather than its background conditions. Indeed, it is still a dealbreaker approach. Put another way, in the same way Dsouza notes about making one's consent depend on *future* matters – 'wash the dishes *afterwards*' – (which he rejects), here the complainant is wronged 'by the fact that the [...] event did not come to pass, rather than by the sexual act'.[57]

Instead, to remain focused on the central idea of non-consent – the encounter to which the complainant did or did not agree – I suggest the following formulation. We can call this 'defined consent':

> Whether the complainant agreed to the sexual activity should be determined with reference to the complainant's understanding of the sexual encounter of which it was a part, including any factors they understood to be a defining or crucial feature of that encounter at the time.

Put into the structure of non-consensual offences, the scope of a sexual encounter is necessarily limited to those matters framed in relation to the time the act mentioned in the offence – e.g., penetration – takes place. On this basis, past and future conditions – if merely triggers for the consent's validity – would be excluded.[58]

Defined Consent in Practice

We can see further how this approach looks in practice by reading some recent case law in this way. The cases of contraceptive sabotage would be regarded as involving consent to *sex-with-a-(viable)-condom*. The case of non-withdrawal is read in the same way: the complainant chose to have *sex-without-internal-ejaculation.* On this reading, these cases do not depend on the idea of conditional consent – that unfulfilled preconditions invalidate consent.[59] Instead, the existence of such explicit conditions is evidence of the fact that, for the complainant, these matters were defining features of the sexual encounter to which they agreed; likewise in the vasectomy situation. Reconsidering the sex worker case, a condition of payment may be evidence that the complainant at the time conceived of the sex as *sex-with-a-bona-fide-customer* – that is, someone with the intention and means of paying. This logic also provides a plausible account of the reasoning we saw in *McNally*: that there was no consent because the complainant 'chose to have sexual encounters with a boy'. She did *not* choose to have 'a sexual encounter with a girl'.[60] As was put simply when the non-consent idea was originally recognised back in 1850: in these cases, the complainant agreed to one thing, the defendant did another. As such, there was no agreement to what happened.[61]

Viewing matters this way avoids the conceptual difficulties that have troubled the courts. The issue of what the *individual* took as a core part of the encounter agreed to is a factual, evidential issue, rather than a metaphysical or moral question: what did the complainant picture themselves as agreeing to? This – along with what the defendant realised (or should reasonably have) about the complainant's consent – is a question of the kind juries already answer in criminal law whenever we ask them to establish the state of mind of complainants and defendants.

Some Common Objections Answered

Part of the worry has been that if we do not draw the line *somewhere* substantive, we bring a whole range of new conduct within the scope of criminal law. However, as emphasised already, not *every* single misconception or white lie in the circumstances of sexual relationships would negate consent. Nor even all those which *would* have made a difference to the complainant had they known. Consent is negated only where the matter formed a core feature of the encounter envisaged by the complainant at the time of the sexual act. Even then, criminalisation would only follow where it is also found that the defendant lacked a reasonable belief in consent. The more obscure (by general standards) a view of what was a key part of the encounter, the less likely it is that the defendant will have, or ought *reasonably* to have realised its importance (absent a particularly express statement from the complainant). Before that, its actual importance to the complainant would also be more difficult to establish to a jury. This already limits the scope of the offences and ensures that those matters which do make it through fit with their core justification: a culpable violation of the complainant's consent.

The defined consent framework can also put into perspective some often-raised concerns regarding discriminatory criminalisation. Reading the cases on gender/gender history within this framework avoids implying a challenge to the authenticity of trans or gender non-conforming people – as has been argued against the dominant reading of so-called 'gender fraud'.[62] There is no need for the 'fraud' label at all because deception is not the basis of culpability on this framework: the issue is that what happened differed from the complainant's idea of what they were agreeing to, and the defendant knew this (or ought reasonably to). This is about the complainant's consent, not the validity of the defendant's self-identity or the way they perform it.

Further, while justifying these convictions on the basis that gender and/or biological sex[63] is closely connected to the nature of a sexual act per se – as the courts currently do – does commit the law to a narrow, arguably hetero- and cis-normative view of sexual relations,[64] the defined consent approach does not invite the courts to make any such judgement. In looking to the definition of the encounter envisaged by those involved, that matter is properly left to people themselves to decide.

There may be concern that this nonetheless leaves the door open to criminalisation based on 'bigotry' – where consent is premised on racial heritage, or again, gender/gender history, for example.[65] Perhaps, then, the problem of discriminatory attitudes has merely been moved from the minds of judges to complainants. However, this placement is important, because here we come across the principle of sexual autonomy. From here, I suggest, we can tackle the concern head-on: respecting this core value of sexual offences means respecting the right of individuals to make choices we do not agree with – even those we find morally problematic. This is especially so given that criminalisation is based on a further element of a lack of (reasonable) belief in consent which, as already noted, works to ensure that liability only arises for culpable violations of sexual autonomy.

Conclusions

The law's take on sex in circumstances of deception or mistake has a long legacy of failing to respect sexual autonomy. In a way, this seems unsurprising, given that even the courts' modern approach can be traced back to Victorian times, in both its content and rationale. After all, that was a time which entertained the idea that there was an obligation on women to submit to intercourse with their husbands.[66] But today, when sexual offences are purportedly grounded in a modern view of sexual autonomy and choice, we can, and should, do better.

In looking backwards, the courts have sought to draw lessons from previous cases. However, I suggest that the lesson to be learned from the history traced in this chapter is, instead, this: if we are to achieve a principled approach to sexual consent, we must shake off the historical legacy of judicial line-drawing and place the decisions about the scope of a sexual encounter where they belong – in the hands of the people themselves. The defined consent approach allows us to do this in a clear and practical way. The courts' longstanding worries about the dangers of doing so are – and always have been – misguided.

Table of Cases

Assange v Swedish Prosecution Authority [2011] EWHC 2849 (Admin); [2011] 11 WLUK 63.
Barrow (1868) LR 1 CCR 156.
Bennett (1866) 4 F & F 1105; 176 ER 925.
Case (1850) 1 Den 580; 169 ER 381.
Clarence (1888) 22 QBD 23.
Dica [2004] EWCA Crim 1103; [2004] QB 1257.
Dee (1884) 15 Cox CC 579.
Elbekkay [1994] EWCA Crim 1 (unreported transcript).
R (on the application of F) v DPP [2013] EWHC 945 (Admin); [2014] QB 581.
Flattery (1877) QBD 410.
Hegarty v Shine (1878) 14 Cox CC 145.
Hogben (Lee) (unreported: sentenced 23rd April 2019, Bournemouth Crown Court).
Jheeta [2007] EWCA Crim 1699; [2008] 1 WLR 2582.
Kashur v. State [2012] CrimA (Jer) 5734/10 (Israel).
Lawrance [2020] EWCA Crim 971; [2020] 1 WLR 5025.
Lewis (Andrew) (unreported: sentenced 2nd October 2020, Worcester Crown Court).
Linekar [1995] QB 250.
Lock (1872) LR 2 CCR 10.
McNally [2013] EWCA Crim 1051; [2014] QB 593.
R (on the application of Monica) v DPP [2018] EWHC 3508 (Admin); [2019] 2 WLR 722.
R v R [1991] UKHL 12; [1992] 1 AC 599.

Rosinski (1824) 1 Moody 19; 168 ER 1168.
Saunders (1838) 8 C & P 265; 173 ER 488.
Sinclair (1867) 13 Cox CC 28.
Williams (1838) 8 C & P 286; 173 ER 497.
Williams [1923] 1 KB 340.

Notes

1 The non-consensual offences are found in the Sexual Offences Act 2003: Sections 1 (rape); 2 (non-consensual penetration); 3 (sexual assault); and 4 (causing another to engage in sexual activity without consent).
2 *R v Rosinski* (1824) 1 Moody 19; 168 ER 1168.
3 *R v Saunders* (1838) 8 C & P 265; 173 ER 488; *R v Williams* (1838) 8 C & P 286; 173 ER 497.
4 *R v Bennett* (1866) 4 F & F 1105; 176 ER 925; *R v Sinclair* (1867) 13 Cox CC 28.
5 *Sinclair*, p. 29 (Shee J).
6 *Bennett*.
7 See, for example, *R v Dee* (1884) 15 Cox CC 579, p. 585 (May CJ).
8 *R v Case* (1850) 1 Den 580; 169 ER 381, p. 382.
9 Ibid., p. 382 (Wilde CJ).
10 *R v Flattery* (1877) QBD 410, p. 413.
11 *R v Clarence* (1888) 22 QBD 23, p. 44.
12 The case has since been departed from for bodily harm offences involving sexually transmitted infections, distinguishing consent to sex from consent to risk of harm: *R v Dica* [2004] EWCA Crim 1103; [2004] QB 1257.
13 First introduced for underage girls in Offences Against the Person Act 1861, s49. Extended to women (of 'good moral character') in Criminal Law Amendment Act 1885, s3(2). Extended to all women in Sexual Offences Act 1956, s3. It was quietly repealed by the Sexual Offences Act 2003.
14 For theoretical analysis of this idea, see Emily C. R. Tilton and Jonathan Jenkins Ichikawa, 'Not What I Agreed To: Content and Consent', *Ethics*, 132.1 (2021), 127–54.
15 *Clarence*, p. 44 (Stephen J), pp. 28–29 (Wills J). On husband impersonation, see e. g., *Dee* (1884); clarified in Criminal Law Amendment Act 1885 s.4; restated in SOA 1956 s.1(2) and Criminal Justice and Public Order Act 1994 s.142.
16 See *R (on the application of Monica) v DPP* [2018] EWHC 3508 (Admin); [2019] 2 WLR 722, [52].
17 *Dee*, p. 587 (May CJ).
18 *Elbekkay* [1994] EWCA Crim 1 (unreported). In the surgical fraud category, see *R v Williams* [1923] 1 KB 340 (agreement under pretence that intercourse with a singing teacher was a procedure to assist with breathing).
19 *Clarence*, p. 59.
20 Ibid., p. 44.
21 *Linekar* [1995] QB 250, p. 255.
22 Law Commission, 'Consent in Sex Offences', Annex C to Home Office, *Setting the Boundaries: Reforming the Law on Sexual Offences*, 2 vols (2000), II [5].[5]; Criminal Law Revision Committee, Fifteenth Report, *Sexual Offences* (1984), [2].[25].
23 Home Office, *Setting the Boundaries: Reforming the law on sexual offences*, 2 vols (2000), I pp. i–iii.
24 Ibid., I [2].[7].[2].
25 See *R v Jheeta* [2007] EWCA Crim 1699; [2008] 1 WLR 2582, [24].

26 *Assange v Swedish Prosecution Authority* [2011] EWHC 2849 (Admin); [2011] 11 WLUK 63; *R (on the application of F) v DPP* [2013] EWHC 945 (Admin); [2014] QB 581.
27 *McNally* [2013] EWCA Crim 1051; [2014] QB 593, [24].
28 Ibid., [26].
29 *F v DPP*, [26].
30 [2020] EWCA Crim 971; [2020] 1 WLR 5025, [35]. For a detailed examination of the roots of this test, see Kyle L Murray and Tara Beattie, 'Conditional Consent and Sexual Offences: Revisiting the Sexual Offences Act 2003 after *Lawrance*', *Criminal Law Review*, 7 (2021), 556–74.
31 *Lawrance*, [37].
32 Ibid., [32], quoting *McNally*, [26] [sic].
33 Ibid., [37].
34 Ibid., [42]. This idea had first been discussed, but not decided, in *Monica*, [48]; [71]. For an argument against this interpretation of the SOA 2003, see Murray and Beattie, pp. 569–72.
35 *Clarence*, p. 43. For the view that these concerns were originally rooted in a desire to secure the sexual freedoms of men, see Lois S. Bibbings, *Binding Men: Stories About Violence and Law in Late Victorian England* (Abingdon: Taylor and Francis, 2014), p. 140.
36 *Lawrance*, [34].
37 *Clarence*, p. 29.
38 *Monica*, [52] (Lord Burnett CJ).
39 *Clarence*, p. 44.
40 *Elbekkay* (unreported transcript). See also *Monica*, [59].
41 *Case*, p. 382; *Williams* [1923], p. 341 (she 'did not know that what he did was wrong'). See further, *R v Lock* (1872) LR 2 CCR 10 – not a case of fraud, but the young boys, because of their age, were said to lack understanding of the 'indecent and immoral' nature of the act (p. 12).
42 *Hegarty v Shine* (1878) 14 Cox CC 145, p. 148 (Ball C).
43 *McNally*, [25]. The court described the physical nature of the acts (oral and digital penetration) as the same whether carried out by a boy or a girl.
44 *Lee Hogben* (unreported: sentenced 23rd April 2019, Bournemouth Crown Court); *Andrew Lewis* (unreported: sentenced 2nd October 2020, Worcester Crown Court).
45 Beatrice Krebs, 'Rape, Consent and a Lie about Fertility', *Journal of Criminal Law*, 84.6 (2020), 622–25 (pp. 624–25).
46 For an argument that this is the central wrong of rape see, e.g., John Gardner and Stephen Shute, 'The Wrongness of Rape', in *Oxford Essays in Jurisprudence*, ed. by Jeremy Horder (Oxford: Clarendon Press, 2000), pp. 193–217.
47 See Mark Dsouza, 'False Beliefs and Consent to Sex', *Modern Law Review*, 85.5 (2022), 1191–1217 (pp. 1196–98).
48 Daniel Dennett, *Content and Consciousness* (London: Routledge, 1968), p. 21. See also, Heidi M. Hurd, 'The Moral Magic of Consent', *Legal Theory*, 2 (1996), 121–46 (p. 125).
49 Dsouza, p. 1196. For analysis of the way in which we give content to our consent, see Tilton and Ichikawa.
50 For critical examination of the relevance of 'common sense', and its use in recent case law, see Murray and Beattie, esp. pp. 559–61.
51 Jonathan Herring, 'Mistaken Sex', *Criminal Law Review*, 7 (2005), 511–24 (p. 517). See also Tom Dougherty, 'Sex, Lies, and Consent', *Ethics*, 123 (2013), 717–44.
52 *Lawrance*, [34].
53 Tilton and Ichikawa, p. 142 (emphasis added).
54 Dsouza, p. 1198.
55 Ibid., p. 1207.

56 Ibid., p. 1206.
57 Ibid., p. 1201.
58 As there is still *some* harm to sexual autonomy, it may be justified to apply a version of a tainted consent offence. Perhaps reviving a (gender neutral) form of procurement under false pretences most recently seen in SOA 1956, s3.
59 This is how they are currently framed by the Crown Prosecution Service: *Rape and Sexual Offences* – Chapter 6: *Consent*, 21 May 2021 <https://www.cps.gov.uk/legal-guidance/rape-and-sexual-offences-chapter-6-consent> [accessed 7 May 2023]. See also Carole McCartney and Natalie Wortley, 'Under the Covers: Covert Policing and Intimate Relationships', *Criminal Law Review*, 2 (2018), 137–56 (p. 149).
60 *McNally*, [26].
61 See *Case.*
62 See Alex Sharpe, 'Criminalising sexual intimacy: transgender defendants and the legal construction of non-consent', *Criminal Law Review*, 3 (2014), 207–23.
63 *McNally* is ambiguous on whether the issue is gender identity, gender history (biological/birth sex), or both. On the defined consent approach, the matter would depend on how the complainant defined the encounter.
64 See generally, Alex Sharpe, *Sexual Intimacy and Gender Identity 'Fraud': Reframing the Legal and Ethical Debate* (Abingdon: Routledge, 2018).
65 Alexandra Brodsky, '"Rape-Adjacent": Imagining Legal Responses to Nonconsensual Condom Removal', *Columbia Journal of Gender and Law*, 32.2 (2017), 183–210 (pp. 194–95). An example often given is a conviction under Israel's rape by deception law for misrepresentation of Jewish Israeli lineage (*Kashur v. State* [2012] CrimA (Jer) 5734/10 (Israel)).
66 While disputed, this influenced at least some of the judges in *Clarence* (see, e.g., Pollock B, pp. 63–64). It was eventually rejected beyond doubt in *R v R* [1991] UKHL 12; [1992] 1 AC 599.

Bibliography

Brodsky, Alexandra, '"Rape-Adjacent": Imagining Legal Responses to Nonconsensual Condom Removal', *Columbia Journal of Gender and Law*, 32.2 (2017), 183–210

Criminal Law Revision Committee, Fifteenth Report, Sexual Offences (1984)

Crown Prosecution Service, *Rape and Sexual Offences – Chapter 6: Consent*, 21 May 2021 <https://www.cps.gov.uk/legal-guidance/rape-and-sexual-offences-chapter-6-consent> [accessed 7 May 2023]

Bibbings, Lois S., *Binding Men: Stories About Violence and Law in Late Victorian England* (Abingdon: Taylor and Francis, 2014)

Dennett, Daniel, *Content and Consciousness* (London: Routledge, 1968)

Dougherty, Tom, 'Sex, Lies, and Consent', *Ethics*, 123 (2013), 717–44

Dsouza, Mark, 'False Beliefs and Consent to Sex', *Modern Law Review*, 85.5 (2022), 1191–1217

Gardner, John, and Stephen Shute, 'The Wrongness of Rape', in *Oxford Essays in Jurisprudence*, ed. by Jeremy Horder (Oxford: Clarendon Press, 2000), pp. 193–217

Herring, Jonathan, 'Mistaken Sex', *Criminal Law Review*, 7 (2005), 511–24

Home Office, *Setting the Boundaries: Reforming the Law on Sexual Offences*, 2 vols (2000), II

Hurd, Heidi M., 'The Moral Magic of Consent', *Legal Theory*, 2 (1996), 121–46

Krebs, Beatrice, 'Rape, Consent and a Lie about Fertility', *Journal of Criminal Law*, 84.6 (2020), 622–25

Law Commission, 'Consent in Sex Offences', Annex C to Home Office, *Setting the Boundaries: Reforming the Law on Sexual Offences, 2* vols (2000), II

McCartney, Carole, and Natalie Wortley, 'Under the Covers: Covert Policing and Intimate Relationships', *Criminal Law Review*, 2 (2018), 137–56

Murray, Kyle L., and Tara Beattie, 'Conditional Consent and Sexual Offences: Revisiting the Sexual Offences Act 2003 after Lawrance', *Criminal Law Review*, 7 (2021), 556–74

Sharpe, Alex, 'Criminalising Sexual Intimacy: Transgender Defendants and the Legal Construction of Non-consent', *Criminal Law Review*, 3 (2014), 207–23

Sharpe, Alex, *Sexual Intimacy and Gender Identity 'Fraud': Reframing the Legal and Ethical Debate* (Abingdon: Routledge, 2018)

Tilton, Emily C. R., and Jonathan Jenkins Ichikawa, 'Not What I Agreed To: Content and Consent', *Ethics*, 132.1 (2021), 127–54

14 Op-eds and Fashion Shows

The History and Future of Consent Education in Ireland

Caroline West

Content Notes: This chapter contains discussion of sexual violence and non-consent.

Historically a majority Catholic country, Ireland has undergone an enormous shift in individual and cultural approaches and attitudes towards sexual violence. This chapter assesses how consent education in Ireland has developed in the context of rapid cultural change, and also explores what the future of consent education may look like, from visual activism to using textiles as a conduit for consent education. Active* Consent, an interdisciplinary team based at the University of Galway but operating nationally, has led the way in consent education in Ireland through workshops at university and secondary school level. Using the work of Active* Consent as a guide, this chapter explains how consent education can be developed from hostile beginnings into widespread acceptance using creative methods that reach across various demographics. Highlighting what has worked in an Irish context may be beneficial to consent educators in other locations, as consent education can be strengthened by collaboration across continents.

From Resistance to Acceptance

Cultural change began to gather pace rapidly in Irish society from the 1990s onwards as rape in marriage was outlawed in 1990, divorce was legalised in 1995, and sex education in secondary school was introduced in 1999. The 2017 Criminal Law (Sexual Offences) Act cemented the definition of consent in Irish law while society adapted to consent education. Despite this progress, the acceptance of consent education had a rocky start. The 2016 announcement of consent classes for students in student accommodation in Trinity College Dublin was met with backlash in the media. Journalist Fionola Meredith wrote an op-ed in the *Irish Times* suggesting that these mandatory classes were 'demeaning and infantilising'. Her op-ed was accompanied by the headline '*Sexual consent classes: Neo-puritan preaching won't stop rape*' and sub-headline: '*Lessons on correct way to have sex is a gross overstepping of individual boundaries*'.[1] The classes were framed as 'compulsory lessons on how not to be a rapist', which misses the point of positive consent workshops,

DOI: 10.4324/9781003365082-18

especially in the context of minimal sex education at second level schools (ages 12–18) and cultural discomfort in having open conversations on consent and sexual violence.

While some may attempt to argue that there is no need to have consent education, data from the Active* Consent Sexual Experiences Survey (2020) of 6000 third level university students aged 18–21 found that 29% of women, 10% of men, and 28% of non-binary third level students reported non-consensual penetration by incapacitation, force, or threat of force, with 44% of the participating students experiencing other non-consensual sexual behaviour. Furthermore, 77% of female students reported experiencing some form of sexual harassment since beginning college, and students with a disability were particularly vulnerable, with 33% of this demographic experiencing non-consensual penetration by incapacitation, force, or threat of force, and 85% experiencing sexual harassment. 90% of non-binary students shared that they had experienced sexual harassment since beginning college. 41% of first-year students had not disclosed the incident to anyone, with some of these participants stating that they did not disclose because they were not aware of support services available to them.

These statistics clearly show the prevalence of sexual violence experienced by young people today and indicate the need for consent education that is inclusive of all genders, relationships, and orientations. Addressing this need, Active* Consent is a national programme based in the University of Galway, whose goal is to mainstream effective, relevant, engaging, practical, and feasible consent education and skills training with 15–24-year-olds. The approach is built on a base of research on needs and experiences and evaluated through outcomes and impact. Resources are underpinned by Active* Consent's unique Irish research evidence which has been published in five research reports.

Working in this area for over ten years, Active* Consent has adopted a positive sexual rights approach to consent and sexual violence, and the Active* Consent ethos is to promote the achievement of positive, active consent communication, while being cognisant of the need to address sexual violence and harassment. The programme utilises an interdisciplinary approach to support positive sexual health promotion and education that is evidence-based, dialogical, and draws centrally on the creative arts in the design and implementation of all interventions across the programme. The Active* Consent programme now collaborates with almost all HEIs (higher education institutions) in Ireland and Northern Ireland, providing training for a wide range of organisations including Student Unions, schools, the Gardai (Irish police force), sports organisations, and external expert groups. Active* Consent's theory of change indicates that by working directly with young people and supporting these organisations, meaningful and sustainable change can happen in the lives of young people. The consent framework used by Active* Consent promotes consent as OMFG (ongoing, mutual, and freely given) which was a framework developed in conjunction with third level students (usually aged 18–21).

To date, over 53,000 third level students across Ireland and Northern Ireland have participated in this workshop. Initially the workshops were in person, but due to the pandemic, a 30-minute online version of the 1.5 hour in-person workshop was developed. This resource has been successfully embedded in orientations for first-year students in the majority of higher education institutions across Ireland. Feedback from students has been positive, including comments such as: 'I'm not as alone in how I feel as others are feeling the same way', 'it taught me that it isn't as scary to give or receive consent as I thought before', and 'this gave me better language to talk about the topic of consent'.

Consent education must take a holistic approach that does not solely place the responsibility of learning about consent on the shoulders of young people. Educators and parents must be included to support young people but also to foster a society-wide openness to discussing sexual violence and harassment, and Active* Consent recognises the parent as the primary educator of the child. For many parents and their children, the prospect of talking about topics related to sexuality is daunting, and negative press reports heighten anxiety about how to discuss sensitive issues they feel they know little about. For this reason, Active* Consent designed a parents seminar that aims to: address parental anxieties about consent, sexuality, and intimacy; understand the influences and context within which adolescents may be starting to explore their sexuality; share some of the exercises in the workshop, so they are clear as to the content, language, tone, and intended learning outcomes of their children's engagement with the workshop; and promote conversations about consent and sexual media at home by sharing relevant resources to enable their children to safely navigate and explore their sexuality.

Outreach team lead at Active* Consent Dr Siobhan O'Higgins facilitates the parents seminar. She outlines the philosophy behind its creation:

> If a child asks a question, we need to be honest and answer that question – if they are old enough to ask, they are old enough to hear the answer. We also need to check that they understand our responses and if they need more information. Sharing factual information that also reflects our values can help satisfy children's infinite curiosity and may well reduce their vulnerability. Talking early and often to our children is even more vital now that we are giving them access to a world of sexual media, on average by the age of nine years old. They need to be able to decipher the sexual messages that they are bombarded with.
>
> (Siobhan O'Higgins, personal interview, 2022)

Some of the feedback from parents gathered during the pilot of the Active* Consent workshop, with ten different schools and 993 pupils across the country, was extremely positive, with 100% of parents stating that they would recommend the seminar to other parents, and 100% agreeing with the statement 'the seminar has increased my confidence in communicating with my child/children about sexual media – in particular pornography'. Alleviating parents' anxieties can help build a consent culture across every aspect of society, which in turn empowers young people, educators, and policy makers.

Addressing Digital Sexual Violence

In a world increasingly mediated through rapidly changing technology, socio-cultural and individual understandings of digital sexual violence have expanded our knowledge of the spectrum of sexual violence. Active* Consent has responded to the changing nature of sexual violence by addressing the positives of digital intimacy and the nature of online sexual violence. This approach recognises that there are many positive reasons why people might choose to engage in online intimacy, but that issues such as cyberflashing, sharing of nudes without consent, and digital victim blaming are also prevalent.

Countries such as the UK often use the term 'revenge porn' to describe the non-consensual sharing of intimate images. However, Active* Consent has chosen to use the terminology 'image based sexual abuse' (IBSA) or alternatively 'intimate image abuse'. The reasoning behind the adaption of this descriptor is because this kind of content is not pornography; pornography can be filmed consensually by professional workers and labelling non-consensual material as pornography equates it with entertainment. The images might also depict sexual assault or be taken without the victim's knowledge; naming this as abuse can assist victims in identifying their experiences and understanding that this behaviour is a form of abuse, and not something minor to be dismissed. IBSA is a violation of bodily autonomy, privacy, consent, and boundaries; therefore, it can have the same impact as other forms of sexual violence. Jessica Ringrose, Laura Harvey, and Sonia Livingstone have highlighted how IBSA has impacted concepts of heteronormativity, masculinity, and femininity, and described how images are used as social capital within schools. IBSA and sharing nudes also impacted perceptions of sexual morality and involved risk-taking, blame, and stigma.[2]

Since 2020, IBSA is now illegal in Ireland under the Harassment, Harmful Communications and Related Offences Act. This law creates an offence that deals with the taking, distribution, publication, or threat to distribute intimate images without consent, and with intent to cause harm to the victim, and will carry a maximum penalty of an unlimited fine and/or seven years' imprisonment.

Active* Consent workshops on digital intimacy and IBSA were first trialled with a cohort of rugby players at a rookie camp for those hoping to go professional. Before the workshop, participants completed a pre-survey workshop where most stated that they knew peers who had been victims. Post-workshop, the survey question 'I am confident that I know how to get help if image based sexual abuse happened to me' had the largest increase, with 18.2% of participants that 'agreed' or 'strongly agreed' pre-workshop increasing to 100% post-workshop. 100% of respondents would recommend the workshop to a friend and felt more confident in supporting a friend if it happened to them.

The IBSA workshop was piloted further with the National College of Art and Design (NCAD), based in Dublin. In this pilot, members of the Student Union and faculty staff were trained as facilitators who would roll out the workshop for first-year students. Additionally, students were invited to enter a poster designing competition which would raise awareness of IBSA and be displayed in an exhibition on the college grounds. The winning poster depicted hands holding a phone showing a blurred image being endlessly forwarded. Entries were showcased on both Active* Consent and NCAD's social media platforms such as Instagram. This approach was chosen to empower students to become agents of change in their environment as advocated by Kathleen Krause, Stephanie Miedema, Rebecca Woofter, and Kathryn M. Yount.[3] By engaging students in a creative campaign, they have a sense of ownership over the discourse produced and through the use of art they produce visual methodology, with which their peers can engage. This method also allows for greater accessibility through image descriptions. The use of alt text or subtitles has been deployed across Active* Consent social media, but it is essential to include this in all possible situations in order to support accessibility and different learning styles.

Andrew Grace, NCAD Student Union Welfare Officer at the time of the exhibition, explains how beneficial the experience was:

> Overall, the experience was fantastic as it was an easy way to reach students, especially in a creative manner, and since IBSA is a new term, it was great to use a visual method to raise awareness of it. It's a new way for students to consider consent not just as a lecture but as a discussion and a visual discussion as well. The students reacted fantastically to the exhibition, and it allowed them to really interact with the message and be informed visually with new terms and information about online sexual violence.
>
> (Andrew Grace, personal interview, 2022)

This experiment shows that visual methodology is crucial in reaching a wider audience with consent messaging and highlights the role that art can play a role in tackling sexual violence on campus while empowering students on a personal level.

The Future: Beyond Workshops

In response to the evolving public awareness and discourse about sexual violence and sexual harassment, the Irish government developed a National Consent Framework, which was renamed in 2020 as the Framework for Consent in Higher Education Institutions: Safe, Respectful, Supportive and Positive – Ending Sexual Violence and Harassment in Irish Higher Education Institutions. In 2023, each third level institution will employ a Sexual

Violence and Harassment Prevention and Response Manager, and the post holders will collect data on sexual violence and harassment on campus, as well as rolling out consent workshops.

While that process develops and we await what that data collection brings, other methods of consent education can be considered. As the pandemic proved, in-person attendance for workshops is not always guaranteed; therefore, consent educators must be innovative in designing resources that are engaging and go beyond the time and spatial limits of a workshop to create consent education that is accessible for all. Active* Consent has begun exploring the potential for consent education through drama, stalls on campus, social media, and podcasting.

Drama

While the workshops and training for professionals and parents have received positive feedback, it is important to be contextually sensitive and mindful of the diversity/heterogeneity of experiences across the community. This includes developing additional resources that work with different audiences and learning styles. Drama can offer different ways to engage with difficult topics and provide a space for participants to reflect on the nuances of sexual violence and consent. *The Kinds of Sex You Might Have in College* has been in development since 2014, initially devised by Active* Consent team lead Dr Charlotte McIvor and a cohort of third-year Drama and Theatre students.

Performed by a four-person ensemble of actors who play multiple roles, the drama brings audiences through a range of sketches that dramatise sexual scenarios and viewpoints that individuals may encounter during college life across different genders, sexual orientations, and relationship statuses. The scenes address male, female, and non-binary experiences of non-consent, online hook-ups, street harassment, and a rape that occurs after a night out. The scenes are interspersed with statistics from Active* Consent regarding sexual violence and harassment and social norms in consent attitudes, including differences related to gender and sexual orientation.

The 2019–20 Irish national university theatre tour was disrupted by the pandemic, but in 2022 over 1600 secondary school students and over 2000 students at 19 third level institutions engaged with the play. Significant improvements were observed between the pre- and post-show consent attitude/literacy scores, demonstrating the power of emotional theatrical engagement to educate audiences about sexual violence.

Interactive Information Stalls

Taking a positive sexual rights approach enables students to engage with sex positive consent messaging, rather than a sole focus on the traumatic and the negative. At the University of Galway's Shag Week in November 2022, Active* Consent hosted an information stall themed around the idea of healthy relationships. While education on red flags and unhealthy behaviour in relationships is of course important, it is also essential to share information on what healthy relationships and green flags look like.

Green flags come in three categories: sexual behaviour, general behaviour, and gut feeling. Active* Consent asked students to write on a green post-it note and share what they thought was a relationship green flag. Some students reported that they had never heard of green flags and found that they learned a lot from reading other students' responses on the wall of green post-its. Making it a positive event focusing on the good side of relationships meant that students engaged with the idea that consent is not just related to sexual violence but to the fun and pleasurable sides of sex and intimacy. Students gave examples of general behaviour such as 'apologises when wrong', 'asks for consent', 'doesn't judge my body', 'communicates', 'emotional maturity', and so on.

Students also shared their sexual green flags, leaving responses such as 'they don't judge me for having previous partners', 'aftercare', 'asks what you want to do', and 'gets an STI test'. Creating content that can be translated across various platforms allows for different learning styles to engage with the same message; therefore, the green flag activity was simultaneously an in-person activity, social media content, a student radio takeover that played songs about sex and consent in-between discussions of green flags, and a news website article that reached over 17,000 views.[4] This allows for engagement on individual and societal levels with high engagement numbers across a variety of demographics, furthering accessibility.

Social Media

Active* Consent, along with other consent educators, recognises the power of social media to expand on consent messaging students receive in school and university, allowing for an engaging dive into consent culture. Alexandra Black, creative content producer and campaign lead for Active* Consent, explains why social media is a force for good when it comes to reaching beyond the classroom:

> It's often the case that the students that *don't* go to the workshop are the ones who would benefit the most from it – so how do we reach them? A targeted social media campaign means that they might see one of our ads or posts and feel a little more curious about the topic of consent than they previously did. We have also worked with content creators and social media influencers in the past, which has proved really beneficial in reaching young people who may otherwise be hesitant about participating in a workshop or one of our other learning resources. Even a quick glance on our social media accounts can give students an idea of the kind of content and messages they can expect from our workshops – which is always trauma-informed and most importantly, sex positive (which can be quite rare in this field). Once they get that initial impression of us, the

> idea of going to a consent workshop and learning more is potentially less daunting for them.
>
> (Alexandra Black, personal interview, 2022)

Social media influencers have enjoyed a stratospheric rise in popularity over the past decade, and consent education can also benefit from the parasocial relationships between influencers and followers. The 2021 ‘Start Here’ campaign, which provided tips on how to support friends who disclose sexual violence, was boosted by influencers sharing this content on their platforms. This campaign was a result of Active* Consent research that found that 79% of young people who have experienced sexual violence will tell a friend before they tell anyone else. Social media also holds the power to reach audiences of a scale that could never fit in a classroom. Similarly, the 2022 ‘Consent is for Everyone’ campaign targeted 17–25-year-olds across Instagram, Twitter, and TikTok, and within six weeks reached 1.5 million impressions. TikTok was the strongest platform for this campaign, showing that it is important to be up to date with new and developing methods of social media communication.

Alexandra notes how consent education through social media allows for a rapid response to real life events:

> Social media also allows us to keep up with current affairs and cultural moments around consent and rape culture (such as a celebrity facing allegations of sexual assault, or harmful relationship dynamics in shows such as *Love Island*). When this happens, I often notice a bump in interest or engagement online which always makes for a good opportunity to amplify support services for survivors of sexual violence, and other beneficial information. Handling these moments delicately is very important, as we never want to re-traumatise anyone or alienate people by how we respond to these events. Young men in particular can be vilified by popular online discourse around rape culture, and we always want to invite young men into the conversation around as agents of positive change – because we can’t end rape culture without young men being a part of that change.
>
> (Alexandra Black, personal interview, 2022)

Alan Berkowitz suggests that messages that are gender neutral allow more men to engage with the content without feeling attacked or automatically positioned as rapists.[5] This is crucial as engagement from men in workshops can be lower than other genders, and social media could be the key to creating large-scale consent campaigns that are inclusive of all genders.

Podcasting

Continuing the approach of utilising different methods to reach distinct audiences, podcasting has proved to be an effective way to expand on consent education. While much is made of the assumed relationship between consent and pornography, the rest of society and the media benefits from scrutiny also. The *Green* Light* podcast from Active* Consent explores how consent, sexual violence, and relationships are depicted in and shaped by popular culture, from Hollywood and television shows to music and memes. Featuring special guests such as author Louise O'Neill, film director Lenny Abrahamson, and intimacy coordinator Ita O'Brien, the podcast has covered topics such as victim blaming, stalking, and consent in pop music. Podcasting has surged in popularity over recent years, and the *Green*Light* podcast has achieved over 6000 downloads for nine episodes in over ten countries, demonstrating that passive listening and public pedagogy are effective ways to build on specific resources such as workshops and in-person training. Podcasting can transform consent education into praxis that provides a relational and accessible approach. Using the power of the voice, lived experiences can be understood in deeply personal ways; activist Alber Saborío fuses their Honduran and Irish lived experiences to create spaces for victims of sexual violence to find healing through art.[6] Using podcasts to spread awareness of healing groups, activists like Saborío reach victims in ways that traditional means such as therapy may not, and podcasts allow for those outside the sphere of academia to reach a wider audience.

The advantages of a podcast include a listener being able to engage in an environment that is comfortable and familiar to them and listening in their own time and at their own pace. Polyvocal approaches that include many perspectives, such as the live *Green*Light* podcast that platformed guests speaking about their childhood experiences of consent and pop culture from Ireland, the US, and India, allow listeners to engage with differing perspectives and apply these to their own learning.[7] Podcasts are 'a medium located at the precise intersection of the digital and non-digital' and offer an avenue to enhance both critical thinking skills for listeners and ethnography for researchers.[8] Passive listening provides a gentle avenue into difficult conversations such as sexual violence, as the listener is in control of how they receive the message.

While these methods have proved to be engaging, consent educators must continue to be creative as our understandings of sexual violence change over time. Textiles may provide a way to build on existing resources. In 2011 activists organised a 'slut walk' in response to the Toronto Police Service constable remarking that 'women should avoid dressing like sluts in order not to be victimised'.[9] Thousands of people attended, and the protests spread across the globe thanks to social media. Textile activism has grown globally, from the use of glitter to protest sexual violence in Mexico, with pink glitter used to highlight the refusal to stay silent about sexual violence.[10] Activism through textiles offers a way for victims, activists, and educators to expand on public discussions of sexual violence and consent, particularly as clothing has long played a role in how we understand and respond to sexual violence. In making invisible violence visible, textile activism can be utilised by consent educators to expand their messaging to new demographics.

Textiles and Consent Education

The question 'what was she wearing?' is a common refrain when victims disclose sexual violence, which can prevent them from taking their disclosure further, as witnessed though the twitter hashtag #WhyIDidntReport. Rape myths are the mechanism that people use to justify dismissing an incident of sexual assault from the category of 'real' rape, and clothing has long been an integral part of perpetuating rape myths. Martha R. Burt suggests that:

> acceptance of rape myths leads to more restrictive definitions of rape and is thus rape-supportive, because such beliefs deny the reality of many actual rapes. Rejecting these assaults as not being "real" rapes makes rape prosecution harder, the victim's recovery more difficult, and the assailant's actions safer. Rejecting or disbelieving rape myths has the opposite effect. It leads to including more concrete instances with the definition of what is a real rape.[11]

Thus, clothes are more than just fabric; they are perceived to hold the power to cast someone as a 'deserving' victim of sexual violence or as an 'innocent' victim, depending on how society interprets their clothes at the time of the assault. Claire Gravelin, Monica Biernat, and Caroline Bucher suggest there is a gender difference between men and women, with men more likely than women to say that clothing was a factor in blaming women for rape.[12] Mutia Husna Avezahra and Tutut Chusniyah suggest that strong religious beliefs were another factor driving the acceptance of clothing as a component of rape and rape myths.[13]

In considering how dress codes for girls and young women can contribute to sexism and rape culture, Maria Ezcurra and Claudia Mitchell found that clothes can be a vehicle for change and resistance to rape culture, stating that 'dress can also become a site of resistance so that it can move from being an instrument of social control regulating the bodies of girls and women into an empowering strategy for challenging social norms'.[14]

In 2018, a rape trial in Ireland saw a defence lawyer reference the type of underwear the 17-year-old victim was wearing, informing the jury that: 'you have to look at the way she was dressed. She was wearing a thong with a lace front'.[15] The 27-year-old defendant was found not guilty, and protests across Ireland ensued with many protestors holding up lace underwear and chanting 'this is not consent'.

Social media was also utilised by people outraged at the verdict as they shared photos of underwear under the hashtag #thisisnotconsent, and this method of digital activism led to well-attended protests across the country alongside media attention. For a country that historically did not talk about sexual violence, this was a seismic shift in how victim blaming was perceived and challenged. Sarah Held suggests that textile activism creates 'self-empowerment through the co-creation of agency' for survivors and can provide a pathway to healing and societal change, and collective action that is united through textiles can help enact cultural change and resistance to the acceptance of sexual violence in society.[16] Combined with social media, textile activism proves itself to be a deeply powerful visual approach to sexual violence.

This case also resulted in a campus exhibition in Dublin City University (DCU) in 2020. The Student Union Welfare Officer Aisling Fagan decided to address the trial verdict by creating a washing line display of various kinds of underwear, from thongs to jockstraps. This was accompanied by posters stating: 'This is not consent', and 'My clothes don't determine my consent'. The exhibition was strategically placed in a building with high footfall, ensuring maximum visibility as students and staff walked under the display. Aisling outlines the impact on students:

> The idea was just to have it there and not give too much explanation as to what it is to allow students to come up with what they thought it was. Obviously if you see underwear hanging up in the middle of your student building you are going to ask some questions, so having the posters dotted through it allowed students to connect the dots and realise the message was about consent, and that it doesn't matter what you're wearing or who you are, your clothes do not determine your consent. I found it very interesting standing back and watching people walk through and see them looking up initially confused but seeing it dawn on them what it was about. They would stop and discuss it with their friends, take photos and were really intrigued by it. The idea was that they had to walk by it and couldn't ignore it, which for me is an important element of consent education – we can't ignore sexual violence.
>
> (Aisling Fagan, personal interview, 2022)

Aisling states she found that most responses were extremely positive, especially from survivors, and the use of fabric such as underwear allowed students to tangibly engage with the concept of consent and victim blaming. Aisling suggests that this exhibition had greater engagement than consent workshops because it was physical and immersive, and underwear is relatable to most people. However, a few days into the exhibition, some male students under the influence of alcohol were filmed tearing down the display. Aisling describes the reaction to these young men's actions:

> It was very upsetting and triggering for many people to see the display being attacked. Some people said, "oh it's just boys being boys", but that is the whole point – this is the whole reason for this exhibition. It was just such a slap in the face, but we used this as a talking point to explain why we need to address victim blaming and the excusing of sexual violence. These boys couldn't even respect this piece of property, so what kind of respect will they have for other people and for victims?
>
> (Aisling Fagan, personal interview, 2022)

While those responsible did eventually apologise, their actions raised awareness of challenges to consent education initiatives, which resulted in a concerted effort from other students to rebuild the exhibition on a larger scale than before with more exhibits on display.

This use of textiles as protest and awareness-raising is evidenced further in the exhibition 'What Were You Wearing?', displayed at the United Nations headquarters in New York from July 2022.[17] Both the exhibition and speeches from participants were recorded in video format and posted online, further increasing the potential for consent and sexual violence education via social media. This decision also increased international accessibility, which builds space for a multitude of voices to be heard in this conversation. The clothes range from dresses to jeans, and participants outlined how they were asked what they were wearing before they were shown any empathy for the assault. Rape culture can be maintained through a focus on clothing, but consent culture can be enhanced through the use of clothes to challenge rape myths.

Conclusion

Consent education in Ireland has evolved alongside a national and international cultural shift in understandings of the spectrum of sexual violence across the lifespan, in the family home, institutions, and on campus. A positive sexual rights approach has proven to be effective, allowing students to embrace a nuanced concept of consent and understand what sexual wellness means to them. Utilising different resources such as workshops, art, dramas, social media, podcasts, and in-person activities has allowed many students to engage positively with consent narratives suited to their particular learning styles. Universal design learning, peer-to-peer engagement, and accessibility is essential for developing consent education that uses multiple platforms to cut across intersectional barriers such as class, non-native language speakers, or neurodiversity. While Active* Consent has worked in the Irish education system, an international approach to consent can draw on a multitude of diverse approaches using a variety of methodologies to challenge rape culture. Future resources can be developed by incorporating textiles and understanding the power of a tactile, tangible approach. In addition to being well-suited to prevention efforts, art can be a powerful means of recovery from sexual violence and survivors should be an essential part of trauma-informed consent education. Threads and the act of weaving them together are symbolic of the person crafting their own individual identity, sexuality, and community. Having proved effective in the area of sexual rights, fabric holds the power to create space for conversations on consent and healing from sexual violence. Consent and sexual violence take many forms; it is no wonder that a kaleidoscope of approaches is ideal for challenging them. Whether it is via fabric, a post-it, or the spoken word, consent education in Ireland is here to stay.

Notes

1 Fionola Meredith, 'Sexual consent classes: Neo-puritan preaching won't stop rape', *Irish Times*, 29 January 2016, Opinion <https://www.irishtimes.com/opinion/sexual-consent-classes-neo-puritan-preaching-won-t-stop-rape-1.2514519> [accessed 14 August 2022].

2 Jessica Ringrose, Laura Harvey, and Sonia Livingstone, 'Teen Girls, Sexual Double Standards and "Sexting": Gendered Value in Digital Image Exchange', *Feminist Theory*, 14.3 (2013), 305–23.

3 Kathleen Krause, Stephanie Miedema, Rebecca Woofter, and Kathryn M. Yount, 'Feminist Research with Student Activists: Enhancing Campus Sexual Assault Research', *Feminist Framings of Sexual Violence on College Campuses*, 66 (2017), 211–23.

4 Caroline West, Alexandra Black, and Eva O'Byrne, 'Consent Matters Whether You've Just Met or You've Been Together for Years', *The Journal*, 3 December 2022, Opinion <https://www.thejournal.ie/readme/sexual-consent-5936392-Dec2022/> [accessed 3 December 2022].

5 Alan Berkowitz, 'A Grassroots' Guide to Fostering Healthy Norms to Reduce Violence in our Communities: Social Norms Toolkit', Alan David Berkowitz, 2013 <http://www.alanberkowitz.com/articles/Social_Norms_Violence_Prevention_Toolkit.pdf> [accessed 14 August 2022].

6 Caroline West, 'Episode 11: Gender Killer on the Loose', *Glow West*, June 2022 <https://www.glowwest.org/episodes/episode-10-bulelani-mfaco-jgkcz> [accessed 14 October 2022].

7 Caroline West and Alexandra Black, 'Green*Light: Live! Ep03', Green*Light, 17 February 2022 <https://tortoiseshack.ie/green-light-podcast/> [accessed 14 October 2022].

8 Markus Lundström and Tomas Poletti Lundström, 'Podcast ethnography', *International Journal of Social Research Methodology*, 24.3 (2021), 289–99 (p. 290).

9 Stacey Hannem and Christopher J. Schneider, *Defining Sexual Misconduct* (Regina, SK: University of Regina Press, 2022), p. 58.

10 Tom Philips, 'Mexico's "Glitter Revolution" Targets Violence Against Women', *Guardian*, 26 August 2019 <https://www.theguardian.com/world/2019/aug/26/desperation-and-rage-mexican-women-take-to-streets-to-protest-unabated-sexual-violence-glitter-revolution> [accessed 17 October 2022].

11 Martha R. Burt, 'Rape Myths', in *Confronting Rape and Sexual Assault*, ed. by Mary E. Odem and Jody Clay-Warner (Oxford: SR Books, 1998), pp. 129–44 (first publ. in *Acquaintance Rape: The Hidden Crime*, ed. by A. Parrot and L. Bechhofer (New York: Wiley, 1991), pp. 26–40).

12 Claire Gravelin, Monica Biernat, and Caroline Bucher, 'Blaming the Victim of Acquaintance Rape: Individual, Situational, and Sociocultural Factors', *Frontiers in Psychology*, 9 (2018), 1–22 (p. 10).

13 Mutia Husna Avezahra and Tutut Chusniyah, 'The Internalisation and Normalisation Process of Rape Myth Acceptance: A Qualitative Study', *Psychology Research on Education and Social Sciences*, 3.2 (2022), 57–74.

14 Maria Ezcurra and Claudia Mitchell, '(AD)Dressing Sexual Violence: Girls and Young Women Creatively Resisting through Dress', in *Disrupting Shameful Legacies*, ed. by Claudia Mitchell and Molestane Relebohile (Leiden: Brill, 2018), pp. 155–76 (p. 156).

15 'Irish outcry over teenager's underwear used in rape trial', BBC, 14 November 2018 <https://www.bbc.com/news/world-europe-46207304> [accessed 2 February 2023].

16 Sarah Held, 'Textile Healing – Feminist Resistance Against Sexualized Violence and Femicides Through Activist Art', *Journal of Textile Design Research and Practice*, 10 (2022), 175–94.

17 United Nations, 'What Were You Wearing?', 2022 <https://media.un.org/en/asset/k16/k16igyxy27> [accessed 14 August 2022].

Bibliography

Active* Consent, 'Sexual Experiences Survey' <https://www.consenthub.ie/research/sexual-experiences-survey-2020/> [accessed 14 August 2022]

Avezahra, Mutia Husna, and Tutut Chusniyah, 'The Internalisation and Normalisation Process of Rape Myth Acceptance: A Qualitative Study', *Psychology Research on Education and Social Sciences*, 3.2 (2022), 57–74

BBC, 'Irish Outcry Over Teenager's Underwear Used in Rape Trial', 14 November 2018 <https://www.bbc.com/news/world-europe-46207304> [accessed 14 August 2022]

Berkowitz, Alan, 'A Grassroots' Guide to Fostering Healthy Norms to Reduce Violence in our Communities: Social Norms Toolkit', *Alan David Berkowitz*, 2013 <http://www.alanberkowitz.com/articles/Social_Norms_Violence_Prevention_Toolkit.pdf> [accessed 14 August 2022]

Burt, Martha R., 'Rape Myths', in *Confronting Rape and Sexual Assault*, ed. by Mary E. Odem and Jody Clay-Warner (Oxford: SR Books, 1998), pp. 129–44 (first publ. in *Acquaintance Rape: The Hidden Crime*, ed. by A. Parrot and L. Bechhofer (New York: Wiley, 1991), pp. 26–40)

Ezcurra, Maria, and Claudia Mitchell, '(AD)Dressing Sexual Violence: Girls and Young Women Creatively Resisting through Dress', in *Disrupting Shameful Legacies*, ed. by Claudia Mitchell and Molestane Relebohile (Leiden: Brill, 2018), pp. 155–76

Hannem, Stacey, and Christopher J. Schneider, *Defining Sexual Misconduct* (Regina, SK: University of Regina Press, 2022)

Held, Sarah, 'Textile Healing – Feminist Resistance Against Sexualized Violence and Femicides Through Activist Art', *Journal of Textile Design Research and Practice*, 10 (2022), 175–94

Gravelin, Claire, Monica Biernat, and Caroline Bucher, 'Blaming the Victim of Acquaintance Rape: Individual, Situational, and Sociocultural Factors', *Frontiers in Psychology*, 9 (2018), 1–22

Krause, Kathleen, Stephanie Miedema, Rebecca Woofter, and Kathryn M. Yount, 'Feminist Research with Student Activists: Enhancing Campus Sexual Assault Research', *Feminist Framings of Sexual Violence on College Campuses*, 66 (2017), 211–23

Lundström, Markus, and Tomas Poletti Lundström, 'Podcast Ethnography', *International Journal of Social Research Methodology*, 24.3 (2021), 289–99

Meredith, Fionola, 'Sexual consent classes: Neo-puritan preaching won't stop rape', *Irish Times*, 29 January 2016, *Opinion* <https://www.irishtimes.com/opinion/sexual-consent-classes-neo-puritan-preaching-won-t-stop-rape-1.2514519> [accessed 14 August 2022]

Philips, Tom, 'Mexico's "Glitter Revolution" Targets Violence Against Women', *Guardian*, 26 August 2019 <https://www.theguardian.com/world/2019/aug/26/desperation-and-rage-mexican-women-take-to-streets-to-protest-unabated-sexual-violence-glitter-revolution> [accessed 17 October 2022]

Ringrose, Jessica, Laura Harvey, and Sonia Livingstone, 'Teen Girls, Sexual Double Standards and "Sexting": Gendered Value in Digital Image Exchange', *Feminist Theory*, 14.3 (2013), 305–23

United Nations, 'What Were You Wearing?', 2022 <https://media.un.org/en/asset/k16/k16igyxy27> [accessed 14 August 2022]

West, Caroline, 'Episode 11: Gender Killer on the Loose', *Glow West*, June 2022 <https://www.glowwest.org/episodes/episode-10-bulelani-mfaco-jgkcz> [accessed 14 October 2022]

West, Caroline, and Alexandra Black, 'Green*Light: Live! Ep03', Green*Light, 17 February 2022 <https://tortoiseshack.ie/green-light-podcast/> [accessed 14 October 2022]

West, Caroline, Alexandra Black, and Eva O'Byrne, 'Consent Matters Whether You've Just Met or You've Been Together for Years', *The Journal*, 3 December 2022, Opinion <https://www.thejournal.ie/readme/sexual-consent-5936392-Dec2022/> [accessed 3 December 2022]

15 Consent Wars? Towards a Critical-Governmentality Approach to Consent in Post-Roe America

Sudeshna Chatterjee

> I just reject the idea that as a woman I need abortion to be successful or to be as thriving as a man in my career … I don't think I need to sacrifice a life in order to do that.[1]

Phoebe Purvey is a 26-year-old Texan who supports a legal ban on abortion and is representative of a minor, vocal group of youth who have been at the driving seat of the anti-abortion rights movement. A recent *New York Times* article captured this youth-led movement – and the resounding logic underlying it that the feminist aspirations for emancipation and growth should not posit the right to life and the right to work in oppositional terms, and that the anti-abortion movement should be framed as 'life-affirming' rather than 'pro-life', a matter of human rights that views women largely as victims of the abortion industry and not as perpetrators of crimes against foetal selfhood.

Another story reported by the BBC similarly highlighted *Students for Life*, a group with more than 120,000 young anti-abortion Americans who view outlawing abortion in the United States as not just about religion, but also about justice for the 'pre-born', which is how the movement frames foetal subjecthood. According to Jess Meeth, a young activist who was born in China under the country's one-child policy and was adopted at about seven months by a white single mother from Pennsylvania, 'with China's one-child policy, and Roe v. Wade, the right to life, the right to be born, was completely taken away', she said. 'That was the commonality that I saw: the right to life been being ripped away'.[2]

These cases are theoretically interesting in disrupting a number of binary-coded assumptions about agency, consent, and subjecthood in a democratic polity. For one, it creates a crucial complication in the widespread assumptions regarding the composition of the anti-abortion movement – of it being framed through a white, male, Christian gaze that made legislation and adjudication on women's bodies, regardless of the consent of the governed, permissible. Secondly, in circulating arguments about foetal agency, pre-birth human life, and/or (il)legitimacy of individual choice vis-a-vis that life, the anti-abortion movement centres consent as a process through its erasure for some and reaffirmation for others. In a context that is largely perceived as

DOI: 10.4324/9781003365082-19

undemocratic imposition, for undemocratic intent, and through undemocratic discourses, the anti-abortion movement draws momentum not in spite of the notion of public and individual consent, but through it. By expanding the timeline of human life (and subjecthood), it pivots reproductive health and rights-based actions/decisions into a space where the individual right to consent does not hold because it violates the ultimate fundamental right: the right to life. Additionally, this emerges as a moment where categorised framings of consent as a collective act versus a personal act are no longer sufficient. The binary framings of consent as 'consent of the governed' at a macro-polity level versus individual/behavioural consent at a micro/local level are too simplistic, as are liberal, binary-coded assumptions about life/death and freedom/oppression, which necessitates a biopolitical and governmentality lens of analysis – situating consent (or its absence) as a power process and system rather than just a political outcome or transactional moment.

This chapter aims to establish the foundations of a critical-governmentality approach to consent by examining post-Roe America's contemporary discourses on reproductive rights, more specifically the right to abortion. Consent is central to governmental legitimacy, political obligation, and citizenship, and is a fundamental principle of democratic ideology on one hand and a 'qualifying element' for legal judgements on the other. While classical texts of liberalism extensively theorise how consent is closely tied to political legitimacy and forms the core of the social contract – an idea that is enshrined in the US constitution – several critical theoretical works have nuanced consent, the modalities of its constitution and operation in liberal democracies, and its complicated relationship with power, from an individual to a systemic level.

Moving beyond simplistic binary framings of consent as a matter of the 'individual' or the 'public', and/or its (un)justified absence or presence, my work draws on critical feminist and decolonial approaches to frame consent through a governmentality lens. This, I argue, enables us to view consent not simply as a means or an end, as a justifiable 'common good' or as an embodiment of 'manipulation/corruption' – but as a system, a body of assumptions, processes, and aspirations, inextricably tied to and co-constitutive of (gendered-racial) subjecthood and power, even when it is 'absent'. Drawing from discursive legal and public justifications and oppositions for the overturning of Roe v. Wade, this chapter highlights how several paradoxes imbricated in a liberal democracy and in liberal systems of consent pave the way for circulating logics re Roe v. Wade and its overturning. This chapter interrogates the assumptions underlying Western liberal consent, as circulated through norms regarding life, statehood, and the social contract; modalities/strategies of consent expressed through technologies of power; and outcomes and aspirations of liberal systems of consent as manifested through gendered-racialised democratic subjecthood.

In feminism and gender studies, the study of consent has been framed mostly in terms of individual, bodily autonomy of women, and more specifically sexual consent. The #MeToo movement is a great case in point, which as a worldwide movement against sexual harassment and rape culture, disrupted the idea of consent as an irrevocable, absolute truth – digging deeper instead into what is perceived as consent and whose consent counts. While complicating consent might have been the epitomising win for #MeToo, I conclude this chapter by asserting that to disrupt coloniality and power hierarchies, the goal is not to stop at consent, but to start with it and to continually, systematically, and historically interrogate who (gets to) consent(s), why, to what, when, and how.

Literature Review

Social Contract, Consent, and Liberal Democracy

Academics have long discussed the foundational role of the 'consent of the governed' in liberal democracies, and its varied embodiments in systems of power and in political processes. Classical liberal texts theorise how consent is closely tied to political legitimacy and forms the core of the social contract. Political theorists view consent as the crucial bridging device between the individual and the community, and between liberalism and democracy. According to Benjamin Barber, 'the doctrine of consent was originally intended to give obedience a justification rooted in the interests of individuals rather than in the authority of states (in the rights of the ruled rather than the rights of rulers)'.[3] This was largely based on a consent theory of power or the notion that power was 'diffuse or heterogeneous, rather than monolithic and homogenous' and relational rather than self-generated.[4]

While consent might have been closely intertwined with or even formative of democracy, 'by making all political legitimacy a function of popular will', the doctrine of consent did not necessarily entail democratic arrangements.[5] This complicated fit is important to understand the conceptual framing of consent. Barber elucidates how the forces in the twentieth century that created the greatest pressures on individual liberty resulted from too little democracy and too much liberalism.[6] While liberal democracy finds a way to offer up consent as a bridge between the individual and community, right and utility, and liberty and justice, justice without consent is heteronomy which is incompatible with the moral responsibility and autonomy of the liberal self. And this is where consent emerges as significant – by consenting to the substantive rules and roles individuals agree to subsume in a polity, they are able to obey and yet remain free. Democracy, then, as it emerges from consent theory, protects freedoms from popular will through voluntarism.

While some of his theorisation appears to be too simplistic in building a linear narrative of history, Barber does nuance consent as being of three distinct types (original, periodic, and perpetual) which take on various shades and hence so do their corresponding versions of liberal democracy.[7] The crux of Barber's argument remains that consent negatively qualifies liberal democracy, whereby politics becomes 'purely defensive; the model political act is resistance to encroachment on a private sphere defined by the autonomous and solitary person'.[8] Despite consent's best efforts to bridge the individual and the community, it fails to create equilibrium which leads him to advocate for an alternative formulation of liberal democracy premised on participation and not consent.

Feminist-Decolonial Critiques of Liberal Consent and the Social Contract

Barber's critique on liberal consent lays some important foundations for complicating consent. Feminist works on consent broadly span anywhere between abstract theorisation of consent as a constitutive element of political/social/legal order to its pragmatic application in real-life contexts. For instance, Maria Drakopoulou writes that feminist critiques contend 'that women neither consented to the original social contract nor to the sexual contract said to have preceded it and according to which they voluntarily subjected themselves to men'.[9] The contract did not include women and hence resulted in the creation of power structures and political processes that easily allowed domination and the exploitative usage of reproductive labour and resources, tying gender, sexuality, and reproduction intimately to the nation state.[10]

Studies at the intersection of feminism, governance, and law on the other hand critique consent by juxtaposing women's social reality with legal realities. Drakopoulou cites several works to elucidate how

> judicial interpretations of the legal requirement of female consent in cases of annulment of arranged or forced marriages, and likewise those of "sexually transmitted debt" involving wives as sureties, are seen as sustaining and reinforcing representations of women as immature or inexperienced, and as either too dependent on men, or as their victims in need of protection.[11]

In the context of the #MeToo movement, I have previously formulated how shifts in norms regarding what consent was post-#MeToo did not happen for all women.[12] The conversation excluded many such as sex workers, who were viewed as ceding unfettered and irrevocable consent by virtue of their work, and transgressions against whom still did not illicit public demands for accountability.

Not only is the social contract gendered but it is racialised too, embedded deeply in colonial-racial hierarchies. Katharyne Mitchell writes that liberal norms of the universal, disembodied individual are actually based on a specific biological, gender and/or racial norm, as a result excluding other identities: 'biological differences from the "universal", individual, stripped-down white male body renders non-universal bodies nonindividuals and hence eternally configured outside the boundaries of the political community'.[13] Similarly, Charles Mills describes how

> unlike what social contractarian tradition in political philosophy claims, the contract was not entered into by "equals" … it is not a contract between everybody ("we the people") but between just the people who count, the people who really are people ("we the white people"). So it is a racial contract.[14]

David Theo Goldberg similarly argues that race is integral and central to the conceptual, philosophical, and material emergence of modern nation states, from voyages of discovery to post-apartheid moment.[15]

Reproductive and Racial Justice

Reproductive justice (RJ) has been theorised from a range of disciplinary perspectives such as social work;[16] law; politics and feminism;[17] and biomedical technology and healthcare.[18] Loretta J. Ross and Rickie Solinger defined RJ as that which goes

> beyond the pro-choice/pro-life debate and has three primary principles: (1) the right not to have a child; (2) the right to have a child; and (3) the right to parent children in safe and healthy environments. In addition, reproductive justice demands sexual autonomy and gender freedom for every human being.[19]

While RJ includes a broad range of issues from contraception to new reproductive technologies (NRTs), abortion has garnered the most political attention. Much of the abortion rights movement has been framed by liberal feminism. First wave feminisms focused on access to contraception while during second wave feminism, both liberal and radical feminists supported legalisation of abortion, with the former identifying law as a principal tool and the latter situating reproductive health and rights and decisions in context of socio-economic factors. Other theories, many of which emerged during third wave feminism, framed RJ a bit differently. Critical race theory focused on racism and systemic inequities that lead to material social inequality and not just bodily autonomy, and the disproportionate impact the lack of RJ has on women of colour.[20] This intersectional[21] lens has also been a contributing factor for transitions in framing reproduction from a rights-based to justice-based language.[22]

Political discourses and contention on abortion rights is hardly a recent matter in the United States. Legal scholar Carol Sanger writes about abortion being at once a heavily politically contested issue and one intimately tied to stigma which has prevented women from speaking about this issue in the past, in turn impacting the nature of legislative/political discussions that occur about abortion in the public sphere. Sanger fleshes out the scope of abortion: all that it is about, starting from medical procedures and biological health, rights (of the woman, of the foetus, of states, federal government, and of doctors), and religion.[23] Decolonial and anti-racist feminists have added an intersectional lens to elevate abortion as a social/racial justice issue, one that cannot and should not be disentangled from the racial hierarchy that is imbricated with the American state and polity.[24] Since Black women's barriers to reproductive autonomy included limitations to 'healthy pregnancies and births, and raising children to adulthood in safe environments', any just reproductive rights framework would have to be cognisant of positive rights which impose affirmative duties on the state to actualise these rights. The right to privacy and government non-intrusion, then, is not sufficient for a racially equitable model of reproductive justice.[25] Anti-racist scholars warn against the racialisation of the anti-abortion movement through the spread of misinformation about abortion as genocide, by co-opting the motto Black Lives Matter, and through deployment of the slavery narrative, aspiring to rope in 'progressives' on abortion to the pro-life side of things. Here recognising the central role Black women's reproductive labour played in sustaining racialised economies becomes crucial to centre Black women's autonomy as a primary objective in these discourses.[26]

Theoretical Framing: A Critical Governmentality Approach to Consent

Governmentality as a concept was coined by French philosopher Michel Foucault, and emerged within post-structural thinking. It aims to make sense of how technologies of power are connected to the political rationality underpinning them, and is best understood as organised practices (rationalities, mentalities, and techniques) through which subjects are governed. Central to many of Foucault's works, it plays a decisive role in his analytics of power, going beyond simplistic liberal binaries (such as consensus/violence), and linking the technologies of self to the technologies of domination/power and constitution of the subject to the formation of the state.[27] One such political rationality is biopolitics, which takes the ordering and administration of life as its subject. Biopower is the way in which biopolitics is implemented in society, representing a significantly transformed definition of power as something positive and life-enabling, rather than negative or repressive.[28] A governmentality approach to consent would thus treat it not as a tangible outcome or as a separate, discrete act in opposition to coercion, but as an entire system of power that is not only a precondition for the Western democratic state but is co-constitutive of democratic subjecthood and the statehood apparatus on a continuing basis.

If the premise of social contract theories is the idea that individuals consensually volunteer to enter into statehood in the interest of preservation of life, a governmentality approach to reading contemporary discourses on Roe v. Wade helps break the binary of consent/coercion to understand how interacting discourses between life, state sovereignty, and accompanying modalities of biopower at various levels of governance constituted the central mission of the social contract – to save certain forms of life and let certain others perish. Whether abortion is a 'right' or moral/legal incursion is the wrong question to ask, since 'both' arguments draw not on the permissibility of the act but rather on its moral and legal (il)legitimacy in a polity. The question then is not merely whether there is consent but rather whether there ought to be consent. And this makes consent an issue beyond individual autonomy and making tangible decisions; it becomes tied inextricably to power, democratic subjecthood, and to foundational questions about whose consent counts. Hence any conversation on autonomy, will, and consent of the governed necessitates understanding the vehicle/regime of consent and its dynamic, non-static, and complicated relationship with the polity. To this end, my theoretical arguments are organised along two lines: first, understanding how consent is constitutive of the polity – which is further reflected in norms about life, statehood, and the manifestation and implementation of the 'original' social contract – in this case through the US constitution. Second, technologies of power that shape consent, including binary-coded political and religious discourses and reproductive rights and racial justice discourses.

Polity and Consent: Norms Regarding Life, Racial-Gendered Statehood, and Social Contract

The celebrated decision in 1973 that inscribed the right to abortion as a fundamental constitutional right prior to the viability of life centred decisional autonomy as well as physical consequences in the interest of bodily integrity.[29] The discourse at the time ranged from constitutional protection of women's right to privacy under the fourteenth amendment to state intervention conditional upon context and as balancing act between protecting the health of pregnant women and the 'potentiality of human life', and to outright dismissal of the legitimacy of the court to prioritise a mother's right to privacy and choice over potential foetal life.[30] Justice Bluckmun, who delivered the judgement, did not agree with Roe's argument for the unrestricted and unlimited right to abortion for women: 'only a compelling state interest' justifies regulations limiting fundamental rights such as privacy and legislators must therefore draw statutes narrowly 'to express only the legitimate state interests at stake'. In this case, that would be contingent on the threshold of defining the origin of human life, which in turn was pegged as the 'capability of meaningful life outside the mother's womb', or viability, which occurs at about 24 weeks of pregnancy.[31] Justice White and Renhquist explicitly dissented to Blackmun's interpretation of the constitution, stating that the constitution creates no legal ground to 'prioritize' one form of life over the other and in allowing for 'whimsical' grounds for extermination of life, this was valuing 'the convenience of the pregnant mother more than the continued existence and development of the life or potential life that she carries'.[32]

What is easy to see is that despite varying definitions of what constitutes biological life, life remained central to both sets of arguments. With life being the sacred motivator for the social contract, and liberal consent being defined in negative/defensive terms vis-a-vis that life, the very fabric of liberal democracy is inherently and undeniably tied to biopower. Here, what specifically necessitates complication is the viability of life and its origin. A genealogy of reproductive rights and justice bears testimony to the fact that our ideas about life and reproduction have changed over time. Religions, especially Christian ethics, have historically played an expansive and important role defining life in these discourses on the right to abortion, in socio-political control over reproduction. For instance, according to medical historians, before the 1920s, many Christian churches (including both Catholic and protestant sects) relied on a theory of natural law dating back to the teachings of Thomas Aquinas to argue against contraception. Basically, the theory goes, the human body and its organs were designed by God for heterosexual reproduction; to interfere with this design was not only immoral but sacrilegious or going against the word of God. Both Islam and Judaism upheld these normative values over life 'but their religious influence on secular society and its laws in most industrialized nations was limited by the marginalization of Muslims and Jews there'.[33]

Abortion is more stringently regulated than contraception, especially among some religious sects in the US. Contemporary understandings of conception and life are shaped by developments in reproductive theory, in genetic/medical technologies, and foetal pharmacology.[34] This in turn led to competing moral guardianship claims from

> those who claim moral guardianship over the embryo and foetus as God-given people, those who wish to access and control embryonic and foetal development including reproductive physicians and geneticists and the woman growing the foetus and typically bearing the brunt of daily responsibility for the person born.[35]

This moral claim is central to understanding how consent (or its absence) plays out in discourses on abortion. Consent as the function of the liberal self then necessitates incursion into that space to be read or approved as coercion. Understandably, then, theorising the origin and viability of foetal selfhood vis-a-vis the individual space and body is crucial to legitimise or delegitimise individual and women's consent in abortion rights debates.

Technologies of Gendered Forms of Consent and Reproductive Power

Neoliberal Binaries

A liberal framing of consent views consent as discrete from coercion; inevitable and unavoidable in democracy; a rightful precondition for freedom. Several critical feminist works have called out this binary in studies on sexual violence.[36] Whether this be individual consent or system-wide, periodic or perpetual consent, it is posited to be a zero-sum game and relational, meaning it can only be exercised through interactions with some other actor and only one can possess it over the other. While delineating the rich body of feminist literature that dismantles this is beyond the scope of this chapter, what is particularly valuable to this case is how discourses surrounding Roe v. Wade and its overturning in the US are similarly framed in binary terms: as a matter of federal vs state; Christian vs Other; right to life vs right to privacy; medical issue vs socio-political issue.

As discussed previously, the 1973 ruling was upheld as enshrining women's rights in the constitution. Going by the spirit of the law, and on the assumption that the constitution in liberal democracies is the manifestation of the 'original' social contract, the judgement was an indication of gendering the contract, of inscribing women's collective consent. The pushback and resistance against this argument was the idea that in doing so, the judiciary had overreached its power and stepped into legislative territory that the people had not consented for the role of the judiciary to be. For instance, in their dissent statements, Justice White and Rehnquist wrote that they found

> nothing in the language or history of the Constitution to support the Court's judgment. The Court simply fashions and announces a new constitutional right for pregnant mothers [410] U.S. [179], [222] and, with scarcely any reason or authority for its action, invests that right with sufficient substance to override most existing state abortion statutes. The upshot is that the people and the legislatures of the 50 States are constitutionally disentitled to weigh the relative importance of the continued existence and development of the fetus, on the one hand, against a spectrum of possible impacts on the mother, on the other hand.[37]

This goes hand-in-hand with arguments about whether abortion is a matter of right to life or right to privacy and autonomy, further sustaining the binary coding of reproductive/gender determinism versus autonomy of the individual and faith-based versus scientific articulations of biological life. Roe v. Wade was founded constitutionally on the basis of the fourteenth amendment-inscribed right to privacy. Anti-abortion activists on the other hand have consistently used biological life as the end goal of their mission, qualifying the movement and its resultant legislations as 'pro-life' through terms such as 'heartbeat'. For instance, state Senator Bryan Hughes stated 'the heartbeat is the universal sign of life … If a Texan's heartbeat is detected, his or her life will be protected'.[38] Clearly this indicates a strong belief that life begins at conception, differing from the 1973 Roe v. Wade ruling that adopted and inscribed a temporally scalar approach to its definition of life, as discussed above.

Religious Discourses

A *New York Times* report in late June also highlighted how overturning Roe v. Wade was a major spiritual victory for 'many conservative believers and anti-abortion groups grounded in Catholic or evangelical principles' in the US. According to Archbishop William E. Lori, chairman of the United States Conference of Catholic Bishops Committee on Pro-Life Activities, 'it is more than celebration … It is a moment of gratitude to the Lord, and gratitude to so many people, in the church and beyond the church, who have worked and prayed so hard for this day to come'.[39] Margaret H. Hartshorn, the chairman of the board of Heartbeat International, a network of anti-abortion pregnancy centres, hailed it as the 'phenomenal work of the Lord', and Bart Barber, the new President of the Southern Baptist Convention, decried pending work in states where abortion was still legal at large to ensure 'justice and protection for pre-born babies in those jurisdictions'.[40]

However, painting abortion ban as a Christian mission alone is oversimplistic and ahistorical. Even right-wing Christianity has a complicated and non-uniform relationship with abortion. According to Randall Balmer, 'white evangelicals in the 1970s did not mobilize against *Roe v. Wade*, which they considered a Catholic issue'.[41] Citing a 1968 conference organised by *Christianity Today* and the *Medical Christian Society*, Balmer notes that delegates could not agree upon the inherently sinful nature of the act but understood 'the necessity of it and permissibility for it under certain circumstances', making choice and consent conditional. While the overturning of Roe v. Wade today is widely perceived as the vindication of religious conservatism, evangelical leaders post-1973 did not challenge the ruling immediately but went a step ahead to articulate the boundaries of consent around women's bodies that should not be transgressed: 'if there are compelling psychiatric reasons from a Christian point of view, mercy and prudence may favor a therapeutic abortion'.[42] Protestant leaders welcomed this liberalisation of the abortion law, upholding it as religious liberty, human equality, and justice.

Clearly this 'Christian point of view' and regard for 'human equality' was not reflected in other issues and for others within the American state. As Balmer argues, the pet project of the evangelicals at the time was racial segregation. According to a report by Katherine Stewart for the *Guardian*,

> Among their [the religious right's] core concerns was the fear that the supreme court might end tax exemptions for segregated Christian schools. Jerry Falwell and many of his fellow southern, white, conservative pastors were closely involved with segregated schools and universities – Jones went so far as to call segregation "God's established order" and referred to desegregationists as "Satanic propagandists" who were "leading colored Christians astray." As far as these pastors were concerned, they had the right not just to separate people on the basis of race but to also receive federal money for the purpose.[43]

This elucidates the interactive, integrated systems of exploitation and exclusion resulting from biological racism and religion – and how the definition(s) of the scope of what constitutes 'human' then becomes a space as well as a biopolitical tactic in service of continuance of the exclusionary boundaries of the original social contract.

Abortion as Racial Justice

The interactions between liberal subject, liberal statehood, and liberal consent are even more complicated when it comes to race. This is indicative of not only an exclusive, gendered social contract that protects and uplifts only some lives and reserves the right of a few to participate in original and periodic consent, but also paves the way for understanding how the right to consent is distributed and negotiated through modalities, rationalities, and technologies of power including colonising/racial politics; it ultimately allows us to understand consent as a strategy and space for racial ordering of the sociopolitical hierarchy. This necessitates not just reading Roe v. Wade and its overturning as a matter of reproductive rights but as reproductive justice, and in context of the racial contract enforced through eugenics.

American sociologist and reproductive justice scholar Dorothy Roberts writes that 'to understand how the United States of America became a country without the constitutional right to abortion, look to the history of Black women's long fight for reproductive autonomy'.[44] In *Killing the Black Body: Race, Reproduction, and the Meaning of Liberty*, Roberts argues for a more expansive definition of reproductive justice as 'the human right not to have a child; the right to have a child; and the right to parent your child in a supportive, humane, and just society'.[45] For her, legal rights unsupported by conducive socioeconomic factors to practice these rights are useless.

The struggle for reproductive rights has also not been uniform across the board. For instance, with regard to contraception for reproductive control, activists like Margaret Stanger in the US and Marie Stopes in the UK argued that the right to control reproduction was essential to the liberation of women (and their right to vote). On the far end of that spectrum were groups seeking to restrict 'certain populations, including the growing numbers of impoverished people in urban centers and the physically and mentally "unfit"'. A number of European eugenicists like Alfred Ploetz of Germany coined the term 'racial hygiene' in 1895 'to address the declining German birth rate and the increasing number of mentally ill and disabled people in state institutions, all as economic concerns'. As strange bedfellows, Nazi Germany and the Canadian Provinces of Alberta and Columbia passed laws around the same time allowing 'population control' for Jews and forced sterilisation of mentally ill people respectively. Socialist and left-wing political groups in Europe and North America initially 'supported contraception at the turn of the century as a path to working-class emancipation through the elimination of poverty associated with large family size', but the *Socialist Standard* in Canada published in 1930 an analysis that upheld 'contraception as a tool of capitalism that could control labour supply and place the responsibility for eliminating poverty on the shoulders of the poor'. Eugenics politics played out through forced sterilisation of indigenous women in Canada and North America as well. Forced sterilisation campaigns funded by US and Canadian governments led to tens of thousands of indigenous women being forcefully sterilised between WWII and the 1970s.[46] Similarly, African Americans perceived contraception as a menace and focused not on the reduction (and erasure) of Black lives, but 'sought protection for motherhood through welfare rights and access to decent housing and education'.[47]

A core element of Black women's struggle for reproductive justice has been to move beyond a simplistic rights-based language and to fight not just for rights to their bodies, but for the body politic, forcing them to view the problem in a more complicated, structural way than white women-led second wave feminism's reproductive rights struggle, due to entrenched systemic socioeconomic racism. Dorothy Roberts in an interview with *Vox* highlighted how Roe v. Wade might have protected against abortion ban laws but did not provide support for women to access them. That went with hand-in-glove bipartisan efforts to reduce welfarism and combined with the war on drugs in the 1980s that disproportionately affected the Black community. Hence, the advocacy battle cry for the 'right to choice' was necessary but not sufficient, since it did not take into account structural impediments to having reproductive freedom.[48]

Lawmakers and reproductive rights advocates are decrying the disproportionate impact abortion bans will have on people of colour, especially Black women. About 40% of women who get abortions in the US are Black. According to Cecilia Lenzen, Black women

> already face higher risks of health complications or death related to pregnancy or childbirth. Taking away the right to abortion care will likely lead to an even higher risk of health complications and mortality, higher teen pregnancy rates and increased financial burdens.[49]

Given the eugenic foundations of the fascist projects in Europe and colonial projects around the world, any deliberations on reproductive control are inevitably and unavoidably a racial conversation. Reproductive control, albeit of various kinds, was used to justify the racial social control, racial status-quo, racial hierarchies, and racial systems of oppression. That entailed protecting/preserving white life, while enslaving/eradicating non-white lives, thus positing the definitions of what constitutes human life and who qualifies as valid participants to the social contract as a power tool deployed by the state.

Concluding Thoughts

This feminist-decolonial framing of Roe v. Wade nuances consent and reproductive rights. A governmentality approach to reproductive rights helps nuance liberal consent and understand this moment of US history as one that has devolved paradoxically from the individualistic, liberal-democratic gender and race neutral foundations of state, and as one that must be read as inherently a matter of not just gender but racial justice as well. This chapter also highlights various modalities and rationalities of the discourses surrounding Roe v. Wade in the contemporary US. A negative definition of consent as something defined in term of boundaries and as transactional has undoubtedly seen some major wins in recent years in vindicating individual rights, but it is not sufficient to rest at that. Liberal consent is based on various assumptions about life, subjecthood, and power, all of which have been historically exclusive for women and more importantly Black women and women of colour. If the constitution of the US is taken to be a signifier of the social contract, it challenges the boundaries of who the consenting body politic was/is. If the original social contract is exclusive, the way forward has to be change wrought through electoral politics and other expressions of perpetual and periodic consent. This must not simply apply to other precarious, 'non consenting' subjects such as the LGBTQ+ communities but also must be designed to continuously interrogate systemic manifestations of racial, gender, and economic inequalities for any change to be sustained and meaningful. The fight for reproductive justice is inherently a racial question and there are many lessons of reproductive justice through allyship and anti-racism that remain left to be learned and shared through this process of collaborative reflection in the abortion rights movements.

Notes

1 Ruth Graham, 'The Pro Life Generation', *New York Times*, 3 July 2022 <https://www.nytimes.com/2022/07/03/us/pro-life-young-women-roe-abortion.html> [accessed 14 September 2022].
2 Rihanna Croxford and Chelsea Bailey, 'Anti-abortion Gen Z-ers see cause as social justice', BBC, 8 August 2022 <https://www.bbc.com/news/world-us-canada-62273461> [accessed 14 September 2022].
3 Benjamin Barber, 'Liberal Democracy and the Cost of Consent', in *Liberalism and the Moral Life*, ed. by Nancy L. Rosenblum (Cambridge, MA: Harvard University Press, 1989), pp. 54–68 (p. 56).
4 Ian Atack, 'Nonviolent Political Action and the Limits of Consent', *Theoria: A Journal of Social and Political Theory*, 111 (2006), 87–107 (p. 89).
5 Barber, p. 56.
6 Ibid.
7 Original consent obliges individuals to civil society and the state; periodic consent entails periodic rehearsal of consent, primarily through elections; perpetual consent entails consent to each and every collective action such as laws.
8 Barber, p. 59.
9 Maria Drakopoulou, 'Feminism and Consent: a genealogical inquiry', in *Choice and Consent: Feminist Engagements with Law and Subjectivity*, ed. by Rosemary Hunter and Sharon Cowan (Abingdon: Routledge-Cavendish, 2007), pp. 9–33 (p. 10).
10 Ruth Miller, 'Rights, Reproduction, Sexuality, and Citizenship in the Ottoman Empire and Turkey', *Signs*, 3 (2007), 343–73.
11 Ibid., p. 10.
12 Sudeshna Chatterjee, '#MeToo from the Margins: Rethinking Consent-Coercion Binaries with Commercial Sex Work in India', *Feminist Formations*, 33 (2021), 291–302.
13 Katharyne Mitchelle, 'Geographies of identity: the new exceptionalism', *Progress in Human Geography*, 30 (2006), 95–106 (p. 97).

14 Charles W. Mills, *The Racial Contract* (Ithaca: Cornell University Press, 2022), p. 3.
15 David Theo Goldberg, *The Racial State* (Malden, MA: Blackwell, 2002).
16 Jessica Liddell, 'Reproductive Justice and the Social Work Profession: Common Grounds and Current Trends', *Affilia*, 34 (2019), 94–115.
17 Carol Sanger, *About Abortion* (Cambridge, MA: Harvard University Press, 2017); Loretta J. Ross and Rickie Solinger, *Reproductive Justice: An Introduction* (Oakland: University of California Press, 2017).
18 Annette Burfoot and Derya Gungor, *Women and Reproductive Technologies* (Abingdon: Routledge, 2022).
19 Ross and Solinger, p. 9.
20 This chapter, in drawing from decolonial and feminist frameworks, does not use 'women of colour' and 'Black women' interchangeably. While the broader critiques presented here are influenced by several strands of anti-racist theorisation, specifically in the case of Roe v. Wade and reproductive justice in the United States, I draw on pathbreaking Black-feminist scholarship to elucidate how anti-blackness, reproduction, and statehood are inextricably tied in the United States. This should not be read as the only way in which social contract is exclusive.
21 The idea that various biological, social, and cultural markers of identity such as gender, sexuality, class, and race interact on simultaneous levels to create multiple and related systems of domination and oppression. In this chapter, I try to tease out gender and race intersectionality that helps understand how abortion and reproductive justice are not simply matters of gender equality, but of racial justice as well. For more, see Kimberlé Crenshaw, 'Demarginalizing the Intersection of Race and Sex: A Black Feminist Critique of Antidiscrimination Doctrine, Feminist Theory and Antiracist Policies', *University of Chicago Legal Forum*, 1 (1989), 139–67.
22 Lisa Ikemoto, 'Reproductive Rights and Justice: A Multiple Feminist Theorists Account', in *Research Handbook on Feminist Jurisprudence*, ed. by Robin West and Cynthia Bowman (Cheltenham: Edward Elgar Publishing, 2019), pp. 249–63.
23 Sanger, pp. 4–6.
24 Dorothy Roberts, *Killing the Black Body: Race, Reproduction and the Meaning of Liberty* (New York: Vintage Books, 2017); Jill C. Morrisson, 'Resuscitating the Black Body: Reproductive Justice as Resistance to the State's Property Interest in Black Women's Reproductive Capacity', *Yale Journal of Law and Feminism*, 35 (2019), 35–56.
25 Morrisson, p. 36.
26 See Saidiya Hartman, 'The Belly of the World: A Note on Black Women's Labors', *Souls*, 18 (2016), 166–73.
27 Michel Foucault, *Security, Territory and Population: Lectures at the College de France 1977–1978*, ed. by Michel Senellart, trans. by Graham Burchell (New York: Palgrave Macmillan, 2007).
28 Rachel Adams, 'Michel Foucault: Biopoliotics and Biopower', *Critical Legal Thinking*, 10 May 2017 <https://criticallegalthinking.com/2017/05/10/michel-foucault-biopolitics-biopower/> [accessed 14 January 2023].
29 Roe v. Wade (1973) 410.U.S.113 <https://supreme.justia.com/cases/federal/us/410/113> [accessed 2 September 2022].
30 Ibid.
31 Ibid.
32 *Mr. Justice White, with whom Mr. Justice Rehnquist, joins, dissenting*, C-Span <http://landmarkcases.c-span.org/pdf/Roe_White_Dissent.pdf> [accessed 2 September 2022].
33 Burfoot and Gungor, p. 47.
34 For instance, contemporary reproductive theory that shapes how we understand conception today involves the ability to see and understand microscopic gametes, and medical management of pregnancy through computerised imaging, foetal pharmacology, and surgery. See Burfoot and Gungor, pp. 51–52.

35 Ibid.
36 See Chatterjee.
37 Justice White and Justice Rehnquist, 1973.
38 Cecilia Lenzen, 'Facing higher teen pregnancy and maternal mortality rates, Black women will largely bear the brunt of abortion limits', *Texas Tribune*, 30 June 2022 <https://www.texastribune.org/2022/06/30/texas-abortion-black-women/> [accessed 1 September 2022].
39 Elizabeth Diaz, 'For Conservative Christians, the End of Roe Was a Spiritual Victory', *New York Times*, 25 June 2022 <https://www.nytimes.com/2022/06/25/us/conservative-christians-roe-wade-abortion.html> [accessed 5 September 2022].
40 Ibid.
41 Randall Balmer, 'The Religious Right and the Abortion Myth', *Politico*, 10 May 2022 <https://www.politico.com/news/magazine/2022/05/10/abortion-history-right-white-evangelical-1970s-00031480> [accessed 1 September 2022].
42 Ibid.
43 Katherine Stewart, 'How the Christian right took over the judiciary and changed America', *Guardian*, 25 June 2022 <https://www.theguardian.com/world/2022/jun/25/roe-v-wade-abortion-christian-right-america> [accessed 3 September 2022].
44 Fabiola Cineas, 'Reproductive rights have never been secure. Ask Black women', *Vox*, 13 July 2022 <https://www.vox.com/23205101/abortion-rights-reproductive-justice-black-women> [accessed 1 September 2022].
45 Ibid.
46 Leonardo Pegoraro, 'Second-rate Victims: the forced sterilization of indigenous peoples in the USA and Canada', *Settler Colonial Studies*, 5 (2015), 161–73.
47 All quotations from Burfoot and Gungor, p. 51.
48 Cineas.
49 Lenzen.

Bibliography

Atack, Iain, 'Nonviolent Political Action and the Limits of Consent', *Theoria: A Journal of Social and Political Theory*, 111 (2006), 87–107

Balmer, Randall, 'The Religious Right and the Abortion Myth', *Politico*, 10 May 2022 <https://www.politico.com/news/magazine/2022/05/10/abortion-history-right-white-evangelical-1970s-00031480> [accessed 1 September 2022]

Barber, Benjamin, 'Liberal Democracy and the Cost of Consent', in *Liberalism and the Moral Life*, ed. by Nancy L. Rosenblum (Cambridge, MA: Harvard University Press, 1989), pp. 54–68

Burfoot, Annette, and Derya Gungor, *Women and Reproductive Technologies* (Abingdon: Routledge, 2022)

Chatterjee, Sudeshna, '#MeToo from the Margins: Rethinking Consent-Coercion Binaries with Commercial Sex Work in India', *Feminist Formations*, 33 (2021), 291–302

Cineas, Fabiola, 'Reproductive rights have never been secure. Ask Black women', *Vox*, 13 July 2022 <https://www.vox.com/23205101/abortion-rights-reproductive-justice-black-women> [accessed 1 September 2022]

Crenshaw, Kimberlé, 'Demarginalizing the Intersection of Race and Sex: A Black Feminist Critique of Antidiscrimination Doctrine, Feminist Theory and Antiracist Policies', *University of Chicago Legal Forum*, 1 (1989), 139–67

Croxford, Rihanna, and Chelsea Bailey, 'Anti-abortion Gen Z-ers see cause as social justice', BBC, 8 August 2022 <https://www.bbc.com/news/world-us-canada-62273461> [accessed 14 September 2022]

Diaz, Elizabeth, 'For Conservative Christians, the End of Roe Was a Spiritual Victory', *New York Times*, 25 June 2022 <https://www.nytimes.com/2022/06/25/us/conservative-christians-roe-wade-abortion.html> [accessed 5 September 2022]

Drakopoulou, Maria, 'Feminism and Consent: A Genealogical Inquiry', in *Choice and Consent: Feminist Engagements with Law and Subjectivity*, ed. by Rosemary Hunter and Sharon Cowan (Abingdon: Routledge-Cavendish, 2007), pp. 9–33

Foucault, Michel, *Security, Territory and Population: Lectures at the College de France 1977–1978*, ed. by Michel Senellart, trans. by Graham Burchell (New York: Palgrave Macmillan, 2007)

Goldberg, David Theo, *The Racial State* (Malden, MA: Blackwell, 2002)

Graham, Ruth, 'The Pro Life Generation', *New York Times*, 3 July 2022 <https://www.nytimes.com/2022/07/03/us/pro-life-young-women-roe-abortion.html> [accessed 14 September 2022]

Hartman, Sadiya, 'The Belly of the World: A Note on Black Women's Labors', *Souls*, 18 (2016), 166–73

Ikemoto, Lisa, 'Reproductive Rights and Justice: A Multiple Feminist Theorists Account', in *Research Handbook on Feminist Jurisprudence*, ed. by Robin West and Cynthia Bowman (Cheltenham: Elgar, 2019), pp. 249–63

Lenzen, Cecilia, 'Facing higher teen pregnancy and maternal mortality rates, Black women will largely bear the brunt of abortion limits', *Texas Tribune*, 30 June 2022 <https://www.texastribune.org/2022/06/30/texas-abortion-black-women/> [accessed 1 September 2022]

Liddell, Jessica, 'Reproductive Justice and the Social Work Profession: Common Grounds and Current Trends', *Affilia*, 34 (2019), 94–115

Miller, Ruth, 'Rights, Reproduction, Sexuality, and Citizenship in the Ottoman Empire and Turkey', Signs, 3 (2007), 343–73

Mills, Charles W., *The Racial Contract* (Ithaca: Cornell University Press, 2022)

Mitchelle, Katharyne, 'Geographies of Identity: The New Exceptionalism', *Progress in Human Geography*, 30 (2006), 95–106

Morrisson, Jill C., 'Resuscitating the Black Body: Reproductive Justice as Resistance to the State's Property Interest in Black Women's Reproductive Capacity', *Yale Journal of Law and Feminism*, 35 (2019), 35–56

Mr. Justice White, with whom Mr. Justice Rehnquist, joins, dissenting (1973), C-Span <http://landmarkcases.c-span.org/pdf/Roe_White_Dissent.pdf> [accessed 2 September 2022]

Pegoraro, Leonardo, 'Second-rate Victims: The Forced Sterilization of Indigenous Peoples in the USA and Canada', *Settler Colonial Studies*, 5 (2015), 161–73

Roberts, Dorothy, *Killing the Black Body: Race, Reproduction and the Meaning of Liberty* (New York: Vintage Books, 2017)

Roe v. Wade (1973) 410.U.S.113 <https://supreme.justia.com/cases/federal/us/410/113> [accessed 2 September 2022]

Ross, Loretta J., and Rickie Solinger, *Reproductive Justice: An Introduction* (Oakland: University of California Press, 2017)

Sanger, Carol, *About Abortion* (Cambridge, MA: Harvard University Press, 2017)

Stewart, Katherine, 'How the Christian right took over the judiciary and changed America', *Guardian*, 25 June 2022 <https://www.theguardian.com/world/2022/jun/25/roe-v-wade-abortion-christian-right-america> [accessed 3 September 2022]

16 Afterword

Sophie Franklin, Hannah Piercy, Arya Thampuran, and Rebecca White

Content Notes: This chapter contains discussion of police violence against people of colour, especially black people, and police violence against women.

Sudeshna Chatterjee's concluding chapter in this volume highlights a key point that has recurred throughout the contributions: the necessity of intersectional approaches for scholarship on consent. Chatterjee argues that consent as a reproductive justice issue is inherently tied to racial justice, and that the social contract is also fundamentally a racialised (indeed, a racist) one. As she writes, 'to disrupt coloniality and power hierarchies, the goal is not to stop at consent, but to start with it and to continually, systematically, and historically interrogate who (gets to) consent(s), why, to what, when, and how'.[1] These questions must take into account not only gender and sexuality, which have traditionally been emphasised in scholarship on consent, but also race, class and socioeconomic status, cultural backgrounds, and the impact of colonialism and capitalism. A collection like this opens up many new questions and pathways for future research; here, we focus on one issue that underscores the importance of intersectional thinking on consent for future work in this field: the relationship between policing and (non-)consent. This issue is not new; contemporary discussions are indebted to decades of activist work by Black feminist abolitionists like Angela Davis, Mariame Kaba, and Ruth Wilson Gilmore, whose ongoing calls to abolish the police have received renewed attention in the past few years.[2] While the Black Lives Matter campaign has protested police violence against Black people since it was founded in 2013 by three Black women, Alicia Garza, Patrisse Cullors, and Opal Tometi, after the 2012 shooting of 17-year-old Trayvon Martin, this movement gained global attention following the murder of George Floyd on 25 May 2020. Calls to defund the police in North America have rightly focused on the institutional racism of the US police force (stemming, in part, from enslavement and its legacies), while in the UK attention has turned to institutional misogyny, following a series of high-profile cases of police officers murdering, raping, and/or abusing women. The violent police response to protests and vigils in the wake of the rape and murder of Sarah Everard by a serving Metropolitan police officer amplified anger and calls for abolition – even as the UK Conservative

DOI: 10.4324/9781003365082-20

government introduced laws limiting the right to protest and paving the way for further police intervention in protests. While recent calls to abolish the police in the UK have been criticised as an example of white feminism addressing an issue people of colour have been protesting for decades only when it has been found to affect white women's experiences, an intersectional approach that acknowledges the connections between racism and misogyny can create a more unified movement to defund the police. Such a movement must recognise the specific racialised trauma of people of colour who have experienced long-lasting and ongoing violence at the hands of the police, affirming both similarities and disparities in experiences of 'who (gets to) consent(s), why, to what, when, and how' in relation to policing.[3]

The question of who gets to consent is fundamental to British conceptualisations of policing, which have historically been underpinned by a commitment to a form of collective consent.[4] Often misattributed to Sir Robert Peel, UK Prime Minister in the 1830s and 1840s, and founder of London's Metropolitan Police Force in 1829, the notion of 'policing by consent' was in fact formulated by Charles Reith in the 1940s to emphasise the interrelation between police and community: 'the historic tradition that the police are the public and that the public are the police'.[5] Notably, the UK Government underlines on the gov.uk website the collectivity of the consensual agreement: it is not possible for an individual to 'withdraw [their] consent from the police, or from a law'.[6] If an individual is prevented from retracting consent, then upon which collective, made up of whom, does consent depend? And, if there is no voluntariness either way, is this really consent?

In recent years, policing by consent has been increasingly interrogated. In 2022, Chantelle Lunt founded the Operation Withdraw Consent (OWC) project. In its press release, Lunt, who left the police force in 2018, writes:

> Policing by consent is a myth. The Public did not consent to the explicit targeting of people based solely on their race, gender or sexual orientation. We never consented to the enforcement of one set of laws for us, and another set for the rich and powerful.[7]

Lunt articulates the violence involved in policing by consent, which claims to rely on the shared trust and mutual consensus of a nebulously defined public, yet prevents individual revocation and remains tacit in its boundaries. In 2022, the Metropolitan Police appointed Baroness Louise Casey to oversee an independent investigation into its culture. Published in March 2023, and ultimately finding the Met to be institutionally racist, misogynistic, and homophobic, Casey writes in the final report that 'the Met has become unanchored from the principles of policing by consent. Consent is not passive but relies on the police operating with transparency, to be willing to explain their decisions and their reasons for it.'[8] Casey finds that many members of society, who are specifically targeted and dehumanised by the police, are excluded from the unwritten social contract of 'policing by consent'.[9]

This non-consent lies at the historical roots of British policing and has incited reformist activism from the nineteenth century onwards. Peel's formation of the Metropolitan Police was anteceded by the Royal Irish Constabulary (RIC) in 1814, a paramilitary organisation designed to (aggressively) curb Irish rebellion and which, tellingly, became the template for colonial policing. Although the RIC was deliberately contrasted with the Metropolitan's 'policing by consent', the demarcation of the two forces became increasingly illusionary. From the 1840s, the overlap between them indicated a tension between policing by consent and policing by coercion that has endured to the present and shaped contemporary scrutiny of, and activism against, the police. Josephine Butler's protest against the Contagious Diseases Acts (1864–1869), which enabled (police)men to abduct any suspected prostitute and incarcerate her in a 'Lock' Hospital (where she would forcibly undergo gynaecological examinations by male doctors), foreshadows both ongoing police predation of women and anti-carceral feminism.[10] Alongside this entrenched misogyny, the classism and racism detected by the Casey Report stems from the RIC and the policing of empire; as Jennifer Fleetwood and John Lea note, following the Second World War 'the British state responded to colonial immigration with colonial policing merged with domestic traditions of general repression of the working class. The result was the current institutional racism of stop and search' (whereby black individuals in the UK are six times more likely than white individuals to be apprehended).[11]

Out of this historical framework, British police reform and abolitionism have been galvanised, re-ignited in 2020 by the growth of the Black Lives Matter movement and calls to defund the police in the US, and granted greater urgency by the social inequalities engendered by COVID-19. Scholars including Koshka Duff speak alongside platforms such as Abolitionist Futures, exposing the 'epistemic gulf between those who experience themselves as *protected* by the police and those who are *policed* by them'.[12] Where reformers seek to improve policing, abolitionists demand elimination, attacking the normalisation of violence and threat that creates the 'appearance of consent' in maintaining police authority.[13] Mediating reform and abolition, calls to defund the police argue for resources to be diverted to public health and education, for example, with policing retained as 'a subordinate part of a welfare approach to social harm'.[14]

Critics of abolition and defunding (including current Labour Leader, Sir Keir Starmer) contend that US paradigms for police decapitalisation conflict with the UK framework. Where, in the US, defunding is 'meaningful against a backdrop of expanding budgets', this 'logic does not fit the reality of the UK, where police budgets are shrinking' and where forces are already often responsible for providing preventative social support.[15] Serious crimes – such as terrorism – test the viability of abolition and defunding, while care needs to be taken to avoid the 'policification' of social services (which can themselves be historically mired in discrimination towards disenfranchised and minoritised communities).

Nevertheless, in challenging policing as an institution that is imagined to be consented to automatically and unequivocally by the public, incarceration within the ideological is also resisted; scrutiny of policing, as practice and concept, becomes a liberation, enabling alternative social praxis to be imagined. Indeed, this balance between policing and protest is itself implicit in Reith's very ideal of 'policing by consent' – for 'consent is only meaningful if there is the genuine option to *dis*sent'.[16]

The murder of George Floyd, and the subsequent momentum of the Black Lives Matter movement, intersected with a particular moment in our global histories, where private and public bodies, and the body politic, became inextricably enmeshed. As many bore witness to the harrowing surveillance of the racialised body, a global pandemic was unfolding, a health crisis that heightened sensitivity to our own bodies, to how we encounter and occupy space with the other – a relationality uniquely experienced in the shared isolation of lockdown conditions. But what we also bore witness to was the stratification in health conditions and the conditional access to care: the parallel encounter with the treatment of minoritised, marginalised populations in carceral systems and the disproportionate deaths of said populations unprotected by medico-legal systems.

Protest culture during the pandemic acquired new forms in response to a rapidly evolving environment of bodily policing in public space, one which redefined the very scope of consent. Activism about healthcare access was staged by racial justice and abortion rights activists, at a time when pressures on medical institutions widened existing, entrenched gaps in healthcare. The overlaps in these activist movements exposed the amplified vulnerabilities of bodies coded with multiple marginalities – black women, for example, had a higher mortality rate than white and black men in COVID-19 outcomes, and there was particular tension over timely access to abortions during the pandemic.[17] These movements demanded a radical redress of the medical, legal, and carceral systems, envisioning a culture of consent solidified through the expression 'my body, my choice', albeit in various intersectional iterations (recalling Iqra Shagufta Cheema's exploration of divided feminist responses to the cultural expression of this slogan, *Mera Jism, Meri Marzi*, in the Pakistani community).

Strikingly, cross-national protests fuelled by opposition to lockdown, vaccination, and masking policies circulated in the same space, at the same time. The abortion rights slogan 'my body, my choice' was alarmingly appropriated by COVID anti-vax and pro-life movements (often with overlaps between the two), couching it in the discourse of 'bodily autonomy' while, in the same breath, violently refusing the principle being extended to *certain* bodies in medical and legal practice.[18]

These movements have largely been viewed – and denigrated – as products of particular political and/or religious affiliations: the stronghold of largely right-wing or populist sentiments across the US and Europe.[19] They have also been discredited as a dangerous product of the conspiracy culture circulating pervasively across social media at a particularly disrupted and disputed period in public healthcare policy. However, this picture of protest culture elides the roots of medico-legal mistrust amongst racialised, minoritised populations. Arya Thampuran's chapter in this volume brought to the surface the violent history of medical experimentation amongst the Inuit community to enhance Canadian military competence in the Arctic. In America, Tom Sorell and Jethro Butler recall the infamous Tuskegee Study, in which 400 black men were used as a control group of untreated sufferers of syphilis, where informed consent was foreclosed and the men who subsequently contracted the illness were left untreated.[20] One could also recall the eugenicist sterilisation campaigns in the US for control of racialised and disabled populations.[21] These have sowed the seeds for enduring suspicion of, and a reckoning with the boundaries – and boundedness – of, the term 'consent' as it has come to be coded through the intersecting axes of race, sex, and space.

Indeed, historically entrenched but endemic healthcare inequities created a breeding ground for COVID-19 conspiracies to gain traction; this was fuelled by the likes of the Rebecca Project, which aligned itself with a particular form of religious conservatism that inspired fears over contraceptives like Depo-Provera.[22] The Gates Foundation also became the subject of a suit of allegations – variously discredited – against its history of medical testing on minoritised populations in 'developing' countries, framing vaccine intervention as birth control and an instrument of state power exercised over reproductive rights.

These fears spread extensively through social media, which seemingly served as a point of contact and connection under isolating lockdown conditions. But the power of technology has also extended into the very possibilities of bodily policing and surveillance. Mandated contact-tracing and medical data tracking apps that gained a stronghold during the pandemic have raised concerns over the right to individual voluntary withdrawal, when such technology is framed as a relationally oriented public good, in a notable echo of the concept of 'policing by consent'. The 2022 overturning of Roe v. Wade in the US, with intersectional ramifications to legal discourse that Chatterjee's chapter unpacks, has additionally amplified anxieties over 'femtech' such as menstrual/fertility tracking apps, often framed as equipping and empowering women with embodied knowledge, but which have particular challenges for data privacy and protection in a climate of highly regulated reproductive rights.[23]

Against this backdrop, it becomes particularly prescient and pressing to develop theoretical and practical frameworks that can accommodate the ever-evolving scope of consent studies. This collection has offered the kind of intersectional, decolonial prism which enables us to collectively think and work *through* these complexities of consent circulating within and across various, individually nuanced spaces.

Notes

1 Sudeshna Chatterjee, 'Consent Wars? Towards a Critical-Governmentality Approach to Consent in Post-Roe America', in *Consent: Legacies, Representations,*

and Frameworks for the Future, ed. by Sophie Franklin, Hannah Piercy, Arya Thampuran, and Rebecca White (Abingdon: Routledge, 2023), pp. 218–33 (p. 220).

2 See *Abolition. Feminism. Now.*, ed. by Angela Y. Davis, Gina Dent, Erica R. Meiners, and Beth E. Richie, Abolitionist Papers, 2 (Chicago: Haymarket Books, 2022); Angela Davis, *Abolition Democracy: Beyond Empire, Prisons, and Torture* (New York: Seven Stories Press, 2005); Angela Davis, *Are Prisons Obsolete?* (New York: Seven Stories Press, 2003); Ruth Wilson Gilmore, *Change Everything: Racial Capitalism and the Case for Abolition*, Abolitionist Papers, 4 (Chicago: Haymarket Books, forthcoming 2023); Ruth Wilson Gilmore, *Abolition Geography: Essays Towards Liberation*, ed. by Brenna Bhandar and Alberto Toscano (London: Verso, 2022); Ruth Wilson Gilmore, *Golden Gulag: Prisons, Surplus, Crisis, and Opposition in Globalizing California* (Berkeley: University of California Press, 2007); Mariame Kaba, *We Do This 'Til We Free Us: Abolitionist Organizing and Transforming Justice*, Abolitionist Papers, 1 (Chicago: Haymarket Books, 2021).

3 Chatterjee.

4 'Collective consent' has often been used in the context of technology, with Nighat Dad and Shmyla Khan defining it as 'the consent experienced in the public sphere where the individual does not have the power to define the consent'. Consent, for example in digital spaces, is 'experienced as a collective based on external decisions, and at times predetermined decisions, of what constitutes consent in those spaces'. See Nighat Dad and Shmyla Khan, '*Mera Internet, Meri Marzi*: Alternative Imaginings of Consent in Pakistani Online Spaces', in *Gender Hate Online: Understanding the New Anti-Feminism*, ed. by Debbie Ging and Eugenia Siapera (Cham: Palgrave Macmillan, 2019), pp. 69–83 (p. 77).

5 Charles Reith, quoted in Clive Emsley, 'Peel's Principles, Police Principles', in *The Future of Policing*, ed. by Jennifer M. Brown (Abingdon: Routledge, 2014), pp. 11–22 (pp. 12–14).

6 'Definition of policing by consent', Home Office, 10 December 2012 <https://www.gov.uk/government/publications/policing-by-consent/definition-of-policing-by-consent> [accessed 23 May 2023]. Countries including Australia, Canada, and New Zealand (all notably former colonies of the British Empire) also adopt a 'policing by consent' approach.

7 'OWC Press Release', Operation Withdraw Consent, 2022 <https://docs.google.com/document/d/17wzOP-zzzFKUxfl9fyrkd1M60ID-XUTYvKbmYRlck88/edit> [accessed 23 May 2023].

8 Baroness Casey of Blackstock, *Final Report: An independent review into the standards of behaviour and internal culture of the Metropolitan Police Service*, March 2023, p. 18 <https://www.met.police.uk/SysSiteAssets/media/downloads/met/about-us/baroness-casey-review/update-march-2023/baroness-casey-review-march-2023a.pdf> [accessed 23 May 2023].

9 Ibid., p. 7.

10 See Elizabeth Bernstein, 'The Sexual Politics of the "New Abolitionism"', *Resources for Feminist Research*, 18.3 (2007), 128–51. Where carceral feminism advocates enhanced prison sentencing for crimes directed towards gender and feminist issues, anti-carceral feminism posits that such measures uphold patriarchal power systems, arguing instead for the re-allocation of police funding towards preventative social and health services.

11 Jennifer Fleetwood and John Lea, 'Defunding the Police in the UK: Critical Questions and Practical Suggestions', *Howard Journal of Crime and Justice*, 61.2 (2022), 167–84 (p. 173).

12 *Abolishing the Police*, ed. by Koshka Duff (London: Dog Section Press, 2021), pp. 10–11. See also <https://abolitionistfutures.com/defund-the-police>.

13 Duff, p. 14.

14 Fleetwood and Lea, p. 174.
15 Ibid., p. 171.
16 Duff, p. 14.
17 Tamara Rushovich et al., 'Sex Disparities in COVID-19 Mortality Vary Across US Racial Groups', *Journal of General Internal Medicine*, 36 (2021), 1696–1701; Neva Bojovic, Jovana Stanisljevic, and Guido Giunti, 'The impact of COVID-19 on abortion access: Insights from the European Union and the United Kingdom', *Health Policy*, 125 (2021), 841–58; Rishita Nandagiri, Ernestina Coast, and Joe Strong, 'COVID-19 and Abortion: Making Structural Violence Visible', *International Perspectives on Sexual and Reproductive Health*, 46 (2020), 83–89.
18 Tina Rulli and Stephen Campbell, 'Can "My Body, My Choice" anti-vaxxers be pro-life?', *Bioethics*, 36 (2022), 708–14.
19 Christian Fuchs, 'Bill Gates Conspiracy Theories as Ideology in the Context of the COVID-19 Crisis', *Communicating COVID-19* (Bingley: Emerald, 2021), 91–144.
20 Tom Sorrell and Jethro Butler, 'The Politics of Covid Vaccine Hesitancy and Opposition', *Polit Q*, 93 (2022), 347–51.
21 Alexandra Mina Stern, 'Forced sterilization policies in the US targeted minorities and those with disabilities – and lasted into the 21st century', *The Conversation*, 26 August 2020 <https://theconversation.com/forced-sterilization-policies-in-the-us-targeted-minorities-and-those-with-disabilities-and-lasted-into-the-21st-century-143144> [accessed 30 May 2023].
22 Amit Prasad, 'Anti-science Misinformation and Conspiracies: COVID–19, Post-truth, and Science & Technology Studies (STS)', *Science, Technology, and Society*, 27 (2022), 88–112 (p. 98).
23 Renate Klar and Dirk Lanzareth, 'The ethics of COVID-19 tracking apps – challenges and voluntariness', *Research Ethics*, 16 (2020), 1–9; Elliot Mbunge, 'Integrating emerging technologies into COVID-19 contact tracing: Opportunities, challenges and pitfalls', *Diabetes and Metabolic Syndrome: Clinical Research and Reviews*, 14 (2020), 1631–36; Zikan Dong et al., 'Privacy Analysis of Period Tracking Mobile Apps in the Post-Roe v. Wade Era', *ASE '22: Proceedings of the 37th IEEE/ACM International Conference on Automated Software Engineering*, 203 (October 2022), 1–6.

Bibliography

Bernstein, Elizabeth, 'The Sexual Politics of the "New Abolitionism"', *Resources for Feminist Research*, 18.3 (2007), 128–51

Bojovic, Neva, Jovana Stanisljevic, and Guido Giunti, 'The Impact of COVID-19 on Abortion Access: Insights from the European Union and the United Kingdom', *Health Policy*, 125 (2021), 841–58

Casey of Blackstock, Baroness, *Final Report: An independent review into the standards of behaviour and internal culture of the Metropolitan Police Service*, March 2023 <https://www.met.police.uk/SysSiteAssets/media/downloads/met/about-us/baroness-casey-review/update-march-2023/baroness-casey-review-march-2023a.pdf> [accessed 23 May 2023]

Chatterjee, Sudeshna, 'Consent Wars? Towards a Critical-Governmentality Approach to Consent in Post-Roe America', in *Consent: Legacies, Representations, and Frameworks for the Future*, ed. by Sophie Franklin, Hannah Piercy, Arya Thampuran, and Rebecca White (Abingdon: Routledge, 2023), pp. 218–33

Dad, Nighat, and Shmyla Khan, '*Mera Internet, Meri Marzi*: Alternative Imaginings of Consent in Pakistani Online Spaces', in *Gender Hate Online: Understanding the*

New Anti-Feminism, ed. by Debbie Ging and Eugenia Siapera (Cham: Palgrave Macmillan, 2019), pp. 69–83

Davis, Angela, *Abolition Democracy: Beyond Empire, Prisons, and Torture* (New York: Seven Stories Press, 2005)

Davis, Angela Y., Gina Dent, Erica R. Meiners, and Beth E. Richie, eds, *Abolition. Feminism. Now.*, Abolitionist Papers, 2 (Chicago: Haymarket Books, 2022)

'Definition of policing by consent', Home Office, 10 December 2012 <https://www.gov.uk/government/publications/policing-by-consent/definition-of-policing-by-consent> [accessed 23 May 2023]

Dong, Zikan, Liu Wang, Hao Xie, Guoai Xu, and Haoyu Wang, 'Privacy Analysis of Period Tracking Mobile Apps in the Post-Roe v. Wade Era', *ASE '22: Proceedings of the 37th IEEE/ACM International Conference on Automated Software Engineering*, 203 (October 2022), 1–6

Duff, Koshka, ed., *Abolishing the Police* (London: Dog Section Press, 2021)

Emsley, Clive, 'Peel's Principles, Police Principles', in *The Future of Policing*, ed. by Jennifer M. Brown (Abingdon: Routledge, 2014), pp. 11–22

Fleetwood, Jennifer, and John Lea, 'Defunding the Police in the UK: Critical Questions and Practical Suggestions', *Howard Journal of Crime and Justice*, 61.2 (2022), 167–84

Fuchs, Christian, 'Bill Gates Conspiracy Theories as Ideology in the Context of the COVID-19 Crisis', *Communicating COVID-19* (Bingley: Emerald, 2021), 91–144

Gilmore, Ruth Wilson, *Abolition Geography: Essays Towards Liberation*, ed. by Brenna Bhandar and Alberto Toscano (London: Verso, 2022)

Gilmore, Ruth Wilson, *Change Everything: Racial Capitalism and the Case for Abolition*, Abolitionist Papers, 4 (Chicago: Haymarket Books, forthcoming 2023)

Gilmore, Ruth Wilson, *Golden Gulag: Prisons, Surplus, Crisis, and Opposition in Globalizing California* (Berkeley: University of California Press, 2007)

Kaba, Mariame, *We Do This 'Til We Free Us: Abolitionist Organizing and Transforming Justice*, Abolitionist Papers, 1 (Chicago: Haymarket Books, 2021)

Klar, Renate, and Dirk Lanzareth, 'The ethics of COVID-19 Tracking Apps – Challenges and Voluntariness', *Research Ethics*, 16 (2020), 1–9

Mbunge, Elliot, 'Integrating Emerging Technologies into COVID-19 Contact Tracing: Opportunities, Challenges and Pitfalls', *Diabetes and Metabolic Syndrome: Clinical Research and Reviews*, 14 (2020), 1631–36

Nandagiri, Rishita, Ernestina Coast, and Joe Strong, 'COVID-19 and Abortion: Making Structural Violence Visible', *International Perspectives on Sexual and Reproductive Health*, 46.1 (2020), 83–89

'OWC Press Release', Operation Withdraw Consent, 2022 <https://docs.google.com/document/d/17wzOP-zzzFKUxfl9fyrkd1M60ID-XUTYvKbmYRlck88/edit> [accessed 23 May 2023]

Prasad, Amit, 'Anti-science Misinformation and Conspiracies: COVID–19, Post-truth, and Science & Technology Studies (STS)', *Science, Technology, and Society*, 27 (2022), 88–112

Rulli, Tina, and Stephen Campbell, 'Can "My Body, My Choice" Anti-vaxxers be Pro-life?', *Bioethics*, 36 (2022), 708–14

Rushovich, Tamara, Marion Boulicault, Jarvis T. Chen, Ann Caroline Danielsen, Amelia Tarrant, Sarah S. Richardson, and Heather Shattuck-Heidorn, 'Sex Disparities in COVID-19 Mortality Vary Across US Racial Groups', *Journal of General Internal Medicine*, 36 (2021), 1696–1701

Sorrell, Tom, and Jethro Butler, 'The Politics of Covid Vaccine Hesitancy and Opposition', *Polit Q*, 93 (2022), 347–51

Stern, Alexandra Mina, 'Forced sterilization policies in the US targeted minorities and those with disabilities – and lasted into the 21st century', *The Conversation*, 26 August 2020 <https://theconversation.com/forced-sterilization-policies-in-the-us-targeted-minorities-and-those-with-disabilities-and-lasted-into-the-21st-century-143144> [accessed 30 May 2023]

Index